To Madeline
From: Susannah

MW01386040

Lift Up a Standard is a sketch of the life and labours of Rev. R. C. Horner and the resulting formation of two denominations: the Holiness Movement and the Standard Church of America. When Laurence Croswell and his son Mark offered to compile this document they did so out of a dedication and appreciation for the saints of the past who gave their lives for the spread of the gospel. They did extensive research and conducted interviews with several individuals, sparing neither time nor effort to produce an authentic record of the workings of God through the instrumentality of men and women totally committed to His service. This book is based on facts regardless of errors in judgments, faults, and failures but also stressing the triumphs and victories of Christian living.

—Rev. Earl Conley, General Superintendent (1962–1986),
Missions Director (1986–2004), the Standard Church of America

As you read the history of the Standard Church of America your heart will be warmed and challenged by the sacrifice of men and women who caught God's vision for the kingdom and in some cases were literally willing to "surrender all" to see God's work go forward. It is humbling to read how men and women mortgaged their farms, sold land, livestock, and personal possessions to begin and financially support Brockville Bible College, which would become the training center from which pastors and laity would go out into the "harvest fields." It is also humbling to hear how they "considered it all joy" so that family, neighbours, and friends could experience the unspeakable joy of knowing Jesus as their personal Lord and Saviour.

Lift Up a Standard is the story of "a people of God" and their rich heritage in Christ. My prayer is that you will know more of God's wonderful blessing, Spirit-filled anointing, and amazing grace, and why as Wesleyans we rejoice and give thanks to God that through our merger this rich heritage has now become part of our history together. To God be the glory!

—Rev. Donald Hodgins, District Superintendent,
The Wesleyan Church, Central Canada District

I appreciate the diligent research Laurence and his son Mark have put into telling the story of Ralph Horner and his legacy. As one who was raised within the religious-cultural milieu of the Standard Church the opportunity to read of the people who shaped and served the church has helped me to better understand the forces that influenced my thinking. It has also given me a greater appreciation for the story of Methodism in Canada and how the history of Horner and the Standard Church flows out of a multitude of factors at work within the religious culture of the late nineteenth century.

Laurence, an insider, has written as one who understands and cares. However his insider status, with the help of his son and their excellent research, did not detract from the ability to objectively tell the story. This important book will be of benefit to anyone who wishes to enter into the significant stories of followers of Christ who were used to make a difference in the world around them. As well, the reader will gain a better understanding of the events that shaped the past and eventually led to the merger with the Central Canada District of The Wesleyan Church in January of 2004.

—Rev. Dr. Peter Rigby, Kingston Standard Church, Assistant District Superintendent, Central Canada District, The Wesleyan Church

Lift Up a
STANDARD

The Life and Legacy of Ralph C. Horner

Laurence Croswell
Mark Croswell

CONTENTS

PREFACE
SPIRITUAL HERITAGE

Growing up as a pastor's son in the Brockville Standard Church, I heard many stories about the early days of the church. Anecdotes about "Hornerite tea" (milk and hot water), black dress uniforms, people getting blessed, and explanations why my mother wore a watch rather than an engagement ring always intrigued me. As a teenager, I remember riding on the Zion Hill Youth Camp bus and listening to Rev. Eldon Craig tell stories of a preacher by the name of Ralph Horner. About this time a memorial archives was placed in the facilities of Centennial Road Standard Church celebrating the history and founder of the Standard Church, Bishop Ralph Horner. I remember looking at the pictures and enjoying the atmosphere of the room.

When my grandfather, Leonard Croswell, passed away in October of 2003, interest in my spiritual roots piqued even more. I was chosen to read the eulogy my dad had written. He told of Grandpa's first encounter with a Standard Church evangelist, Rev. W. Jackson. Revival services were scheduled at the Balsam Grove school house, near Newbrook, Alberta. Rev. Jackson was schooled in preaching by Ralph Horner. My grandfather had been impressed with Rev. Jackson's first words, "I may be a stranger to you, but I am not a stranger to God."

Knowledge of my church history was never thorough, and I had no real historical sense of the culture, people, and beliefs that had shaped me. When my dad mentioned in passing that he was thinking about writing a history of the Standard Church, I told him I was interested in helping, partially because of the "history teacher" in me, but also because I wanted to know more about my own spiritual heritage. I started my journey by reading a master's thesis, "Ralph Cecil Horner, Product of the Ottawa Valley," written by C. Roy Fortune.[1] I began to research the Horner era, searching old newspaper files, reading files in the Ontario Archives in Toronto, sifting through Pentecostal, Free Methodist and Standard Church denominational archives, and motoring across Ontario and western Quebec for interviews with longtime Holiness, Free Methodist, and Standard Church people. My goal: to find out what made Ralph Horner who he was and what influence he still had on churches a hundred years later.

Without a doubt, the personal interviews turned this book from a project to a passion. One of my first interviews was with the late Rev. Gordon Hammond. I was inspired by many of his stories and challenged by the dedication of these early pioneer missionaries. I am indebted to my friend, Paul Perry (his mother was a Horner), who introduced me to Ralph Horner's relatives and Ottawa Valley people who knew stories about Ralph Horner. After meeting these people and hearing their stories, I felt a strong sense of conviction that I have very little understanding of what it means to really sacrifice and serve God fully. I want to dedicate this book with my dad to all the Holiness Movement and Standard Church pastors, evangelists, and lay people who have laboured for God and truly "took up their cross daily" to follow the Lord Jesus Christ.

—MARK CROSWELL

ACKNOWLEDGEMENTS

I was born in 1944 and grew up on a homestead near Newbrook, Alberta, across the road from the Standard church and campgrounds. My grandmother, "Aunt Nellie" Croswell, had been converted in the 1928–1930 revival that took place in the Balsam Grove schoolhouse one mile from our home; everyone in my father's family was touched in some way by the move of the Spirit that took place in that pioneer community. My spiritual roots go back to the beginnings of the Standard Church in western Canada. I made a personal commitment to be a follower of Jesus Christ on the old campgrounds when I was a twenty-year-old young man about to launch into a career of education. After teaching school in Edmonton for two years, I moved to Brockville, Ontario, in 1967 to attend the Brockville Bible College and became pastor of the rural circuit of Wilton and Violet. The next year I became pastor of the Brockville Standard Church, later known as Centennial Road Standard Church; I was lead pastor for forty years. When the Standard Church merged with The Wesleyan Church in 2004, I realized that much of our spiritual heritage would fade with time unless someone took up the project to record the history. While writing, I came to realize that many of the pioneer "Hornerite" preachers, missionaries, and evangelists were heroes of faith who should be honoured for their labour and sacrifice.

There are several people I would like to thank who made this book possible:

Mark Croswell: history teacher at Bay View Secondary School, Richmond Hill, Ontario. Mark is my oldest son and spent countless hours diligently collecting and filing stories from interviews, archives, newspapers, libraries, personal diaries, and dusty boxes of record books. Mark would not allow any shortcuts in our research and gently cajoled and encouraged me to continue rewriting, reviewing, and reorganizing the vast amount of material we eventually collected and stacked in boxes and notebooks in my basement office. This book is not only a tribute to Mark's exhaustive research but also to his dedication and determination to record and honour our spiritual roots. Mark reviewed the past and believes Romans 8:28—that God works all things out for good for those who believe and love God.

Rev. Earl Conley: Standard Church pastor, missionary, Bible college teacher, and general superintendent. During his tenure as editor of the *Christian Standard*, Rev. Conley accumulated, organized, and documented historical vignettes, highlights, and dates of the Hornerite movement. Without his careful documentation, much of the early history and growth of Standard Church foreign missions would have been lost. Sadly, before this manuscript was presented for final publication, Rev. Conley was suddenly taken from this life on November 23, 2011. I had the honour of preaching his funeral message, appropriately entitled, "Let Us Rise Up and Build."

Brian Phillips: personal friend. Brian scanned many of the pictures from old, less-than-ideal-condition snapshots, magazines, and scrapbooks. His patient work of image processing and revitalization has enhanced and recorded historic pictures from our past for generations of people to view in years to come.

Central Canada District of The Wesleyan Church and the leadership of District Superintendent Rev. Donald Hodgins: CCDWC has encouraged and sponsored the writing of this book to record the spiritual heritage and contribution to God's kingdom of the Holiness Movement and Standard churches in Canada, northern USA, foreign missions, and eventually The Wesleyan Church.

Aaron Perry: editorial consultant and proofreader. I have known Aaron since he was a boy attending Zion Hill Camp, and then as a student at Bethany Bible College (now Kingswood University) and Asbury Seminary. He has since become a successful author and editor and has been accepted for his doctoral studies in organizational leadership at Regent University, Virginia. He is currently serving on the staff at Centennial Road Standard Church in Brockville, Ontario. It is fitting that Aaron should have a part in the publication of this book since his family lives near Clarendon school in Quebec, where Ralph Horner attended and began his amazing revivals; his mother is Kathryn (Horner) Perry, a distant relative of Rev. Horner. Aaron has deep roots in the Standard Church.

Wesleyan Publishing House: Thank you Wesleyan Publishing House for allowing me the opportunity to publish *Lift Up A Standard* with you. Your patience and help has been most appreciated. And Mary McNeil, you were awesome to read and correct this manuscript with such detailed diligence and correct the myriad of capital letters, conference titles, and punctuation marks!

My family: My family has supported me for forty years as senior pastor of Centennial Road Standard Church. Without them the story of the Standard Church would have been different, and this book would never have been written. I have a supportive wife, Faye; two terrific sons, Mark and Darren; a marvelous daughter-in-law, Lauri; and now the joy of my life, grandchildren: Austin, Abigail, and Sadie. You are the greatest family and I love you!

—LAURENCE CROSWELL

1

EARLY LIFE IN
THE OTTAWA VALLEY

One sunny day in July of 2008, my son Mark organized a motor trip for our family to visit the childhood home of his maternal grandmother, Evelyn Montgomery, in the beautiful, rolling farmlands of Pontiac County in western Quebec. Since Mark is a history teacher and has spent considerable time researching his genealogy, he was anxious to visit the old landmarks where his grandmother had grown up. As we meandered along the peaceful country roads bordered by luxurious fields of corn and hay, we realized we were in "Horner country." It was on one of these peaceful farms on Highway 148, three miles west of Shawville, that Ralph Cecil Horner was born and raised—a farm he later managed but eventually left to become an evangelist. Mark's family roots had brushed up against the very locale where Ralph Horner began his remarkable life and ministry. Grandma Montgomery, then Evelyn Armstrong, attended Radford School in Clarendon (the original school burned to the ground), where Ralph Horner some thirty-five years before had completed his elementary education.

One of Canada's foremost homegrown evangelists, R. C. Horner is both revered and reviled. But while achieving a consensus about feelings for the evangelist may prove elusive, one thing is certain: few Canadian evangelists have ever exceeded the influence he has brought to the evangelical church in Canada. His life is one of triumph and tragedy, success and adversity, but in all things, resolve and perseverance. What follows is an attempt to relate his story, beginning with his humble origins in Shawville, Quebec, to becoming bishop of the Holiness Movement Church and the springboard for other spiritual awakenings across Canada and northern USA.

Little is known about Ralph Horner's early life and personality. Information that does exist is based on a few archives, his personal memoirs, and oral tradition. Of northern Irish Protestant descent, Ralph Horner was the eldest son and fourth of eleven children born to James Horner and Ellen Richardson, second-generation famers.[1] The Shawville United Church parish register, signed by his parents with an X (indicating illiteracy), declares he was born December 24, 1853, and baptized by Rev. L. Houghton, Wesleyan minister, July 13, 1854.[2] This date is supported by his gravestone in Merivale Cemetery, located at the Merivale United Church in Ottawa. His wife, Annie Horner, who published his memoirs, stated he was born December 22, 1854, and many biographers have quoted this incorrect date.[3]

PIONEER LIFE IN PONTIAC COUNTY

Ralph Horner's home—Pontiac County, Quebec—was isolated from the Ontario side of the valley physically, culturally, and economically by the mighty Ottawa River. Transportation networks and improved agricultural techniques were slow to infiltrate. Early roads were often two ruts winding through the bush. The railway arrived in 1886, and even though certain manufacturing facilities and cheese factories followed, Roy Fortune noted, it was too little, too late: Clarendon Township would never completely overcome its isolation, conservatism, and marginalization.[4]

Despite the isolation, Clarendon was one of the most prosperous of Pontiac's townships, and the Horner and Richardson families were among its most wealthy.[5] However, farm responsibilities and the unavailability of high school did not help Ralph to complete his education much beyond the primary grades. Although most parents considered it valuable to provide some education for their children, school was not a high priority since most girls would become housewives and the boys would become farmers or loggers. Ralph dropped out of school before graduating, and only returned to complete his elementary education in 1878 at the age of twenty-five.

At sixteen years of age, Ralph Horner unexpectedly found himself managing the two-hundred-acre family farm after his father, James, was killed when kicked by a horse. The responsibility of caring for his mother and his surviving nine brothers and sisters still living at home fell on Ralph's shoulders.

The death of James was a great shock to his family. Ralph recollected how his father announced at six that evening he would die at twelve that night. For six hours Ellen and her children watched and listened to the laboured breathing of the injured James and the steady ticking of the old family clock. Every hour he became weaker as death approached. Ralph said that when his father was nearing the "bank of the River," he and his brothers and sisters were taken from the room. Ralph went outside around the house and got near the window so he could hear his father's throaty breathing; the "death rattle" sounded like beautiful music to him, for it meant his father was still living. James died at the time he said he would, and young Ralph recalled that "the solemn realities of the great eternity lingered with him."[6]

"It would have been an easy matter at any time during the next year to have led me to Jesus for Salvation," Ralph Horner wrote in his memoirs, but it seemed to him "that he was never in a place up to the day of his decision to be saved, where Christians had faith and power to bring him under enough conviction to seek salvation."[7]

After the death of his father, his mother, Ellen, reported that "Ralph nobly assumed . . . the heavy responsibilities of home."[8] Since Clarendon Township had a reputation for fights and violence, Ellen taught her boys how to box. Early photographs and accounts depict Ralph as an imposing man, muscular and sturdy, with piercing eyes and a ruddy complexion and reddish whiskers. Charles Lynch, columnist for the *Ottawa Journal* reported that "Ralph Horner of Radford, Quebec, in his earlier days was a man of physical power to be reckoned with in the hotels and shanties along the Ottawa River. He was five feet eleven inches tall and weighed 235 pounds, was well known, and was not averse to displaying his fistic power, or on taking a drink when the occasion arose."[9] Ralph's memoirs claim he was "corrupted" by his parents' hired help, and as he grew older he was known to brawl in the taverns of Pontiac County. "A number of times," he confessed, "I had drunk and danced all night . . . with the people of the community."[10] It is unknown whether Ralph was an Orangeman, but according to J. Lloyd Armstrong almost every man and boy over the age of sixteen in Clarendon was a member of the Orange Order.[11]

Ralph's younger brother, George, was also stocky, sturdy, and strong (despite being whipped by Ralph for sassing his mother).[12] Known as "Red Roaring George,"[13] he was described as "a man of brawn and muscle, burly, broad shouldered and weighing 220 pounds."[14] The story is told of George taking grain to the grist mill at Massham to grind and sell to his customers. The Horners took good care of their horses and George stopped at Quyon, Quebec, to have supper and feed his team. While at the hotel, someone told him that Morrie, a member of the Knights of Columbus, was bragging that he could beat any Orangeman in a boxing match. George, goaded into taking up the challenge, said, "You had better go get him." The bare-knuckled fistfight took place outside the hotel. Morrie hit George, but he would not go down. The men slugged it out for several hours — some claim the fight went on for six hours. When it finally ended, it was declared a draw. Unfortunately, Morrie died six months later. Neighbours said it was from a blow delivered by George's fist.[15] George later accompanied his brother, Ralph, during his outdoor tent meetings serving as unofficial bodyguard and bouncer, and was known as "Horner's Policeman," intercepting drunks or hooligans who would attempt to injure Ralph or disrupt the meetings.

Winters would find Ralph and George, along with many of the local farmers, employed in the valley lumber camps to supplement their farm income. Ralph reported the shanties were wicked places where men entertained themselves with vulgar songs and card playing. Excessive drinking in the shanties became such a social problem that major operators prohibited its consumption in their camps.[16] Gambling was also a vice and many lost their wages at the card table, sadly returning home with little money for provisions and support for their families. It is little wonder wives dreaded the card-playing episodes of the lumber shanties and condemned any form of playing cards as sinfully wicked. (My [Laurence] grandmother, "Aunt Nellie" Croswell, whose husband, Fred, worked the winter lumber camps in those years, would not so much as allow a deck of cards to enter her house.)

Religious Life in the Valley

To understand Ralph Horner, one must understand the religious life of the Ottawa Valley. When settlers first arrived, most were Irish Anglicans accustomed to defending Protestant "superiority" against the "Catholic hordes."[17] It was the Methodist circuit riders who first brought the "Word of God" to the early pioneers. These saddlebag preachers followed the settlers on horseback, on foot, in canoes, or on snowshoes to conduct the sacraments, perform marriages, and baptise new infants and converts. Goldwin French described these circuit riders as "preachers and administrators whose deficiencies in education were more than offset by their zeal and self-sacrifice."[18] It was not work for the faint of heart, but the Methodist circuit riders made a significant contribution to the religious life of the valley and most Christians living there traced their spiritual roots to the early days of the Methodist Church.

The growth and success of the Methodists in North America during the early to mid-nineteenth century had been impressive. When Francis

Asbury arrived in America in 1771, Methodists numbered 10 preachers and 600 members; when he died in 1816 after forty-five years of relentless preaching virtually every day and conducting meetings and conferences, the Methodists reported 695 ordained preachers and 213,735 members; a million people, one-eighth of the entire population, attended Methodist camp meetings, the nineteenth-century equivalent of megachurches.[19] In Ontario, census figures reveal Methodists increased in number from 2,550 members in 1812 to nearly 650,000 in 1891. That's 30.9 percent of the entire provincial population. Across Canada, 17.5 percent (840,000) claimed to be Methodist.[20]

The growth engine for Methodism was primarily revivals: a minister preached revival and success was talked in terms of revival. "The Methodists paid their preachers only a nominal stipend, gave them no job security, and told them to avoid arid theology: 'Always suit your subjects to your audience, and choose the plainest texts you can.'"[21] Preaching was simple and straightforward and language generally plain, direct, and colloquial.

Revivalism was also characterized by preaching that called for a crisis conversion experience establishing an intimate relationship with God. This was followed by a "second work of grace," entire sanctification, also a conversion-like experience known as the "second blessing" whereby the child of God presented himself as a living sacrifice to God, sought cleansing from inbred sin, and was filled with the Holy Spirit. Methodists utilized mass revival services to evangelize, invigorate, and rekindle the spiritual intensity of the church.[22]

CAMP MEETINGS

A primary method for revival during the early 1800s was through large, open-air gatherings in isolated rural areas known as "camp meetings." Camp meetings lasted for several days and were under the control of leading clergy and families at prearranged sites. Tents were pitched in a clearing, encircling a preaching stand and rough benches. During camp meetings, theology was largely ignored and preaching focused on an individual's personal rebirth and spiritual growth to a purer way of living whereby the power of the corrupt world would be broken.[23] Free from outside influences, and with the encouragement of friends and neighbours, attendees would be moved upon to forsake their former manner of life and seek a higher spiritual experience; in doing so, many would weep, shout, shake, and faint. These experiences became spiritual markers and defining moments for adherents. Leading the camp revivals were anointed preachers, usually from surrounding churches and districts, who, from training and experience, directed the emotional energy of the meetings to provide seekers opportunity to make critical, spiritual decisions usually at an altar of prayer.

CLARENDON

The Methodist saddlebag preachers began visiting Clarendon, Quebec, in the 1820s. Early meetings were held in private homes and later in the schoolhouse at Clarendon Front. Considerable growth took place between 1851 and 1881: "Circuit-riding preachers met the needs of rural residents who craved a more emotional religion, one which seemed to seek reform and cater to the needs of the common man. . . . Most of the Horners who had been Presbyterian and then Anglican, converted to Methodism."[24]

CONVERSION

Ralph Horner's family was nominally Methodist. Despite the fact that his grandfather, Ralph Sr., had been a staunch Anglican who read the responses in church, and his wife, Jeannie Brown, was a faithful Presbyterian, Ralph Horner confessed, "I had very little early teaching in the truths of Christianity. . . . I attended Sunday school in my boyhood until I was old enough to teach a class. Being absent one Sunday, my class was given to another teacher, at which I was offended and left the school. I became desperately wicked in my manner of life, but I retained a strong fear of God and a profound respect for Christians." Ralph goes on to say, "I never was deeply troubled about the salvation of my soul as many have been whom I have known. I do not remember ever losing any sleep over my transgressions of God's laws. I can remember deciding that I would become a Christian when I would settle down in life."[25]

A Methodist camp meeting was conducted near his home, and twenty-two-year-old Ralph (likely out of curiosity) decided to attend the Sunday services.[26] A motto printed over the stand made a favourable impression on the young man: Clarendon for Jesus. The prayers and testimonies of those who had been converted on the campgrounds deeply moved Ralph. He recalled,

> When I saw young men lead their companions into the woods, and heard them pray with them until they were saved, my heart commenced to melt. . . . What I saw and heard was so interesting to me, that I remained on the camp grounds all day. . . . I said in my heart that I wanted that kind of religion. . . . In the night service when sinners were invited to the penitent form (altar) to seek the Lord, I went forward to repent of my sins. I was very anxious for someone to come and tell me what I should do to be saved. . . . I mourned over my sinful heart and life for two days.[27]

The next day Horner returned to the camp. Horner told his counselors that the more he prayed the more lost he felt. At this moment a wise friend spoke to him and led him to salvation:

> "The Son of Man is come to seek and to save that which was lost," he said.
> Instantly I felt that there was hope for me.
> He asked me, "Do you believe that Jesus is able to save you?"
> I said, "Yes."

"Then," he said, "Do you believe that He is willing to save you?"

I said, "Yes."

The next question was, "Do you believe that He saves you now?"

There was no feeling that He did save me. The struggle for a few minutes was desperate. . . . The promise of God was before me and my cry went out, "I believe He saves me now!"

Immediately I declared to all present that I was saved.

Upon returning home from the prayer meeting, Ralph said, "God appeared in every star. The whole earth seemed to be full of His glory."[28]

When Ralph reached home that evening, he took out a Bible and began to pray and worship. His mother, hearing her son's voice in praise, quickly dressed and came from her room in tears, and soon she too found salvation in Jesus. Ralph reported that in a few days, all in his home were saved. "We sang, prayed and praised God in our new joy. Anger, strife and worldliness gave place to prayer, praise, and great rejoicings."[29] It is essential to understand Ralph's conversion experience, because for him it was a defining spiritual moment. "I was born in revival," he would later testify, and it was this revival experience that transformed him from his former life of carousing and fighting, and that he attempted to re-create during all his future preaching as an evangelist. For him this was true "scriptural conversion."

ENTIRELY SANCTIFIED

About two months after Ralph Horner was converted, he attended a workers' meeting on another campground and learned there was a second work of God's grace for his life: entire sanctification. A worker explained to Ralph there was a second experience available whereby he might receive a greater fullness of God's presence and be delivered from his inner battle with self when tempted or provoked. Ralph related that he was astonished at hearing there was perfect deliverance, and he remembered that his soul, his head, and his nature cried out at once, "I must have it now."[30] People were asked to go in groups and seek the experience. Ralph recalled that he could not go quickly enough and determined to call upon God with an audible voice. Two questions were posed before prayer:

"Do you believe that it is for you?"
I said, "Yes."
"Can you trust Jesus for it?"
My heart cried, "I can trust Him for anything."[31]

Ralph testified that instantly the second work of grace was wrought and God seemed to let the whole heavens upon him, and the witness of the Spirit was clearly received. Ralph Horner explained that for a few years after his experience of entire sanctification, he did not hear another sermon on the doctrine and experience, and made very little personal progress. The only help he received, he said, was in telling it to others. But the experience not only freed him from the power and pull of sin, but also empowered him for soul winning. "Perfect love made me groan for power to reach the perishing masses and lead them to Jesus," recalled Ralph. Many times he remembered pleading with God for the unsaved and for His people, and being overpowered by the Spirit until all his physical strength was suspended.

"Entire Sanctification had cleansed me from all inbred sin and filled me with perfect love," Ralph testified. "The baptism of the Holy Ghost and fire put energy and might into every faculty of my mind and soul. It was to me the 'Tongue of Fire' to preach the reconciling Word."[32]

NEW FAITH TESTED

Tragedy struck the Horner home a few months later that would test their newfound faith and trust in God. Scarlet fever raged through the community. Ralph was first in his home to come down with the illness, but he recovered. His second youngest brother, Willie, was next; Willie died within four days, singing, "Come, Holy Spirit, Heavenly Dove." Soon the youngest brother was stricken with the fever as well and died about three days later. Ralph reminisced about those days of grieving: "God made our home a heaven on earth, dividing it to give us more of an interest in the upper and better place He has prepared for us. Our home was a place of prayer and thanksgiving. We were considered at once the people of God, and the unsaved knew that our house would no longer be a place of ungodly amusement. When our neighbours came to see us they expected me to pray with them, and when I went to their homes they looked for the same."[33]

CALL TO PREACH

Upon conversion, Ralph Horner immediately felt a strong call to preach—to labour for the salvation of those who were lost. But, he insisted, "I did not feel called to devote my life to the Christian ministry"—despite the fact he was strongly aware of Christ constraining him to labour for the salvation of the perishing. It did not seem to be a cross to bear for him to go and conduct a prayer meeting or service of worship in the community. In fact, he had not been converted more than two weeks when he was scheduled to conduct his first public worship service. One of Ralph's sisters, who lived ten miles away, was eager to hear first-hand of her brother's experience and invited Ralph to conduct a church service in her home. Ralph recalled that he was eager to enter into the service. During the first two weeks of his Christian experience he had learned a tune to one hymn in the Methodist hymnbook, which he would use along with a brief prayer. The service was likely to be very short, he thought, but young Ralph was so eager to tell of his experience with the saving grace of God that he thought the preliminaries were quite long enough. Ralph, himself, was amazed at the liberty he received to testify to those assembled in the service and he felt as a father at home talking to his children. Public speaking came easily to Ralph.

After that first meeting, there was such a spirit of revival on the people that Ralph was convinced it was impossible to leave them without other services. The congregation requested that he meet them on Sunday morning, and Ralph consented to do so. The same revival spirit continued Sunday morning. It became necessary for Ralph to meet the people every Sunday, which he did until other calls became too numerous for him to continue in the one location.

When it became known that Ralph had commenced a revival and established a mission, he was considered by many to be a preacher already. He accepted all the work that was offered him and he was ready to conduct three services on Sunday and all the prayer meetings within his reach. "It was a delight to walk three or four miles to conduct a prayer meeting at night after a day's hard labour," he wrote. "But God had not called me to the Christian ministry."[34]

The winter season found Ralph employed as usual in the lumber woods and living in a shanty. Ralph conducted hymn sings at night and on Sundays—a distraction for the men accustomed to whiling away the long, cold evenings, playing cards, gambling, drinking, singing their vulgar songs, or proving their manliness with feats of strength.

When Ralph Horner returned from the woods, he continued to take meetings. One night after a meeting, he was disappointed because he had not been given opportunity to speak; it was then God spoke to Ralph's heart and asked him if he would leave all and go to preach. "The call," said Ralph, "was as clear to me as my conversion and the entire sanctification of my nature. . . . All my desires for secular employment left me. . . . I had no desire for anything else only spreading the glad tidings of Jesus to all mankind, and leading the people of God into the experience of Christian Perfection."[35]

But Ralph found it difficult to tell people he was called to preach. The most difficult matter was to leave the farm. His mother depended on him for the operation of the business—and it was a prosperous farm. Ralph's younger brothers and sisters looked up to him like a father, for Ralph had acted as a parent in governing the home. Moreover, Ralph would be rejecting the land and inheritance that was his birthright. There was a second reason: Ralph had a speech impediment—he had a lisp during casual conversation[36] and could not articulate certain sounds in the English language.[37] The third reason was his lack of schooling: he was twenty-five years old and had not completed his elementary education.[38]

PREPARATION FOR MINISTRY

Ralph Horner was aware that if he would follow his call to preach, it would be necessary to further his education. He had never studied anything of grammar, geography, or British and Canadian history. It was somewhat humiliating, he confessed, to enter a class of little girls, but once he settled it in his mind, God blessed him, for in eight months he completed all that was taught in the public school. During the year, he still availed himself of every opportunity for ministry, conducting services, even organizing a "Sabbath school" in the little country school and leading weekly prayer meetings.

Ralph spent the following year in "special evangelism." During the year, Rev. Hammond and Rev. Knox, ministers of the Methodist Church, urged Ralph to enter the Methodist ministry. They assured the young preacher that he would find the probation course useful and that they were in need of evangelists in their Conference.

October of 1879, found Ralph enrolled in Renfrew High School, across the Ottawa River in Ontario, to complete his high school matriculation. During the year, he boarded in the home of Methodist pastor Rev. William Craig, who, according to Ralph, pleaded with him to take the Preliminary Course of Study for entering the Methodist ministry. Conflict had already begun in Ralph's mind that he was called to the office of an evangelist and could not engage in pastoral work. Rev. Craig endeavoured to explain that the Course of Study for Probationers was the best possible course for an evangelist, and constantly affirmed that the Methodist Church was in great need of evangelists and that Ralph could have a large field of ministry.[39]

About the first of February 1880, and after much persuasion by Rev. Craig, Ralph Horner commenced work on the Preliminary Course of Study for Probationers for entry into the ministry of the Methodist Church. The Conference gave Ralph permission to be employed during the year under a district chairman. Ralph did not conduct any regular Conference work until sometime in the middle of August 1880. He was appointed by the Methodist hierarchy to preach at home and oversee the Clarendon circuit where he was born and raised. A daily routine was established of visiting, praying, and attending to his studies. Ralph Horner conducted most of his first ministerial duties in Clarendon, but soon he was called upon to preach revival services farther afield in the circuit. Alumette Island, across from Pembroke, was first. Ralph reported in his memoirs that when he closed the special services on the island, nearly all the Protestant people (about thirty individuals) were "scripturally converted." Next he was called to Zion Church, at nearby Shawville. He was on the Clarendon circuit for two years, and two hundred thirty members were received on probation into church membership.[40]

COLLEGE YEARS

In 1882, Ralph Horner was received on trial for the Methodist ministry. Since it was customary for probationers to go to college after travelling for two years, he chose to study theology from 1883 to 1885 at Victoria

College, located then at Cobourg, Ontario. Although some had cautioned him that college was a place where young preachers lost their salvation, Ralph decided to remain only so long as he was assured that he was retaining all his Christian experience. Ralph reported that his professors did not try to hinder him in any way and soon he was meeting with students in the vestry of the church to discuss the doctrine and experience of entire sanctification. According to Ralph, many of the students, as well as the pastor of the church, sought and found the experience of holiness. Revival spread beyond the college and, claimed Ralph, 150 were received on probation for membership in the Methodist churches.[41]

When two years expired, Ralph testified he left Victoria College in a "great revival flame." He entered the summer evangelistic campaign full of the love of God and anointed to preach the gospel of Jesus Christ. That fall, he entered the National School of Elocution and Oratory in Philadelphia, Pennsylvania. He completed the two-year course in one year, graduating with his bachelor of oratory. He had overcome his speech impediment and was a commanding figure to behold: with posture-perfect stance, one foot slightly forward in order to move at will, he spoke slowly, deliberately, and powerfully.[42] But he said he did not neglect opportunities to win souls for Jesus. He took several opportunities to preach and remained in the spirit of revival.

Three years of college had not dampened Ralph Horner's passion for evangelism. If anything, it fuelled a deeper desire and resolve to conduct revivals and lead men and women to Christ and then into the deeper experience of surrendering their lives entirely to God in purity and holiness.

Ralph Horner's early years were shaped and influenced in many ways by the culture of the Ottawa Valley, his life events, and nineteenth-century Methodist revivalism. But it was his conversion and experience with entire sanctification that transformed him. They were, for him, scripturally true Methodist experiences. And it was God's call to evangelism that drove him to give up wealth, culture, and family obligations to preach these doctrines. It later placed him in conflict with the Methodist Church.

EVANGELIST NOT PASTOR

When Ralph Horner graduated from college in 1886, many perceived that the spiritual fervour of the Methodists was diminishing. In Canada, critics attributed that loss to the merger in 1884 of the Wesleyan Methodist Church, the Methodist Episcopal Church, the Primitive Methodist Church, and the Bible Christian Church to form the Methodist Church. This union marked the culmination of a fifty-year effort to secure denominational consolidation of the Canadian forces of the Methodist Church. Although union seems to have initially accelerated the numerical growth of the Methodist Church between 1884 and 1890, especially in the budding towns and cities, success bred its own set of problems. No sooner was union attained than many of its initial gains were lost as large sections of the membership body broke off to join the rise of new evangelical religious sects.[1] Evangelistic passion and emotionalism waned as leading Methodists became intent on keeping the denomination respectable.

The increased growth, prosperity, and influence of the Methodist Church resulted in a shift into the cultural mainstream of society through the establishment of successful urban churches in cities and towns—metropolitan centers that were becoming increasingly more powerful and important. Moreover, by the mid to late nineteenth century, society was becoming more diversified socially and economically. The Methodist Church was finding it more and more difficult to "work both sides of the track in an increasingly stratified society."[2] "They created a professional clergy trained in formal seminaries rather than in their former on-the-job apprenticeships, and became increasingly more concerned with impressing polite society. These professional priests not only softened many of Methodism's once-austere rules and rituals, they also shifted their focus from preaching the Word to reforming society and doing good works."[3]

HOLINESS REVIVALS

As to be expected, the more conservative church members reacted against this toning down of expression and zeal—especially those from the Methodist Episcopal Church, who had originally evangelized among the rural communities and represented a more enthusiastic style of revivalism. Conservative Methodists began to find expression in a renewed emphasis on holiness. General Superintendent Dr. Albert Carman undoubtedly recognized this concern and (perhaps to alleviate some of these growing fears and from a personal concern himself) delivered an outstanding message and plea to the whole membership of the Methodist Church to enter anew into a life of holiness. The message "Holiness Our Hope" was published in 1884, in which he argued that only holiness could make the union successful.[4]

This discouragement of spiritual passion during the late nineteenth century brought about a series of changes to the nature of Canadian Methodism. Change is seldom tolerated without a corresponding reaction. In response to these changes, conservatives within the Methodist Church embraced what has been referred to as the "Holiness Revival"; eastern Ontario was home to a significant proportion of the Holiness Movement in Canada. The period of most intense activity regarding the issue of holiness took place between 1880 and 1900.

A number of forces combined to help create these holiness revivals. By 1875, Methodists were becoming a middle class church and began to enjoy political influence. The level of Methodist social prestige is suggested at the 1886 General Conference by the presence of the prime minister (John A. MacDonald), the premier of Ontario (Oliver Mowat), the provincial minister of education, as well as the chancellor and vice chancellor of the University of Toronto.[5] The influx of new middle class men to the ministerial force began producing a new breed of ministers from the seminaries. Younger faculty knew little of John Wesley and became enamoured with German higher criticism and English Darwinism. Subsequently, the holiness message was often neglected. This served to strengthen the conviction by the conservative wing that these new and foreign elements were threatening traditional Wesleyanism.

Industrialization and urbanization began to intensify. Major philosophical differences developed between city churches (with their new-found wealth, rented pews, robed choirs, architecture, musicians, and liturgy) and the numerous rural churches (with their emphasis on revivalism, free expression, personal involvement, and outbursts of enthusiasm). Modern churches gradually relaxed their prohibitions against worldly amusements, fine dress, and dancing. The lifestyles of church members enjoying their new social position bore little resemblance to the stern conduct codes of their early Methodist forebears. The social elites who controlled pews often sought to dominate church affairs, including the selection and message of the minister. Furthermore, in many Methodist churches there was a breakdown and neglect of the small group class meetings with their accompanying personal accountability.

Added to all this, the 1850s saw a subtle change in the nature of the camp meeting, one of the traditional venues for the highly emotional, religious experiences associated with Methodist conversion and entire sanctification. Although camp meetings reached the height of their success in the early part of the decade, during the same period there were calls to establish permanent campsites in order to make them more respectable. Within twenty years, a transition had occurred and permanent sites were developed, some with large tabernacle-auditoriums surrounded by clusters of summer cottages. The nature of the camp meeting began to shift from a place of revival preaching to that of a vacation in the country.[6] Preachers were asked to avoid talk of hellfire and damnation, and emphasize revival preaching that was sober and sincere. By the 1870s the nature of the camp meeting had shifted to where the benefits were more social and recreational than religious.[7] In his memoirs, Ralph Horner told of going to a camp meeting held on the old grounds where it had been for years. Each family had its own cottage, and the camp had dwindled into a yearly resort where they met to visit. There was a large grocery where candies, cakes, and soft drinks were served.[8] Methodism was becoming preeminently a middleclass institution and assumed it could best serve all segments of society by remaking the world in its own image, including the camp meeting.

CONCERNED METHODISTS

This shift in values and emphasis caused great concern among conservative, orthodox Methodists. For them it seemed the church was going to hell and nothing but a "Holy Ghost revival" could stem the tide of worldliness and save it from higher criticism, Darwinism, and popular Christianity with its church fairs, drunkenness, Sabbath breaking, and card playing. Lola Willows in her memoirs wrote of the "cold and worldly people who professed religion" in the Methodist Church.[9] War was on and those who loved the old paths became defenders of the faith. In a letter written to Harold Pointen, retired Holiness Movement preacher Rev. S. A. York examined why he and others participated in the holiness revivals. The origins traced to a feeling of dissatisfaction in the minds of a segment of conservative people and ministers within the Methodist Church after the union of 1884, especially as to the neglect of preaching the doctrine of entire sanctification as a second work of grace. This manifested itself in the banding together of like-minded people calling for special meetings of prayer, testimony, and exhortation. Conventions were organized in which local preachers and itinerant ministers were called upon to take leading parts. According to Rev. York, ministers actively participated, but laypeople furnished the initiative. For example, at a Methodist camp meeting at Holford, Ontario (near Jasper), Rev. York recalled overhearing a conversation between two members of the church:

"Joe, what do you think of this new doctrine of Holiness?"

"Oh Rachel, this is no new doctrine, it is Methodist doctrine and Bible doctrine. I received the experience myself two years ago at Hecton camp meeting but because there was so much opposition to the doctrine, I failed to testify to the experience which I received, and it has leaked away."[10]

MASS EVANGELISTS

Another trend began to develop during the 1850s: the rise of the "professional evangelist," patterned on the preaching style of Charles Finney (1792–1875). Finney adopted the Methodists' "anxious bench," offering congregants an opportunity to publicly declare their faith; he prayed in the colloquial, common language of the people and allowed free expressions of emotionalism. Unlike Finney, however, the new professional evangelists were not appointed to any particular congregation or circuit, but travelled full time from church to church, city to city, camp meeting to camp meeting. This new approach to mass evangelism took place to stem the tide of rising worldliness and liberalism and call Christians to the fundamentals of faith and holy living. In 1857, Phoebe Palmer and her husband, Dr. Walter C. Palmer, held large revivals in Hamilton, Oakville, and Toronto, as well as the Maritimes. Phoebe Palmer had an experience with entire sanctification, and her published books and preaching—identifying sanctification as a second blessing distinct from that of the initial experience of regeneration—were influential in how Methodists would interpret John Wesley's teaching on the subject.[11] Revivalism also gained momentum in the later quarter of the nineteenth century with the arrival of mass evangelists D. L. Moody and Ira D. Sankey and their emphasis on conversion and a deeper spiritual life. Preachers like these opened the way for a new breed of preacher—the professional evangelist as opposed to the preacher assigned to a church or circuit.

HORNER CALLED TO EVANGELISM

It is likely Ralph Horner saw himself as this new breed of preacher and requested the Methodist Conference to leave him without a circuit. He felt God had called him to evangelism and not to pastoral ministry. Despite assurances by the president, Rev. T. G. Williams, that he would "do all in his power to open up the way,"[12] the Stationing Committee of the Montreal Conference ignored his request and appointed him to the Cobden-Locksley Circuit in the Pembroke District. Horner refused to accept the appointment. "I had tested my call to special evangelism, and I was settled. I was obliged to disobey the Conference, or do violence to my own conscience," he wrote. "I entered special evangelism at once."[13] In response, Horner claimed Chairman Williams "brought to bear upon me the terrors of the law of the Church."[14] But in the second half of the year, according to Horner, Williams pleaded with him "as father would plead with a prodigal boy" to take the circuit.[15] Horner's refusal marked the beginning of conflict between him and the Methodist Church.

ORDINATION: MONTREAL CONFERENCE 1887

When the Fourth Session of the Montreal Conference met at Sydenham Street Methodist Church in Kingston, Ontario, on Wednesday, May 25, 1887, among the first items of business was that of probationers for the ministry who were to be received into full connection with the Conference and ordained.[16] Evidently there had been considerable discussion concerning Ralph C. Horner, provoked, no doubt, by his refusal to accept the Conference appointment of 1886 to the Cobden-Locksley Circuit. An extract in the minutes of the proceedings reads, "The case of R. C. Horner was referred back to the Pembroke District for the purpose of amending the minutes in the case."[17] The amended minutes acquiesced to Horner's request to be engaged in evangelistic endeavours: "Brother Horner, having travelled three years and attended college two years, completing the prescribed course of study, having finished his probation, answered all the disciplinary questions; moved by Brother Allum, seconded by Brother Shortt, that Brother Horner having finished his probation, he be recommended to be ordained to the ministry of our Church, and in view of his marked ability and use-fulness in the evangelistic work, this District in its judgment believes that he should be permitted to labour in that work."[18]

Subsequently, the Annual Pembroke District Meeting of the Con-ference convened and prepared for the business of recommending Ralph Horner for ordination and full membership. Horner was asked if he could answer the questions for ordination. He answered to the contrary: "I have spent six years on probation and will spend six more rather than be ordained in the regular way."[19] Ralph recounted that he was definite in explaining his calling was to special evangelism. He could not be ordained to do regular pastoral work. Horner was asked to appear before the ministers in a private session of the District. In the private session, members of the District were straightforward as well: they said there was no unwillingness on the part of Conference to ordain Ralph Horner for evangelistic work, but they could not do so, since there was only one form of ordination. Ralph recalled an aged minister was brought into the session to convince him that the office of pastor and evangelist were one and the same. Moreover, the chair-man continued to reason with Ralph as follows: if the Conference was willing to give him evangelistic work, and if the Conference was will-ing to trust him, should not he be willing to trust the Conference?[20] According to Horner it was stated and emphasized by members of the

District, including the chairman, that the Conference was willing to give him evangelistic work if he would accept ordination in the regular way. If the Conference was willing to set him apart for evangelism, should he not trust his brethren when they were willing to trust him? "These and other questions were asked," Horner contended, "until I was ashamed to refuse any longer."[21]

Ralph Horner was convinced to proceed with ordination. He later reasoned that members of the Conference were eager to ordain him in this way because the Methodist Conference was divided: on one side, there were many who supposed that in a short time he would desire to be in regular pastoral work, and the controversy would cease; on the other hand, there were others who were very much in favour of special evangelism and looked to Ralph for his emphasis on revival.[22] In fact, General Superintendent Rev. Albert Carman and a number of more traditional conservative church leaders initially promoted Horner's holiness crusades.[23] Thus, despite the short but public disagreement with some officials of the Montreal Conference, Ralph Horner was ordained to the Christian ministry with seven other candidates in the Methodist Church. The ceremony, conducted by the president, Rev. T. G. Williams, was held in the Sydenham Street Methodist Church, Kingston, Ontario, on Sunday morning, May 29, 1887.

EMERGING EVANGELIST

Ralph Horner was appointed as one of two Montreal Conference evangelists placed under the direction of the Evangelistic Society. Minutes from the June 6, 1888, Montreal Conference held in Dominion Square Methodist Church, Montreal, record a glowing report: "Two Evangelists, Revs. D. Winter and R. C. Horner, have been labouring under the auspices of the Society during the year. Cheering reports of satisfying and soul-converting power have come from the circuits where they have laboured. The large increase of 2,272 members in the

Conference during the year is in some measure due to the earnest and God-honoured assistance given the Pastors by the Evangelists."[24] Writing his memoirs, Horner recorded accounts of a number of the evangelistic revivals he organized and conducted during this period in and around the Ottawa Valley. Horner's preaching style was powerful, for he was endowed with a prodigious charisma that commanded the attention of the hundreds who flocked to hear him preach. His memoirs report all-night services and what he described as "waves of Pentecostal power that overwhelmed the people." He had acquired a reputation for holding meetings characterized by high levels of noise, excitement, and "manifestations." His reports of these meetings can be accepted as typical. Of one meeting in the year 1887–1888 he wrote:

God manifested his power more mightily under my preaching, so that the people commenced to fall under the power of God. God sent cyclones of power and fire, and the people became so hungry for it that they could not be induced to go home without it. God poured out His Spirit on them in every service. One night I went to my room at twelve o'clock and had supper; returned to the service at one o'clock, and it was still going on as I had left it, without any leader. The people fell by the score under the power of God. Some laughed, some cried, but most of them lay as if they were dead. As soon as they were able to creep on the floor, they reached their friends and cried to God for them. They had such power with God and over men that those whom they prayed for would fall over at once. It was an easy matter to count sixty or seventy under the power of God on the floor. I left the service about half-past one without any leader. I never knew what time the service closed.[25]

HORNER'S PREACHING

It is interesting to note that Ralph Horner's services were beginning to take on distinctives that would characterize his movement for years to come, even after his death. He was typical of the itinerant preachers who were the "genius of Methodism," "plucked from the common folk" who "spoke to people's hearts" using the "language of ordinary people and focusing on preaching rather than engaging in arid theological debates."[26] Much of what is recorded about his theology and methods during these early years is found in his own memoirs.[27]

First: His theology was based primarily on Methodist interpretations of the New Testament with a slight variation—he emphasized three stages of spiritual progression rather than two:

1. *Regeneration.* An initial work of grace occurs when the Holy Spirit convicts a sinner of sin and grants the seeker forgiveness and eternal life through faith in Jesus Christ—he is justified and born again.

2. *Entire Sanctification.* A second work of grace as described by John Wesley (also called the second blessing, Christian perfection, or holiness) occurs when the born-again child of God gives himself entirely over to God, seeks and is granted deliverance from the will to sin, and is filled with perfect love.

Entire sanctification, according to Horner, was "an instantaneous operation of the Spirit in the human soul, through the atoning merit of the Saviour's blood, by which the root and seed of all sin is destroyed, the whole soul restored to the image of God in righteousness and true holiness, and the witness of the Sprit received as clearly as to justification."[28]

"The children of God," Horner taught, "are to be made perfect in this life, under the preaching of the Gospel by men who have been called and are sent of God."[29]

3. *Baptism of the Holy Ghost.* There was a third work of the Spirit that Ralph Horner emphasized, slightly diverging from mainstream Wesleyan theology and giving rise to the emergence of Pentecostalism within the

Holiness Movement. The Baptism of the Holy Ghost occurs, he taught, the Holy Spirit baptizes the cleansed life with "fire from on high" and anoints (energizes) the recipient with power for soul winning and service. This was not unique to Horner; a number of American Pentecostal holiness revivalists also espoused a similar doctrinal emphasis.

Horner personally experienced what he taught; he summarized his threefold doctrinal stance in his own testimony: "Regeneration was my salvation from all my transgressions of God's law. . . . Entire sanctification destroyed all the depravity I inherited from Adam. . . . The anointing [was] a qualification to do wonders and miracles in the name of the Lord. . . . This baptism of the Holy Ghost and fire put energy and might into every faculty of my mind and soul. It was to me the 'Tongue of Fire' to preach the reconciling Word."[30]

Thus, the recurring content of Ralph Horner's sermons was formed around one of these themes: salvation, entire sanctification, and baptism by the Spirit. His messages were simple and straightforward; he delivered them with passion and conviction.

Second: His services were emotional and developed around a symbolic decision on the part of the seeker to come forward, kneel at the altar (or "penitent form"), and cry out to God. Horner described how he would preach and exhort all present "to come to the altar of prayer to seek salvation. . . . Their conviction for sin was deep and pungent. They wept and cried for mercy, and were scripturally converted. As soon as some of them received the converting grace of God, they could not rest day or night until others were saved. I had nothing to do only tell them there was such an experience as entire sanctification. They sought and found it at once. They were as clear on their entire sanctification as on their justification. They had the witness of the Spirit."[31]

Third: Ralph Horner developed a distinct manner of preaching. He preached extemporaneously without notes and without a pulpit. His platform style was an extension of his personality—crisp, forceful, and to the point. His sermons were not exegetical teaching lessons. They were generally exhortations focused on a central theme (a text read at the beginning of the message); illustrated by stories and testimonials, delivered in short, succinct sentences and phrases, and punctuated with interjections such as "Glory!" or "Hallelujah!" They were intended to prepare and encourage seekers to make their way to the altar of prayer at the end of the message.

Fourth: Horner encouraged congregational participation. Congregational members expressed approval and agreement with significant points in the sermon with hearty interjections of "Amen!" and "Praise the Lord!" Services were noisy. Concluding altar services were a cacophony of voices praying simultaneously with loud exuberance; tears would flow; some would rock back and forth on their knees; others would express joy with bursts of holy laughter or dancing in the Spirit. A more controversial symbol of God's power at work in Horner's services began to emerge: falling prostrate to the ground or floor as evidence that God was enduing His people with power from on high. Ralph Horner claimed he never encouraged physical manifestations, but he did maintain that under the mighty outpouring of the Holy Spirit such scenes would follow.

TENT PURCHASED

It was during this time that crowds became so large that churches were too small to hold the congregations that would gather. To accommodate the crowds, Horner resolved in 1887 to purchase a huge tent and take his message to the fields for the summer season. Success came instantaneously.[32] The novelty of the tent brought many to the services, but more came to see the manifestations, especially people falling under the power of God. Others came because Horner reminded them of the "good old days"—when the Methodist Church had the "fire." The calls for the tent became so numerous that it seemed impossible to remain long enough in one place to complete all the work that needed to be done. At no time was there any attempt on Horner's part to indicate how many people were brought under the influence of his preaching, but attendance throughout the Ottawa Valley came to be numbered in the thousands.[33] Horner's hometown paper, the *Shawville Equity*, on June 27, 1887, provided some idea of the growing interest and size of the crowds in these tent crusades:

> The revival services . . . have been largely attended throughout the week, and an ever increasing spirit of religious fervour has been manifested. The arrival of Mr. Waddell, the gentleman who led the musical part of the service in Ottawa, has lent a new interest to the meetings. This gentleman is possessed of a fine tenor voice, and the pathos with which he is enabled to render the many appropriate selections at his command, often proves effective, where the most earnest exhortation fails to convince. Mr. Horner's tent is capable of accommodating about 600 persons; but on Sunday evening last it afforded inadequate room to seat all the assembly which was present. The after meetings are being well attended, and many are seeking forgiveness at the Saviour's feet. Although not his original intention, Mr. Horner will probably remain for the balance of the week.

MEDIA COVERAGE INCREASES

As crowds increased and Rev. Horner's fame increased, media coverage throughout the Ottawa Valley increased as well, reporting the revival services with growing interest and more detailed coverage. The *Ottawa Advertiser* reported on Ralph Horner's meetings on Friday, September 14, 1888, as follows:

> The Rev. Ralph Horner, who is a native of Clarendon, Pontiac, and is well known in Pembroke, having laboured in the

Methodist Church some years ago, is creating great excitement in the County of Carleton. Last winter there was a great sensation in the same county owing to Mr. Horner's meetings having been attacked by persons who did not believe in them, and Mr. Horner pelted with eggs. This time nothing of the kind has occurred — the excitement being purely of a religious nature. The singular feature of the affair is that many fall over as in a trance and remain in this condition for some time. At a great "field meeting" in a grove near Stittsville, on Sunday last, there was an immense crowd of well dressed, comfortable looking people — young men and maidens, children, old men and women. On the platform were Rev. Mr. Richardson, of Carp, Rev. Mr. Ryan, of Montreal, and three local preachers, besides Rev. R. Horner. Rev. Mr. Ryan preached the first service and strongly defended "prostration," — as the trance-like condition is called — and spoke strongly in favour of outward manifestations of religion. Then Mr. Horner arose to lead the experience meeting. At once, a few came forward to testify. After a few minutes, Mr. Horner said: "It's no use one at a time; we'll never get through. The Lord can hear all."

The scene that followed these words of Mr. Horner was described by a reporter of the *Ottawa Journal* who was on the spot and saw it:

An almost indescribable scene followed. Fifty were speaking or praying at once. All around people were on their knees, clapping their hands, swaying back or forwards, praying or uttering cries of Jesus. Here and there one would fall over. It might be a big man or it might be a girl. There was nothing spasmodic or repulsive about the collapse, but simply, apparently, a sort of relaxation of the muscle, which might last for a few minutes. Near the Journal representative was a young girl on her knees. For a time she simply clapped here hands regularly, each time saying, "O Blessed Jesus," until she quietly sank over on one side and remained in a sort of trance for five minutes. Asked afterwards what her feelings were, she said she could hardly tell, but she just felt so full of happiness that she did not know what to do.

During the intervals between the regular meetings, side meetings were held at various spots on the grounds, at which people prayed and sang hymns. At one time as many as seven of these were in progress at once, each shared in by, from fifty to one hundred and fifty people. The work goes on in other parts of the country, and has called forth some opposition from Methodists themselves.[34]

IMPACT OF HORNER'S EVANGELISM

There was a definite curiosity by the public to hear and read more news about Horner and his tent revivals. Some reported that Horner's preaching was effecting a profound change on people. The *Athens Reporter*, a newspaper sympathetic to Horner and his holiness revivals (the editor was an Episcopal Methodist), reported that "Mr. Horner's plain practical preaching had done much good. He told the people in plain English that sin is sin and . . . that Christ was a mighty saviour that could save to the uttermost. . . . Skeptics were astounded at the transformation of people who had used tobacco for years giving it up completely while other converts were willing to go to their neighbours and make wrongs right between them."[35] In her memoirs, Jane Conley told how her father changed after attending Horner's services: he gave up tobacco and commenced to read the Bible and became active in church work. Fred Vickery of Lyn, Ontario, composed a poem in 1890 that testified how the ministry and message of Ralph Horner transformed him in services held at nearby Crosby:

> The words of truth stuck in my heart,
> From which I never could depart.

> I "took him in" from head to foot;
> He kept on preaching, had no book;
>
> He seemed to know that I was there,
> He made my little heart quite bare.
> His preaching surely did me good.
> I went to hear him when I could.[36]

It was apparent Horner's emotion-filled revivals were instrumental in the conversion of sinners and that dramatic changes were occurring in their lives as they went on to entire sanctification.

OPPOSITION MOUNTS

During Horner's second year as Conference evangelist, opposition began to mount by Methodist clerics and local newspapers. Some claimed he was preaching unsound doctrine; local pastors complained Horner was holding services without their permission in direct conflict with Methodist Discipline; others considered the emotional conduct unbecoming and embarrassing—especially to middle and upper class congregations. Other critics condemned Horner for "mesmerizing" his congregations.

As to be expected, reporters began to review Rev. Horner's revivals with suspicion. The *Pembroke Observer* published the story of a letter written by Mr. George Burroughs of Fallowfield to the *Ottawa Journal* encouraging the newspaper to "assert most positively" that Mr. Horner causes the people to enter into this state of prostration "simply through mesmerism and to strongly dissent from the same." Mr. Burroughs claimed that "Mr. Horner's mesmeric influence produces hysteria," and that he himself "combated it at more than one revival meeting." He further said that he was "prepared to back up his contentions by depositing with the editor of *The Journal* the sum of $50, to be used in support of Methodist missions, if he failed to prevent genuine prostrations at any of Mr. Horner's meetings." The *Journal* took up Mr. Burroughs' challenge to scrutinize Horner's revival services: they demanded an investigation in the interest of public morality and true religion. Crossely Hunter (an active Methodist) attended Horner's meetings and said he saw "women prostrated by intense excitement, violent hysteria and the whole congregation howling like a lunatic. . . . Horner is terrible earnest and possesses an uncommon degree for the faculty of impressing his earnestness upon the minds of others, but it is doubtful if the unwholesome excitement can be productive of lasting good. It is unquestionable he is fitting more weak minds for the lunatic asylum than erring souls for heaven."[37]

Some pursued opposition through legal injunctions. Horner recalled in his memoirs being invited to a field of labour where there was opposition: "Before the tent was up, some of the members of the church ordered me to take it away. They went to the Reeve to have me driven out of the place. I was there to remain and I always liked opposition. It made me courageous. It convinced me that I was greatly needed in a place. I was in a hurry to get everything in readiness to commence the battle in the name of Jesus."[38]

Most criticisms were meant to discredit and marginalize Horner, but, as usual, the coverage only served to advertise the meetings and more people flocked to hear the holiness evangelist expound his doctrines of repentance and sanctification.

PRANKSTERS AND SKEPTICS

Horner tent meetings were also vulnerable to pranksters. Some came to create havoc by throwing eggs or untying ropes from tent pegs. Some came to heckle. Others came to disrupt the services. Revivals and tent meetings often faced outright ridicule and sarcastic mocking. But again, like the media coverage, commotion and opposition only served to publicize the meetings and some of the antagonists often became converted themselves.

Ralph Horner told of conducting a series of services where a skeptic came to hear his sermons so he could criticize them to his neighbours. He came night after night, but one night thought he would stay home (perhaps to rest); however, he came under such strong conviction, he made his way back to the ongoing service. When he arrived, the church was full, and he was obliged to sit in the front seat. The "penitent form" became jam-packed with seekers, and the front seats began to be used for prayer as well. Ralph noticed the skeptic was left standing alone, "and I felt inspired to say to him, 'You, sir, go and kneel there and seek the Lord.' He went and knelt in the place and commenced to repent of his sins. He did not seek long until he was scripturally converted to God. As soon as he was converted, he commenced to drive to the neighbours' houses with a large double sleigh and bring people to services."[39]

Horner's meetings were met at times with physical violence. Horner's first major physical incident on record occurred June 25, 1888, in the Hazeldean Methodist Church. Men from Hazeldean, Gouldbor, Huntly, Nepean, and March townships created a ruckus outside the church. The men allegedly assaulted Rev. Mr. McDowell, who had tried to dissuade their disturbances. After several court appearances, Police Magistrate G. W. Rochester fined the young men ten dollars each or ten days imprisonment (*Ottawa Journal*). On September 4, 1888, the *Pembroke Observer and Advertiser* reported that "there was a great sensation in the county of Carleton when Horner's meetings were attacked and pelted with eggs by persons who did not believe in them."[40]

At another series of services, Ralph related how rowdies came one night to break up the meeting. They brought with them a man, feared by many, who claimed to be the greatest rowdy in three townships; he was rough and raunchy, sufficiently intoxicated that the pranksters thought he would follow any instructions they gave him. But, said Ralph, "the man to break up the meeting was the first to go forward to seek salvation." It was said in the community that "if he could go to town and come home sober, it would be evidence that he was saved."[41] And he did.

HOLINESS AWAKENING

Ralph Horner had begun a whirlwind of revival activity up and down the small villages and communities of the Ottawa Valley in towns such as Renfrew, Arnprior, Pembroke, and Carleton Place. His influence grew as his gifts and abilities as a preacher were honed. "His year in Philadelphia studying oratory and elocution stood him in good stead, but he appears as a man naturally endowed with the capacity to sway great masses and to arouse a high state of emotional excitement. . . . Though his own account of his revivalist work was probably highly coloured, the fact that he was viewed by the church authorities as a seriously disturbing influence offers support to the claims which he set forth respecting the success attending his work."[42]

But many in the media, the establishment, and inevitably the Methodist Conference were beginning to question his methods. Ralph Horner rationalized his methods by arguing that those who resisted them were ignorant of the manifestations of divine power that had attended the rise of Methodism. The Ottawa Valley had been the scene of numerous spiritual awakenings, but Evangelist Horner's revival meetings soon became questioned within the Methodist Church:

Like many evangelists, he had little interest in the denominational labels of people to whom he preached. . . . He built up a
following outside as well as within the church, and the effect of
this was to weaken denominational attachments among those
within the church. . . . From the beginning, Horner refused to
go where he was told or to consult with his superiors about his
work. . . . If he co-operated with those ministers who worked
with him, he was prepared to wage bitter warfare upon those

ministers who offered him resistance; he invaded local churches without any direction from the pastors in charge and, at times, competed directly with regular Methodist services. . . . Even more serious, from the point of view of church government, Horner refused to conform to the accepted practices of the Methodist religious service.[43]

Ralph Horner had become a controversial leader of the holiness renewal in the Ottawa Valley. The forces of ecclesiastical opposition and censorship would continue to dog his efforts and eventually lead to his expulsion from the Methodist Church.

CONTROVERSY GROWS

Ralph Horner became a leading voice for the church in what the conservative wing viewed as the threat of modernism and liberalism. His preaching struck a chord with rural folk living on the various family farms along the Ottawa Valley or in the small bustling towns and villages that serviced the hinterland around them. Dissatisfied with how their spiritual needs were met, many longed for renewal and a more personal encounter with God. Ralph Horner emerged as one who would help fill that vacuum. He was charismatic and attracted large crowds with his passionate, fiery preaching. A number of his associates and disciples — Ella Birdsell,[1] Ida Mason, James Findlay, Nellie Judd (from the Judd sisters), Susi Williamson (later Mrs. James Findlay), and Rev. John Scobie — were conducting holiness revival services, often in Methodist churches, throughout rural eastern Ontario and western Quebec in places such as Lake Eloida (north of Athens), Ebenezer, Burrits Rapids, and Shawville. In his memoirs, Horner recalled that the winter season (1892–1893) was spent in churches, "except for a few weeks I spent drilling a class of evangelists."[2] Although Ralph had mentored and encouraged half a dozen or more sincere young lay preachers in evangelistic ministries, many in the Methodist Conference judged them to be without theological grounding and felt they were bringing offence to the Methodist cause, reputation, and membership. Despite this, Horner's pupils continued to preach and cause tension among the Methodist ranks.[3]

METHODISTS ATTEMPT TO CURTAIL WORK

In 1890, the Methodists made a serious attempt to rein in their enthusiastic evangelist at the Montreal General Conference. Horner and his associates were about to be censured by their Methodist superiors intent on keeping the denomination respectable.[4] Methodist leaders argued that most professional revivalists "were out of harmony with modern, progressive society, were often ill informed, and had little lasting influence on expanding church membership."[5] The report of the special committee on evangelistic work in the 1890 Montreal Conference identified a concern: incorrect teaching of Scripture, which had done much harm and lessened the power of the church. The committee recommended petitioning the General Conference to provide some efficient method for the instruction of evangelists in doctrine and training and allow only accredited evangelists to be employed by ministers on their circuits. The discipline committee of the General Conference responded to the concern and set forth the following rules regulating the activities of evangelists in the Methodist Church of Canada:

- Article 176—No evangelist shall be employed whose teaching is not in harmony with our doctrinal standards or whose work tends to lessen attachment to our church.
- Article 177—No annual conference shall appoint a minister or a probationer as an evangelist without clear evidence that he is called of God to that work.
- Article 178—No minister or probationer shall enter the field at large as an evangelist without the consent of his Conference.
- Article 179—Superintendents of circuits employing evangelists, other than recognized ministers of the Methodist Church, shall engage only those that are amenable to the church and labour under the supervision of the pastor where they are employed.

- Article 180—When a minister is employed as an evangelist, arrangements shall be made by which he shall receive a regular salary from contributions paid into a fund for that purpose.

STATIONED AT PORTAGE-DU-FORT

In addition to applying the rules for evangelists in the Methodist Church, the Montreal Conference stationed Horner in 1890–1891 to the Portage-du-Fort circuit near Shawville.[6] Although the placement at Portage-du-Fort was an attempt to curtail and control Horner and his special interests, it was not a punishment: it was a large circuit named after the lumbering town across the Ottawa River from Renfrew and extended back into the bush land adjacent to Horner's hometown.[7] But Ralph felt betrayed. He refused to accept the position and resisted all attempts to control his evangelism. His response was simply to hire a supply minister in July 1890 and continue his independent evangelism. The Conference refused to accept the replacement and Horner was instructed to return immediately to Portage-du-Fort. Nevertheless, after discussion and afterthought, the Conference relented and appointed him once again as Conference evangelist. Ralph reported his results were greater that year than any previous year he had experienced in the ministry. "They prevented me from labouring in some places . . . but God opened doors in the Conference that year which no man could shut. . . . In the first place where I pitched my tent after Conference, God poured out His spirit upon the community for many square miles."[8]

MARRIAGE

Despite the pressure of conducting a busy summer and fall schedule of camp meetings and campaigns, Rev. Horner found time for one other assignment. On November 27, 1890, he married. His wife was

Miss Annie E. McDonald, daughter of Kenneth McDonald of Fallowfield, Ontario. Miss McDonald had been one of Mr. Horner's converts at Carp and had preached as an evangelist for a year prior to her marriage. His marriage was like his life—on the run! Ralph said in his memoirs that his friends . . .

> Among the most holy people in the ministry and laity had been advising me for a number of years not to live a single life. . . . I told the Lord, a short time after He saved me, that I would not associate with women; that if I ever needed a partner in life I would trust Him to get me a good one. The time had now arrived when it seemed good to the Lord to do so. There was no engagement; it was all in the Lord . . . the lady was assisting the pastor in revival services where I was labouring. I took him sixty miles to assist in solemnizing the marriage, and he was anxious to find out who my intended was. Neither he nor any others had any suspicion. We did not purchase any new clothing for the occasion, and there was no time lost from soul-winning on account of it. We were on our way for the next service and marriage was solemnized where we remained over night on the way.[9]

Annie became a faithful, loyal companion for many years until her husband's death in 1921, and she stood beside him during the highs and lows of his illustrious but controversial career.

PRESSURES APPLIED BUT REVIVALS CONTINUE

When the newly married couple reached the city where they were to have special services, Ralph Horner and his bride were met with renewed opposition from the established church. The ministers had sent word to press the resolution of the Conference Special Committee that no chairman of a district should allow Rev. Ralph Horner to labour in his district because he did not go to the pastoral work assigned him at Portage-du-Fort. The resolution, recalled Ralph, worked against him all year. "It did not deprive me of work, but it kept many away from the services and produced prejudice against me in the minds of many people." In one city (location unnamed), the services were not allowed in the church proper, but were assigned to the basement, which was dark, cold, and dreary. It was here, however, that Ralph Horner received one of his greatest personal blessings: "I was won- drously baptized with fire during my stay, and God gave me a vision of hundreds flocking to Jesus. I knew that I was soon to have a flaming revival." Sure enough, at his next field of labour, Ralph reported the power of God falling on the congregation: "We had reached the place where God had let me see so many coming to Jesus, when He had baptized me with fire."[10]

When the Pembroke District convened early in May, 1891, Horner went to the chairman and made known his intention to continue evan- gelistic work. The chairman reprimanded him for not taking the Portage-du-Fort Circuit and expressed the opinion that Horner should acknowledge his act of insubordination and seek forgiveness or resign, adding the latter was the honourable thing to do. Horner refused to do either. The Pembroke District took no action, but refused to pass his character. "The chairman," said Horner, "laboured to show how dishonourable it would be for me not to resign, and attempted to prove that every person would respect me if I did so." Horner chose to attend Conference without his character having been passed by the District Meeting. It was a serious matter and he noted solemnly, "When the character of a Methodist minister is not passed in a District Meeting, the Conference decides at once that the brother is guilty of some crime."[11]

The Montreal Conference convened on June 4, 1891, and again in the session devoted to ministerial character, Rev. Horner did not pass. There was a motion to form a committee of investigation in regard to Horner's refusal to be stationed at Portage-du-Fort. It was also noted, that this had been his procedure in former years as well, and so it was not a startling event. Ralph Horner was summoned to meet the committee to clarify himself on five points:

1. For having ignored the action of the 1890 Conference in appointing him to Portage-du-Fort Circuit, by not going near it;

2. For having shown disrespect to the chairman of the Pembroke District who had endeavoured to persuade him to accept the Conference appointment;

3. For having treated the District Chairman with contempt when he counselled him either to resign or make redress;

4. For having worked within the bounds of Conference during the year, after that the Conference Special Committee had recommended to the chairman of Districts that he be not allowed to work in any of the Districts;

5. For coming to Conference without having had his character passed by the Pembroke District meeting.

It is not known what was discussed behind the closed door of the committee room. Little evidence can be found in the 1891 Conference minutes. What we do know is that on the morning of June 3, the committee of investigation brought in their report and stated that Rev. Horner should continue to engage in evangelistic work, but the Conference would arrange his meetings, review his finances, and more or less control his activities. The question was then submitted to the Conference for a vote as to whether it would be wise to engage Mr. Horner next year for evangelistic work.

In Horner's memoirs, he claimed exoneration from the charges brought against him. He stated that he was exonerated without a dissenting vote, and the matter was immediately dropped. Ralph saw the action of the Conference as a strong censure of the Special Committee and a keen rebuke against the Pembroke District chairman who had tried to make him resign his standing as a member of the Conference.[12] Conference, however, placed Rev. Horner under the supervision of the Conference president. At the close of Conference, Rev. Horner said he demanded work, but the president said he had none to give him and asked him to rest awhile until application would be sent to him. "I am not tired," Horner replied. Rev. Horner recalled he had an invitation to a camp meeting that commenced in a week: "I went through a form of resting." The camp meeting was only the first of the season. At the close of the camp meeting, Ralph again asked the president for work, but he still had none to give him. "I had a number of invitations," recalled Ralph, "so went on in the power of the Lord and in the power of His might. When we left the camp ground, we proceeded to engage in our gospel tent services for the season."[13]

UNDENIABLE RESULTS

Ralph Horner had placed the Methodist Conference in a dilemma: they could not control his unorthodox preaching methods, but they could not deny the results. His unconventional conduct was overlooked and he was reappointed Conference evangelist for 1891–1892 and again for 1892–1893.[14]

Early reports in the *Christian Guardian* told of Horner's powerful and Methodistic presentation of the Gospel, which brought some to conversion and others to entire sanctification. In 1891, the church at Wilton, in the Bay of Quinte Conference, invited Horner to lead evangelistic services there in his big gospel tent. He went and stayed four weeks. According to the report, "God did marvels for us, not only in the conversion of sinners, though there were about 100, but in the sanctification of believers. . . . Bro. Horner is thoroughly Wesleyan in his teaching in reference to entire sanctification, because he is scriptural. And with one foot, as it were, on Wesley's teaching, and the other on Scripture, he slays all opposers."[15]

Although the writer made effort to reassure readers about Horner's acceptability and compliance with Wesleyan teaching, he nevertheless was preparing them for what came next: "A peculiar feature of our meetings was the number who were prostrated. Sometimes as many as twelve were unable to rise from the altar of prayer, being overcome by the power of God. Some of these were shouting, some praying to God for their unconverted friends and companions. . . . Some of our old members say they have not seen anything like it in over fifty years."[16]

HOLINESS CONVENTIONS

Ralph Horner continued his evangelistic work with a strong emphasis on holiness and entire sanctification. For a time, he appeared to be one of a number dedicated to the promotion of holiness. During a convention from October 4–7, 1892, at Smiths Falls, Horner and a number of Methodist ministers took part in a holiness convention. Leadership included John McDermott Kerr of Toronto, who, for many years carried on evangelistic work while based in the Toronto Conference. Those in attendance formed a holiness association for the continuance of such meetings.[17] Local newspaper, the *Athens Record*, added to the interest and intrigue by announcing, "Rev. R. Horner is to pitch his tent at Smiths Falls on Oct 4th for a brief holiness convention. The editor of the Record will have an opportunity of investigating 'prostration' and witnessing its fruits."[18]

Rev. Nelson Burns was another of these men. He was a preacher of prominence and known for his intellectual prowess; he founded and became president of the Canada Holiness Association and had made wide use of conventions for the promotion of holiness among the evangelical churches of the day. Numerous reports of these conventions appeared in editions of the *Christian Guardian*.

In response to the success of these conventions, the Eastern Ontario Holiness Association (EOHA) was also formed under the leadership of Rev. John Ferguson. The purpose of the EOHA was to promote holiness through publishing a newspaper—the *Canadian Methodist and Holiness*

Era—and conducting holiness conventions to promote the doctrine of entire sanctification. Ralph Horner played a prominent role in organizing EOHA conventions and editing the newspaper.

The *Era*, as it was often called, published news informing readers of what was taking place in the evangelical and holiness movements in and around eastern Ontario, as well as in the US and around the world—holiness books, holiness literature, and other holiness newspapers were advertised. Thus, the paper served to connect the EOHA to the broader influence of the Holiness Movement, especially south of the border. Instruction for readers was provided by printing Bible lessons, sermons, and testimonies. The magazine also provided encouragement to the cause of holiness by responding and providing answers to criticisms of holiness practices and doctrines, maintaining that the doctrine of holiness was taught by Methodist founder, John Wesley.

The organization of holiness conventions was important to the work of the EOHA. These conventions were typically held once a month in various locations and involved preaching by itinerant evangelists assisting the pastor of a local church. Delegates and the interested public would travel far distances from across eastern Ontario to attend. Key organizers such as Ella Birdsell, Ida Mason, John Scobie, F. H. Sproule, and R. Mallett, conducted two services daily. Preaching focused on the encouragement of believers and teaching in the doctrines and discipline of holiness. Altar calls were provided for converting sinners, reclaiming the backslidden, and offering the experience of entire sanctification to sincere believers.

Typical of Horner's role during these conventions was preaching as he did during the Smiths Falls conference, where he gave two addresses—one on "Consecration" and the other on "Repentance of Believers."[19] Horner wrote to say that in response to his sermons people were saved and their lives changed; they gave up alcohol, tobacco, and other things.

Much emotional fervour was associated with these conventions. It was claimed that some of the convention leaders were extremely unorthodox in their teaching and preaching of Wesleyan doctrines. In answer to this widespread criticism, Rev. J. Ferguson, who was also superintendent of the Cobden-Queen's Line Circuit, wrote to the *Christian Guardian*:

> It is insinuated by some parties in the Guardian and elsewhere that we teach doctrines that Mr. Wesley knew nothing about. My only reply is that the parties of most of the 'teaching' are ministers and probationers of the ministry in our church . . . which I think is sufficient guarantee for doctrinal soundness. I would just advise the said parties in the language of one of old: "Refrain from these men and let them alone, for if this council or this work be of men it will come to naught (and the sooner the better) but if it be of God, ye cannot overthrow it, lest happily ye be found to fight against God" (Acts 5:38).[20]

More news coverage added to the intrigue of Horner's evangelistic tent campaigns. Crowds grew at each endeavour. The Committee on the State of the Work within the Conference submitted this encouraging report on the overall spiritual progress of the church: "We are of the opinion that there was never a time when so many professed the blessing of holiness, and never were so many discussing it with a view to its intelligent acceptance and enjoyment. We pray that all our members will enjoy this great blessing and exhibit it in increasing liberality to God's cause, a conscientious discharge of all their duties in the Lord Jesus Christ in sincerity and truth."[21]

ELDORADO REVIVAL

Shortly after the concluding services of the Smiths Falls Holiness Convention in October, 1892, Methodist pastor Rev. R. Mallett[22] organized revival services in the Union Church at Eldorado, about three miles north of Madoc. Rev. R. C. Horner was invited to preach. A spiritual awakening ensued and became known as the "Great Revival." Services became so popular and so well attended that they were continued for eight months into May of the next year. During the winter, large sleigh-loads of people came from miles around in the surrounding communi-ties to attend the meetings. As many as twenty people would pile into one horse-drawn sleigh for the trip.

It seems one night "there was a particularly large crowd when every person had to stand, even those in the seats, because of the press of the people. It was that night that the floor began to settle . . . to a depth of four inches . . . requiring the services of a carpenter the next day, when supports were put in the basement to raise the floor to its original position."[23]

Rev. Mallett reported about the Elorado revival in the March 15, 1893, edition of the *Canadian Methodist and Holiness Era:*

We are in the eighteenth week of the mightiest work of grace ever known in this part of the country. On the 23rd of October, 1892, Bros. R. C. Horner and J. Waddell came to help us start our revival work for the fall and winter. . . . Brother Horner preached every afternoon and evening for about four weeks. When he commenced the state of religion was so low that no one but myself professed holiness, and very few, if any, were sure they were living in a state of justification. The Lord soon began to bless Brother Horner's straight and Scriptural preach-ing on holiness, justification, and power from on high, so that from almost the commencement of our wonderful meetings we have had people seeking, some for pardon, others for holiness, and others for power. Crowds have been so great that on Sab-bath evenings, especially, we have had to ask seekers of holiness to go down to the basement in the after meeting. . . . The influ-ence of the meetings has been felt in Madoc, Marmora, Spring-brook, Thomasburg, Hazzard's Corners, Malone and all over our circuit. Two young men, one of them my son, have been saved, and have given themselves to God for the work of the ministry. Two others have preached with acceptance and power since they got saved, one of them my own daughter. Glory be to God in the highest! We needed local help here on this large circuit very much, and, praise God, He is giving it to us. Many, after hard struggling, have given up drink, tobacco, gold, and other ornaments. The Lord be continually praised for what He has done, is doing, and for what He is still going to do![24]

In yet another report to the *Christian Guardian*, May 1893, Rev. Mallett stated the Lord had given the circuit "the mightiest revival I have ever seen, and now crowns the work by a special act of great liberality" (large gifts freed Zion Church from debt, and practically wiped out the debt of Union Church and McCoy as well). When the news was announced to the Zion congregation, the people rose as one man and joyfully sang a "Praise God from Whom All Blessings Flow." Rev. Mallett reported an increase of about 80 percent in the membership of Zion and McCoy churches. The pastor concluded by saying, "We as a people ought to thank God and take courage."[25]

The revival had a significant effect on one twenty-year-old man by the name of George Christie, who later would become an influential member in the Holiness Movement Church. He was converted to God and was led into the deeper experience of entire sanctification. George Christie was called to public ministry and began preaching in the summer of 1894. He later became editor of the denominational paper, the *Holiness Era*, and manager of the Holiness Movement Book Store on Bank Street, Ottawa. In all, eleven young men are reported to have entered the ministry of the Holiness Movement as a result of the Eldorado revival.

SUSPENDED FROM METHODIST CONFERENCE

The ministers with whom Ralph Horner laboured were ordained Methodists who, like him, were under the discipline and supervision of the Methodist Church. However, a number of laypeople were associated with Horner's movement who were not subject to the same supervision as ordained ministers. To avoid "being injured by unqualified persons or those whose views or methods are likely to be the cause of injury to our work," the Montreal Conference decided in 1893 to license evangelists.[26] Applicants were questioned about theology, loyalty to the church, prostration, and permitting several persons to pray at the same time. More attention, however, was placed on practices than doctrinal issues. In a joint statement, Ella Birdsell and Ida Mason—who had been evangelists since at least 1887—wrote in their defence: "We do not believe that prostration is essential to accompany any degree of grace, and have never had such experience ourselves but could not say but what in some cases, they are of God. We never encourage it, but we dare not discourage lest we grieve the Spirit in so doing. . . . [We] know there are blotches in this holiness movement, and feel like offering the prayer, our beloved founder, John Wesley, did, Lord give us another holiness revival without the blotches, but if we cannot have it without them, send it blotches and all. Amen."[27]

Ralph Horner and his associates had all but sealed their ministerial fate in the months leading to the Montreal Conference convened in Cornwall, Ontario, June 1, 1893. The Conference Committee on Evangelistic Work presented a long report that read in part that "as to the general benefits of evangelistic efforts, we find that although we are assured that souls have been converted and believers sanctified, yet the results, spiritual and financial, have been sadly disappointing." The report went on to say "serious irregularities" were in evidence in the practice and encouragement of simultaneous public prayer and physical manifestations (prostration, ecstasy, immoderate laughter) tending to confusion and disorder. "We find physical manifestations, not calculated to commend our common Christianity to the hearts and consciences of men but tending rather to bring it into disrepute, are common . . . and we judge that sufficient effort is not exerted towards their restraint and control." Furthermore, the report charged, "we find a censorious spirit is exhibited leading to unkind criticisms and condemnation of both ministers and members of our Church . . . and we further find that a spirit of disloyalty to our Church and her institutions is a very painful and frequent outcome."[28] The report recommended that in the future all evangelists undergo an examination according to character, doctrine, methods, loyalty to the church, and views on prostration and laughter. Only licensed evangelists would be permitted on Methodist circuits.[29]

In response to complaints about Ralph Horner's conduct and unconventional methods, including his hiring untrained and unlicensed lay preaching assistants, the Conference Stationing Committee did not reappoint Rev. Horner as Conference evangelist. He was left without any appointment. Female applicants for licensing Ellen Ostrom, Ella Birdsell, and Ida Mason were also rejected. Ostrom was rejected as "an extremist" because of her belief concerning the necessity of a distinct blessing of holiness. Birdsell and Mason concluded, "We will never have the holiness without the blotches until we are prepared to be firm and wise as well as spiritual and fervent."[30] It appears the Methodist Church had no place for Ralph Horner's ministry, and Horner had no place for the constraints of the Methodist Church.

Receiving no appointment did not mean inactivity for Ralph Horner. On the contrary, there was a flurry of activity. No doubt, he realized his work in the Methodist Conference might soon be totally terminated. He continued in special evangelism, independent of Conference appointment or direction, with unabated zeal and enthusiasm. A former Baptist church on Concession Street, (now Bronson Avenue) was purchased in Ottawa by Rev. Horner and his associates to enlarge and formalize his work.

The year 1893 also brought forth Horner's publication of *Notes on Boland*.[31] Dr. J. M. Boland, D. D., of the Methodist Episcopal Church had published a book titled *The Problems of Methodism*, claiming that John Wesley had eventually abandoned the doctrine of holiness and entire sanctification as taught throughout his writings and sermons. Ralph Horner sought to disclose Boland's opinion on the doctrine of holiness as erroneous and unfounded. The June 21, 1893, edition of the *Canadian Methodist and Holiness Era* commended the book in an article entitled "A Book for the Times" and stated, "Our associate, The Rev. R. C. Horner, has written a reply to Dr. Boland's book. . . . It is undoubtedly the most masterly and conclusive reply that has yet been given to Dr. Boland's attack on the doctrine of entire sanctification." It was rather a lofty compliment to the evangelist who was supposedly causing embarrassment and disturbance on the evangelistic field!

DR. ALBERT CARMAN SYMPATHETIC TO HORNER

The general superintendent of the Methodist Church, Dr. Albert Carman, was essentially a moderate conservative both socially and theologically, and felt that Methodism should remain broad enough to provide a congenial home for a diverse range of Protestant beliefs and approaches such as Horner's. Carman had served as the last bishop of the Canadian Episcopal Methodists and, with his respected father-figure image, "he continued to assert an 'Episcopal,' if not dictatorial dimension to his office of general superintendent in the united Methodist cause. Combining unequalled knowledge and experience with energy, skill, and a forceful personality, he assumed a leadership role on the committees and boards which administered the church's operations and was undoubtedly the most influential voice in Methodist councils."[32] Not only was Carman sympathetic to Horner, he also wrote the introduction to his book *Entire Consecration* and declared that he was impressed by the practical parts of Horner's work, although he could neither understand nor endorse the metaphysical parts.

Horner Ups the Ante

Ultimately, however, in 1894 matters escalated so much that even the supportive Carman could not tolerate Horner's outright repudiation of the church's disciplinary authority. In March 1894, Horner published a pamphlet entitled *Conference and Evangelist Relations*. The pamphlet argued that although there was only one form of ordination in the Methodist Church, Horner was ordained by T. G. Williams, the chairman of the Pembroke District, with the understanding that he would be given only evangelistic work. Two paragraphs from the booklet tell of the paradox and misunderstanding that existed between Ralph Horner and the Conference:

My call to preach the Gospel was as clear as my conversion to God. I have never doubted either. I have always positively affirmed that I never felt called to enter the Christian ministry. When I was called upon to relate my conversion and call to the ministry before Conference, I was careful to affirm that I was called to preach, but was not called to enter the Methodist ministry.

It was stated and emphasized by a number of the members of the District, that Conference was willing to give me that kind of work if I would only accept of ordination in the regular way, as they had no other form of ordination. The Chairman of the District asked me if I would not accept of ordination in the regular way, seeing that Conference was willing to set me apart for evangelism. He asked me if I was not willing to trust my brethren, when they were willing to trust me. I asked if it was not time enough for me to lose confidence in my brethren when they would refuse to give me the kind of work for which I was asking. These and other questions were asked until I was ashamed to refuse any longer. I consented to be ordained, but did not fail to say, at the same time, that I would not be stationed on a circuit by the Stationing Committee.[33]

To substantiate his claim and prove that his ordination was for a special purpose, a number of "testimonials" were included from senior members of the District. One of particular interest was that of Rev. William Craig, the pastor with whom Rev. Horner resided while attending high school in Renfrew:

AYLMER, QUE. March 31, 1891

Dear Bro. Horner,

I remember that you refused to be ordained—unless you could have permission to engage in evangelistic work. I remember reasoning very earnestly with you about the matter, and your reply was, "I don't care for ordination. I feel called to this work, and cannot accept ordination unless I am permitted to engage in it." I remember the private District meeting being called, was glad, and attended as an interested hearer. I remember Bro. Hansford being present; remember the questions being asked, if it was not time enough for you to trust your brethren . . . and also the statement was made, "Trust your brethren; you ought to be willing to trust them when they are willing to trust you. They know what you desire, and can't you trust them to grant it?" Thus with the understanding that Bro. Horner was to labour as an evangelist, I voted for his ordination, and this understanding a large number of the brethren of the Conference must have had from the fact that Bro. Horner's name did not occupy two seconds of the time of the Stationing Committee that year. This I know to be a fact, as I was a member of the Committee. His name with Bro. Winter's was put down as an evangelist without debate.

To all whom these lines may concern, I am yours in Jesus,
Wm Craig[34]

Rev. R. C. Horner had decided to make the public aware of the growing controversy concerning the pledge made by the Montreal Conference that evangelism would be his special field of service. He wanted to show how the Methodist Church had broken its promise by stationing him on a circuit and suspending him from evangelistic work. It was obvious some type of reckoning needed to take place to avoid a serious breach between Horner and the church at the next General Conference.

4

Suspended

The concern for decorum and respectability in Methodist churches was growing. In August 1894, E. H. Dewart wrote an editorial in the *Christian Guardian* entitled "Noisy disorder in worship is no evidence of holiness." He lamented the existence of "religious teachers who encourage noisy shouting and physical demonstrations in religious worship, as if they were signs of a sanctified state."[1] Two months later, he again argued that it was possible to have "full consecration . . . without physical demonstration; and . . . noisy display without religious principle."

"Along with the editor, letter writers also claimed to place a high value on holiness, but their use of the term differed from the content implied by Horner and his followers. For Hornerites, it meant a sudden experience of sanctification that erased the effects of original sin and, indeed, freed the one sanctified from feelings of temptation."[2]

The decisive clincher determining Rev. Ralph Horner's future with the Methodist Church may have occurred on the eve of the Montreal General Conference on May 30, 1894. Rev. Horner's burly brother and peace enforcer, George, got into an altercation at a revival service near Ottawa. It was front-page news in the *Ottawa Journal*, obviously an embarrassment to the Methodist Church. The Horner brothers had pitched their tent in the village of Birchton on Richmond Road and large crowds had gathered, the curious flocking to see the prostrations. George kept strict order and requested silence inside the large gospel tent. Apparently, so the newspapers reported, George Horner had on one or two occasions during the meeting asked certain individuals to be silent. One of those whom he accused of disrupting (the paper reported the disruption as "a whispering") was Mrs. James Forward, of Hintonburgh. When George Horner spoke to her, she gave an "emphatic denial to the accusation." After an animated exchange, George attempted to usher her out and a scuffle ensued.

> The scuffle was the signal for a general row. About a dozen men took Mrs. Forward's part, although she is reported to have been pretty well able to take her own part against her sturdy opponent. Outside the tent, Mr. Horner was assailed on all sides, his coat was torn into shreds and he was left without collar or necktie. A few people tried to pacify the disturbance, among them being the evangelist himself, and eventually there was quiet. While the disturbance was going on, the service in the tent never ceased and the exclamations of *Glory*, *Glory* and *Hallelujah* were heard above the uproar. . . . It is very probable that there will be some arrests forthcoming.[3]

CONFERENCE RESOLVE

There is no record of any arrests. The Horner preachers were not known to call police for protection or to make arrests. The publicity only served to increase the size of the crowds. But clearly, many Methodist leaders were embarrassed. The next day — Thursday, May 31, 1894 — the Montreal General Conference of the Methodist Church convened in Kingston, Ontario, and the case of Ralph Horner was the main event as articles were garnered not only from the *Ottawa Evening Journal*, but also from the *Kingston Daily British Whig*, the *Toronto Star*, and the *Toronto Globe*.

During the Friday session the Central Committee met and a resolution was passed to condemn the current state of evangelism:

[T]here have been serious irregularities in the prosecution of our evangelistic work, especially in the following particulars: in the mode of conducting prayer and inquiry meetings, in which the people were permitted and sometimes encouraged to pray simultaneously, tending to disorder and confusion. We find that the physical manifestations not calculated to commend our Christianity to the hearts and consciences of men, but tending rather to bring it into disrepute, such as prostration, ecstasy, immoderate laughter is common, and we judge that sufficient effort is not exerted toward their restraint and control.[4]

In order to strengthen the hands of the Central Committee in carrying out its commission of accrediting evangelists, a Standing Resolution regarding evangelists was passed by the Conference: "This Conference affirms that no evangelist of the Montreal Conference shall conduct evangelistic services on any circuit or Mission in the Montreal Conference without an invitation, or expressed concurrence of the Superintendent of such Charge, and we desire in the clearest way to affirm our conviction that all evangelists in our church must be subject to the Authorities of the church and conform to our usual customs."[5]

The Central Committee presented a form for the examination of all evangelists who would work within the bounds of their district. The form was divided into three sections:

- As to character: A certificate would be furnished from the minister in charge of the circuit/church covering the basics, such as name, age, date of conversion, official position. There was also a section covering general opinions as to the qualifications of the evangelist's gifts, grace, and fruit.
- As to experience and doctrine: Written answers would be secured by the District Committee in any cases where the position, knowledge, or attainments of the candidates were in the least unsatisfactory.

- As to methods of work: The candidate's opinion was also questioned on whether he encouraged or repressed such religious behaviour as prostration, permitting several persons to speak aloud at the same time, allowing for professedly uncontrolled laughter. There was also a question as to whether the evangelist expressed or practiced disloyalty to the regular ministry, services, and financial interests of the church.

To this third section of the report there was also attached the same rider as in section two: that written answers shall be secured by the District Committee in any cases where the position or knowledge or attainments of the candidates are unsatisfactory.[6]

It was apparent the Methodist Church would no longer tolerate the unorthodox practices of Horner and his associates. Amazingly, however, in the evening session, with Horner still in Birchton, Conference proceeded to pass Horner's character, despite stating that his methods had been offensive to many and there were many legal and constitutional questions surrounding him—including whether he would receive a station. A great deal of discussion carried on late into the night dealing with questions concerning Horner. How was he ordained? Was it special? Dr. T. G. Williams, the man who ordained Horner, was brought in and questioned as to whether Horner had received a special ordination; Williams stated that Horner had not. The *Conference and Evangelist Relations* pamphlet was discussed, with Rev. Lawson claiming his statement in Horner's pamphlet was edited through careful selection of sentences. The inappropriate conduct of Horner's services was mentioned and that Horner's followers were criticizing Methodist ministers. Rev. W. H. Graham complained that if a pastor would not let his people "howl and squall" he would be prayed at and charged with not being holy.

The discussion continued until finally a motion was offered instructing the Stationing Committee to station Mr. Horner. The Rev. Chisholm moved that the vote be taken, but the vote failed and the debate continued.

A new motion was offered stating that because Horner had declared he was not called to the work of the ministry he now be summoned to attend the bar of the Conference to answer for this statement. Rev. H. M. Emsley then moved a resolution that the Conference, having heard Rev. Horner's statement and Dr. Williams's reply, declare the accuracy of Williams's statement and declare that Horner was ordained in the usual way. The motion was carried unanimously, and two ministers—Rev. Maveity and Rev. Clipsham—were sent to call Horner to appear before the Conference bar.

The length of debate that evening demonstrates that the Horner controversy was not a simple matter for the Methodist Church to decide either positively or negatively; despite the criticism and controversies, there evidently was ample support for Horner and his work.

SUSPENDED FROM METHODIST RELATIONSHIP

Saturday, June 2, 1894: The ministerial session of the Montreal Conference met to resume hearing the report concerning Rev. Ralph Horner. The Special Committee brought in the recommendation that Rev. Mr. Horner be requested to give up his ordination parchment and Bible and cease to be a minister in the Methodist Church.[7] The committee chairman, Mr. J. T. Pitcher, moved its adoption; nothing was said of Rev. Horner's methods of work, but reference was made to the records of his ordination, which Mr. Pitcher sincerely believed Rev. Horner had misapprehended.[8] A divergence of contrasting views as reported by the *Toronto Globe* was aired on the floor of the Conference:

- Rev. Mr. Chisholm objected to the adoption of the report, inasmuch as Mr. Horner had not had a trial and because the action of the Conference was not strictly legal.
- Rev. A. Lee Holmes thought that if Rev. Mr. Horner's ordination had been misconceived by him and could not enter the regular

work, he should either come into full connection with the church now or resign.

- Rev. Mr. Rilance said that Mr. Horner's method of work was not such as should be approved by the Conference. It tended toward excitement. He regretted that Rev. Mr. Horner had ever come to his circuit.

- Rev. Dr. Shaw said that in 1887 when the subject first came up, Mr. Horner agreed to accept the regular course of the ministers, and said nothing about the position he now held. While working in Montreal as an evangelist he showed an intractable spirit. The Conference was in favour of evangelistic work, but those who would not accept the guidance of the church could not be tolerated.

- The record of the Pembroke District was then read, and Rev. Rilance moved in amendment that the Conference "request" Mr. Horner to resign rather than "require" him to do so. The amendment was not seconded.

- Rev. David Winter thought that the Stationing Committee might either place Rev. Mr. Horner on a circuit or that Mr. Horner should consent to change his methods as an evangelist.

HORNER ARRIVES FOR QUESTIONING

Upon his arrival at Conference, Horner was requested to appear before a Special Committee that had been instructed by Conference to ask two questions to which either a negative or positive answer was to be given without any qualification. With his supporters demonstrating outside the church, Horner faced the Conference:

The Chairman of the Committee asked if Horner had written the pamphlet *Conference and Evangelistic Relations*.

Horner said yes.

Was he prepared to accept the regular obligations of ordained ministers as settled in the church's ordination vows?

Horner answered: Not in the full sense—not as to pastoral work. Would he take a circuit?

Horner responded in the negative.

Horner was then informed that the Conference had already decided that he was not ordained for special evangelism.

Rev. A. C. Courtice said the question was not one of methods and beliefs, but of constitution and ordination. There was not room in the church for two classes of ordained ministers. He hoped Mr. Horner would retire honourably from the ministry. The motion was then put to the house, and the report of the committee was adopted to ask Horner to resign. Dr. Williams moved that the same committee be reappointed to inquire if Rev. Mr. Horner accepted the decision of Conference. Following the report, Rev. Horner was handed a written ultimatum requesting him to resign his ordination parchment.

In a matter of minutes, Rev. Horner handed the chairman the following note: "I will not resign; I believe my work is in this Conference and I wish to be left free to labour as a member of the Conference in evangelism as I have been doing."[9]

Horner's address to the Conference was reported in the *Globe*:

Rev. R. C. Horner faced the Conference with a smile. When he thought he was right he was very determined. . . . He again affirmed that he had never been called to pastoral work. He had spent six years on probation, and would rather spend six more years than take a station. There had been an understanding that he should have only evangelistic work. He said that he loved the church and the discipline. His home was the Methodist Church. He saw the force of the remarks of the ministers regarding excitement and prostration, and knew there was truth in them, but he did not believe in quiet methods. He said his work tended to excitement and fanaticism, but this was the line the Spirit of God took. He was not to blame if men went too far. There were times when he himself shouted, but he never told his people to do so though there was room in the Methodist Church and need of it. He could not cripple himself by denouncing it, and believed there was room in the church for himself and his work. Every man had his own way, and there exists a tendency to make all correspond to one type. He thought the church could bear with him, for he had done and was doing his best for the church, and preach he must.

In reply to a question as to whether he had discouraged the extravagance complained of, Mr. Horner said that he discouraged what he considered extravagance. He believed that prostrations, jerks and laughing might be of God.[10]

After Horner's speech there was a resolution to adopt the finding of the committee, but President Ryckman offered advice. He suggested that the report not be adopted, that they sleep over it, and that they be prepared to act in the next session. When Conference adjourned, many clergymen shook Ralph Horner's hand and several talked very earnestly with him. Many recount that Horner was always treated as a gentleman and genuinely liked by most of the Methodist ministers.

At 12:30 p.m. Horner met with reporters. Speaking slowly and calmly Horner reiterated his position. He said, "The committee asked me to resign, but I said that it was not in my heart to cut myself off from the church of my choice. The Conference must do that."[11] He said he was ordained seven years ago in the church in which the Conference is now held. His ordination was for evangelistic purposes. Once before ordination and once since, he had been given appointments but refused to accept them. He said his work was that of an evangelist. He contended for the old Methodist faith. He did not believe in the new way of securing converts, handing down cards, but he liked to see a man on his knees crying to God for mercy. He was not concerned about what the Conference might do; the brethren had ordained him for evangelistic purposes but had broken faith with him.[12]

It does seem Horner genuinely did not want to leave the Methodist Church, and to their credit the Methodists were doing all they could to keep Horner. But Horner saw the church as drifting from the preaching and practice of early Methodism and consequently was trying to bring the church back to her roots.[13] Horner also believed he was called exclusively to evangelism; anything else meant disobedience to his calling. This is why he could not compromise. The Methodist Church was heading in a different direction and did not have a place for Horner's interpretation of old-style Methodism. Horner meant for his holiness revivals to be a renewal movement in the church, but the Conference saw Horner's actions as insubordination and they could not treat him differently than any other minister.

The Conference was obviously exasperated. However, they were hesitant to drop Horner's name because there were those who believed that if they could harness his talents he could help the church; others feared a backlash by the hundreds of followers who had been saved and sanctified in his meetings. On the other hand, many were frustrated by Horner's defiance in conducting tent crusades without the invitation of the ministers of circuits and without the permission or direction of the Conference Evangelistic Committee.

On Monday, June 4, the Special Committee met with Rev. A. C. Courtice and moved that since Horner declined to accept the expressed methods of the Methodist Church in evangelism he be stationed on a circuit. The discussion that followed was subdued. "Finally, an ex-president of the Montreal Conference arose and said, 'Mr. Horner preaches our doctrines, and we have nothing against his Christian character, it having been passed by Conference; but he will not obey the Conference. We will put his name down for a circuit and if he does not go to it, we will drop his name in silence at the next session.' This the Conference sanctioned almost unanimously."[14]

The Stationing Committee appointed Rev. Horner to the Combermere Circuit, where he had served a term during college vacation. The Conference had presented him with an ultimatum. The door was still open for Mr. Horner: he could accept the circuit and remain within the fold of the Methodist Church, or he could refuse and be stripped of his ordination and standing in the Conference.

Ralph immediately refused to accept the appointment.[14]

REVIVALS CONTINUE, SUSPENSION INEVITABLE

It was obvious Ralph Horner had no intention of curbing his tent revivals with or without the blessing of the Methodist Church. When the Birchton campaign concluded in June 1894, Mr. Horner and his associates pitched their gospel tent in Pembroke and again commenced revival services.

On Monday, July 5, 1894, the Quarterly Board of the Pembroke Methodist Church sent a letter to Dr. E. G. Ryckman, president of the Montreal Conference, reporting Rev. Horner's breach of church discipline in that he was conducting evangelistic services within the Pembroke District. The letter called for quick action. Dr. Ryckman appointed a committee and convened a trial, which Horner did not attend. The committee was then forced to find and meet with Mr. Horner in Pembroke, where he was conducting the revival services:

The president asked, "Why did you not take the appointment given you by the Conference?"

"Did you expect me to go to Combermere?" replied Mr. Horner.

"Did you refuse to go because it was Combermere?" asked Dr. Ryckman.

"No," answered Mr. Horner. "I would not take the best city circuit in the Montreal Conference."

The president then asked, "Will you as a member of the Conference observe the rules of the Conference?"

"I will not," answered Mr. Horner.

Dr. Ryckman continued. "Will you not then resign your position as a member of the Conference?"

"I will not," Mr. Horner insisted.

The president persisted in his questioning. "Mr. Horner, do you then wish to compel the Conference to expel you that you may gain the sympathy of the people and prestige of a persecuted man?"

After a considerable pause, Ralph Horner replied, "I am not thinking of that."[16]

According to Mr. Horner, the committee retired and in a short time a lawyer handed him a copy of the action they had taken. He was suspended from the office and work of the ministry of the Methodist Church up to the next session of the Montreal Conference.[17]

DEPOSITION FINALIZED

In the following year, June 1895, the Montreal Conference indeed sustained the action of the Special Committee and dropped Ralph Horner's name from the roll of the Conference for refusing to devote his time to circuit work assigned him, and persisting in evangelistic efforts at circuits whose superintendents had not consented to it.

On the one hand, the church had been longsuffering but was faced with emerging realities within the Methodist Church that were irreconcilable to what was taking place in Horner's revivals. On the other hand, Ralph Horner was convinced his calling was to do the work of an evangelist; he had defended his position that he had acted with integrity and honesty in his sixteen-page booklet, *Conference and Evangelistic Relations*:

For three years the Stationing Committee appointed me for special evangelism, my name appearing this way each year in the minutes of the Conference. This was done without debate. The fourth year the Stationing Committee put my name down for a circuit, and I did not go to it during the year. When the Conference Special Committee met that year, they recommended by a circular which they sent to all Chairmen of Districts, that no pastor in the bounds of the Conference should employ me for evangelism. The next annual Conference appointed a committee to investigate the matter and report. The committee approved of my course up to date, and the Conference unanimously accepted the report.

The fifth and sixth years I was appointed Conference Evangelist under the President of the Conference and a committee of three, who were appointed by the Conference to arrange my work and pay me a salary. This committee did not act in their capacity. The seventh year the Stationing Committee requested me to ask to be left without an appointment. . . .

If I had not been ordained for special evangelism, I would either have gone to the circuit given me by the Stationing Committee, or surrendered my parchment. I have been true to my ordination vows and agreement with Conference authorities. If any of my brethren have not known that I have always declared positively that I would not do circuit work, it is because a probationer has not the privilege of appearing before Conference personally. I did not fail to let my mind be known in District meeting. If it had been my privilege to have spoken in Conference, I would have spoken as I did in District meeting.[18]

The suspense was over. The deposition from the ministry of the Methodist Church was final. Rev. Ralph Horner, resolutely believing in his call to do the work of an evangelist, announced his position as follows: "It must be understood first of all that I am not a pastor. I am an evangelist. I was ordained such. I never was on a circuit. Last year Conference removed me from the position of Conference evangelist or rather abolished the position, but the question was not touched. . . . At the present time I am a minister of the Church, but have no responsibilities for work toward it. When I was ordained, I refused to take a circuit, believing I was called to evangelistic work. Consequently, I am now free to do as I please."[19]

The Methodist Church of Canada and the Eastern Ontario Holiness Movement experienced a watershed year in 1894: two high-profile ministers—Rev. Ralph Horner, evangelist, and Rev. Nelson Burns, founder and president of the Canadian Holiness Association—were suspended.[20] They were subsequently stripped of their ministerial credentials in the next Montreal Conference of 1895. The case of Rev. Burns centred around a controversial book he had published in 1889 entitled *Divine Guidance*; Rev. Dr. E. H. Dewart summarized the charge in his column, *Editorial Jottings*: "He has taught a doctrine of Divine guidance, which assumes that each believer may receive such revelations of truth, on all points, directly from the Holy Spirit, as virtually supersede Scripture and reason."[21] Rev. Burns was given opportunity to renounce his theology and remain in the Conference, but he refused to retract his "erroneous views and vow himself in full accord with the Methodist doctrines and usages."[22] Rev. Horner was deposed for insubordination and not fulfilling his circuit posting to Combermere.

Not only did the Methodist Church lose two influential preachers, but from this time forth, Methodist ministers participating in holiness conventions were looked upon with suspicion. Furthermore, the Methodist Church would shy away from any association with holiness teaching on entire sanctification.

HOLINESS MOVEMENT CHURCH

When Ralph Horner's name was dropped from the roll of the Methodist Church, there was a surge of activity on the part of his followers. Many who had been converted during his services and ministry rallied around him, strongly urging him to organize a separate body on holiness principles, to which they pledged their loyal support. Moreover, others who had been in the Eastern Ontario Holiness Association and had been sympathizers with Rev. Burns also encouraged Horner to organize a separate denomination. "If Horner did not form a new church fellowship, what would become of the holiness people, his converts and the converts of other like-minded holiness ministers and evangelists?"[1] The personnel and infrastructure were in place from the Eastern Ontario Holiness Association: a sizable membership, evangelists, ongoing meetings, and the regular publication of the *Holiness Era*.

Rev. Horner found himself in a dilemma. On one hand, there was a large following of loyal adherents who vowed disassociation from the Methodist Church; on the other hand, he had been very public and adamant in stating he loved the Methodist Church with its doctrine and discipline, and that he was a loyal member of the Conference. Recall the interview with the reporter from the *Globe and Mail*: "The committee asked me to resign, but I said that it was not in my heart to cut myself off from the church of my choice."[2] It would seem that Horner, by his own admission, had no desire to form a new denomination, but rather to preach and evangelize under the umbrella and auspices of the Methodist Church. Nevertheless, it became increasingly necessary for Horner to reposition himself to provide a home for his large following and continue his revivals.

NEW HEADQUARTERS, NEW ORDINATION

The process began when Horner and his associates purchased a church on Concession Street (now Bronson Avenue) in Ottawa to serve as headquarters and a focal point from which to organize and continue operations. His suspension from the Methodist denomination, however, deprived him of the rights and privileges of ordination. He immediately communicated with a friend in the Rochester Conference of the Wesleyan Methodist Connection advising him of his dilemma with a view to receiving ordination privileges in his Conference in order to continue work in Canada. The president of the Conference wired Horner, "Meet me at Ogdensburg on my way to Conference." Rev. Horner and the president met and travelled together to attend the Rochester Wesleyan Conference in Westfield, New York.

The Rochester Conference questioned Ralph Horner as to whether the Canadian church would ever join the Conference in the United States. Rev. Horner stated that he could not give any promises. Furthermore, he stated he would work under the discipline and rules of the Holiness Association established in Canada, and not that of the Rochester Conference. Surprisingly, the Rochester Conference ordained Ralph, but it would appear "the Connection" was searching for a convenient "in" to plant churches and increase denominational presence in Canada.

Ralph Horner returned to Canada and used his ordination privileges to continue his work and ministry. Reverends F. H. Sproule and J. C. Irvine—two ordained ministers of the Methodist Church—joined the Horner movement, and the Rochester Conference agreed to accept their names as well and place them on the ministerial role with full ordination privileges.

RAPID GROWTH

In July 1894, the first circuit of the new Holiness Movement was organized in Pembroke, and Mr. S. J. Shields, a young probationer of the Methodist Church, cast his lot with Mr. Horner. He was thus conferred with the distinction of receiving the first appointment to the first circuit. Other districts began to ask for pastors and evangelists to serve among them. Young men and women began to volunteer for placement, presenting themselves for service to Mr. Horner, who became their recognized leader. Ralph Horner assigned them work and gave them general rules of conduct to govern their new tasks. By 1895, a number of circuits were formed; pulpits were filled by twenty-five to thirty ordained preachers called to the ministry and in sympathy with the doctrines and discipline as formulated by the new religious body.[3]

A ripple effect was taking place: new holiness churches, independent of the Methodist Church, began to organize as enthusiastic converts travelled outward from the Eldorado revival to nearby communities. The *North Hastings Review*, February 1895, announced revival services to be held in nearby Madoc: "Evangelist Horner, of Holiness fame, who created such a ripple in Methodist circles on the Eldorado Circuit a short time ago, has commenced a series of meetings in the old Methodist Church building in this village, meetings to be held nightly."

A holiness church was organized in Madoc when local men rented (and later purchased) the old Methodist church on Division Street from the Salvation Army.[4] As the church became established, a number of those attending from nearby Eldorado (many remembering the great revival with Ralph Horner in 1892) were eager to have their own place of worship as well and erected a church in their village. The *North Hastings Review* reported in July 1895: "The adherents of Evangelist Horner have withdrawn from their respective churches and have decided to organize churches themselves in Madoc, Eldorado neighbourhood and Huntingdon." Some months later the *Review* again reported: "The new church built by the followers of Rev. R. C. Horner on the Eldorado Circuit was dedicated on Sunday last, December 7, 1895. There was a large attendance at all services and prostrations innumerable were in order. The church starts entirely debt free."[5] Two new holiness churches soon formed nearby and the movement fanned out to Ivanhoe, Stockdale, Wooler, Foxboro, and Roblin.

James R. Kennedy's history of the growth and strength of the Holiness Movement Church (HMC) in the Lombardy area probably was typical of many church plantings within the newly emerging denomination:

> As they grew in size and strength, the Hornerites of the Lombardy area wanted a more permanent forum for their preachers than the schoolhouses and camp tents. The local followers decided in 1896 to have their own place of worship. A one-acre site was purchased, from a Methodist, on the north side of the Portland road west of the intersection of the two major streets in the village. With the help of the congregation a frame church was erected that spring . . . a plain prayer hall that allowed everyone of any means to participate. All buildings on the site had to be "plainly built and without ornaments, such as memorial windows, spires . . ." All pews had to be free for all, none could be rented. These covenants demonstrated how the new denomination was clearly a church for the ordinary person. It fitted Lombardy area with its community of farming folk of modest means like a glove.[6]

Evidence of these new holiness churches being established is scattered throughout local and personal histories. According to Roy Fortune's research, it appears most of the followers lived primarily in small towns or villages—95 percent of the members and 94 percent of the adherents.

Only 5 percent claimed they were from the larger towns of Ottawa or Pembroke.[7] Some question the accuracy of these demographic percentages, since several factors play a role in how the numbers can be interpreted; the church had many sympathizers who attended the holiness revivals but still remained committed to the Methodist Church. The lack of evidence on the matter makes any hypothesis mere speculation. Nevertheless, given the scale of the holiness awakening and personal popularity of Ralph Horner in eastern Ontario, the number of adherents in the movement by 1896 was near five thousand.[8]

OPPOSITION

There was, of course, immediate opposition from the press and the Methodist Church:

> The Holiness Movement received a mixed response from local residents. The atmosphere of their meetings was considered bizarre. As one observer put it (*Rideau Record*, Nov. 15, 1894), if one may judge by the volume of noise, the frequenters of the canvas tabernacle [were] having a howling good time. . . . Entertainment went hand in hand with the informal and spontaneous sermons. It provided local people with a respectable alternative to the taverns, and it was a much more regular event than the fairs and the Orange parades.[9]

Methodist churches were not pleased with the expansion and growth and influence of these new holiness churches—understandable, since it was from their membership that many of these holiness churches were drawing converts and members. The Pembroke District of the Methodist Church expressed its entire disapproval of the new church and called upon "our people to stand loyally by the church until the facts of the case are understood."[10] *Pilgrimage of Faith*, a history of churches in Madoc Township and village, reports that former Methodist minister Rev. Mr. Hagar circulated a printed letter of counsel to his "loyal, devoted, old Methodist friends in that vicinity of the true position of Mr. Horner." He said he could not believe that the Methodist people would be found "ready to scuttle the old ship on which so many had embarked, and which had borne so many safely into harbour." He was convinced, if the facts were studied carefully by the people, they would be slow to aid a project to destroy the church that had so tenderly cared for them. He concluded by saying that he was not for strife, but for peace, and that the great kindness shown him by the Methodist people of Madoc Township led him "to give them this information lest for want of proper knowledge, they be led astray. At one time Rev. R. C. Horner was a Conference evangelist, but now he is a suspended minister in active conflict and hostility towards the church and conference."[11]

ATTEMPT TO INCORPORATE

The fledgling holiness churches in eastern Ontario continued to grow, and in 1895 new candidates for ordination were presented to the Rochester Conference. But the Conference refused to accept them. Horner was advised to incorporate the church in Canada and instigate ordination privileges.

The new movement had begun with only one permanent building in Canada: the Concession Street property in Ottawa that had served as a centre for holiness meetings. Many services throughout eastern Ontario were held in local schoolhouses and often conducted by the female teacher who was among the early converts. Rev. S. A. York, years later, declared that God placed His hand upon a number of these talented, educated young women, separating them from secular employment and sending them forth as "flaming heralds of the cross."[12] These women unselfishly sacrificed their lives, and it is believed no missionary department of the church showed greater fruits for its labour than that of the young female evangelists who pioneered many of the new works. The movement spread west to southern Manitoba and opened new work at Crystal City in the wake of the noted Methodist evangelists the "Judd Sisters."[13]

First Annual Conference

On December 27, 1895—under the name the Wesleyan Methodist Connection of Canada—the first annual Conference of the new movement met in the Mission Hall on Concession Street. Rev. Ralph C. Horner presided and Rev. J. C. Irvine was appointed secretary. Three ministers presented themselves for enrollment: Rev. Ralph Horner, Rev. F. Sproule, and Rev. J. C. Irvine. In addition there were sixty-eight probationers who presented themselves for membership. Following the enrollment, and in keeping with the established custom of the Methodist Church, all members underwent an extensive examination of character. Rev. Horner then read the Twenty-Three Articles of Religion that had been previously prepared; they were adopted. The second motion resolved that a committee be appointed to deal with the matter of incorporation.[14]

The Second Annual Conference

On April 28, 1896, the second annual Conference met, heard encouraging reports, and continued with the proceedings of incorporation.

Another issue, however, surfaced—a harbinger of things to come—church discipline. Rev. Horner, the president, gave Conference an address on discipline. Discipline meant personally submitting to the rules of the movement; the new discipline would pervade into every area of preachers' lives. As a starter, the next report on the Conference floor was the Advisory Committee on Matrimonial Relations—the extension of the Book of Discipline into the marriage of preachers. The following rulings were decided:

- That all members of Conference who are engaged to be married appear before a committee (appointed for the purpose) before further steps are taken toward matrimony.
- That all members of Conference who are already married appear before said committee to make known the attitude of their wives and families toward the Movement.
- That all members of Conference are prohibited from corresponding with the opposite sex, save in purely business or pastoral matters.

A series of questions were composed by the Committee on Matrimonial Relations to be asked of all married and engaged men. The questions were deemed helpful for couples to consider before entering the ministry in a church that depended heavily on pioneering and opening new works; the thinking was that they would sift out any not fitted for the rigors they might face. Ministers were queried about their spiritual experience, agreement of spouse (or spouse-to-be) to joining in the ministry, children, debt, and means of support. Also, those intending to be married were asked if their spouses were willing to submit to the hardships connected with the work. Hardships included things such as no parsonages and no salary. The upside is that the faint of heart and unequally yoked would be weeded out; the downside is that they were asked publicly in front of Conference—no opportunity for private counselling, questioning, or advice . . . and perhaps honest evaluation.

It must be emphasized, however, that conditions were difficult, and the opening up of "new fields" called for courage and sacrifice. Thus, it was important for the unity and progress of the church for wives to be in unity with their husbands: entirely sanctified; accepting of the service styles; in agreement with the holy living requirements, especially the plain dress codes. Becoming a preacher in the new movement required an all-out dedication. The questions asked of wives indicate some of the hardships and criticism faced by the ministers. Tom Eades—grandson of Rev. George Christie, one of the earliest of Horner's converts—tells what it was like to be a holiness preacher in the new movement: "The opening of 'new fields,' it should be pointed out, was not work for the faint of heart; it was not the more settled life of the church pastor. . . . Loud mockery on the street, heckling and other interruptions of services by the occasional hurled stone or rough prank were more the style of this time, as the locals sought amusement at the expense of these 'holy rollers.' Some measure of courage was a condition of the work."[15]

The bar of confidentiality was set from the beginning. Reverends R. C. Horner and F. H. Sproule, along with Brothers T. G. Kenney and Henry Jarvis,[16] satisfactorily answered the questions. Sproule and Jarvis confessed to having other means at their disposal. George Horner and Andrew Lasher answered the questions satisfactorily and expressed their indebtedness to the Holiness Book Room (obviously their new appointment) and indicated their families desired to join with them in the ministry. William Greer confessed his wife was not saved and was not strictly in favour of him leaving home. Herbert E. Randall indicated he could not satisfactorily answer the questions until he would have an interview with his intended. If matters were satisfactory, he would then disclose her name. And on and on went the questioning of young men answering the queries posed by the Matrimonial Committee.

CAMPAIGN OF PROTEST

On June 1, 1896, Bradley and Wyld, solicitors for Ralph Horner and his followers, published a notice that "application will be made to the Parliament of Canada at the next Session thereof for an Act to incorporate a Religious Body to be called and known as the Wesleyan Methodist Connection of Canada."[17] The document became known as the "Horner Bill."

When the Honourable Mr. MacDonald (BC) rose in the Canadian Senate to introduce "an Act to incorporate the Wesleyan Methodist Connection of the Dominion of Canada" on September 15, 1896, he lit the fuse of a social and political bomb.[18] Methodists held a great deal of the religious power and control in Ontario, and when Horner was deposed from the Methodist Church, the church used both press and politics in an attempt to prevent Horner from having any influence in Canadian society.[19]

The Methodist Church attempted to portray an outward image of calm and unconcern. The Montreal Conference presented a public façade of nonchalance, claiming that very little had come of the cessation of Horner and his followers: "He has drawn a few malcontents during the year together with one minister but little effect has resulted in any of the churches through the action of the gentlemen."[20] To offset any criticism of their actions and portray confidence, the Montreal Conference reported in their *State of the Work Report*, May 30, 1895, "We are glad to note that after providing for all losses, we are able to report an increase in membership of over three hundred during the past year."[21] But behind closed doors, the announcement caused a flurry of correspondence between the headquarters of the Methodist Church and its superintendent, Dr. Albert Carman, along with his lawyers and advisors. Dr. Carman strongly opposed Horner's new society because it caused division within Methodist churches—members were encouraging fellow Methodists to leave the church for the new movement.

The *Holiness Era* strongly criticized Methodism for moving away from an emphasis on revival and conversion. An article published on March 24, 1897, was indicative of their criticisms: Methodists had "lost their zeal and are afraid to preach hell to sinners and holiness to believers." They have adopted "methods of medicine vendors on the street." They strive to "humour people" and "induce them to make professions of faith to Christ when they have no real conviction of sin. The Holy Ghost has not revealed to them their true state of sin nor has He witnessed to them that they are born again. Take such people in your church and they make a fine strawberry social brigade."[22]

In some cases there were actual protests embarrassing to the Methodist Church. The *Kemptville Advance*, December 12, 1895, reports of one such protest in Leeds County. Apparently "Hornerites," as they were now called, had gone to a Methodist church while the service was in progress and marched around the outside in a procession not unlike Joshua and the people of Israel marching around the city of Jericho. The article stated that Hornerites intended to keep up their pilgrimage for seven days. Members of the congregation were at a loss to know what the protest meant.

The Methodists needed some people of influence to help combat the perceived membership bleed and blizzard of criticisms levelled at them. The Hon. Oliver Mowat was such a man. Mowat, a director of the Upper Canada Bible Society and president of the Evangelical Alliance, had been premier of Ontario for most of the latter quarter of the nineteenth century. He had joined Prime Minister Laurier's federal cabinet in 1896, a few days later becoming a senator. Mowat now began to use his considerable political influence to prevent Horner from obtaining a charter for his new denomination.

One word caused the fracas: *Methodist*.

On June 23, a petition was sent to the Senate and the House of Commons signed by the presidents of all the Methodist Conferences across Canada that this bill be disallowed. John MacLaren, counsel for the Methodist Church, sent a letter to Dr. Carman on August 17, 1896, urging that the church set to work at once to have friends canvass every member on the Private Bills Committee; he advised that ministers and laymen in their respective counties write the members of the committee; he also suggested that interested Methodist members of Parliament be aroused by deluging them with telegrams of protest and added, "a member usually fears a single man of influence in his own constituency more than a hundred men outside of it." Finally he urged Carman to go to Ottawa and speak as the representative of the whole church.[23] Carman also received another letter the following day from MacLaren: "Begin at once among MPs who would likely be canvassed by members of the

Horner Movement . . . so that they will realize that it is a matter in which our whole church is interested."[24] The Methodist Church launched a massive campaign of protest, urging clergy and laity alike to send telegrams to the members of Parliament in their respective constituencies. It was apparent that Ralph Horner and his followers would become more and more vilified by the church and the press.

Why was there such objection over the use of "Methodist" in the proposed name? Roy Fortune explains:

1. Such a denomination would attract immigrants into Canada from the British Wesleyan Methodist Church, and other Methodists in Britain.
2. This new and inconsiderable organization would spring up at a time when the Presbyterians, Congregationalists, and Methodists of Canada were seeking to form of the three bodies one united church for the Dominion.
3. The largest body which entered the unions of 1874 and 1884, thus forming the present Methodist Church, was the Wesleyan Methodist Church. In no way did the Methodists want this upstart Horner, with whom they had so much difficulty, to undermine their authority or steal their members.[25]

Dr. Carman's private letters reveal that Senator Mowat did his part to prevent incorporation by writing a private letter from the Office of the Minster of Justice advising the Methodist superintendent that the bill had little chance of passing but that "it would be expedient for you to be prepared to resist it all stages."[26] A copy of Horner's "schedule" was supplied Dr. Carman and reported thirty-six circuits; thirty-five preachers; fifty-five evangelists; thirty chapels; 118 places of worship; 1,090 members of Societies; 4,553 adherents; fifty-one Sunday schools; and 1,514 Sunday school scholars.[27]

On September 29, 1896, the Honourable Mr. MacDonald (BC) rose in the Canadian Senate and finally introduced "an Act to incorporate the Wesleyan Methodist Connection of the Dominion of Canada." The bill that had generated such a storm of controversy came before the Private Bills Committee, where it was defeated.[28] Methodist political power and intrigue had prevented the denomination from being incorporated.

Down but Not Out

The politics of the day had prevented the Wesleyan Methodist Connection of Canada from obtaining a charter, but had not quashed the grassroots life of the Holiness Movement. The members were undaunted. In fact, if anything, the defeat of the "Horner Bill" served to accelerate enthusiasm and effort to pursue their cause.

A special session of the Conference was called in Ottawa, December 29, 1896, and a new name was selected and adopted by majority vote: the Holiness Movement Church in Canada (HMC). Much time was also devoted to consolidating the work, establishing rules of conduct, drawing up a model deed for church property, and sending workers to Manitoba.[29] An Incorporation Committee of five ministers and five laymen was appointed for the purpose of investigating and preparing for the matter of incorporation.[30]

A primary concern of Conference was the governance to be used for the administration of the HMC. Worried that the movement was becoming too extreme in its discipline and preventing people from joining, a memorial from the laymen of Winchester Holiness Movement (F. C. Sproule's circuit) was presented asking for equal representation of laymen with members of Conference. The memorial requested that equal numbers of laymen be included in various committees, including the Committee on Pastoral Relations, Committee of Reference to consider important changes during the interval of Conference, committee for the dual role of establishing and managing periodicals, and the committee enquiring into the financial state of circuits and the support of ministers.

The inclusion of laypeople, it was thought, might be able to soften the discipline and increase membership. Ralph Horner, J. C. Irvine, and F. C. Sproule were chosen as a special committee to consider the matter and called upon to present their findings to Conference: J. C. Irvine stated that he had not studied the matter, but in his opinion "layman and preachers each had a part in Church government in early times." F. C. Sproule stated he had not studied the matter, but in his view of New Testament history "there was very little discipline . . . and everything was run on a very loose basis." He was of the opinion that different times called for different government: "It was necessary to arrange church matters to meet the difference in times now." Finally, Horner spoke. He stated that he had "made this a matter of close study." Before he began to study he believed that laymen should have representation in the Conference and church government, "but when he began to search the Scriptures he learned that the government of churches in apostolic times was placed entirely in the hands of Apostles and Elders."[31]

A committee of twenty laypeople and twenty preachers was chosen to make a decision as to whether laymen should be admitted to future Conferences of the HMC. That evening, Conference met for the vote. It was a standing vote without discussion. Reverends Mallet and Irvine moved that laymen be represented in future Conferences. When the vote was counted the motion was lost. Little did the participants realize the future importance of their decision! Horner's views on church polity prevailed, reflecting his preference for the governance model of the Methodist Episcopal Church. But the issue of lay representation would not go away. In fact, twenty years later it became a root cause of major division within the membership and ministers of the Holiness Movement Church. The issue would rise again!

RESTRICTIVE RULES

After the Conference, Reverends Mallett and Horner began exchanging letters. Mallet said he could not work under the existing rules of the HMC and that they needed to be modified; he believed the rules were so stringent they might prevent incorporation.[32] However, the manner in which Mallett expressed his opinion and displeasure was called into question, and Horner removed him and replaced him on the Inverary Circuit.[33] Rev. Mallett did not take his dismissal lightly and wrote of his concerns to the Holiness Movement Conference: "I was driven out of the old church because I would not be a party to falsehood any longer about the observance and enforcement of rules. . . . I found the same deception being carried on from the top to the bottom [of the HMC]. . . . I leave for this reason that I left the old church and the godless and cruel despotism of your rule."[34]

Rev. Mallett went further, claiming Mr. Horner had no power to dismiss him. He denounced the Holiness Movement and Horner personally, accusing him of lying, being a dictator, not to be trusted more than the devil himself. Mallett asked the officials of the Wesleyan Connection in the US to put Horner on trial.[35] Mallett also proceeded to write letters to local newspapers arguing his side of the story.

Horner's response to this was to call the third annual Holiness Movement Conference in March 1897. The first act of the Conference was to state that the Holiness Movement was an independent Canadian denomination and that they were now withdrawing from the Rochester Conference. Witnesses were then called to testify at the Conference, and the conclusion was reached that Mr. Mallet was not treated unjustly, that he had been preaching against the doctrine of the church, and, moreover, had tried to lead the people of the Inverary Holiness Movement to follow him into an independent church. Mr. Mallett's charges against Horner were dismissed. At the same Conference, H. Sproule was removed from the Conference for employing Mallett and speaking against the rules.

HORNER ORDAINED BISHOP

Around late March 1897, Horner was suspended by the Rochester
Wesleyans. Horner was summoned to meet at Syracuse and defend his
case before A. T. Jennings, president of the Rochester Conference. The
Holiness Movement Special Committee met and decided on April 5,
1897, that Horner should attend the session only if the Conference
appeared friendly to him; if it appeared the Conference was biased, the
matter should be dropped.[36] After some discussion it was decided that
Horner would not attend the Syracuse session. At the end of the meeting, almost as an afterthought, it was motioned by N. Scharf and seconded by S. J. Shields that Horner be ordained leader of the Holiness
Movement. Without the consent of the Conference members Horner
became the official leader of the denomination. This obviously must
have raised some issues, because another Conference was called on
May 1, 1897, with S. J. Shields, R. C. Horner, and N. Scharf again
present. There was an amendment made to the HMC discipline on the
election and ordination of a leader: "Provided it is necessary to obtain
a leader before a General Conference the Annual Conference or special
committee may elect a leader."

This move did not sit well with Rev. J. C. Irvine, who protested
Horner's appointment. Irvine was tried at a Special Conference on May
27, 1897; he was accused of violating and neglecting the rules, attempting to cause division in the Chesterville Circuit, disloyalty to Conferences and rules, and imprudent conduct with a woman (disrespectful
and insulting language). Irvine was found guilty and deposed from
HMC.[37]

The HMC had faced its first internal conflicts: lay leadership,
restrictive rules, and appointment of a leader. There was definite fallout
and loss: three of Horner's most experienced and respected ministers
were removed, Winchester Circuit decided to leave the movement, and
a number of members also decided to leave.

New Churches

Despite the setbacks and conflicts, the Hornerite movement continued to increase. Ralph Horner continued conducting meetings and revivals in different parts of the Ottawa Valley and St. Lawrence River counties, as well as in Montreal and other parts of the province of Quebec.

A congregation began services in a small brick school owned by the Roman Catholic parish in Campbell's Bay until a site was donated by William Flood and a log church was erected. George Blackwell and Eddie Hamilton were said to have donated a great deal of time and materials toward the building of the church, and today it is one of the oldest buildings in the village of Campbell's Bay.

In 1897, Horner purchased a small acreage in nearby Shawville for his Clarendon followers to build a church.

G. A. Christie started a church in 1898 across the Ottawa River in Renfrew.

The first edition of *Pilgrimage of Faith* records the growth of Hornerite revivals in the Madoc vicinity: "A convention was held in January of 1898. It was reported to be the most powerful yet held in Madoc. Many souls were saved, sanctified holy, and anointed for the service of God. The old chariot wheels of salvation are still rolling on through the instrumentality of the Holiness Movement. To God be glory. Services three times daily, 10 a.m., 2:30 and 7:30 p.m."

A year later, in 1899, a series of divisions (districts) were formed and presiding elders (superintendents) appointed:[38]

- Ottawa District (Superintendent—Rev. E. Comerford): Ottawa, Billings Bridge, Carp, Munster, North-Wakefield, Carleton Place, Maberly
- Kingston District (Superintendent—Rev. J. J. Nesbitt): Kingston, Inverary, Sydenham, Wilton, North-Shore, Pine Grove

- Athens District (Superintendent—Rev. R. C. Horner assisted by Rev. W. Trotter): Athens, Warburton, Newboro, Lombardy, Prescott, Bishops Mills, Algonquin, Brockville
- Chesterville District (Superintendent—Rev. J. Caverley): Chesterville, Newington, Aultsville, Matilda, Kemptville
- Montreal District (Superintendent—G. S. Paul): Montreal, Ormstown, Coney Hill, Island Brook
- Arundel District (Superintendent—Rev. R. Collins): Arundel, Harrington, Morin Flats
- Shawville District (Superintendent—Rev. A. Warren): Shawville, North Clarendon, Thorne
- Snake River District (Superintendent—Rev. E. Claxton): Snake River, Haleys, Locksley
- Madoc District (Superintendent—Rev. S. Hollingsworth): Madoc, Ivanhoe, Foxboro, Wooler, Roblin

The Hornerite movement had increased numerically and put in place an organizational infrastructure. However, not becoming incorporated had become a barrier to their being accepted as legitimate and subjected their meetings to continued harassment and mockery. Two incidents demonstrated the prevailing attitudes of press and communities.

THE DEVIL IN THE CHURCH

One bizarre prank was carried out by local jokesters at Remington, near Madoc, Ontario, in the fall of 1897. Supposedly a practical joke, the hoax made headlines in the *Tweed News* and was subsequently reported in the *Toronto Evening Star*. The story was published as humour. The Hornerties were presented as "holy roller" quacks not to be taken seriously:

The Devil appeared to a crowd of people in this little church, at one of their evening meetings, materializing before the speaker with an ominous clanking of chains! As there had been an abundance of preaching on the devil and hell fire, it must have seemed an appropriate time for him to appear. In the dim light of the few coal oil lamps this apparition was convincing enough that the service was considerably disrupted and some of those present left rather abruptly.

The explanation of this supernatural visit was really very simple. A beef [sic] had been slaughtered in the community, and as the head of this unfortunate beast had been equipped with a suggestive pair of horns, some pranksters thought to introduce the element of drama into the meeting with the appearance of the Devil himself, through a trapdoor in the floor.[39]

The *Toronto Evening Star* embellished the prank with the theatrics of a ghost story:

The night of which we speak was dark and dismal and one calculated to strike terror into the stoutest of hearts upon slightest cause for alarm. The people came as usual to their place of worship, an old wooden building, through the cracks and crevices of which, the wind blew with many a ghostly and weird sound. . . . As the meeting progressed, and as the preacher arrived at that part of the discourse in which he had occasion to speak of the devil, there arose immediately in their midst, through and beneath the floor, a spectre so awful in appearance that the audience and preacher alike were wholly paralyzed in fear. The latter had hardly ceased speaking when there rang out in a voice terrible to hear, "I am the devil. I'll have you, Ha, ha, ha."

Fire issued from the devil's mouth and nostril, he had two horns coming out of his head, cloven feet and a clanking chain, two flaming eyes and a large appendix at the rear. His ears were perpendicular, and a fiery blaze encircled his whole body. Tall, erect and slim and when he spoke the building shook like an earthquake.

The terrified people and the preacher rushed pell-mell for the door over the seats and one another in their frantic endeavour to rid themselves of so awful a presence. . . . The terrified people fled in all directions, leaving "His Satanic Majesty" in possession of their meeting house.[40]

DISORDERLY CONDUCT

Shortly thereafter, two members of the Conference, Rev. Smith and Rev. Paul, were arrested and imprisoned for keeping a "disorderly house" (a reference to their mode of worship). The movement was incensed about this and about being ridiculed in the secular press. Subsequently, the 1998 Annual Conference passed a resolution that "whereas the Conference has all confidence in the unblemished character of these godly men," they [members of the Holiness Movement] would "maintain their rights [to worship] to the death." Therefore, in view of the fact that as body of Christians they were being "subjected to scandal," they sent a copy of the resolution to their solicitors in Montreal.[41]

INCORPORATION AT LAST

Pranks, secular criticism, and persecution demonstrated that without incorporation the movement would not be taken seriously. For nearly three years, the Incorporation Committee had worked diligently to perform their appointed task and investigate the matter of incorporation. On November 27, 1899, the application for incorporation signed by Solicitor R. A. Bradley appeared in the press:

That application will be made to the Parliament of Canada at the next session thereof for an Act to incorporate a religious body to be called and known as "The Holiness Movement (or Church), and to authorize such Corporation to meet and adopt, frame or repeal constitutions or make regulations for enforcing discipline in said Church, and to empower said Corporation to acquire, receive and take conveyances of such lands, money, mortgages, securities or other property as may be required for the purposes of a chapel or chapels, college or colleges, school or schools or other educational purposes of printing and publishing or house or houses and book depository or depositories in connection therewith and to take and receive the benefit of any gift or devise by will or otherwise in its said Corporate name, and to give said Church all necessary powers connected therewith.[42]

Three days later at the November 30 Annual Conference, Rev. Horner addressed the Conference, outlining four advantages of incorporation:

- Provide exemption from taxation;
- Quiet the public mind (he called it "quieting the Galilean Sea") and silence opposition;
- Do away with possible difficulties in the event of bequeathed legacies; and
- Avoid legal troubles that might arise in Quebec.

Four years had changed the religious environment: "No winds of protest blew this time from the direction of the Methodist Church in Canada; or if they did, they held no prevailing influence in so far as stemming the tide of incorporation was concerned. The door that closed in September 1896, against the 'Horner Bill,' opened again on June 14, 1900, in the passing by the Dominion Parliament an Act to Incorporate the Holiness Movement Church in Canada."[43] The Holiness Movement was now well established across eastern Ontario, and had spread into the provinces of Quebec and Manitoba, and as far away as Ireland and Egypt.

It was in this atmosphere of progress that in 1900, Mutchmor Chapel was born as a plain wooden frame building within walking distance of several mainline Methodist churches. (Mutchmor Street was later renamed Fifth Avenue, which is when the church changed its name to Fifth Avenue Holiness Movement Church.) Although it was the third congregation in Ottawa to be founded by HMC, Mutchmor Chapel "quickly became the hub of this new denomination, the Holiness Movement Church. Annesley College, the Bible School that developed as the new denomination grew, moved to a property a block away from the church. The new publishing house was close at hand, just a fifteen minute walk to the north. Teachers from the Bible School, and the editor of the weekly *Holiness Era* and the youth paper, along with the monthly *Missionary Tidings*, the Rev. G. A. Christie, and their families made Fifth Avenue Church their home congregation."[44]

The infrastructure of the Holiness Movement Church was in place, and its leaders were looking toward new horizons for expansion.

6

THE HORNERITES

Who were the members of the Holiness Movement Church—the Hornerites? The typical members who attended a HMC were those who had been converted by repenting of their sins, usually at the "penitent form" (altar), and had shown great emotion or agony as a sign they were truly sorry for their past lives. Thereafter, they would attend services in an unadorned church or "prayer hall." They would seek or give testimony to the experience of entire sanctification and manifest the presence of the Holy Spirit in their lives by a simple, holy lifestyle. Preaching was fervent, and members "got blest" with physical "demonstrations in the Spirit" while worshiping or praying. They might dance for joy, lift their hands heavenward signifying surrender to God (women often waved hankies), or offer praise to God with ecstatic whoops: "Glory, glory! Praise His name! Hallelujah!" Jim McCumber shouted the praises of God while kicking his foot over his head—even in his old age! Many would quote large portions of the Bible. Members usually addressed or referred to one another as "Brother" or "Sister," expressing solidarity and Christian affection. Although stories and rumours spread that exaggerated and glorified the accounts of saints "getting blest," nevertheless, for many "demonstrating in the Spirit" was real, and preachers would later recount the stories to congregations in sermons, emphasizing, "They lived as high as they jumped."

CASE STUDY: MA BROWNELL[1]

Ma Brownell, as she became known, recalled her first contact with
Hornerites at the Holiness Movement Camp at Bangor, where revival had
spread across the US border a few miles from her home near Malone,
New York:

> I took the morning train, arriving at the camp ground in time for
> the morning service. I sat down on an end seat, with eyes, ears
> and mouth open. I listened to a wonderful message from God.
> That was all I remembered until I came to myself lying out in
> the rain, covered with an oilcloth; the little pattering raindrops
> were whispering the most beautiful things about Jesus. I was
> laughing with childish glee; and for the next few days I just felt
> I was on my honeymoon. . . .
>
> The next morning I was up early and looked over the little
> city of white tents. Right in the midst was one that attracted my
> attention the most; it had been beaten by the storm of years and
> drenched again and again; and in one of the many battles it had
> lost its sides. It bore the scars of an old warrior of the past. They
> had run a pole up through the centre and tied the drooping cor-
> ners to some old stumps. This was the tent that had been assigned
> to the Bishop. While I stood looking and wondering about it, I
> heard a voice in prayer. It seemed to be streaming out of the hole
> in the top of the tent, like a mighty volcano pouring fire and glory
> all over the place until everything was drenched in the volcano.
> People may laugh at this—it was real to me!
>
> As the song service closed he opened his Bible and gave out
> the text. I never can forget, while the years of eternity roll, the
> first time I heard our Bishop preach. All through the service peo-
> ple were laughing, crying, shouting, jumping, running, falling,
> praising God and clapping their hands; the noise was the sound
> of many waters. (Oh I know what heaven is going to be like!)

Some were talking in tongues, and nearly everyone was drunk with the Spirit. When the altar call was given, there was a stampede, about one hundred people fell on their knees, and all began to pray at once. Between the meetings people were praying all over the grounds and I could hear the shouts of victory coming from away back in the woods, from the spice beds of prayer; then I would see the people coming, about meeting time, up out of the wilderness, leaning on the arm of their Beloved.

Every one of the faithful workers was filled with the unction of the Spirit, and had power with God that brought such a depth into the altar services that confessions of guilt and shame were wrung from poor, discouraged, broken-hearted sinners. . . . Often it was midnight before all the seekers were through. They were never allowed to rise, if we could help it, without the victory.[2]

STATISTICS

Statistically, according to the 1901 Canadian Census lists, there were 2,772 people who declared themselves HMC, most living in the Ottawa Valley heartland of Ontario and western Quebec, only 220 living in the west. The HMC, however, reported 11,000 members.[3] Canada, no doubt, did not account for many who attended and considered themselves loyal adherents.[4] Many still reckoned themselves members of the Methodist Church; others were supportive of the HMC but because of the restrictive nature and obligations of membership set forth in the Discipline did not become full members. Roy Fortune's research indicates that members were mostly agricultural labourers (often Irish), rural craftsmen, tradesmen, merchants, and workers in small towns who were slow to drift toward the industrialization occurring in the growing cities (60 percent of Canada's 5.4 million citizens were rural). Ralph Horner obviously had considerable influence among the rural people in the Ottawa Valley, the centre of his revival ministry.

CULTURE OF EXCLUSIVENESS

The HMC also began to reflect what was taking place in many emerging holiness movements across Canada and the United States— a tendency toward becoming exclusive societies, reacting against the encroachments of what they viewed as the "worldliness" of the modern age. Holiness defined itself in opposition to the dominant culture of the day and appealed to converts to defend themselves against unbelievers and "Methodist apostates." The battle lines were drawn, and R. C. Horner sounded the battle clarion "loud and clear" as his editorial in the *Holiness Era* suggests:

> The enemies of Jesus are more numerous and more bitter than ever they have been in the past. They are foaming out their shame. When they learn that the holiness movement is going to move on with increased rapidity, vigour, and power, they will rise up in their hatred, spite and devilishness. We do not know how much it means to be pressing this battle. But we know if we follow the pillar, we will learn that there are hundreds of men in every section of the country that are ready to persecute this way to the death. The war between right and wrong, between sin and holiness, between heaven and hell, and between God and the devil, never was stronger or more persistent than at this time.[5]

Traditionally, Methodists had emphasized simple faith issues that resulted in observable changes in attitude and behaviour. But now the foundations of faith and civilization seemed to be crumbling, and many who longed for the "old paths" began to turn to legalism, defined as the discipline of a separated life, as a way to preserve tradition in the face of massive social and economic change taking place in society. Robert Walker, a Primitive Methodist Conference president, some twenty-plus years previously in his annual address of 1875, grieved over the changing conditions. He had spoken frankly and prophetically of the times as he saw them: "Dress like the world; talk like the world; dissemble like the world; play with the world; join with the world in foolish amusements; go to the theatre and opera with the world; marry with the world; and the great majority of professors who do this are in great danger of finally going to hell with the world."[6]

Hornerites held to this view. Added to this, most tended to be connected socially to rural farms and villages where people resisted change and tenaciously clung to the past. R. Wayne Kleinsteuber, in his analysis of the Holiness Church mentality of the times, reasoned that "for the theologically and morally conservative, who found themselves out of tune with theological higher criticism . . . the temptation to abandon the world to its own devices, raise the barricades as high as possible, and retreat into their own cozy subculture was almost irresistible."[7] Indeed, when Ralph Horner and his thirteen fellow colleagues met on November 25, 1899, in their first General Conference, they not only established the constricting rules of episcopal governance that placed leadership and decision making in the hands of a few, they also set forth stringent rules to restrict how each individual member would live his or her private life. They began to choke the entrepreneurial spirit of the Holiness Movement.

DRESS CODES

It was the area of "dress" that caused the greatest controversy. The HMC began to devote a great deal of attention to codify and control the dress standards of its members. As far back as the 1890s, it is reported that Horner, speaking in Chesterville with "Sister Hamilton," said, "I am seriously thinking of having a certain style of uniform for our people." She replied, "Mr. Horner, no man is going to dress me!" Her reply gives credence to the issue of concern Rev. R. Mallett expressed in 1897 and caused an early division within the Holiness Movement ranks over rules and regulations.

Roy Fortune believes the moment Horner and his followers entered into legalism, they began to sow the seeds of their own destruction.[8] "Come out from among them, and be ye separate," recalls Jim Wood, son of Rev. Barney Wood, as he repeated the words impressed upon him by old-timers at various camp meetings to justify their dress and stern manner of life.[9] The sanctified life began to be equated with how one dressed.

Members were required to wear plain clothing, and no one could be received into the movement "until they have left off the wearing of gold and superfluous ornaments."[10] The practice of plain dress had its merits if applied with wisdom and in the spirit of modesty. But the list became pharisaic and prohibited men from wearing shirts with white fronts, jewelry of any kind, and neckties altogether; for women the list included everything from large sleeves and corsets, to fancy hats, netting, high-heeled boots, and fashionable hairstyles. All were off limits.

In her book *Athens Was Her Home*, local historian Edna B. Chant recalls her grandfather telling of a camp meeting (Lake Eloida) he attended when a young man; the preacher told the women to burn their corsets. The preacher told them they were a cursed invention, and all who wore them would deform their bodies and burn in everlasting fire. A bonfire was lit, and when the meeting was over, a mass of twisted corset steels was glowing in the coals, as several women had thrown their corsets into the bonfire. This would be a symbol of sacrifice for these women who probably saved hard-earned money to buy them.

STRIPPING ROOM

The most controversial practice of the dress standards was the "stripping room." According to oral tradition, Horner's meetings had a stripping room where ladies and gentlemen were expected to deposit their watches, rings, and other jewelry before or after going to the penitent form; hearsay had it these objects were sold to support the ministry. This was obviously untrue, as evident from Horner's memoirs. He told of a converted jeweller wishing to sell his inventory of jewelry; he took it to the firm, who sold it to him, who in turn "did all they could to make him believe that he was becoming fanatical, and that it was no harm to sell it."[11] There is ample evidence, however, that stripping rooms did exist, for Horner himself refers three times to the stripping room in his memoirs. He relates one instance of "two women who each had about one hundred and fifty dollars' worth of gold ornaments and dress [a sizeable sum in those days] . . . they entered the stripping room of Mt. Horeb, and went on to the promised land."[12] Writing of seekers who came to the penitent form, he said, "It was a great cross for them to enter the stripping room until they were humbled before God. They removed their ornaments and appeared in plain attire. It is hard for proud people to see that more than the simplest plainness is bad taste."[13] He also tells of another young woman who "took off hundreds of dollars' worth of gold and ornamentation to find the experience of entire sanctification, and God met her in the stripping room. Others profited by her example."[14] Rev. R. C. Horner emphatically asserted, "Holiness and jewelry do not go together."

PLAINNESS DEFENDED

Plainness was defended in the *Holiness Era*, the denominational periodical, "to act as an outward symbol of the internal reality of holiness, and a Christ-like spiritual life. Following fashion [does] great evil by engendering pride, breeding vanity, inflaming anger and lust, impoverishing families and begetting dishonesty."[15] Furthermore, the 1897 Discipline reasoned, "We should not on any account spend what the Lord has put into our hands, as stewards, to be used for His glory, in expensive wearing apparel, when thousands are suffering for food and raiment, and millions perishing for the word of life."[16] The last motive was valid, and followed John Wesley's admonition to "earn all you can, save all you can, and give all you can." To those who spent money, for example, on elegant clothing and "delicate food," he wrote, "You bind your own hands. You make it impossible for you to do that good which otherwise you might. So that you injure the poor in the same proportion as you poison your own soul. . . . And so this wasting of thy Lord's goods is an instance of complicated wickedness; since hereby thy poor brother perisheth, for whom Christ died."[17] Unfortunately, many holiness people around 1900 misinterpreted Wesley's call for plainness: it was about saving to give to the poor and evangelizing the lost—not an outward symbol of inward holiness.

TESTIMONIES

It must not be supposed, however, that dress codes were arbitrarily foisted on reluctant members against their will. Testimonies such as Jane Conley's often bore enthusiastic endorsement of the rules:

> I once loved to be dressed up in style, although I never put on any kind of makeup. I felt this false appearance was no improvement to the way God created us. The Bible tells us we are created in His image and likeness and I am sure we cannot make ourselves any better. Now I hated the fashionable dresses and hats I was wearing and took off extra ribbon, feathers and flowers from my hats as well as trimmings, ornaments and jewellery. I had combs in my hair with seventy-five rhinestones set in silver. They shone like diamonds. I sold them and put the money on the offering plate. I felt then, and so still, that such things are not becoming to women professing to be followers of the meek and lowly Nazarene. The only ornament I can find allowed in the New Testament dispensation of grace is "the ornament of a meek and quiet spirit, which in the sight of God, is of great price" (1 Pet. 3:2–5).[18]

MORE REGULATIONS

There were other regulations on how to treat the body as the "temple of the Holy Spirit," as instructed in 1 Corinthians 6:19–20. The motives were noble and simple: Be careful where you go, what you do, what you think, and how you respond to others. Their message to the world was: "We are holiness people set apart to God."

But it was the attempt to pair rules with spirituality that bred confusion and bondage to legalism. The Discipline defined regulations that prohibited members from using tobacco ("the very craving for the substance suggested corruption of appetites and morals") and other stimulants—and although the use of coffee and tea as stimulants was not prohibited, almost the same arguments were put forward to warn against their consumption. According to oral tradition, at one convention someone offered tea to the person seated beside Horner. Horner retorted, "He won't have tea. He is converted." Rev. William McDowell recalls that George Horner used to sing this song:

> My coffee for a substitute,
> It came in very handy.
> But when I got fully sanctified,
> You might as well give me brandy.

Hence, the popularity of "Hornerite tea"—hot water and milk!

A number of other standards governed the lives of HMC members. Dancing, card-playing, novel reading, amusements, political involvement, alcoholic drinks, participation in secret societies, and the purchase of insurance were all forbidden. An obituary in the *Holiness Era*, February 10, 1897, tells the story of William Russell, who had connected himself with the Holiness Movement and became convicted of his life insurance policy of two thousand dollars, believing it not to be trusting in God. Unfortunately, while he was working on the OA & PS Railway, he was scalded to death, leaving behind a wife and four small children. The *Holiness Era* stated the family was left to the care of God and the holiness society and that everyone was urged to help.

Keith Dagg, great-grandson of George Horner, told a family story about George's resistance to amusements. His parsonage in the West was across from a skating rink; George told his grandchildren that it was "the devil's playhouse" and commanded them to stay away from it. His daughter remembers sneaking a peek to see, and was very disappointed that it was just a messy dirt floor and nary a devil.[19]

SPIRITUAL DYNAMISM

Despite opposition, negative persuasion, and restrictive legalism, there was a spiritual dynamism within the HMC that propelled growth and momentum. There obviously was a spiritual hunger for revival and personal encounters with God among many of the rural people. *Pilgrimage of Faith* recorded the following events indicating the growth of the Holiness Movement in the Madoc vicinity:

1. A convention was held in January of 1898. It was reported to be the most powerful yet held in Madoc. "Many souls were saved, sanctified holy, and anointed for the service of God. The old chariot wheels of salvation are still rolling on through the instrumentality of the Holiness Movement. To God be glory. Services three times daily: 10 a.m., 2:30 and 7:30 p.m."

2. "The Camp Meeting of the Eldorado District, comprising Eldorado, Ivanhoe, Wooler, Foxboro, and Roblin circuits was announced to be held in Mr. Fred Comerford's grove near Eldorado village. Two gospel tents were to be there, one for preaching and one for camping purposes. Visitors from the other districts would be provided for and welcomed. Together with the preachers and evangelists of the district, the following were expected: the Reverends R. C. Horner; H. Caverly and W. J. Nesbitt. Mr. Waddell and Miss Dora Hamilton are invited to take charge of the singing. Services will be three times daily."

3. In 1908, "a novel sight was to be seen when half a dozen wagon loads of furniture and camping utensils was seen wending southward to the camp grounds at Ivanhoe, where the Holiness Movement Camp Meeting was in session. Bishop Horner is in attendance and large crowds wend their way daily to this great annual event."[20]

GROWTH OF CHURCHES

Keeping in mind that history is recorded from the bias of the writer and his interpretation of what has taken place, it is interesting to read *South Elmsley in the Making 1783–1983*, written by James R. Kennedy, active member of the Ontario Genealogical Society. Kennedy includes a section titled Progress of the Churches, which chronicles, among others, the growth of the Holiness Movement Church in the village of Lombardy and surrounding areas reaching as far as Smiths Falls. Some of Kennedy's research was derived from the local paper of that day, the *Rideau Record* (1888–1897), and records news of the community and editorial impressions:

> The Holiness Movement received a mixed response from local residents. The atmosphere of their meetings was considered bizarre. As one observer put it (*Rideau Record*, Nov. 15, 1894), if one may judge by the volume of noise, the frequenters of the canvas tabernacle (were) having a howling good time . . . the scenes of good-looking young women grovelling on the floor . . ." repulsed him. . . . Entertainment went hand in hand with the informal and spontaneous sermons. It provided local people with a respectable alternative to the taverns, and it was a much more regular event than the fairs and the Orange parades.[21]

James R. Kennedy's history of the growth and strength of the HMC in the Lombardy area was typical of many church plantings within the newly emerging denomination:

> As they grew in size and strength, the Hornerites of the Lombardy area wanted a more permanent forum for their preachers than the schoolhouses and camp tents. The local followers decided in 1896 to have their own place of worship. A one-acre site was purchased, from a Methodist, on the north side of the

Portland road west of the intersection of the two major streets in the village. With the help of the congregation a frame church was erected that spring . . . a plain prayer hall that allowed everyone of any means to participate. All buildings on the site had to be "plainly built and without ornaments, such as memorial windows, spires . . ." All pews had to be free for all, none could be rented. These covenants demonstrated how the new denomination was clearly a church for the ordinary person. It fitted Lombardy area with its community of farming folk of modest means like a glove.[22]

We learn also from Kennedy's history that the local congregation was not large enough to support its own minister; hence, the pastor served Smiths Falls as well. But the Lombardy church influenced several local families into the ministry indicated by the names of several young people attending the Holiness Training Institute in Ottawa: Sala Blanchard, Alice Newman, and Katie Jones became Holiness leaders and ministers. Camp meetings and conventions provided the main means of outreach and growth:

Camp meetings remained the main evangelical forum for the people in the rural areas. Meetings were held at local Lake Eloida in Kitley and were attended by Hornerites from the Lombardy area. Strict dress and others codes of discipline were practiced at these meetings. No one smoked, drank, swore or criticized their friends and neighbours. To many, it provided relief and relaxation as well as a spiritual rejuvenation which the other churches were not able or willing to offer. In 1913, a three-day Holiness Movement convention was held at Lombardy. Large crowds from the vicinity and surrounding places attended this event at which Reverend Horner was present.[23]

EVANGELISTS: THE JAMES SISTERS

The HMC, like the Methodists of the same era, envisioned a strong role for women in their ministry, and indeed Ralph Horner suggested in his *Entire Consecration* that women could be eloquent speakers and as gifted as men.[24] Two sisters, Lola J. Willows and Eva James, became icons in the Holiness Movement and later Standard churches. "Sister Willows," as she was known, and her sister, Eva James, were familiar preachers in the circuit of holiness conventions and camp meetings, sounding their clear trumpet call whether in word or song to follow the "good old paths" of holiness. Their family roots extended back to the very beginnings of the HMC: John James and his wife, Mary Argue, had settled in the Stittsville area just west of Ottawa; they had five sons and four daughters, two of which were Lola and Eva. In her book, *The Two Sisters*, Lola Willows recorded vignettes of the early sights, sounds, and spirit associated with Ralph Horner and the Holiness Movement of that day:

Father and mother were staunch members of the Methodist Church. As time passed it grew to be a cold and formal church. While we were still young, Rev. R. C. Horner started to hold revival meetings. Holy Ghost conviction settled on the people, so much so, that some were prostrated by the power of God. Both father and mother were gloriously converted. My mother would get so happy she would dance, and father would run around the church. This was too much for the cold and worldly-minded people who professed religion. They strongly opposed such demonstrations. The "war was on," and the happy "defenders of the faith," rather than grieve the Holy Spirit, were willing to go to the bush and chop down trees for lumber to build another church where they could have freedom to worship God.

We held a meeting every month in our home, and on that day, usually Thursday, father would seat the large dining room with chairs and planks, and mother would set the table for all who came from a distance. The yard was filled with horses and buggies. The house was often so full that many had to stand outside. The saints would get the holy laughter. Some would shout the victory. Some were prostrated by the power of God. Many sinners were saved in those meetings and they will rejoice all through eternity. The country was stirred for miles around. Our home was always open to receive the "prophets of the Lord." And many times, I think, we "entertained angels unawares."

Oh, those shining faces! Can I ever forget them and the testimonies of praise to God? Hundreds tracked out into the Light and they lived and died burning and shining for Jesus. No wonder that many churches were built! Whole communities were changed. Old store bills were paid-up and old grudges were dissolved and enemies reconciled. Is it any wonder there was such rejoicing? The people shouted with a great shout and the noise was heard afar off. These people were not popular with the worldly crowds or with formal church-goers. They were called "Hornerites" in derision. And, like the early Methodists, you could tell a Hornerite as far as the eye could scan. They could pray and get the glory down like Elijah did on Mount Carmel. There the fire fell and the prophets of Baal were put to flight. Glory!

Preaching was definite. We were told very plainly that there was a heaven and a hell. People were urged to seek definite experiences. Every Christian was urged to seek a clean heart and every one with a clean heart was exhorted to pray and wait before God until the mighty baptism of the Holy Ghost was poured out upon his soul. It is no wonder that preachers and missionaries came out of that effort. Ontario was stirred.[25]

THE CHURCH SPREADS WESTWARD

John A. MacDonald's dream of the Canadian Pacific Railway was realized on November 7, 1885, with the driving of the "Last Spike" at Craigellachie, British Columbia. A ribbon of steel united Canada from sea to sea, and the West was opened to settlement. The Movement, as the church was often called, first opened in southern Manitoba in the early 1890s at Crystal City seemingly in the wake of the Judd sisters, noted Methodist evangelists.[26] In the autumn of 1897, nearly three years prior to incorporation, a work was also started in Winnipeg, Manitoba, by Rev. S. J. Shields, a charter member of the church. The first annual Western Conference was held in Crystal City in the fall of 1899.

The main impetus for the growth and spread of HMC churches in the West, however, was Clifford Sifton's goal, as minister of the interior in Wilfred Laurier's Liberal cabinet between 1896 and 1905, to fill up the West with farmers. Sifton was determined that railway lands be opened for farming homesteads. My grandparents, Fred and Helen (Nellie) Croswell[27] were part of that land settlement, departing by rail from Parry Sound, Ontario, to file entry for a homestead in South Melfort, Saskatchewan, on December 28, 1904. And so did many members of the Holiness Movement Church. Membership in the West was largely a reflection of the westward migration from the Ottawa Valley heartland. Holiness Movement churches began to dot the landscape of Manitoba (Portage la Prairie, Crystal City, Kilarney) and Saskatchewan. Rev. J. H. Southcomb in his short history of the Holiness Movement in Saskatchewan wrote:

Shortly after the twentieth century, there was a tremendous migration of settlers into western Canada, thrilled by the prospects of one hundred and sixty acres of land for ten dollars and another one hundred and sixty acres for a low price. Among those who came west were numbers of members from the Holiness Movement Church in eastern Canada, a quite a few settled in southwest Saskatchewan. . . . Many who are in heaven and many yet on the way will thank God for the early holiness preachers and people who amid hardship and suffering proclaimed the message of full salvation. . . . There were no churches, no parsonages, no campgrounds when they came. Through work, sacrifice, and faith, they gave us what we have today.

All of the Holiness Movement churches which were in the southwest, were around Swift Current and within a radius of one hundred miles, so the area was naturally called the Swift Current District. To the west and south of Swift Current was the Tompkins circuit, about sixty miles away, and south forty miles was the Admiral and Cadillac circuit. . . .

In the fall of 1909, John Elliott Jones and his wife and four sons and three daughters moved from Shawville, Quebec to homestead at McCord, Saskatchewan. Others . . . came out to settle in the same area. . . . These early pioneers really loved the Lord, so they did not wait until the church sent them a pastor, but held services among themselves in homes until a minister came. These services were usually led by Mr. John Elliot Jones or Uncle Billy McDowell, and were blessed and honoured of God. The Christians were faithful in attendance at the Sunday services and the midweek prayer meeting. . . .

In 1910, the health of Rev. J. E. Cooke gave out in eastern Canada and the doctor recommended a change in climate, so he came out and took a homestead on the Wood River, just a mile east of the present town of McCord. Here he not only farmed but laboured as a pioneer preacher . . . and the Lord wonderfully owned and blessed his labours. Many will thank God that Brother Cooke ever moved to McCord. Times were hard, and many times the men of the congregations wore overalls to church, but the blessing and presence of the Lord were always there. The people were not long without a church. In

1913, lumber was hauled forty miles from Vanguard and a house of God was erected. Later, a parsonage was built, and cemetery commenced where many of the early settlers are buried.[28]

Other churches sprang up in Saskatchewan: Swift Current, D'Arcy, Keatley, Melfort, Nipawin, Love, Cadillac, Admiral, Glengary, Wellard, Tompkins, Cannington, Manor, and Alida. Churches were established in Alberta: Edmonton and Wildwood. Eventually Holiness Movement churches were located as far west as Vancouver, British Columbia. Houses of prayer were built and camp meetings established to continue the traditions of the Holiness Movement as preached and practised in the heartland of the Ottawa Valley, where Ralph Horner first held his revival services.

BIBLE COLLEGE AND BOOKSTORE IN OTTAWA

Ralph Horner believed young men and women needed to be trained for the evangelistic ministry in the Holiness Movement. He initially conducted the first training school for preachers in 1895 out of his house in Ottawa. He trained evangelists to preach like he preached. A year later in 1896, a Bible school was established and conducted by Rev. Horner at 480 Bank Street, Ottawa. In 1907, the school moved to a beautiful old home at 910 Bank Street, Ottawa, and became known as Annesley College—in honour of Susannah Annesley, John Wesley's mother. The naming of the college after the "mother of Methodism," particularly during the women's suffrage movement in Canada, obviously encouraged and honoured the many women who attended and were sent out to evangelize. One of the first teachers assigned to teach with Rev. Horner at Annesley College was Rev. S. A. York.

RELIGIOUS PUBLICATIONS

Ralph Horner was an avid writer, and following John Wesley's pattern for distributing literature (magazines, booklets, and pamphlets) into the hands of as many people as possible, he established the book room as one of the first institutions of the emerging church. He began using his house in 1892 to edit and publish the *Holiness Era*, which later became the official organ of the Holiness Movement Church. This paper, supported by subscribers only, served as the initial means of disseminating the movement's doctrine and discipline (regulations for members to live by). Rev. Horner established a printing house in 1897 at the 480 Bank Street property in Ottawa. The Holiness Movement Press moved into high gear, publishing not only the *Holiness Era* but also numerous pamphlets and books for wide distribution at camps and conventions:

- *Saved to the Uttermost* (based on Hebrews 7:25), in which Horner asserted, "Jesus can save a man to the uttermost. . . . Jesus takes all the sin out of men, but He does not do it until they repent of it."
- *The Root*, based on five sermons Horner preached that taught the doctrine, "There is only one way of having the victory—the root must be destroyed."
- *The Feast*, a series of sermons printed yearly from the annual Feast of Pentecost
- *Gospel Tent Hymns*
- Holiness Movement Church Catechisms
- "We Are Happy Today," Horner's famous gospel song, still sung at holiness camp meetings and conventions[29]

LAKE ELOIDA CAMPGROUND ACQUIRED

Ralph Horner did not neglect equipping, training, and indoctrinating his ministers and evangelists before sending them forth "on fire" to their various fields of labour. He needed a retreat grounds to do so, and Lake Eloida became an ideal location.

Lake Eloida campground was located on the north shore of Lake Eloida, a few miles north of Athens, Ontario. It was a picturesque lake surrounded by a ring of maple and evergreen trees. A country road running east and west along the shore of the shallow, mud-bottomed lake gave easy access to the grounds. There were few boats and no swimming near the campgrounds to distract from the services. Lake Eloida camp provided a serene, picturesque retreat for personal revival and renewal—five flat acres that fronted on the lake, suitable to pitch a gospel tent with room to build a line of joined-together two-story cottages on either side, and space behind to hitch numerous teams of horses. Anyone who has viewed the scenic autumn grandeur of the sparkling lake framed along the shoreline with the glorious reds and yellows of sugar maples, sprinkled with garnishes of evergreens, will agree the lake is a jewel to behold.

The grounds were donated in 1899 by Mr. Andrew Henderson, a very religious man, dedicated to the work of God and the Holiness Movement. He had built what was known as the "show barn of the whole countryside." People came from miles around to read with wonder the texts painted in white on the great red barn: on one end, "Where shall I spend Eternity?" and on the other, "The gift of God is eternal life through Jesus Christ Our Lord." The tract of land later became known as the "Hornerite Camp Ground," and became a favorite location for the bishop to gather his pastors and workers for a ten-day retreat where he would indoctrinate them with his preaching on entire sanctification and the baptism of the Holy Ghost and fire.

The first cottage was built in July 1899 by Otis Bullis. Others began to follow his example, building two rows of cottages, each one adjoining, like a village street, with the great gospel tent pitched in the center, the lake at the front, and the road at the rear. Hundreds of people came with their horses and buggies each Sunday during camp meeting. Many came to worship and praise God and find spiritual renewal. Others came to meet their friends from afar, while others came to view the spectacle of Hornerites getting blessed, dancing in the Spirit, and falling prostrate in the straw. Visitors would contrast sharply with the Hornerite women in their somber black or navy blue uniforms, their prim collars, and ubiquitous small-brimmed sailor hats. It was reported in 1902 that Lake Eloida camp drew a crowd from thirty miles on each side, there being about a thousand in attendance. Places to tie horses were at a premium, nearly every fencepost and tree being utilized. Mr. Horner was in charge, with special ministers and evangelists taking part as well. Lake Eloida was a perfect place for a camp meeting, for even on the warmest days there was a gentle breeze from the spring-fed waters of the lake.[30] The fervent amens and hallelujahs would echo and ring about the countryside for miles around.

Many stories and tales grew and abounded by those not acquainted with the Lake Eloida camp meeting culture and spiritual customs, especially the altar services. One writer, known only as Harold, tells how he reluctantly attended the Hornerite camp at Lake Eloida with his brother. He stated he did not want to go to any of the meetings, but went down to the shore of the lake and tried to study history. He maintained the Hornerite preachers went among the crowd with sticks, making them pray. If a person did not pray hard enough to suit them, they would beat him with the stick. He claims he could hear one man while beaten shouting, "Amen! Amen! Glory! Amen!" The ministers kept shouting at the people, "Keep it up! More! Pray harder!" and so on. It made a good story, but obviously the gentleman did not understand what was taking place. He was hearing sounds emanating from the altar service at the end of the preaching. He stated he could hear the shouts, wailing, and moaning of the congregation.[31] The cacophony of voices at the altar of prayer, the shouts of "Glory!" from the blessed, the groans of those bent low in earnest repentance, and the thumping of clenched hands on the wooden altar and seats by desperate seekers might easily have fed the imagination of anyone not acquainted with altar services at a holiness camp meeting.

Lake Eloida became the mecca of the Holiness Movement.

RENEWAL MOVEMENT

The Hornerites became one of many fringe holiness sects in the late nineteenth century reacting to worldliness in the church. They were a renewal movement, emphasizing aggressive evangelism and entire sanctification, which they felt were characteristics of true Methodism. Their focus on holiness, however, began to detour from the core heart issues of perfect love for God and neighbour, and expressed itself more and more in outward legalism, especially dress codes. Moreover, the church adopted an autocratic governance that devolved much authority onto one office, that of the bishop. Subsequently, creativity and entrepreneurialism began to wane; moreover, when growth began to subside and decline, it was easy to point fingers at one source, that of the bishop. Nevertheless, Rev. Horner acceded to their request to form a new fellowship of holiness people, "never doubting that Divine wisdom and strength would be given commensurate to the task set before him."[32]

OVERSEAS MISSIONS

From early beginnings, the Holiness Movement Church in Canada had a profound interest in foreign missions. Many had a deep passion for the lost in other parts of the world. At the Conference held in the fall of 1898, it was decided that December 25, Christmas Day, would be General Missions Day across Holiness Movement churches. Missionary sermons were to be preached at all places of worship, and an appeal made for missionary offerings. A Church Missionary Fund had been established.

IRELAND

Overseas missions really began in Ireland, although it was not considered to be a foreign mission. A contact visiting Canada had requested Mr. Horner send someone "to help quicken the spiritual life of Ireland" (remember, many Ottawa Valley members of the HMC were of Irish ancestry). Reverends McConnell and Wright answered the call. Rev. McConnell formed the first Holiness Movement Society in Ireland at Ballymena. He wrote in 1898, "Belfast is ready to be opened and workers are needed."[1] By 1905, Allan Moore reported in the 1948 edition of the *Holiness Era*:

We are grateful to God for another prosperous year of His work in Belfast. Since last conference the work has constantly advanced. Sisters Ardill and Barkely had a blessed revival in the beginning of the year in the old Park Road Chapel. Then Bro. Dearn had a good tent campaign during the summer on the Shankhill Road. These efforts resulted in the erection of another hall in the latter place to accommodate the splendid congregations gathered there during the meetings. Since then we have built a second temporary hall in another part of the city and by the time this report is ready there will be three places of worship with a congregation of two hundred in each, where we hope to settle down to have three powerful revivals. We want to open up two additional places of worship here before spring. If the workers are forthcoming, and God continues to lead, we shall have them. Will you not all join us in prayer that the arm of the Lord may so be manifested that next year's report, whosoever may live to hear it, will vastly exceed this one?

The Irish work was important, for it became a stepping-stone to foreign missions work in Egypt. Practically all early HMC missionaries sent to Egypt travelled by way of Ireland, where they remained for a month or more (sometimes a year) for rest and spiritual preparation.

EGYPT

It was to the Conference of 1898 that Rev. H. E. Randall wrote from Ireland, stating there was "an opening of the door to the foreign field and any workers who were ready may leave without delay. Some should leave England for Egypt and the Soudan by the first of the year." Rev. Randall accepted the call himself, left the British Isles and arrived in Egypt by midsummer 1899. Years later the Young People's Missionary Society reported the pioneer work of Rev. Randall in Egypt:

He was studying Arabic at Alexandria in preparation for going to the Soudan when the Wissa brothers from Assiout [later spelled *Assiut*] met him and were impressed by his spirituality. They were adherents of the Presbyterian Mission work but were hungering for experiences of grace not yet attained and were classed as Reformers. They invited Mr. Randall to go to Assiout to hold meetings. This he did. As the Presbyterian Mission had built a new church, they allowed the company of men who sought Mr. Randall's leadership to use their vacated church for Sabbath services. This group also secured another meeting place more centrally located where they conducted services nightly. Mr. Randall had all freedom in preaching to them the doctrines of the Holiness Movement Church. He was well received by the Egyptian people and was zealous to see the church organized and reaching out to the villages.[2]

Soon the Egyptian brethren urged the opening of a school for girls. Rev. Horner approached Miss Edith Burke, Miss Cora Van Camp, and Miss Carrie Reynolds about going to Egypt. They sailed from Montreal via England to Ireland, where they spent a month in evangelism: They arrived in Alexandria, Egypt, on December 2, 1899. Two days later they proceeded to Assiout, where they were cordially received by Rev. Randall and a native brother. They were soon surrounded by people who spoke no English, and they realized how handicapped they were with the rudimentary Arabic they had learned in Kingston. They made use of interpreters, however, and in time with diligent study and work, acquired a working knowledge of the language.

Miss Van Camp was an experienced teacher, and they with the assistance of the other two female missionaries, organized the School for Girls in Assiout. To their surprise the rooms were filled to capacity: 150 girls and a few boys. Three Egyptian teachers also helped in the school, and in 1901 Miss Elma Cannon, who was an outstanding teacher from Ontario, joined the staff as well. Straightaway the school began to have a positive influence on Egyptian children from all classes of society and continued to do so for many years.

HMC missionaries were pioneers in breaking new ground for women speaking in public. Miss Cora Van Camp related how it began:

How strange it was in this land of the Pharaohs! We women were a spectacle to the people of Upper Egypt. The men came in large numbers to meet us. Of course the women did not come. Brother Randall and we sisters sat on the long bench while opposite us the brethren sat. They had been listening to Brother Randall for some weeks. In order to get time for the study of Arabic we appointed a special hour for a little service of prayer and Bible reading. God did bless us in giving forth the message and a blessed spirit of prayer came on all so that finally we sisters were invited to speak publicly in the night services. What a victory that was for women preachers fulfilling Acts 2:17–18.[3]

The women's work gained momentum as Miss Van Camp continued pioneering. She conducted the first women's meeting at Nakhala in 1901 with thirty or forty women, and three or four took part in prayer. Participation by women was surprising to many Egyptians. In 1902, one of the missionaries wrote that the doors were opening on many sides and calls were coming requesting preachers. Carrie Reynolds recalled later that while stationed at Aboutiz, she was entreated by a chief of one of the villages across the Nile to go over and help his people. She consented to go for an open-air meeting each Sunday, returning to her own village again in the evening. And thus the village work grew as more and more villages appealed to the missionaries for services.

Reading the reports and diaries of these missionaries, one cannot help but appreciate that many early HMC missionaries were heroes of faith. Their stories are exciting and filled with adventure! More young women from Canada responded to the Macedonian call: Miss Lydia Bradley and Miss Emma Barkley gave needed assistance to the School for Girls in Assiout. One young woman especially notable in her service to village churches, Edith Burke, was stationed at Nakhala. Rev. Randall wrote about his visit to Miss Burke's station:

> While spending a few days with Sister Burke at Nakhala to assist
> a little in the revival there, we were kept on the go from house
> to house during the daytime and at each place the neighbours
> would come in and make a good congregation. There would also
> be listeners on the roofs. The method of visitation followed by
> our diligent little sister is so thorough that nearly all the streets
> in that large town are entered and every few square rods become
> the centre of a lively prayer meeting from time to time.[4]

The first "Pentecost Meeting" was held in 1903, where there was reported to be a great spirit of prayer and manifestation of God's power. The doctrines of the church were printed in Arabic, as well as a church paper, the *Bugle of Holiness*, with five hundred subscribers.

The Egyptian work was progressing, and by 1903 six young Egyptian preachers expressed the need for a Bible school. Rev. Trotter began a training school in the basement of the mission home—the beginning of the Holiness Movement Bible College.

In January of 1906, the first Egyptian church was opened and dedicated in Akhmin. The church seated 600 with a gallery for 250 more. Opposition to the church began to break down as many became convinced of God's power and experienced salvation. A young Egyptian woman, Aneesa, who was almost blind, attended the church. She was educated in the American Girls' College and reportedly was "well blest" in her Christian experience. She insisted on testifying at the church service. Canadian women had overcome the Egyptian custom forbidding women to speak in church, and now an Egyptian woman testified in a service of praise and worship.

By 1907, the work had become strong enough that Rev. Trotter, who was in charge of the work, assembled the eight missionaries on the field, along with a few of the native Egyptian workers from the training school he had started in the mission home, and formed the first Egyptian Holiness Movement Conference.

At home in Canada, Miss Sarah Longhurst, at age forty-six, volunteered for service in Egypt; she and Miss Clara Maclean arrived in Alexandria in the fall of 1907. The girls' school in Assiout was opened for boarding pupils in 1908, and Miss Longhurst, after a few weeks of ministering in the villages, returned to the school, where she would work for many years.[5]

Back home, the church was encouraged greatly to pray for and support the work in Egypt. The 1910 Manitoba Conference urged the children to be involved in the missionary endeavours: "To them we must turn for new workers; interest them now; have them save their spending money to help support children in the mission schools; teach them to pray for our missionaries so that they may be rooted and grounded in God and grow to perhaps be missionaries in a few years."[6] This missionary zeal "brought forth fruit in prayer and effort." Miss Bradley wrote from Egypt that she had chosen a young girl from the Assiout school for the Stittsville Sunday school to support. Later in 1910 she reported they had helped in the work among women. Three children were being supported in 1910, and by 1915, forty-eight girls had Canadian sponsors and the enrollment was 184 students, seventy-three of them boarders.

In the 1914 annual Conference statistical report, the work had grown to thirty-nine mission stations, forty-two places of worship, an average Sunday attendance of 3,662, with twelve missionaries, and forty native workers. The Egyptian work had done exceedingly well.[7]

CHINA

No account of missionary pioneering is more moving and challenging than that of Rev. Asa B. Van Camp and his all too brief missionary labours in China. Reading his tattered little diary is deeply moving. Many of these unsung men and women in the HMC, such as Rev. Van

Camp, were motivated by a passion to reach the lost that transcended all personal comfort and ease; they took the injunction to be a living sacrifice seriously.

Asa Van Camp, a schoolteacher, joined the HMC Conference consumed with a passion to reach China's millions without God. He pleaded with Conference to allow him to go to China, but they would not consent to his going alone. It was too dangerous. During the Boxer Rebellion in China (1898–1901), thousands of "Boxers" (a secret society that practiced martial arts and believed they had magical power such that foreign bullets could not harm them) roamed the countryside. They attacked Christian missions, slaughtering foreign missionaries and Chinese converts. In 1902, Asa rehearsed his call to China at Conference and with much feeling spoke on the subject so dear to his heart. At last in 1903, Rev. R. C. Horner responded: "Mr. Van Camp had on his heart heavily for years the perishing masses of that vast country of China. I restrained him until it seemed cruel to do so any longer and I had to say, 'You may go.'"[8]

On his journey across the Pacific on board the *Empress of India* en route for China in October 1903, Asa made this entry in his diary: "I pray that God may rejuvenate, renovate, and smash me up and give me a Chinese tongue. I could sacrifice all knowledge of English if so doing I could have my influence correspondingly increased among a people toward whom are my purposes and desires for good. Much as I love the English language, it may all go, Lord—and all the vain things that charm me most, I sacrifice them to His blood."[9]

After his arrival in Shanghai, Rev. Asa Van Camp wrote home: "I feel so much at home—perfectly in love with the Chinese—I feel like getting my arms around the waiters and telling them how much the Lord Jesus is to me. O, my poor heart overflows! I am determined to walk with God and honour Him. With Eternity hinging on these few short years of toil, Lord Jesus make me faithful in my stewardship."[10]

It was the early missionaries like Asa Van Camp who helped lay the foundation for the great spiritual house-church movement China experienced near the end of the twentieth century. Among the missionaries at Shanghai, Mr. Van Camp met some warm Christian friends, one of whom was Rev. A. P. Quirmbach of China Inland Mission. Rev. Quirmbach was well acquainted with the Chinese language and was known for his prayer and evangelical fervour. These two men, in company with others, set out for the province of Hunan, about one thousand miles inland. They ate their food with chopsticks and slept on hard bunks all the way up the Yangtze River. They arrived in Changteh, Hunan, in January 1904, where the two men lived and laboured together.

Mr. Van Camp was a tireless student and made remarkable progress in the Chinese language. He loved the Chinese and made himself one of them. Tragically, in January, 1905, Rev. Asa Van Camp contracted a violent strain of smallpox. He arrived at the Presbyterian hospital in Changteh on January 9, but in spite of loving care died on January 18. Before entering hospital, the last entry to his diary on January 5 reads, "Pain in my bones and back of my eyes, but Glory be to God I rejoice in my Saviour." He was only thirty years old but left a wonderful impression on the missionaries in the city, as well as the native Chinese who knew him. Dr. O. T. Logan wrote a letter of condolence to his parents, Mr. and Mrs. Byron Van Camp, in Winnipeg, Manitoba. The letter is a beautiful tribute to Asa and records some of his last words, which he dictated shortly before death, later published in a small book entitled *Gems of Thought*:

Dear Mother, have gone to be with Jesus. Weep not for me, we shall meet again. Mother, your prayers, your humility, your love, changed my hell to heaven. Father calls, I'm away.

"Dear Father, farewell. I'm the first to lay the burden down.

"Sister Cora (Assiout, Egypt)—Cora toil on. Thy path will be hard sometimes, but I know you will overcome and enter into His love.

"Mr. Horner, I shall work no more. Now [I] will be praising Jesus throughout eternity."

Dr. Logan, seated at Asa's deathbed, reported: "As I listened to the thunder, and saw the lightning that occurred at the time of his death, I said to myself, this is God's announcement of our brother's triumph: the thunders are the palms of victory; the lightnings are God's fiery chariots escorting our brother to glory, while the accompanying rain is earth's tears of sorrow for its loss."[11]

Who would pick up the torch for China? It was another of the young female heroes so prevalent in the Holiness Movement Church—Miss Edith Burke. After labouring in Egypt for eight years, she came home on furlough. She was troubled because no one was going to China to pick up the task Mr. Van Camp had laid down. She volunteered to go. The mission board refused to send her alone, so in 1909, she worked her way to the western coast of Canada and prayed for her fare to China. She arrived all alone in Shanghai and proceeded inland to Ching Kiang, where she remained in the home of Dr. Cox to study the language for one year until Miss Tillie Danford joined her in 1910. Writing in 1928, Miss Danford recalled the burden of her call to China she had received many years before in 1909:

Twenty-five years ago last September God healed me, soul and body. Then within two months, I had His call upon me to leave home and go out as an evangelist. In the following January I went to Ottawa, where Bishop Horner had a school for training and preparing young men and women who were called of God to preach the Gospel. Those were great days to my soul. Praise God for the blessed privilege of attending such a place! At the close of the term Bishop Horner, under divine guidance, sent me and a co-worker to our first circuit. God blessed our feeble efforts and gave us souls at every place we laboured.

I spent six years in evangelistic work, and it was during that time that I received a definite call to China. At times it would seem that I must be mistaken: what could I do in China? After fasting and prayer, God helped me to decide. I knew it meant China or hell. Jesus helped me to make a complete sacrifice.

I started for China in 1910. It took grace and courage and strength from God to bid adieu to my parents, brothers, sisters and all for that dark land. God promised His grace would be sufficient, and (Praise Him!)I have proved it over and over again. . . . No matter what the trials or the conflicts are, I have never doubted my call to China. My blessed Saviour has proved a very present help in every time of need. Whenever I felt tired and lonely this was always followed by a very special nearness to Him.[12]

Miss Danford's diary is full of suspense and faith. It was decided that since Mr. Van Camp had died in Changteh and the city did not have a strong gospel witness, the women would establish their work there. It was a crowded city with a population of about half a million people. Rev. S. G. Caswell and Rev. S. A. Graham were sent to join the two ladies, but when they arrived in Shanghai from Ireland, they were surprised to find out by telegram that Miss Burke and Miss Danford had gone inland to Hunan a week ahead! Proceeding by steamer up the Yangtze River to Hankow, where they engaged a native junk to carry them to Hunan, the two men, without knowing a syllable of Chinese, found their way after eleven days to the walled city of Changteh. They were escorted by the boat captain through the narrow streets to the Presbyterian mission, where they were hospitably entertained by Dr. and Mrs. Logan. The next day they were taken to see the two female missionaries and were happily welcomed. Miss Burke was eager to start preaching at once, as she had been a student of the language for a whole year. The HMC owes much to the Presbyterian missions and China Inland Mission for the kindness they bestowed: they welcomed the HMC missionaries into their hearts and entertained them in their homes until they succeeded in procuring a place to rent in Changteh and open a mission.

CHANGTEH MISSION

The Changteh Mission was a commodious building huddled up against the city wall near the south gate, but it was dark and damp inside. The lower part was used for meetings and the upper part was used for living quarters. The two missionary women lived there for three years, "labouring day and night in prayers and tears, studying and helping the poor women who came to visit them daily. . . . Much praise is due these faithful ladies for their untiring labours there."[13]

That spring, Reverends S. G. Caswell and S. A. Graham went farther into the country and joined Mr. Chapman, the faithful brother who nursed Asa Van Camp during his illness. They remained with him until the fall of 1911, when the great Chinese Revolution began and the country was turned into turmoil and confusion. The Chinese were determined to throw off the yoke of the Manchu rulers. The British and American consuls advised all female missionaries to move to safer quarters. Rev. Graham accompanied Miss Burke and Miss Danford to the relative safety of Hankow, but the city was full of soldiers and the hospitals full of wounded. The HMC missionaries joined the Red Cross and went to work in the International Hospital to care for the wounded. When the war was over in April 1912, the Manchu dynasty was overthrown and the missionaries returned to their former places of service.

ANSIANG

Late in the summer of 1912, missionaries Caswell and Graham attempted to push farther afield and opened a mission at Ansiang, an island on Tung Ting Lake about seventy miles northeast of Changteh. They opened a small rented chapel on the street, but it was difficult to attract more than just a few children who came to ask questions about the strange men. However, one young man and his father from the countryside began to attend and became earnest believers. The young man was baptized and became an evangelist. Unfortunately he contracted tuberculosis and died; so did his father, but both died in the Christian faith.

The work in Ansiang was tedious, but in the fall of 1913 the arrival of new recruits cheered everyone's hearts. Mary Irwin, Mildred McCreary, and Helena Freeman arrived in China. They were met enthusiastically at Shanghai by Rev. S. G. Caswell, and he and Miss Freeman were married a few days later. Mary Irwin and Tillie Danford also joined the mission to assist Rev. Graham in Ansiang. They were the first foreign women to be seen. Opening a day school for children and nursing the many sores and sicknesses that abounded did much to break down the prejudice that existed against them. Tillie Danford also adopted a Chinese orphan named Hsuing Chin Uin, whom she cared for and taught with all the devotion of a mother. Hsuing later graduated from Yale College at Changsha—a credit to his foreign mother, who laboured faithfully for his good.

The mission work in Ansiang continued to progress slowly until a large property was purchased in the heart of the town and a large building was erected in 1915 to serve as chapel and school. When this new facility was opened, great crowds flocked to the services and Bible classes. A day school was opened and the first enrollment nearly filled the school to capacity—some had to be turned away. A great work began in the city and many were converted and turned away from their idols to serve the one true God and His Son, Jesus Christ. (Anyone acquainted with the superstitions in which these people were entangled cannot help but rejoice greatly upon learning of these conversions.)[14]

NEW PROPERTY IN CHANGTEH

In 1913, a property was purchased on the main thoroughfare in the city of Changteh. HMC missions raised seven thousand dollars for the erection of the Van Camp Memorial Home, in memory of Asa Van Camp who had given his life for the work in China. "A Brief History of Holiness Movement Missions" recorded, "Rev. R. C. Horner deserves great credit for his services and enthusiastic support in raising this money."[15] Rev. S. G. Caswell moved into the new building with his young bride, Helena Freeman, and they enjoyed many years of missionary service in the city. From this centre, native workers, Bible women, and Christian students were raised up to serve God. A new chapel was also built on the property; part of its upper story was used as a school for small boys and girls.

WAR

The year 1914 brought about the horrors of World War I. Much commotion was felt throughout the provinces of China. Propaganda from many sources was broadcast to the people. British and American diplomats employed the services of their subjects in every district to distribute large quantities of literature; daily telegrams were sent for publication. Missionaries not only carried out their daily mission routines but were also employed to assist considerably in the war effort.

The civil war followed with its long train of bloodshed:

Nearly the whole country was again at war. A reign of terror existed in the province of Hunan. The whole province was overrun by armies and large bands of brigands and robbers. The people suffered terribly. They looked to the mission halls for protection. Our missionaries felt the strain very much, for day and night they were called to render medical aid and shelter refugees. The brigands kidnapped children and women, destroyed whole villages, looted, killed and cruelly oppressed the people. Happily in the midst of all this chaos the noted Christian General Feng-U-Hsiang arrived with his forces and made his headquarters in the city of Changteh for three years. Our missionaries had a feeling of security as they listened to the soldiers singing hymns as they marched around the city at 6 o'clock every morning. Order was restored and a strong Christian influence prevailed making it easy to carry on mission work. Hundreds of soldiers embraced the Christian faith and received Christian baptism at the hand of our missionaries.[16]

Missions Flourished

A 1915 HMC Conference report states: "We have 10 missionaries in Egypt and it costs $150 for a single fare; we have 7 missionaries in China, single passage costing $300." These early HMC missionaries were men and women who knew the meaning of sacrifice and willingly gave their lives for the sake of the gospel in lands far away from home and family.

In 1959, two biographers, Nettie Hill and Norma Eves, paid tribute to the brave endeavours of early HMC missionaries: "No tales of frontline heroism are more thrilling, and no fiery preacher more convincing, than the action-packed lives of men and women who carry the Christian faith to the four corners of the world. . . . And we rejoice in the part our band of loyal missionaries had . . . since our first messenger was sent from Canada to the regions beyond."[17]

STORM CLOUDS

To say that Ralph Horner possessed a strong personality is an understatement. Oral histories surrounding Horner's personality are full of anecdotes that at first glance seem contradictory: his strong will and abrasive manner on the one hand; his gentle, caring nature and charisma on the other. All agree, however, his authority was not easily challenged. Horner had integrated most aspects of the hierarchical and administrative polity of the Episcopal Methodist Church into the governance of the HMC. Pastors and evangelists had input in theory, but the bishop's word was always final. Subsequently, as the bishop of the HMC, Horner controlled and ruled all aspects of church government: he wrote the rules of the church and curriculum for the school; he chaired the meetings, controlled the business, decided the placement of pastors, and edited the *Holiness Era*. The challenge this presented for the HMC was that Horner by nature and gifting was not the pastoral type. He had less interest in training pastors for local churches than teaching preachers to be evangelists like himself. Rev. Fred Patterson related to Rev. Eldon Craig how Horner taught his preachers to pray and speak; he would stop them in the middle of their prayer or preaching and correct them: "No, say it right."

Horner's leadership became an issue in the stationing of pastors. He wanted to train evangelists who would conduct revivals: preach on a circuit for six months to two years and then move on. The late

Rev. John Woodland also stated that pastors were not allowed to own property. This, coupled with being stationed on a circuit for such a short while, kept pastoral families in a state of instability, making it difficult to establish any sense of normality. An example of Horner's indiscriminate moving took place when Manly Pritchard, while stationed on the Shawville Circuit, made provision for the coming winter, equipping and readying himself and his family during the fall. On December 20 he received a note from the bishop stating he was appointed to the Wooler Circuit and was to be there in less than two weeks beginning January 1. Woodland wondered how he could pick up his belongings and move his family (by horse and train in those days) when he was set for winter in Shawville and didn't know whether any preparations had been made at the other end.

HORNER RESIGNS

The first major challenge to Horner's authority occurred February 1, at the 1905 General Conference held in the Mutchmore Street Chapel, Ottawa. Horner acknowledged there had been a complaint made against him in his official capacity as bishop that, he said, had neither been proven nor exonerated, and, therefore, he reasoned, "the only honourable mode of procedure was to tender his resignation," which he read to the Conference. Conference immediately proceeded to investigate the charges embodied in R. C. Horner's communication. The next day Horner's resignation was refused. The grievance was made by Wilfred Flower, who had written to Conference concerning Horner's lack of confidence in Flower's Christian experience and ministry (apparently Flower had taken steps toward matrimony without permission).[1] The matter was resolved privately and Horner resumed his work as bishop of the HMC. It is interesting to note that the bishop's response to the conflict was to resign rather than fight; no doubt he knew his resignation would not be accepted, but by threatening to resign he would force his critics to back down. This would not be the last time Horner would use this tactic.

LEAVE OF ABSENCE

In May of 1907, R. C. Horner requested a leave of absence from the HMC.[2] According to Conference minutes, Horner requested an absolute rest from work for six months—not surprising since he had worked at a pace few others could have sustained. Was he now totally exhausted? Was his health declining? Was there undisclosed conflict? The most obvious reason seems to be that there was an underlying conflict, since, immediately after the request for leave was granted, a committee was appointed to wait on the bishop to see if "a more harmonious state of affairs could be arrived at."[3] At any rate, the leave lasted from 1907 to 1910—much longer than the six months requested.[4] The leave was significant, for in the fall meeting of the General Conference Special Committee, appointments were made to continue the operations of the HMC:

- General Conference Committee Chairman: W. J. Dey;
- Editor and associate editor of *Holiness Era:* W. J. Dey and S. J. Shields;
- Teacher (principal) to take charge of the college: S. A. York;
- Interim bishop until Horner would again assume the bishopric: A. T. Warren.[5]

These appointments were significant and constituted a watershed for the HMC. The reins of power were, in effect, transferred. With his leave, Horner lost control of the church infrastructure, and pastors would get a taste of life without him. Moreover, as Horner would ultimately learn, it would be difficult to regain power after relinquishing it.

There has been speculation as to another motive for Horner's leave of absence. Many claim he requested his leave to have time to write his book *Bible Doctrines* in response to the rise of Pentecostal revivalism that was beginning to blaze across Canada. There is good reason to believe this. Horner requested a private secretary of his choosing, and it was decided that each member of Conference would contribute five dollars for support of a private secretary.[6] The rise and growth of the Pentecostal movement, as we shall see, appealed to the same spiritual clientele of the Holiness Movement, since many of Horner's followers were leaving the HMC and joining with the Pentecostals. Interestingly, it was mostly the adherents and not the members who were leaving (see graph below).[7]

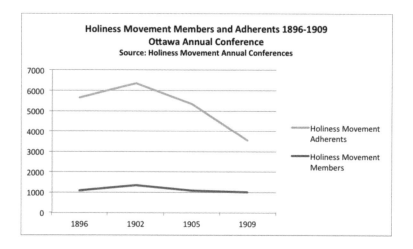

THE THIRD FORCE

As the growth of the Holiness Movement Church began to plateau and decline in some churches and camp meetings, Pentecostal revivalism, or the "third force," began to gain momentum, and many from Ralph Horner's holiness revivals began contributing to their spiralling growth. Thomas William Miller reported in his history of Canadian Pentecostals, "Hornerites were among the first to respond to the Pentecostal message when it reached Ontario."[8] Free Methodist writer Rob Clements said, "Historians today often point to Horner as the missing link between Pentecostalism and Methodism."[9] Gordon Atter, in his history of the Pentecostal movement, noted, "Many of the early Pentecostal leaders in Canada had been members of the Holiness churches."[10] The terminologies familiar in holiness circles became a part of the language of Pentecost.[11] Ralph Horner's third blessing, the "baptism of the Holy Ghost" and its ensuing physical manifestations, was an easy bridge to the Pentecostal baptism of the Holy Ghost with its evidence of speaking in tongues (glossolalia) along with the familiar manifestations of prostration, shouts of praise, dancing, and singing in the Spirit.[12] Demonstrations common in Horner's revivals became familiar scenes in many Pentecostal services.

Robert Edward McAlister, a name familiar to students of Canadian Pentecostal Church history, was an early Hornerite who played a foundational role in the early growth of the Pentecostal Assemblies of Canada; in fact, he has been called the father of Canadian Pentecostalism.[13] He was born in the Ottawa Valley into the large Presbyterian family of James and Margret McAlister (they had thirteen children), and became a convert around 1900 at the age of twenty in the Cobden Holiness Movement Church.[14] Sensing a call to the ministry, he became one of Horner's young holiness preachers. He was gifted and to further his training attended God's Bible College in 1901, a small holiness school in Cincinnati. But poor health during his second year of studies forced McAlister to return home. After his recovery he began preaching for the Holiness Movement Church. In 1906 he heard of the Azusa Street Revival in Los Angeles. Out of an awakened interest, he boarded a train and headed to California to attend the meetings. He experienced the baptism of the Holy Spirit and received the gift of speaking in tongues. He came back, witnesses reported, "on fire for God," preaching the baptism of the Holy Ghost wherever he went. In 1911, McAlister published a Pentecostal paper known as the *Good Report*, sending out as many as 45,000 copies a month. Later that year, he and some likeminded clergymen organized a well-attended conference and revival in Ottawa resulting in the establishment of the first Pentecostal Assembly in Ottawa (Bethel Pentecostal Assembly).[15] From Bethel, the Pentecostal message spread. "In the same year, new churches were established in various locations along the Ottawa Valley . . . places where McAlister had preached for the Movement."[16]

Roy Fortune also maintains that after 1906, several of Horner's pastors and evangelists had definite Pentecostal connections, and some became pastors and evangelists within the Pentecostal movement.[17] Fortune relates how his wife's grandmother, Mrs. Albert (May Anderson) Peever, was a graduate of Horner's college and became a founding member of the Kinburn Pentecostal Church in 1911; her brother, David Anderson, was a Holiness Movement preacher. "I am convinced," Fortune writes, "that Horner had an influence on many other Pentecostals in Eastern Ontario."[18] Rev. Ken Bombay, Pentecostal Assemblies of Canada pastor, evangelist, and Bible college teacher with many Holiness Movement connections, concurs that many Pentecostal churches have HMC roots.[19]

A revival in the city of Toronto, Ontario, under the leadership of Pastor and Mrs. A. Hebden, broke out in 1906 at their independent mission located at 651 Queen Street East. Although the Hebdens were unaware of the Pentecostal revivals taking place, many Pentecostal scenes became common in their meetings. Many were filled with the Spirit and went home to carry the Pentecostal banner to new communities. These people were from all religious persuasions, but most came from holiness churches—Methodist, Holiness Movement, Free Methodists, and New Mennonite.[20] Their holiness theology largely shaped the theology of early Pentecostals in Ontario.[21]

The loss of former friends, associates, and converts must have been an emotional blow to the aging Horner. During his early years of preaching, the *Pembroke Advance* reported that Rev. Ralph Horner, Rev. Walter Russell—along with evangelists Ida Mason, Ella Birdwell, and Nellie Judd, and other Christian workers—witnessed the wedding of James Findlay of Beachburg, and evangelist Susie Williamson. The wedding was officiated by Rev. John Wilson, formerly of the Methodist Church, on December 9, 1889, at the home of the bride's sister in Athens, Ontario.[22] The wedding write-up reveals these young evangelists had been a close-knit group of friends who had served together during the initial stirrings of holiness preaching within the Methodist Church and the Eastern Ontario Holiness Association. But a 1908 baptismal record[23] reports that long-time HMC friend and evangelist Ida Mason was baptised by immersion, along with several others, at Singleton Lake by Robert McAlister, Pentecostal preacher, and Alex McCready of "McCreadyites" fame. Alex McCready had moved to the John Singleton house at Lyndhurst and began holding Pentecostal-style camp meetings at Singleton Lake.[24] Other names included in the baptismal record were those of Vernel, Cora, and Clarence Cross—probably a family connection to Adelaide Cross, whose name also appears on the 1898–1901 Conference rolls of the HMC, and who conducted tent meetings during the 1890s at Seeley's Bay, Ontario, with Evangelist Eli, another of the young female Hornerite evangelists. These names represented friends of Horner who had laboured with him during his early years but were now being won and recruited into the Pentecostal movement.

An examination of church minutes and records reveals that a number of Horner's preachers and evangelists were striking out in a different venue under the banner of Pentecostalism. The Pentecostal Assemblies were open to the entrepreneurial spirit of these young men and women, and they in turn carried the spirit of Ralph Horner's meetings with the same manifestations across Canada. Clare Fuller, in an unpublished paper, reports that about 15 percent of the early Pentecostal leadership in Canada came from Holiness Movement Church backgrounds.[25] This percentage is amazing because the Pentecostal Assemblies became Canada's largest evangelical denomination. The PAOC numbered 513 members in 1911, and by 1920, census statistics indicate that 7,000 Canadians identified themselves as Pentecostal.[26] Horner's spiritual children were moving beyond their restrictive bonds of legalism and governance. By 1915, the Laymen's Committee of the

HMC reported that, according to their statistics, membership in Ontario and Quebec had not increased from that of twenty years before, but had actually declined over one hundred members; adherents had left by the thousands.[27] The committee was attempting to pin the loss on Bishop Horner, since he was the public face of power and leadership; however, many believe there was an exodus of many holiness people open to the "new winds" of the emerging Pentecostal revivals being conducted across the country.

In the West, a revival in Winnipeg also had its roots in the great holiness revivals of 1906. A. H. Argue, a young businessman from Winnipeg, told of the days when large crowds were on fire for God because of the preaching of holiness evangelists. He heard of the baptism of the Holy Spirit, left his business, and travelled to Chicago to seek this experience. Returning, he opened his home for holiness people who were seeking this experience as well. Soon a hall was secured to contain the crowds. It was not long until the revival spread throughout the prairies. Soon A. H. Argue found himself fully engaged in the ministry and gave up his private business activities.[28]

Pentecostalism in Alberta traces back to holiness roots as well. The Pentecostal message came to Alberta in 1917 when Rev. John McAlister (brother to Robert) met with a group of Holiness Movement believers in the home of Mr. and Mrs. Edgar Taylor for revival meetings and Bible study. A number of them received the Pentecostal baptism of the Holy Spirit. The work grew from that small group. In 1919, they occupied the sanctuary of what became Edmonton Central Pentecostal Tabernacle, situated on a small obscure corner of town at 114 Avenue and 93 Street. The sanctuary was enlarged by taking down partitions and still the church was packed for services. Central Pentecostal, with its Holiness Movement roots, became the mother church for planting many of the Pentecostal churches found in Edmonton and vicinity.

Rev. David Mainse of *100 Huntley Street* television fame—a student of Brockville Bible College and Eastern Pentecostal Bible School,

Peterborough, Ontario—traces his spiritual roots directly back to Ralph Horner. "David's father was Rev. Roy Mainse, HMC missionary to Egypt and pastor who was present at the 1959 merger of the HMC with the Free Methodists. His mother's uncle was the Rev. Manly C. Pritchard, respected preacher who remained with the HMC in 1918. Perhaps more than any other evangelical in Canada, David Mainse has tried to bring various denominations and sects together into one worshipping whole."[29]

Not only did a number of pastors and evangelists switch alliances, some early Pentecostal missionaries also traced their beginnings to the HMC. Rev. Herbert E. Randall, Ralph Horner's first missionary appointment to Egypt in 1899, visited the Hebden Mission in Toronto while on furlough. He received the Pentecostal baptism of the Holy Spirit with speaking in tongues, an experience he says he long sought.[30] In October of 1907, he opened the Ingersoll Pentecostal Mission. Of particular interest and significance is that a talented high school senior, Aimee Kennedy, learned of Randall's meetings just before Christmas as her father James Kennedy was driving her home in a horse-drawn cutter. A sign hanging in a storefront advertising the meetings caught her attention and drew her into the services. She made a commitment to Christ and in years to come became better known as Aimee Semple McPherson, evangelist and founder of the International Church of the Foursquare Gospel.[31] Randall later teamed up with Robert McAlister (they would have been well acquainted as former ministers of the HMC) and H. L. Lawler, another missionary on furlough from North China, during the winter of 1910–1911 at Queen's Hall in Ottawa and conducted meetings under the banner of the Apostolic Faith.[32] Later, Randall returned to Egypt as a Pentecostal missionary. While he was in Egypt, another of McAlister's periodicals, the *Morning Star*, was sent to Randall for translation and publication into Arabic. Herbert Randall's mission work in Egypt had become Pentecostal.

HORNER'S RESPONSE

It makes perfect sense that during this period of growing discontent and migration by a considerable number of holiness people to Pentecostalism, Bishop Horner should remove himself from his duties as bishop in 1907 to write his *Bible Doctrine*—a clarification of his entire doctrinal position on the "second blessing" of entire sanctification and the baptism of the Holy Spirit as experienced by the apostles at Pentecost. "This is the baptism of the Holy Ghost for service and warfare for Jesus," he wrote. "They know their foes are mighty, but oh! They see these stores of exhaustless power. They seek it and get it, and know by the witness of the Spirit that they have it."[33] His teaching was a divergence from mainline Wesleyan doctrine, which taught that entire sanctification and the baptism of the Holy Spirit were received simultaneously. Although he did not deny that those so baptized in the Spirit would perform signs and wonders, the manifestation of such gifts were merely *possible* "signs of the baptism" and not necessarily features of it. Thus, he rejected both a central feature of the Pentecostals and their chief "distinctive," that of speaking in tongues.[34] Nevertheless, his emphasis on the baptism of the Holy Spirit left his followers open to the spiritual winds of Pentecostal revivalism.

HORNER RETURNS TO CONFERENCE

It was during the fifth General Conference of 1910 that Ralph Horner emerged from his leave of absence. He arrived late on May 10, the day Conference convened at the Mutchmor Chapel in Ottawa. The Conference was obviously expecting him because a committee was appointed to wait on the bishop and see if he was sufficiently rested to assume responsibilities and if so to invite him to come and take charge of the Conference.[35] Upon arrival, Bishop Horner proceeded to chair the next order of business: the examination of ministerial character.

Committees had already been formed by interim president A. T. Warren and were accepted by Conference. That evening, Warren was obviously back in the chair; Conference minutes were signed by Warren and he appears to have chaired most sessions until May 12.

Then the unthinkable happened. Warren suddenly resigned in the afternoon session and asked John Dey to take the chair. That evening he gave his reasons. He said, "Whereas he had only been asked to take the bishop's place while he was resting, and only voted in by a small Conference committee, and as Conference was now in session and Bishop Horner had not resumed his work, he thought it was now time for General Conference to do something in a unanimous way as to placing a man in this position."[36] Conference moved to adjourn.

The next day with Dey in the chair, Bishop Horner arrived in Conference and was asked to resume chairing the Conference. The committed then reported on Brother Horner relative to his resuming his former position in the work after his period of resting. Horner indicated that he would resume his work if Conference gave him permission to employ help or helpers as the work required. From then on Horner and Warren played tag team chairing the Conference. Warren's request was ignored, and no vote was taken for him to become interim president in the bishop's absence. The stage was set for conflict over leadership — and who was responsible for the slowing down of growth and loss of membership in the HMC.

MOMENTUM SLOWS

Why was the HMC losing momentum? Why was it losing members? The simplest reason was to pin blame on the leadership of the bishop. But the reasons were more fundamental. The movement was aging and growing more conservative. Few could grasp what was taking place. Four reasons are postulated for the decline and eventual demise of the HMC.

1. PROVINCIAL MINDSET

In retrospect one can see that the HMC was not adjusting and transitioning to changes taking place in twentieth-century North America. In the early 1900s, modern conveniences—such as washing machines, sewing machines, and new store-bought clothing—were becoming readily available, and they could all be ordered from the convenience of the Eaton's catalogue! The HMC reacted to these changes rather than accommodate them, or even use them to their advantage. Oral tradition reports Bishop Horner would not ride a train or streetcar on Sunday. The HMC reacted to modernization rather than embracing changes that would help to spread the gospel.

In the period between 1901 and 1911 almost two million people immigrated to Canada, many settling in the West. This was an open mission field to thousands of Eastern Europeans right on their doorstep. In 1903–1904, there was an economic boom and many were employed in the construction and transporting of materials to build new roadways and railroads. Industrialization led many to head from the farms to the overcrowded cities to seek employment. There was a growing divide between the rich and the poor who could not afford the new modern conveniences. Urbanization was growing, but the HMC remained rural—provincial, not open to change. With its rural mindset, the Conference clung to conservative codes and morays, hindering transition from a rural base to an urban base as was happening in the rest of the country.

2. RESTRICTIVE GOVERNANCE

Horner's view on church polity reflected his endorsement of the Methodist episcopal model of governance. Episcopal polity is a form of church governance that is hierarchal in structure; the chief authority rests in a bishop. Churches having episcopal polity are governed by bishops who have authority over dioceses, Conferences, or synods (in general referred to as a Judicatory). As well as performing ordinations, confirmations, and consecrations, the bishop supervises the clergy within his jurisdiction, often prescribing their work and locale of service. The danger of episcopal governance is the potential for muzzling the vision and creativity of laypeople within the church. As James E. Wilson would express so passionately to the Board of Directors Committee of the HMC in just a short while, "The worthy ambitions and holy aspirations of our young men are crippled by our ecclesiastical government which has them tied down." He later added, "I believe laymen are anxious for the spread of the Gospel, and are willing to sacrifice for the salvation of souls. Laymen should have a place in all our councils as New Testament Christians, and should be allowed to put their God given thought and spirit into the ears of all, even the General Conference."[37] The HMC was missing out on the ministry of a host of lay leaders who, following the model of 2 Timothy 2:2, might minister, witness, and teach others also. A more democratic form of governance would have allowed for more control and modulation of Horner's dogmatism and provided some outlet for the frustration generated by his take-charge tendencies.

3. RULES AND MORE RULES

One cannot read the minutes of HMC Conferences, Annual and General, and the *Book of Discipline* without sensing that every effort was made to control, restrain, and direct every detail in the lives of preachers within the movement. A section of the 1907 Discipline was entitled "The Duty of Preachers to God, Themselves, and One Another," which covered everything from fasting weekly to drinking water and eating no more at each meal than was necessary; there was also a question on "denying oneself every pleasure of the sense." Preachers and people were enjoined to observe the strictest economy in dress, furniture, and high-priced carriages. The motives were noble: so that one might have means to give while there were those perishing for the Word of life or suffering for food and clothing. But enforcing the rules gave rise to judgment and legalism. Who could live up to all the rules?

As already noted, the Discipline regulated how long a preacher could remain stationed in one location or circuit. The bishop formed a committee to counsel and advise him in the appointment of preachers. But in so doing, he would not allow any preacher "to remain in the same station more than two years successively, excepting the Presidents, Principals, or Teachers of the Seminaries of learning."[38] Families were in a constant state of flux and instability.

Perhaps the most personal intrusion was that of approving or disapproving the marriages and engagements of preachers and preachers-to-be. Marriages and engagements were closely scrutinized (see chapter 5 for questions and procedure). Probationers preparing to preach in the Holiness Movement Church, "who . . . entered into the marriage relation before the completion of their probation [at least two years], might be licensed by a Presiding Elder . . . but would not be stationed on a Circuit for at least three years after their restoration"—a long delay for couples eager to serve God together as pastors or evangelists![39] Marriages were carefully examined, and not all young couples were willing to relinquish control over their personal and family lives.

4. CHAINS OF LEGALISM

Hindsight is always 20/20. Hundreds of people in the rural settings of Ontario and Quebec were led to experience salvation and sanctification through the ministry of the HMC. But legalism became a fly in the ointment. The infinite number of dress codes and regulations became stumbling blocks to the greater purpose of evangelism, especially in the larger towns and cities. Urban people were less conservative about dress and jewelry. Other movements began to ease their legalistic requirements and jumpstart from rural, small-town holiness revivals and churches to establish vibrant evangelistic works in the cities. Ralph Horner and his movement might have enjoyed greater success in the urban centers were it not for the rigid rules and constraints bogging them down in legalistic quagmires. Rev. R. T. Williams, in his last quadrennial general superintendent's address to the Church of the Nazarene at Oklahoma City (1940), warned that legalism "is a very subtle force that works its devastation unsuspectingly in the hearts of men, resulting in the weakening of a whole institution: Legalism is the enemy to be feared. Legalism gives more attention to law than it does to human beings. It emphasizes the letter of the law. In other words it is law without love. No church can survive unless it fulfills the law of love, both in experience and practice."[40]

S. Lewis Johnson warned of the paralysis of legalism as one of the most serious problems facing the orthodox church today:

> One of the most serious problems facing the orthodox Christian church today is the problem of legalism. It was a serious problem facing the church in Paul's day. Regardless of the age it is the same. Legalism wrenches the joy of the Lord from the Christian believer, and with the joy of the Lord goes his power for vital worship and vibrant service. Nothing is left but cramped, sombre, dull and listless profession. The truth is betrayed, and the glorious name of the Lord becomes a synonym for a gloomy killjoy. The Christian under law is a miserable parody of the real thing.[41]

During interviews with second- and third-generation children of former Holiness Movement families, many shared freely about the regulations, especially the clothing rules foisted on them while growing up. Some accepted them gracefully and with sympathetic understanding and respect for their parents, while others reacted with bitterness and resentment. Most agree that Rev. Horner probably made a decisive error in allowing legalism to overtake his focus; his evangelistic outreach became hindered by an emphasis on keeping rules instead of reaching lost souls. Many pointed to the church uniform as one of the most damaging decisions to impede the movement's growth. Ralph Horner was a gifted evangelist whom God had mightily used, but things began to unravel as the emphasis shifted from evangelism to control and maintenance.

Frustrations with Bishop Horner

There was increasing frustration with Bishop Horner's leadership. Bishop Horner called things as he saw them and often made decisions on the fly. He would change his mind if circumstances changed. He had no patience with disloyalty and would move opposition out of the way without consultation. Some perceived him as deceptive, and the perception became more important than reality for those who opposed him. The episcopal governance combined with Horner's dogmatic, choleric personality made for the potential of toxic relationships between churches, pastors, and laity.

Bishop Horner's business dealings within the church also caused tension; tradition suggests Horner was a shrewd businessman. The most significant conflict was the attempt by the HMC to purchase the stock from the book room. The bishop had been manifestly successful in his operation of the book room and printing plant. The Ottawa Annual Conference of 1905 recognized "Mr. Horner's ownership of all books purchased, edited and compiled by him with the exception of the Holiness Movement Hymn Book."[42] However, on May 10, 1910, at the fifth General Conference, it was decided that Conference should take over the contents of the book room from Rev. Horner, making it their own property; it was moved that General Conference offer Horner the two building lots west of 480 Bank Street in exchange for the contents of the book room. Obviously Horner was not in total agreement, for in the evening session a motion by the Book Room Committee was accepted by Conference that the book room continue in its present status.[43] The Special Committee of General Conference met in Ottawa on January 24, 1911, to hear from Bishop Horner concerning the proposal: a letter was read from Horner stating that he would take the lots as part payment. Rev. Horner valued the entire stock of books, including plates for hymnbooks, periodicals, and catechisms at $8,021—a significant sum in 1911. There was contention about the price, for after much discussion it was resolved to offer Horner $7,000 cash for the entire stock. Horner refused the offer and said he would take his books out of the book room.[44] The contention continued, and at a later date he decided instead to donate the books and would not accept a lesser payment of $5,000.[45] No doubt these types of episodes made working with Horner extremely frustrating, for in the General Conference of July 29, 1913, held in Kingston, Ontario, a resolution was passed to give Rev. Horner a gift of $7,000 (the exact amount offered by the committee for the stock). Quite obviously the gift was in payment for the books and plates, but it was couched in glowing terms to honour Bishop Horner and made no mention of his gift to the bookstore: "Whereas our beloved Bishop has devoted his life in long and arduous labours among us and has spared neither time or means in pushing the work and all its departments, and whereas he has been the chief educator of the work in its varying departments—spiritually and temporal, be it resolved that this General Conference in heart-felt gratitude for his services, grant the said Bishop a donation of seven thousand dollars, said amount to be taken out of proceeds for the sale of the property at 480 Bank Street, Ottawa when said property is disposed of."[46]

Some members of Conference, however, criticized (perhaps resented) the gift and said Horner had given the books to Conference, refused a $5,000 payment, and afterward took $7,000 for them. Herman R. James later defended the action and explained that Bishop Horner had given the books to Conference as a gift and refused $5,000 payment for them. Then the $7,000 was offered not as a payment but as a present, in consideration of his life's services. "He refused a payment, but was obliged to accept a present."[47]

Despite the glowing words and generosity of Conference, whispers of discontent were growing among a number of Holiness Movement clergy and laity.

By 1911, the reach of the Holiness Movement was slowing and in many places stalled. Growth had extended beyond the Ottawa Valley base to outposts in Montreal, Toronto, New York State, Michigan, Saskatchewan, and Alberta. Works also had been established in Belfast, Ireland, as well as missions in Egypt and China. Biographer Tom Eades estimates there were about 3,800 members (3,000 in Canada) and, given the strict requirements for membership, there probably were an additional three or four times as many adherents (estimated at least 10,000).[48] It was an amazing growth in a short time. But despite the growth and rapid expansion of the HMC, there was a growing discontent with the stifling leadership and the obvious loss of momentum.

ROAD TO CARLETON PLACE

The years between 1901 and 1913 were known in Canada as the boom years. This time span witnessed the greatest percentage of increase in Canada's total population. Clifford Sifton's policy as minister of the interior (1896–1905) for filling the "Last Best West" with farmers from eastern Ontario, the United States, and Eastern Europe had transformed the prairies. Settlers came in large numbers, and by 1905 two new provinces—Alberta and Saskatchewan—had linked the gap between Manitoba and British Columbia in the westward expansion of confederation. Members of the HMC had ridden the trains west during this boom and established churches in Manitoba, Saskatchewan, and Alberta. Could the HMC effectively reach the exploding population of western Canada, portrayed as the "Land of Promise" by the federal government? A full two million people had immigrated to Canada during the period between 1896 and the First World War, mostly to the West. American author Albert Hubbard, visiting Winnipeg in 1913, was astonished at what he saw: "Business booms and bustles," he wrote. "Skyscrapers go up overnight. You remain away from Winnipeg six months and when you come back you have to hire somebody to conduct you around the town."[1] Edmonton, Calgary, Regina, and Saskatoon were in a state of frenzy over perceived economic opportunity and spiraling land prices. The West was a mission field ripe for evangelism!

A University and the Role of Laymen

There is little wonder that a memorial was sent from the Manitoba and Alberta Conferences to the General Conference of the HMC in Kingston on July, 28, 1913, requesting steps be taken to organize a college and university system for the Movement. One campus would be located in the West. The proposal, of course, had great merit, for to reach this bustling frontier the church must educate and train westerners. The memorial suggested the new college-university would upgrade students' education to high school matriculation and continue with university and college courses. Furthermore, the memorial requested that when the "valuable property" on 480 Bank Street was sold, a portion of the funds would be designated to help with the endowment of a chair and possibly help build the school. The memorial went on to request permission to appoint a committee of laymen and preachers from the western conferences to select a site for the western university campus.

The controversy in the memorial was the inclusion of laymen. Recall that Bishop Horner agreed with the idea of creating and building a university to train leaders, but they would be schooled in the episcopal governance of churches. Some of the laity saw this as an affront to their call and entitlement to more lay involvement in the decision-making process of the HMC.

Adding to the controversy, a memorial had been sent from the Alberta Conference in regard to a pamphlet commending lay representation in Conference entitled *Freely Chosen Representation*, written by Harold R. Morgan and published in Ottawa, July 22, 1913. The pamphlet had been distributed at the Alberta Conference and the memorial stated, "We disapprove of the passing of his [Harold Morgan's] moral and religious character in Conference until he repent of having issued this pamphlet." The memorial was ignored by General Conference, but it would soon resurface in a most uncongenial manner.

As Conference proceeded, a decision was made to obtain the necessary information for founding a university. The memorial to establish a western university was adopted. It was decided that two college boards of directors would be formed, one for the East and one for the West. The board of directors for the West would include five elders and two laymen; the board of directors for the East would include ten elders and three laymen, one of whom was James E. Wilson.

Conference proceeded smoothly with no apparent factions surfacing. The HMC seemingly was thinking ahead with vision to break their current logjam in growth and expand their work in western Canada. A motion to sell 480 Bank Street was carried. Some of the proceeds were to be loaned at no interest to build a new printing house; a tithe of the proceeds would be given to the western work to help in their proposed university. The college and university board of directors in the East were directed to sell the existing college property in Ottawa.

The selling of properties and establishing a university system was forward thinking, but it stirred resentments among laymen. What role would they play in the dreams and new horizons of the HMC? Were they part of the church or not? Would they simply donate money without having any input and decision-making authority? Somewhere between Conference and February 28, 1914, the property at 480 Bank Street was sold, since a letter was received from James E. Wilson on that date explaining his resignation from the board of directors, objecting to the sale of the property and instituting an endowed university under the sole control of General Conference. The power of the lay trustee board was "solely to sign papers," he protested, "and had no voice at the General Conference. . . . The General Conference showed no faith in the Trustee Board." Wilson was gracious in his letter both in tone and testimony, stating he had "for a long time felt deeply the need of a better standard of education for our young men," but he was uncompromising in his criticism of no lay representation: "480 Bank Street is an accumulation of all our charities, and should therefore be spent in the best possible way for the good of all. . . . At a meeting of the Trustee Board and representatives of the General Conference a year ago the Trustees showed their disapproval of the proposal of the Conference in regard to this property and the Board did not have another opportunity to further express itself. . . . We were simply presented with the papers for our signature."[2]

HORNER RESIGNS AT FEAST OF PENTECOST

Matters came to a head at the Feast of Pentecost held that spring at Stittsville, Ontario, on May 18, 1914. Bishop Horner, now sixty years old, unexpectedly placed a letter of withdrawal in the hands of the General Conference Special Committee, removing himself as bishop and minister from the church he had helped found: "To the General Conference Special Committee, I hereby withdraw from all Conference relations of Annual and General Conference, and I at once cease to preach in the Holiness Movement Church."[3]

A puzzled Special Committee convened immediately in the Stittsville parsonage on May 18 at 6:30 p.m.[4] When asked why he had withdrawn from relations with the HMC, Bishop Horner's reasons in substance were as follows:

1. Doctrinal stance on church polity: the paper published and distributed by P. Morgan concerning lay delegation to Conference. The Alberta Conference of the HMC had sent a memorial condemning the paper, but the General Conference in session, July 1913, had remained silent on the question. Since Horner's views were staunchly episcopalian and did not include lay representation, the silence of the Conference, he felt, amounted to inferred agreement with the propositions in Morgan's pamphlet.

2. Winds of change: the bishop sensed that certain preachers present at the Feast of Pentecost were pressing for a change of leadership and governance in the HMC. He would not be part of it.

To complicate matters, another pamphlet, *Important Facts for a Truth Loving People*, had been written by James E. Wilson to the Special

Committee relative to a new form of government. It too was wholly opposed by Bishop Horner. The letter had been "read in a tent in the presence of many members of Conference and others . . . thereby causing additional agitation."[5] More significantly, the dispute was now public. Interestingly, W. J. Watchorn, a Horner loyalist, attempted to provide leadership in Horner's absence at the Feast of Pentecost to keep things moving and orderly.[6] The General Conference Special Committee appointed two of its members to meet with Mr. Wilson and asked him to withdraw his writings. He gave them a letter stating he would do anything he could to help the cause of God among them: "The General Conference Special Committee may depend upon me to withdraw my writing for a reasonable time in order for the General Conference to meet."[7]

After considerable deliberation on May 20, the Special Committee delivered a letter to the bishop expressing their "severe disapproval" of his curt resignation.

The next day, the Special Committee again met on the campground, and after prayer and consideration the members decided the best thing to do under the present situation was to advise "Brother R. C. Horner that if he would write out a withdrawal of his withdrawal as Bishop and member of Conference," they would consider it. One wonders why. Whether this was the correct response to the predicament is debatable. There already was division among Conference members over leadership and church polity, and the Committee was well aware of it. Had not Horner correctly read the spiritual and political thermometer of the HMC and acted responsibly? His resignation was straightforward—a window that would never open again. Bishop Horner received the letter from the Special Committee and returned the following response:

Bro. Claxton, Chairman of the Committee:
    I withdraw my withdrawal.
    Signed, R. C. Horner

However, the matter was not settled as quickly as the Committee might have hoped. Recall that Horner had previously resigned in 1905 because of complaints against him in his official capacity as bishop. The matter was solved quickly, the charges dropped, and he was reinstated as bishop. But not this time. This time a letter of chastisement was written expressing disproval of the bishop's actions and also a legal bind:

Dear Brother,

We the General Conference Special Committee, now in session, having at length deliberated in the present situation caused by your withdrawal, do hereby wish to express our severe disapproval of your action in the matter. The strife, division, and contention, occasioned by the same, we deem to be one of the most serious nature, and one of the worst blows the Movement has ever received. Had this occurred at any other time than at the Feast of Pentecost, it would not, or might not have been so serious; but, to spring such an issue upon this Committee at this Feast of Pentecost is, we deem, extremely serious. Under the circumstances and in view of the clause of Discipline which declares on page 57, question 3, "If a Bishop cease from traveling at large among the people, shall he still exercise the office among us in any degree?" Answer: "If he cease from travelling without the consent of the General Conference, he shall not thereafter exercise the office in the Holiness Movement."

We see no way of accepting, or allowing, the withdrawal of your withdrawal.

Moreover, as this Committee has made provision for the filling of the vacancy made by your withdrawal, and for the carrying on of the work until General Conference convenes, we see no other way to proceed. This is not only the opinion of this General Conference Special Committee, but the expression of a number of members of the Annual Conferences.

Do not think that the above-mentioned has occasioned no sorrow or grief to this Committee. With hearts almost breaking over the present situation, and for the cause of God which we represent, we have labored, having had this work thrust upon us and can see no alternative.

E. Claxton, Chairman

P. O. Wiseman[8]

The Committee was desperate to bring about healing and unity. They proposed a plan to be read and signed by Bishop Horner and the Committee and all others concerned for reconciliation who by mutual agreement would participate in a general apology. Bishop Horner would apologize for dissension and trouble caused by presenting his withdrawal at the Feast of Pentecost, and also for the reflection cast on the work of the Special Committee; the brethren would take back unkind or improper words that may have been advanced relative to Brother Horner. The plan for reconciliation read, "Thus we all heartily confess to and forgive one another where anything amiss has occurred."

Next came what the Committee thought was the solution to the dilemma of Bishop Horner: "Also owing to Brother Horner's advanced age and many years of strenuous labour, and as he has consented to the following office, we do this with the understanding that at the next General Conference whether it be regular or special assembly, that Bro. Horner be promoted to the office of Life Honorary Bishop."[9]

The Committee was proposing that a younger man be ordained who would have the authority of the bishop's office. The deliberations, they claimed, had proceeded according to the Discipline and usage in this matter. The Committee then proposed that the agreement be read twice in a public meeting at the earliest convenience in this Feast of Pentecost.

The proposed agreement concluded with signatures:

Done at Stittsville, the 22nd day of May, 1914.

Signed: E. H. Claxton, D. Anderson, W. J. Watchorn, M. C. Pritchard, W. A. McCracken, Johnston Price, G. A. Christie, P. Wiseman.[10]

It was understood by the Committee that a memorial to General Conference would be formulated relative to the appointment of Bishop R. C. Horner to the position of honorary bishop, and presented to the Ottawa Annual Conference for their approval or disapproval.

One signature was still needed: R. C. Horner.

From a rational point of view, the plan seemed to be a practical offering by the Committee, for it would give (at least the appearance of) a reasonable, compassionate plan to honour the bishop and provide for his needs. Hopefully this would placate Horner loyalists. But the bottom line was that it would also remove him from the administrative affairs of the denomination. After all, they reasoned, Bishop Horner was sixty, appeared to be in need of rest, and was in declining health. But Horner's supporters would have none of it! To them it was a devious plan to oust the bishop, take control of the HMC, and still appear kind and gracious. Years later, in the 1960s, Rev. Eldon Craig, curious about the division, interviewed an aging Rev. G. L. Monahan, who claimed he counseled Horner not to accept the title, telling him it was symbolic with no function. On the other hand, the plan freed Horner from all the administrative duties of the denomination (not his forte) and allowed him to do what he did best: preach and conduct evangelistic crusades. It was the pleasure of the Committee that Rev. W. G. Ketcheson should meet Rev. R. C. Horner, present him with the proposed reconciliation and offer, and obtain his signature.

What takes place next is difficult to discern and is open to conjecture and opinion. A meeting took place between Rev. Ketcheson and Bishop Horner in regard to the proposed plan and signature. We neither know for certain what transpired nor what was said, except that what both men claimed were later contradictions. Rev. Ketcheson claimed he read the document to Bishop Horner repeatedly for three consecutive days and made suggested alterations; Bishop Horner claimed he did not personally read the document.[11] At any rate, Bishop Horner signed the agreement, insisting he did not know what was contained therein. The two men were at an impasse as to who said what. And R. C. Horner continued to function as bishop of the Holiness Movement Church.

OTTAWA ANNUAL CONFERENCE 1914

When the nineteenth Annual Conference convened on October 27, 1914, in Ottawa, there was much anticipation. Bishop R. C. Horner was in the chair. Business proceeded as usual. But much was going on behind the scenes. Records reveal that a private meeting took place on October 30 with the Special Committee to settle differences between Rev. Horner and Rev. Ketcheson.[12] Rev. Ketcheson submitted in writing the contradictions as he saw them. However, nothing could be proven and it was a case of "he said, I said." The committee did not see how anything could be ascertained by the two testimonies and recommended Brother Ketcheson overlook the contradictions he claimed concerning Rev. Horner.

During Conference, it was decided that the report of the Investigating Committee not be inserted in the Conference minutes.[13] Nevertheless, the minutes read that the Investigating Committee was not able to bring about a satisfactory settlement relative to the existing contradictions between Reverends R. C. Horner and W. G. Ketcheson.[14]

Most important, no memorial was sent to General Conference that Bishop R. C. Horner be "promoted" to the office of Life Honorary Bishop. Later reports reveal that Horner refused to put the motion to the Annual Conference for consideration, declaring that the General Conference Special Committee had been illegal in its proceedings because the western brethren had not been notified of their action.

Things were heating up! A Special General Conference was called to meet in Smiths Falls, December 25, 1914, to deal with the troubling issues.

Gananoque Meeting

A special committee was appointed to examine the bishop and meet him in Gananoque before the Smiths Falls General Conference. They believed Horner to be guilty of charges. They notified him to appear on December 29 at the Smiths Falls Conference for trial. The Lay Committee later reported that Horner ignored the notice and proceeded to lead the Conference, which opened as scheduled.[15]

1914 Special General Conference

The stage was set for confrontation. The Special General Conference came to order in Smiths Falls, Friday, December 25, 1914. Bishop Horner was in the chair and minced no words as to why the Conference was called: "To settle existing differences especially in the Ottawa Conference and to bring about a state of peace" within the HMC. After preliminaries and some initial business, Rev. Horner was called upon in the afternoon session to express his mind on the charges brought against him: his contention was that the charges did not come under the Discipline of the HMC. Reverends Samuel J. Shields and William W. Lake would hear none of it and proceeded to appeal the bishop's decision. As debate proceeded, Rev. Ketcheson's letter was read for information.

Bishop Horner then proposed that the brethren from the West constitute a court to judge in the matter. A long, drawn-out discussion lasting two full days into a late Saturday-evening session ensued with amendments and amendments to the amendments, but no unanimous agreement was reached. Sunday was the Lord's Day and no Conference sessions were convened. However, late Monday evening, it was agreed to call upon the "Western Brethren" to become a court to bring forth a judgment. Conference met Tuesday morning, December 29, and formally apologized to the Alberta Conference for ignoring their memorial regarding the pamphlet *Freely Chosen Representation* at the last General Conference. During the afternoon session, Conference recessed until the court was able to present their findings and recommendations on the bishop and the contradictory controversies.

CONFERENCE RESUMES

The recess lasted almost a week until the following Monday, January 4, 1915. On return, the first four days of Conference were spent choosing Rev. E. H. Claxton as chair in the bishop's absence, and procedures and practices regarding the anticipated court decisions. It was not until Friday, January 8, that the court was ready to report and make their recommendations. They made three.

1. ADMINISTRATION OF COLLEGE

An attempt was made to make the bishop more accountable to the college board of directors in regard to expenditures, financial receipts, salaries of staff, and courses taught.

2. ACCOUNTABILITY FOR BOOK ROOM AND PUBLISHING HOUSE

There was to be a full account for the sale of 480 Bank Street, as well as annual reports of business conducted in the book room.

3. DENOMINATIONAL LEADERSHIP

It was recommended that the next General Conference discuss the idea of electing a second bishop. Until the time of the next General Conference, the court recommended that Rev. A. T. Warren, who had fulfilled Horner's duties in 1907–1910, would "assist" Rev. Horner until the 1917 General Conference. This was an attempt by the court to keep Horner in some function as bishop, but also alleviate some of his administrative duties.

The Conference wanted more. The next morning, January 9, members of Conference took the recommendation of the court a step further: they moved that Rev. A. T. Warren become the assistant to Bishop Horner and that the two men arrange their work to best serve the eastern and western works. The motion was carried.

Rev. Horner faced a dilemma. There was obvious division among the members of the HMC. Conference closed on January 9 with a motion of fidelity to one another, but one could sense there were two sides (almost even in number) at odds over the proceedings and plans. One cannot read the minutes without sensing the difficulty Horner was facing—again! On the one hand, if he retired as the Special Committee recommended and became honorary bishop, a sizeable number would not be in agreement over the proposed new leadership and obvious choice of bishop; nor were they in agreement about the loss of the epis-copal governance model that would loom on the horizon. On the other hand, should Horner attempt to lead the church without major admin-istrative and governance changes (some of which he strongly disagreed with personally), another sizeable faction would be unhappy and would continue their agitation.

LAY DELEGATION

As expected, the agreement at Smiths Falls did little to alleviate trou-bles in the HMC. There is no evidence of Horner sharing administrative duties with Rev. Albert Warren in the east. Rev. J. C. Black wrote an article in the January 26, 1915, edition of the *Holiness Era* in support of the laity entitled "How a Layman Entered the Apostolic Succession." The ante was heating up. It was deemed by many that the special session of General Conference had failed to effect reconciliation. A group of laymen felt "necessity" was laid upon them to "undertake, and devise some means, that might prove beneficial, by way of encouragement, to those who have been laboring under the depression of our present administration." To this means they arranged and announced a Laymen's Convention in the month of April (meetings were also attended by some ministers and ministers' wives to give "church sanction" to the proceedings). A resolution was formed and circulated throughout the connections that would be presented to the bishop at the 1915 Feast of Pentecost.

During the Feast held at Athens, Ontario, a deputation of laypeople, members of the HMC, arrived on May 25, 1915, desiring an audience with the bishop. They carried with them the resolution signed by 370 members. (It was a sizeable number of signatures, especially when one considers the transportation and communication modes of the day, but represented less than one-third of the Ottawa Annual Conference membership and 10 percent of the average Sunday morning church attendance.)[16] The Committee waited for an interview to present the following resolution:

Whereas, we the laymen of the Holiness Movement Church find that peace and harmony have ceased to exist owing to certain causes amongst the ministry;

Whereas, we the Laymen of the Holiness Movement Church, find Conference having met at Smiths Falls, Ont., in Dec. 1914, to remedy said causes, but failed to effect a satisfactory settlement;

Be it resolved, that we memorialize Rev. R. C. Horner to call Rev. A. T. Warren from the West at once or, as soon as convenient, to assist in the management of our work in the East;

Be it resolved, that we memorialize Rev. R. C. Horner to call a General Conference not later than July 1st, 1915, consisting of Ministers and Representative Laymen throughout our Connection, that a peaceful settlement of this trouble may be effected;

Be it further resolved, that this Petition be circulated throughout our connection.[17]

Bishop Horner ignored the deputation. Apparently he saw it as a group of disgruntled people stirring up disunity. They took it as a snub.

LAYMEN'S CAMP

Storm clouds were looming larger. A growing number of HMC preachers and people were becoming dissatisfied with the stalemate. Concerned laymen decided to take further steps of action to express their concerns: they organized a Laymen's Camp Meeting of the Holiness Movement Church to be held in Ottawa, September 14, 1915. The Conference wasted little time on preliminaries. J. D. Wilson reported how the Committee was received by Bishop Horner at Athens. The Conference strongly protested against the actions of the bishop in ignoring the deputation. A paper on lay representation was presented, and after a lengthy discussion the Conference went on record to say that "we strongly approve of lay representation in our Annual and General Conferences."

A document expressing the discontent of the laymen was summarized in a pamphlet titled *Synoptical History of the Holiness Movement Church*, and published. Active in the publication was James D. Wilson, aided by a few ministers and ministers' wives. The pamphlet began by rehearsing the origins of the HMC as far back as the year 1893. A statement was made, quoting from a copy of the *Canadian Methodist and Holiness Era*, dated August 2, 1893, as to the origins and advancement of the Holiness Movement:

> [W]e were called, the *Eastern Ontario Holiness Association* . . .
> Rev. John Ferguson was the President, and W. J. Nesbitt served
> in the capacity of Secretary. Those who united in the Association
> were members of the Methodist Church who had been converted
> and entirely sanctified . . . through the instrumentality of the
> Revs. J. Ferguson, Easton, Sproule, Summerville, Winters,
> McAmmond, Earl, Horner, and others whom God used. We have
> also the names of lay-evangelists, of both men and women, as
> Misses Birdsell and Mason, Moke and Coulthart, Messrs. McInnis,
> Scobie, Waddell and Deachman who were powerful under God
> in producing revivals of pure and undefiled religion.[18]

The pamphlet went on to recreate the "golden age" history of the HMC—typical of people who believed the "good old days" were better than the present:

> In the early days of our Church the converts were strong and they died out to sin. When the revival broke out, it spread to all classes of people. The rich and poor, infidels, hotel keepers, and even preachers, acknowledged their sin and found mercy. There was not the seemingly, fruitless, struggling in prayer with seekers to the extent we see this today. Conviction was so strong that many cried out for mercy without being coaxed to pray. Many prayed through to victory while alone, and some in the silent watches of the night. Such as these have stood the test of years, and are to-day the fathers and mothers in our church. In the early part of our work, the camp-meetings and conventions exceeded in glory the camp-meetings and conventions of to-day. The work of the present is too superficial, and as evidence of this, is not lasting.[19]

The pamphlet claimed that Mr. Horner assumed leadership of the Eastern Ontario Holiness Movement and persuaded the association that episcopal governance was scriptural and best. "The Holiness Association in their simplicity submitted to this form of government, and soon learned, to their loss, that they were fast being enchained under bondage." The pamphlet concluded that the present form of episcopal governance and administration was "unscriptural and irrational."[20]

Horner was systematically blamed for the current problems in the HMC, including stagnation and lack of growth. What is striking is the personal nature of the attacks. A section entitled The Office of a Bishop cited New Testament passages to support their insinuations that Horner was not qualified spiritually to lead the church: "A bishop must not be self-willed, that is self-opinionated, arrogant by setting up his judgment above that of all others. Such a man as described here can do little good, and may do much mischief."[21] The most malicious attack was on Horner's family, claiming "a bishop is required to have faithful children or his family converted to God. In the early Christian Church it would have been counted absurd to appoint, or recognize a man as bishop, to govern the church, whose children were not in subjection to himself." The committee was intent on removing Horner at all costs; Horner's children would never forgive the HMC. The section ended with a recommendation: "We are highly pleased with Rev. P. Wiseman's pamphlet entitled, Elders and Bishops, and recommend that it be secured, and read by all who are looking for light on this important subject. Its first introduction has commended itself to our readers, and we pledge ourselves to labour for the extension of its circulation."[22]

The Laymen Convention concluded with a memorial dated October 26, 1915, to "The Bishop and Members of the Ottawa Annual Conference," asking for an audience of the Laymen's Committee in support of said memorial:

Dear Brethren,

We your humble laymen beseech you, by the mercies of God, to grant us the privilege of placing in your hands a Memorial signed by the Chairman and the Secretary of our Laymen's Committee, asking you to grant us your prayerful consideration; as we in this Memorial represent at least about five hundred of our laity in the Holiness Movement Church.

We request of you the privilege of sending a deputation of our Representative Committee to be present in one of your sessions when you see your way clear to give us a hearing in the said memorial.

Kindly inform us, as to the date, when you will be ready to admit us, while we continue yours, humbly and trustingly,

J. D. Wilson (Chairman)
C. W. Tobin (Secretary)
(8 Allan Place, Ottawa, Ont.)[23]

The controversy was becoming epidemic. According to biographer Tom Eades, grandson of Rev. George Christie, discontent was particularly acute among those who had served with Horner the longest. Rev. George Christie, long-time member, had replaced Bishop Horner as editor of the *Holiness Era* in 1910, and Eades recounts, "George was in perhaps a unique position to gauge feelings within the Movement. . . . Ministers dropped in regularly to The Book Room to pick up their literature and supplies, as well as have a chat, to unburden themselves freely, or to receive sympathy and counsel. In addition, he was in regular correspondence with clergy and laity from the far-flung reaches of the church's territory."[24] There was a general sense of unease and restlessness with the direction and leadership of the HMC. "With its system of governance based on the quasi-democratic Methodist model of districts with elected superintendents and annual General Conferences at which the church's course was set, the way was prepared for a clash between Conference and the Bishop."[25]

OTTAWA ANNUAL CONFERENCE 1915

Members of Conference were quite aware that unless they solved their issues, major division was inevitable. The purpose of the Ottawa Annual Conference in October 1915 was to find ways to unify the church and solve problems. The Laymen's Committee memorial and accompanying letter was refused—it was not given a reading in Conference. Tensions heightened. Discussions went so far as to suggest the church be divided geographically with those who supported Horner in one region and those who wanted alternative leadership in another.

TENSIONS CONTINUE

In the spring of 1916, Horner began to respond to the conflict by removing those in opposition to his church polity and leadership. At the Feast of Pentecost, Peter Wiseman was not stationed on a circuit because he had snubbed Horner and conducted a convention beyond his circuit without permission from the bishop (interestingly, something Horner himself had done while in the Methodist Church). Horner made negative comments about Wiseman's work on the Trenton Circuit and Ivanhoe Camp Meeting; he also criticized Wiseman's wife (probably her support of the laymen's movement). This caused considerable tension between Wiseman and Horner, and shock in the HMC; Wiseman was one of Horner's most talented young preachers, and gossip accused Horner of jealousy.

OTTAWA ANNUAL CONFERENCE 1916

Things were quickly coming to a head at the October 24, 1916, Ottawa Annual Conference. Reading the minutes on a surface level, one might not discern the tensions and divisions simmering within the Conference: the secretary reported "seasons of prayer" in which "God came down our souls to greet, while glory crowned the mercy seat," and the "blessing of God was felt upon the assembly." Itinerant ministers were joyously received into Conference, the secretary reporting, "it was a glorious time in Conference": Lloyd Tomlinson shared his victorious testimony; George Kelly told how "God had fired him up so that he preached everywhere he went, even in his sleep!" Contrary to the report of the Laymen's Camp Meeting, it would seem the church was experiencing revival and renewal: in his State of the Work Report, Presiding Elder James Smith reported that there were "great conventions, backsliders restored, great financial movements of over seven hundred dollars raised outside of remunerations to the support of the

Ministry. . . . His faith and hope was strong for the Shawville District"; Reverends Lindsay and A. A. Smith reported similar victories and good reports from their districts.[26]

But something ominous was also taking place: there were an unusual number of resignations and requests for leaves of rest. Pernicious accusations were brewing that Horner and his supporters were purging the Conference of what they perceived as negativity and division. To his credit, Rev. Wiseman apologized to Conference and received forgiveness for his negative comments and attitude directed at Horner. But others refused to apologize or admit their errors and were suspended. A total of ten ministers either resigned or were suspended, and three were given time off for rest. Things would be much quieter now . . . or so Horner and his supporters hoped!

COLLABORATION AND COLLUSION

Between the October Annual Conference and the December General Conference in Carleton Place there was widespread collaboration and collusion. Obviously a movement was underway to oust Horner; a significant number of those who had been removed or retired attended the General Conference. This would have taken substantial coordination and was a major undertaking considering the short amount of time between the conferences and the slow means of travel and communication of the day. There is no indication who led the move to remove Horner. G. A. Christie, in later cross examination, when asked who the leaders of the opposition were, responded only by saying, "We were the presenters of the objections."[27] It is tempting to think members of the lay delegation, because of their opposition to Horner, were actively involved and spearheaded the movement; however, there is no evidence to indicate a direct role. At any rate, the opposition was ready with a plan when General Conference came to order.

DIVISION AT CARLETON PLACE

The General Conference began on December 12, 1916, at the Holiness Movement Church, Carleton Place, Ontario. After singing and prayer the roll was called: fifty-eight elders answered to their names. However, when a motion was made to formalize the Conference roll, S. J. Shields and E. H. Claxton moved an amendment: "Whereas there are appeals to this General Conference to investigate the removal of names of ordained men in the Ottawa Annual Conference in such a way as is considered by numbers as illegal and that said men are strongly persuaded in their minds that they legally are still members of Conference, that General Conference go into a committee of the whole to investigate these matters and bring in recommendations."[28] Appeals were heard by men who claimed they were members of General Conference: J. C. Black, was reported to have been omitted—his character was passed and added to the roll; three members from the Alberta Conference were added—every addition would eventually prove vital. Other names were added: Reverends A. A. Caswell and Allen Moore from the Egyptian Conference were enrolled—Bishop Horner apparently protested placing their names on the roll because quorum would now necessitate including the Egyptian Conference and would increase the number of eligible members from eighty-seven to ninety-seven.[29]

The case of Rev. W. G. Ketcheson was brought before Conference. His name had been dropped from the Ottawa Conference without a trial, and he appealed the action to the General Session now in order. This would be a sensitive issue in light of the recent history of Ketcheson versus Horner in the presentation and signature of the Special Committee's report during the Feast of Pentecost. There was considerable discussion as to including his name; the bishop finally ruled in favour of a two-thirds vote for acceptance. S. J. Shields appealed to the General Conference against this ruling, but A. T. Warren asked for an explanation to be given first from the chairman relative to the two-thirds vote. The appeal was withdrawn to allow Conference opportunity to formulate a ruling relative to what majority it took to sustain an appeal from the decision of the chair. Bishop Horner refused to put the appeal to a vote, so the secretary was requested to make the call, which resulted in thirty-three sustaining the appeal and twenty-two against. The appeal carried by a 60 percent majority. There were now amendments and amendments to the amendments concerning the Ketcheson case. Ultimately, after a great deal of discussion and jostling over procedure, the bishop gave permission to proceed; again the secretary put the motion forward, and a standing vote was taken. Ketcheson was restored to his place in General Conference with right of vote. Seven members protested against the committee's report.

Other names were added after appeals or requests were made to withdraw resignations: W. G. Burns, T. E. Clow, E. G. Schmidt, W. W. Lake, J. J. Snelgrove. It became a contentious issue in that it would be claimed that Ketcheson, Burns, and Ralph had no right to sit as members of the General Conference, inasmuch as the General Conference is composed of those whose names appear as members in good standing of the several annual conferences; there is no provision, it was contended, for any appeal from an Annual Conference to a General Conference, nor can the General Conference order any name to be put on the roll of an Annual Conference.[30]

It is certain by the way Conference was proceeding that these men had been engaged in a plan to remove Horner. There had been secret meetings. Someone was coordinating the effort. It is difficult to believe this entire group of men would have decided without prodding and encouragement to reconsider their Conference status—they were participating in a preplanned scheme and realized their votes would be needed to remove the bishop from office. Crucial votes were being added one by one to the anti-Horner contingent.

HORNER IN TROUBLE

Bishop Horner's leadership was in trouble. Opposition against him was increasing in Conference. When it was moved to proceed with the examination of the chairman's character, the question was asked, "Is there anything against the moral or religious character of this brother?" G. A. Christie responded, "I have objections."[31] Tom Eades writes, "George Christie was now forced, with reluctance, to openly take sides. Recognizing the unworkable situation in which the Movement found itself, with the issue of leadership, a continuing distraction from its mission and drain on its energy, he followed his conscience, presenting a list containing ten points against Horner's leadership in a measured exposition of the problems."[32] Christie's daughter, Grace Eades, maintained her dad was torn by a residual loyalty to Horner given their long association and service together, but the larger good of the church and the furtherance of its mission outweighed personal feelings.[33] That was George Christie's personal conviction on the proceedings.

The bishop was called forward for examination. George Christie, W. H. Bradley, J. Price, and five other men who previously had been taken off the General Conference roll (W. G. Ketcheson, B. L. Ralph, J. C. Black, W. J. Tompkins, and W. G. Burns), indicated they had objections to passing Horner's character. The objections ranged from failure to make apologies as required to the court at Smiths Falls, to changing the board of examiners on the Course of Study and the treasurer of the missionary fund without the consent of General Conference. Most contentious of all was a charge of showing partiality at the last Ottawa Annual Conference in his capacity as chairman, declaring that passing ministerial character was with himself, and that he passed or refused to pass character as he so decided. The Conference went into a committee as a whole to investigate the objections taken against the character of the bishop. Rev. Horner abruptly left the meeting without the consent of Conference. A private interview heard his objections.

The next day, December 12, Conference was presented with written objections raised by the bishop in regard to the legality of anyone raising objections to his character and having a vote on the committee. Confusion began to reign in Conference with interpretations as to the legality of laying charges and voting on said charges.

Two members, dismayed with the proceeding of Conference, arose and walked out. This was cause for an important ruling: a member arose and asked if a member or members could leave the house without permission, and the effect of such upon the Conference. This was occasion for a decision that would be called into question in a later court battle. A resolution was made that according to page 89 of the Discipline: At all times when the General Conference is met, it shall take two thirds of its members to make a quorum for transacting business, be interpreted to mean that if any member, or members of the General Conference leave a sitting or session of Conference without having obtained the permission of the General Conference in sitting, even though sufficient members leave as would otherwise break the quorum, yet their leaving, or having left without permission of Conference will have no effect to break the quorum.[34]

As business proceeded in the afternoon, the question of quorum was again raised by a Conference member as to whether there was a legal quorum or not. It was moved by G. A. Christie and A. T. Warren that the question regarding quorum in the Discipline "be interpreted to mean two thirds of the ordained members who answer to their names at the calling of each session of General Conference when said Conference is legally called."[35] That resolution would come back to haunt Rev. Christie.

HORNER DEPOSED

The controversy concerning Horner was coming to a head. A motion was placed before the Conference by W. H. Bradley and S. S. Buell that these objections, which were "proved and sustained in connection with his administration as Bishop of the Holiness Movement Church in his varied duties as Bishop, clearly revealed the incapability of said Rev. R. C. Horner to properly fulfill the duties and functions in connection with the Bishopric of our church." The motion ended with this resolution: "Be it hereby resolved that said Rev. R. C. Horner by such improper conduct has forfeited his right to retain among us the office of Bishop or Leader in the Holiness Movement Church and that he henceforth cease to exercise the function of such office."[36]

It was a sad day. Several members who had walked out on Conference in protest of the proceedings returned, no doubt to be present for the vote, apologizing for having left irregularly; they were accepted with forgiveness back into Conference. Every vote would be needed. When the vote was put before the house, it resulted in thirty-three yeas and twenty nays. Bishop Horner received only 38 percent support in the vote. But the issue would soon rise as to the matter of quorum—the total number of all ordained members of Conference eligible to vote who were not there.

The Conference declared that the acceptance of the resolution removed R. C. Horner from the office and work of bishop in the HMC, but declared that General Conference still recognized him legally as being an elder in the Conference where he holds his name. Bishop Horner left the proceedings of the Carleton Place Conference. So did about twenty other men.

ELECTION OF A NEW BISHOP

The next session of Conference proceeded to elect a nominating committee. The committee returned with nominations for various General Conference Committees: Missionary, Book and Publishing House, Discipline, Periodicals, and College. All were accepted.

It was now time for the election of a new bishop. The Conference expressed its need of gracious guidance and engaged in a season of prayer. But only thirty-seven of the sixty-eight eligible members remained to vote. The rest either walked out in dismay or disgust at the proceedings or would not take part in the vote. Thirty-four votes were cast in favour of Rev. Albert T. Warren. Rev. Warren was declared elected, receiving a 50 percent mandate by General Conference members declared eligible to vote (including those reinstated)—only 35 percent of the total General Conference membership, the Egyptian Conference included. It was not a strong mandate in any case, and the issue of quorum would be called into question.

R. C. Horner and his supporters would not accept the decision of what they felt was an illegal Conference. Their claim was that two-thirds of all the ordained members were not present to form a quorum. During the sitting of the Carleton Place Conference, Bishop Horner sent the following communication:

To the Chairman (*pro tem.*),
General Conference in session in Carleton Place, Ont.
Dear Sir:

Every legislative and deliberate assembly with a certain number of members has a quorum fixed by statute or by its own regulations. . . .

Take notice that all our conferences are represented in this General Conference. The number of ordained men exceeds one hundred.

Our constitution provides that two-thirds of its members are necessary for transacting business.

Respectfully,
R. C. Horner

R. C. Horner ignored the rulings and election of the Carleton Place Conference and continued to function fully as bishop of the Holiness Movement Church.

10

Two Bishops

Newly elected bishop Albert Warren faced a major problem: Ralph C. Horner continued to function as bishop of the Holiness Movement Church. Horner and his supporters refused to recognize the legitimacy of the Carleton Place Conference and the election of the new bishop.

On January 13, 1917, a letter was written to Horner stating he was no longer the bishop of the HMC. Horner disregarded the letter and maintained possession of the denominational seal, records, and books. He appointed Rev. George L. Monahan as treasurer of the missionary and college funds and collected money for their support; he continued to station preachers to various church appointments. Horner was paying no heed to what had taken place at the Carleton Place Conference. In his mind the proceedings were illegal.

Furthermore, many of his followers regarded what had taken place during the past year as nothing less than unequivocal rebellion. Ma Brownell, one of Horner's ardent supporters, writes in her memoirs: "It is a sad thing to have to record that there was trouble brewing in our beloved Zion. . . . I had seen the lack of obedience and submission had been one of the causes our church trouble. . . . Later, the Bishop and one of his preachers were sitting in a room with me. While the dear old Bishop was talking to him, I could see open rebellion written all over the man's face. When a preacher or worker gets where the bishop can't pull the chain for him to mind . . . he is done."[1]

The stage was set for confrontation and on April 13, 1917, charges were officially laid against Rev. R. C. Horner by Reverends W. J. Tompkins and E. G. Schmidt (neither were members of the Ottawa Annual Conference).[2] The trial was held in Ottawa at the Bronson Chapel on April 24, but Horner was not in attendance. There were eight charges revolving around the fact that Horner was usurping the office and function of bishop; that he and his party had attempted to form a new Kingston Conference; that he was causing trouble and contention; that he was stationing preachers; and that he was now publishing a rival magazine, the *Christian Standard*.[3] After deliberation the Conference suspended R. C. Horner from the office and functions of the Christian ministry of the HMC in Canada.

At this juncture, two persons claimed to be bishop of the HMC and there was general confusion among the ranks of the denomination. Who was the real bishop? A Special Committee was called by Bishop Warren on May 8, 1917. The Committee's goal was to attempt to gain possession of the seal and books and to counteract an announcement in the newly published *Christian Standard* by Horner of his own Special Committee to meet on May 14, followed the next day by the Ottawa Annual Conference. Bishop Warren's committee decided to insert instructions in the *Holiness Era* to preachers and people informing them that the calling of the Ottawa Annual Conference and Special Committee by R. C. Horner and his party was neither authorized nor legal.

Reverends R. M. Hammond and S. J. Shields were chosen to meet with Horner and attempt to gain possession of the seal and books. During the meeting, Hammond and Shields listened to the concerns and demands of Horner, who stated that the General Conference Special Committee was out of order and that he refused to recognize their demands.

Later that afternoon, the Committee delegated Reverends Warren and Shields to interview Rev. Horner, but their conversation revealed that Rev. Horner still maintained the same attitude of mind.

The committee worked late into the evening and made four propositions for settlement of difficulties in the HMC. They included:

1. That Mr. Horner and his party recognize the validity of the General Conference held in Carleton Place, December 1916.

2. That provided the aforesaid be agreed to; the men who laid the charges on Rev. Horner at the Ottawa Conference withdraw the same.

3. That the eastern work be divided into two conferences: the Ottawa and Kingston conferences respectively.

4. That Mr. Horner and his men transfer into the Kingston Conference.

Rev. Horner seemed open to considering some terms of the agreement, but believed that he and his men were being forced to make most of the concessions. Horner stated he would get back to them.

The pressures and tensions were overwhelming Rev. A. T. Warren. He believed he could bear no more, and the next day, May 9, he handed in his resignation as bishop of the HMC. He explained that the responsibilities laid upon him were greater than he had understood and more than he now believed he could conscientiously assume. But the Committee declined to accept his resignation and made provision for the "Eastern work to be made such as would relieve Bro. Warren of this undue responsibility."[4] The Committee carried on.

R. C. Horner wrote his reply to the proposition of the Special Committee. Despite any interesting proposals or white flags, the bottom line was that the Committee would not accept any propositions made by Horner that would not recognize the validity of the last General Conference. Subsequently, they recommended that Conference proceed to fill the HMC circuits with pastors. Furthermore, they resolved that steps should be taken immediately to arrange a meeting of laymen to consider taking necessary steps to establish the legality of their position. Plans were formulated to notify the public through the press, warning that anything Mr. Horner and his men may have done, or might do at their Conference held at Stittsville, Ontario, would be illegal. They also decided in conclusion to obtain legal advice as to the safest way to safeguard the church and people.[5]

Two Conferences

On May 15, two special sessions of the HMC were being conducted simultaneously. Like Rev. Warren and his supporters, Rev. Horner and his men were wasting no time consolidating their position. When the Horner Ottawa Annual Conference came to order, forty names appeared on the Conference roll and thirty answered to their names — a sizeable number of HMC preachers and evangelists. It took little time for the Horner Conference to get to the heart of why the Special Conference had been called: they declared the court of the Carleton Place General Conference Committee illegal.

Rev. Horner made a formal appeal to the Conference concerning the decision of the Carleton Place Conference in which he was suspended from the Christian ministry and deposed from the bishopric of the HMC. He restated his reasons why the Carleton Place Conference was illegal in its undertakings and out of place in its decision. The charges and their repudiation were included in the minutes of the Ottawa Conference for future reference.[6] The repudiation began with an eleven-point recital of various paragraphs from the HMC Discipline regarding the trial of a bishop, what committee may try an elder and his right to appeal, the formation of a Court of Appeal, and the matter of quorum. Following this, R. C. Horner summarized his appeal, stating, "I was declared deposed from the Bishopric of the HMC in Canada:

- Without any trial by a committee.
- Without a chance to appeal.
- Without being in any court.
- Where there was no quorum when I was declared deposed.
- Men took part in the proceedings and voted who were not members of any Annual Conferences.
- There were no charges preferred against me.
- My Ordination was not to the office but to the order of Bishop. Therefore, I could not be deposed when I was not accused of crime."[7]

The Conference went on record to declare that since R. C. Horner was not tried as a bishop before a court formed according to Discipline for the trial of a bishop, members of Conference "do hereby sustain the appeal, and ignore the action of the court in question, and we do hereby declare that Rev. R. C. Horner still retains his ministerial standing." Furthermore, the Conference declared, that "whereas two thirds of the ordained members of the Conferences were not present when Rev. R. C. Horner was declared deposed from the Bishopric of the HMC . . . we do hereby resolve and do hereby declare the action which declared Rev. R. C. Horner deposed . . . was illegal." In their view, Rev. R. C. Horner was still bishop of the HMC.[8] The Conference then proceeded with business as usual.

Despite the bishop controversy, the general spirit of the Conference was upbeat and positive. A motion was accepted to have an ordination service on Wednesday evening to ordain all who had been elected. Ten candidates were recommended for Elders Orders and four candidates for Deaconess Orders; five more names were later submitted for Elders Orders, three for Deacons Orders and four for Deaconess Orders—a total of twenty-six during the Conference for ordination and ministerial deployment.[9] The Horner crowd would not lack for preachers and evangelists.

Plans were made, as well, for Annesly College to continue, and assistance would be provided to aid students in need of financial help. As far as the Horner Conference was concerned, the winds of momentum were in their sails and they were free of the negative elements that had plagued their growth and progress.

The issue of publications was brought before the Conference, and the *Christian Standard* was given official recognition and launching. The committee on literature submitted the following resolution to Conference:

Whereas the original organ of the Holiness Movement Church called the *Holiness Era* has for some time been brought under the influence of one party; and whereas the said *Holiness Era* has used its influence to establish the action of last General Conference in deposing Rev. R. C. Horner from the Bishopric of the Holiness Movement Church which action we have affirmed to be illegal; and whereas the said *Holiness Era* has refused to publish several articles and notices submitted by Rev. R. C. Horner and his supporters, so as thus to become monopolized by the one party of our Church, be it hereby resolved and hereby declared that the Ottawa Annual Conference . . . in order to secure a medium of publication . . . publish another paper which has been well named *Christian Standard*.[10]

One more item was significant and important: the formation of a "Peace Committee." The Conference moved that Reverends R. C. Horner, A. A. Smith, G. L. Monahan, and H. R. James form a standing committee to make proposals of peace to Rev. A. T. Warren and that the Conference would abide by what they agree to. The Horner Conference was extending an olive branch to Rev. Warren and the rival HMC Conference.

The final day of Conference concluded after the ordination service, and six new members were recommended and received as candidates into the ministry. The roll was purged and the published list contained sixty-nine members—a significant percentage of the eighty-five members listed on the roll of the Ottawa Conference of the HMC.

PROPOSALS REFUSED, COURT ACTION TAKEN

It is not known for certain what the Horner Committee sent the Warren Special Committee by way of an offer for peace, but one thing is certain: the Horner Committee would not recognize the legitimacy of the Carleton Place decision to depose Rev. Horner as bishop. The Warren Special Committee replied that they could not accept the Horner position and decided to consult a lawyer to establish the legality of the Carleton

Place Conference; the Committee was in effect deciding they could no longer negotiate with Horner and determined they must pursue a legal civil option to protect the interests of the church. Two days later, on May 18, they met with their lawyer, who advised them to make affidavits. Meanwhile, Horner sent out another proposal via telephone from H. R. James expressing his desire to continue the talks. However, the General Conference Committee felt there was no guarantee Horner would follow any settlement. Moreover, they were of the opinion Horner was making a number of unreasonable requests, such as the destruction of General Conference and Special Committee minutes relating to the affair.

Rev. Horner continued to claim he was bishop and acted in this official capacity. He was featured as "Bishop Horner" on advertising for camp meetings.[11] He still had possession of the denominational seal and Conference books. To combat Bishop Horner's action, the Special Committee filed a court injunction on March 28, restraining Horner from acting as bishop and Monahan from collecting funds as missionary and college treasurer until the trial or other final disposition of this action. The restraint was issued on July 19 by Mr. Justice J. Sutherland at Osgoode Hall, who ruled in favor of the General Conference. The Carleton Place Conference was, in Sutherland's opinion, legal, and quorum meant two-thirds of the members actually present at the meeting. He believed that if Bishop Horner had thereafter wished to contest the action of the Conference, it was incumbent upon him to move the courts to that effect rather than continue to act as though he were still bishop.[12]

From that day forward, R. C. Horner was restrained from acting as bishop of the HMC, and G. L. Monahan from collecting any monies for the missionary and educational funds. The restraint, of course, was appealed by Horner and Monahan, who sought to refute that Warren and York were duly elected to the offices of bishop and secretary-treasurer.[13] The *Statement of Defense and Counter Claim* read, "the Defendants (Horner and Monahan) (are) refrained from doing anything as Officers of the Holiness Movement Church in Canada . . . and ask for a declaration that the Plaintiffs Warren and York were not duly elected to the Offices of Bishop and Secretary-Treasurer of said Church and for an injunction restraining them from interfering in the affairs of the said Church other than as ministers or elders thereof."

The final decision was set for October 3, 1917; the issue would be settled in the Supreme Court of Ontario.

SUMMER OF 1917

Throughout the summer, the legal conflict wore on and various ministers were called upon to make affidavits. Meanwhile, members and adherents of the HMC were trying to digest and understand what was taking place in their beloved denomination. Most were saddened by the proceedings:

In the year 1917 we were sorry to hear of trouble and division in our beloved church. It was a terrible blow to me for I had such confidence in the Christian people and especially the preachers. With sad and burdened heart, I went to the Lord in prayer about it and He revealed to me the way to take. This came to me, "If there should be raised up a people who had to preach on stumps, stones, or in barns would you be willing to follow and worship?" I said, "Yes, Lord." At that time I had not heard a word about another church starting and it was very hard for me to think of forsaking the little church where I found the forgiving love of Jesus.[14]

The first impact of the restraining order was that Horner and Monahan were prevented from providing any leadership in the church that summer. Paul Johnston, grandson of Monahan, told of the impact this ruling had on him and his family. Monahan had been stationed as pastor of the Cobden HMC, but his church was padlocked so he was unable to preach in his own pulpit. The action was so stressful on Monahan's family that his daughter, Johnston's mother, who was nine at the time, would never speak about it.[15] Horner, however, continued to preach at revivals and camp meetings throughout the summer. Jane Conley reported that R. C. Horner preached at the 1917 Ormstown Camp Meeting with "undaunted courage and power." She and her family also spent some days at Chesterville Camp Meeting, where Horner was in attendance: "Many were saved from sin," she reported, "and God was moving on hearts. One woman took sick and could not come into the services. She sent for Mr. Horner to come and pray which he did and she was healed and converted."[16]

Supreme Court of Ontario

The hitherto difficult situation over leadership and direction of the HMC had now become an impossible one. The stalemate could not be resolved internally, but only by outside intervention in a civil court. Ralph Horner was emphatically not in favour of placing the matter before the courts, but Warren and the Special Committee believed that the uncompromising stand by Horner and Monahan on the legality of the Carleton Place Conference gave them no option but to press for a decision by the Ontario Supreme Court. Ralph Horner and his supporters were adamant that injustice had been done by removing him illegally from his position as bishop of the HMC. Affidavits were prepared for the hearing of the trial. Lawyers for the defendants and the plaintiffs were given opportunity to collect affidavits and cross-examine the principal players in the dispute. The trial would settle the dispute between the Holiness Movement Church in Canada: A. T. Warren and S. A. York, plaintiffs, versus R. C. Horner and G. L. Monahan, defendants.

A statement by the defense was prepared to explain the reason for assembling the court. In summary, the defendants alleged that the action of the Conference (Carleton Place) was not legally constituted by reason of absence of a quorum as required by the constitution of the church; moreover, it was not competent for the said Conference to depose Defendant Horner from his office of bishop without a trial as provided by the Book of Discipline. The defendants were asking for a declaration that the plaintiffs, Warren and York, were not duly elected to the office of bishop and secretary-treasurer, and for an injunction restraining them from interfering in the affairs of the church other than as ministers or elders.[17]

Affidavits Filed

Affidavits were prepared and filed with the Supreme Court of Ontario:

Samuel A. York

Ordained member of the HMC and newly elected secretary of the General Conference, Samuel A. York was sworn in in the city of Ottawa, May 22, 1917.

York duly stated that at said General Conference at Carleton Place, 1916, there were sixty-seven members present. On the motion to declare defendant R. C. Horner no longer bishop, fifty-three votes were polled, thirty-three votes for the motion and twenty against, and there were certain members present who did not vote. Furthermore, he stated that thirty-three votes were cast for A. T. Warren's election as bishop and four against it. York also repeated the charge that Horner refused to hand over the church seal and documents to his successor and continued to act in the capacity of bishop of the church. He stated that certain real estate transactions could not take place that were authorized by the Ottawa Annual Conference by reason of R. C. Horner's retaining in his possession and control the church seal and records.

WILLIAM J. TOMPKINS

An ordained member of the HMC of the city of Ottawa, Tompkins took oath on July 18 to say that he had read the affidavit of G. L. Monahan and claimed that when the motion as to quorum was passed, there was a larger number of members present than fifty-four. He stated that he did not believe there were ninety-nine ordained members entitled to attend the General Conference (he would exclude the Egyptian members). The actual number can only be ascertained by a careful examination of the Annual Conference rolls. Moreover, he stated that he "always understood and knows a large number of members who understand that a quorum to transact business consists of two-thirds of the members who are at Conference."[18]

GEORGE L. MONAHAN

Ordained member of the HMC, Cobden, Ontario, George L. Monahan filed his affidavit on July 19, 1917. Rev. G. L. Monahan contended with utter conviction that there was not a quorum necessary for the conducting of business to remove Bishop Horner. He also contended that Ketcheson, Burns, and Ralph had no right to sit as members of the 1916 General Conference in asmuch as there was no provision for a General Conference to put any name on the roll. Monahan claimed there was not a proper quorum present at any stage of said Conference. He charged the Conference with interpreting the ruling in midstream to suit their agenda and attempting to change the provisions of the Constitution. He also claimed emphatically that he and Defendant Horner believed it was "not competent for the Conference to remove the Bishop from office without a trial . . . as provided by . . . the Book of Discipline. . . . General Conference cannot dispense with the right of trial." Moreover, Monahan's affidavit contradicted the accusations that Horner had exercised the function of bishop while under restraint order. Horner, he declared, had not ordained any new ministers and before leaving for Alberta stated that he did not intend to exercise any functions of the church pending the commencement of the action launched against him. Monahan's statements, like his personality, were convincing, decisive, and forceful.[19]

EDWARD J. BISHOP

An ordained member of the HMC, Bishop was called to make his oath in Kemptville, Ontario, on June 20, 1917. He stated R. C. Horner had called a special session of the Ottawa Annual Conference at Stittsville, May 16, 1917. He claimed the Conference was called to "quash the action of the General Conference, which had removed [R. C. Horner] from his office of Bishop." Bishop went on to declare that Horner ordained four men and four women into the ministry, and that he, E. J. Bishop, had been appointed to the Circuit of Carleton Place. This affidavit was to serve evidence that Horner was ignoring the action of the Carleton Place Conference and continuing his work as bishop.[20]

AFFIDAVITS CROSS-EXAMINED

The next two witnesses, G. A. Christie and R. C. Horner, not only offered evidence and statements relevant to the case, but were cross-examined by each opposing party's attorneys. Rev. George Christie's testimony was of particular interest since it was his response to the secretary's question at the Carleton Conference—"Is there anything against the moral or religious character of this brother?"—that got the ball rolling for the removal of Bishop Horner.[21] Rev. Christie had responded, "I have objections."

G. A. CHRISTIE

An ordained member of the HMC, G. A. Christie filed his affidavit on July 9, 1917. George Christie had been a major player in the formation and leadership of the Holiness Movement Church. He had been converted in the great revival of 1892 that had occurred in the Methodist Church at Eldorado, Ontario, initiated by Rev. R. Mallett; the revival services were conducted by Rev. R. C. Horner and continued during the winter and spring months. George Christie became a follower and associate of Rev. Horner and was one of the earliest young men who began preaching with Horner in the summer of 1894. Over the next few years, Christie was greatly used of God in the early days of the HMC, and was instrumental in opening up many new fields and establishing new circuits. George Christie had been appointed editor of the *Holiness Era* and manager of the HMC Book Room and Press. This was a position of great trust in the church, and he was responsible for the hundreds of books, pamphlets, and denominational publications.

George Christie was respected and well liked by most everyone in the HMC. His grandson, Tom Eades, says he was a conciliator by nature. During the crisis facing the church he persisted in his refusal to take sides, consequently facing strong personal criticism, even abuse, from individuals on both sides of the controversy. It was not in his character to retaliate and he bore the criticism with courtesy and forgiveness.[22] It must have been with personal pain and sincere sorrow that he regretfully made his charges against his former spiritual mentor and leader.

On July 16, Mr. Christie faced the imposing George F. Henderson, counsel for the defendants for cross-examination. Christie's affidavit had rehearsed the events leading up to the charge pending against his old friend and associate, R. C. Horner, and stated that Horner had refused to hand over the seal and records of the church as demanded by the Special Committee. He concluded by charging that "unless R. C. Horner is prevented by Order of these Courts [he] will, I believe, continue to act in the capacity of Bishop . . . and continue to do and perform acts and things which according to the Discipline of the said church can only be done by the Bishop."[23]

The court transcripts of the cross-examination indicate that Christie was intimidated and flustered by the bombardment of Mr. Henderson.

His self-confidence and assuredness waned and withered under the barrage of questions; by nature he was self-effacing and retiring. Mr. Henderson knew how to conduct a cross-examination and his questions caused Mr. Christie considerable confusion: his answers reveal a man attempting to carefully think through what he said; he was often hesitant and slow in responding. After one particularly long pause, Mr. Henderson remarked, "You are thinking a long time before you answer each question—so you mean to tell me that you don't know?"[24] Henderson began to poke fun at Mr. Christie's seemingly uncertain recollection of members present at the juncture of Conference concerning the issue of quorum: "Mr. Christie, if this case ever goes to trial before a Judge at a public hearing, would you care to answer that question in the witness box in the way that you have done, remembering that you are a Minister of the Gospel?"

Mr. Christie's testimony of the proceedings to depose Mr. Horner and what constituted a quorum were not convincing. In fact, he may have considerably helped the Horner-Monahan cause. His answer to the question for a proper interpretation of the Resolution he and A. T. Warren had presented to Conference was confusing. "Was there a quorum at the meeting when that Resolution was passed? Did you notice just preceding that two members were leaving?" Mr. Henderson queried.[25] Mr. Henderson continued his merry-go-round of questions, confusing Rev. Christie's understanding of *quorum* all the more: "A proper interpretation of that Resolution would mean two-thirds of those whose names appear on page one (minutes) and at the top of page two (the entire number of members who attended and answered the roll at Conference), is that it? . . . Please explain it since it is your child?" continued Henderson.[26] George Christie appeared bewildered.

Christie paused long before replying. "Well I didn't look at it that way," he finally answered.

Henderson continued his grilling: "I have waited nearly five minutes— is it susceptible of explanation do you think? . . . What did you mean by saying a quorum means two thirds of the Ordained Members who answered to their names? Did you simply mean that those who came in later should be counted in estimating a quorum?"

Rev. Christie continued to answer slowly and deliberately. "I hadn't any thought of excluding any eligible . . ." He did not finish his sentence.

George Henderson continued to confuse George Christie, almost teasing him about his confusion over what constituted a quorum, who had been the leaders of the movement to depose Mr. Horner as bishop, who proffered the objections to Bishop Horner's leadership, and the fact that Mr. Christie had laid ten objections to Mr. Horner's character. At one point, Mr. Henderson, referring to a motion regarding a personal difference between Rev. Christie and Bishop Horner, asked, ". . . you were the one who had the most difficulty with him?" Rev. Christie sheepishly replied, "I wouldn't say that." Rev. Christie hesitantly admitted to having "some difficulty" with the bishop.

Rev. George Christie's vacillating testimony served to add credibility to the claim of Horner and Monahan that the quorum of Carleton Place was not legal.

R . C. HORNER CROSS-EXAMINED

It was now time for the main event: R. C. Horner was examined for the pretrial hearing by Mr. Harold D. McCormick on behalf of the plaintiffs, September 19, 1917. An interesting picture of Horner and how he was handling the difficulty of his preceding days emerges.

At times he appeared defiant. When questioned about being removed from the office of bishop, he responded curtly, "I don't believe it."

At other times he spoke with religious conviction. When asked why he did not appeal the previously taken action by the General Conference in court or otherwise, he replied, "I don't believe it right to go to Court at all. . . . I wanted to keep out of trouble. I didn't want to give any self-defense. I refused to give it in Conference. There are many things there that I could have destroyed (by referral to the Discipline and proceedings that were out of order). I protested against it. The business, I considered illegal. There would not have been anything done. I thought they were reckless on the quorum—they proved it to be—they dwindled lower and lower. Their quorum became less—there wasn't a quorum according to their own interpretation."[27]

There were times when Horner purposely resisted the question and said he was unable to remember what took place. For example, he could not remember how the 1916 Conference was called, where the Conference Journal was located, or who gave instructions to open the college a short time ago. It must be remembered, however, that he had been placed under court injunction not to act as bishop since July 19, 1916, and there is every reason to believe he would not have knowledge as to the conducting of current and recent church affairs. Reading the court transcripts, it is difficult at times to know whether the bishop was being uncooperative and simply answering the questions by the "letter of the law" exactly as phrased, or if he genuinely did not know some of the answers to Mr. McCormick's questions. One thing is certain: he had obvious disdain for being questioned in a civil court of law.

RULING BY THE SUPREME COURT OF ONTARIO

The dates for the trial proceedings—the Holiness Movement Church in Canada (A. T. Warren and S. A. York, plaintiffs) versus R. C. Horner and G. L. Monahan (defendants)—were set for October 3 and 4, 1917, in the city of Ottawa. Members and adherents of the HMC held their breath. The Hon. Mr. Justice Clute presided over the hearings in the presence of counsel for all parties, and would declare a ruling without jury.[28] Pleadings and hearing of evidence were read. The Supreme Court of Ontario declared the ruling:

> The Court doth order and adjudge that a ballot shall be taken under the direction of the Master at Ottawa, as to whether the plaintiff, Warren, or the defendant, Horner, shall be Bishop of

the Church in question in this action, and that those entitled to vote on the question shall be those whose names appear upon the rolls of several annual conferences as of December 1916 according to the list annexed hereto . . . And this Court doth further order and adjudge that whichever shall receive the majority of votes shall be declared elected Bishop of said Church.[29]

It was a pyrrhic victory of sorts for R. C. Horner and his party. Horner had in essence won the battle, but he would lose the war. The court ruling was in his favour—he had won his point that a quorum was in fact two-thirds of the total members of all Annual Conferences—but the battle for votes was now in Warren's favour. Conference records revealed ninety-seven eligible voters: fifty-five from the Ottawa Conference, where Horner received the majority of his support; eighteen from the Manitoba Conference; eight from the Alberta Conference; sixteen from the Egyptian Conference—and much to the chagrin of Horner's men, Justice Clute also added the names of W. Ketcheson, W. Burns, and G. Ralph.[30] Under the direction of the Master at Ottawa, ballots were prepared and sent to a total of one hundred eligible voters.

A battle for the hearts of the ordained clergy ensued. Horner's support was strong in eastern Canada but he was less known in the other conferences; Warren had been superintendent of the western churches, where he was loved and honoured. But how would the Egyptian Conference vote? That would be crucial—never before had the Egyptians been included in General Conference business.

Circular Letters

Herman R. James: In defense of Horner[31]

On the evening of the ruling, a number of the men who supported R. C. Horner instructed Rev. Herman R. James to disclose to the ordained ministry of the Holiness Movement, by way of circular letter, the facts concerning their position. Herman James was a member of the HMC, but his home address was listed as Queens University, Kingston, Ontario; he wrote in a very scholarly, well-informed manner with an obvious knowledge of history and government. "One side of the matter you have heard," he wrote, "the other side we now entrust you to hear patiently." Rev. James tediously and carefully rehearsed the recent history of the HMC beginning with the call for General Conference to meet in Carleton Place, December 12, 1916. His goals were, first, expose the illegality of the proceedings to depose Horner; second, exonerate Horner from the negative charges and malicious innuendo being spread concerning his character and actions; and third, convince the elders of the church that the moral and just action was to support R. C. Horner as bishop.

Rev. James offered insight for each member to consider: "Truth never lies on the surface, but we must search for the circumstances and inner mind, or soul of the fact." In other words, all the facts concerning the accusations heard against the bishop were not known—there was another side to the story. Yes, he admitted, Mr. Horner had made some mistakes, but "some don't make many mistakes because they don't try to do anything. Some never miss because they never aim." However, he stated, "Pathfinders are few in this world; we had better honour and use, not murder them. . . . [W]e are stoutly opposed to impulsive and destructive revolution."

One section of the James letter was entitled "Evil Reports": "The schism in our church is largely a disease arising from the poisonous germ known as evil speaking. If it were a mere difference in opinion with regard to government, strife would be less bitter, and the cure conveniently easy. But nothing can completely repair the breach as it is, only what will stop the mouths of busy-bodies who will persist in circulating 'hearsay reports.' In blackening the founder, they blacken the church and themselves."

The Circular Letter concluded by tabulating twenty-two reasons why "Brother Horner has a right to be Bishop, (and) why you should vote for him." He began with, "He is the founder of the church; as our most powerful Evangelist, he has kept the church alive." He went on to say that "While the church laboured with him, it prospered." He ended with, "He is the Lord's anointed; to condemn him, is to reverse the decision of the Appellate Division of the Supreme Court of Ontario." James also pointed out that Horner "has not been a busybody in agitation. He has published no self-defense." Rev. James concluded his remarks with a lofty exhortation entitled "Brotherhood":

> Now brothers, let us conscientiously and prayerfully turn to our task. If the words, "Last century made the world a neighbourhood; this century must make it a brotherhood" are true; and if we, as a church, would have a part in this great and divine task, then we must not begin the century by a disrespectful deposition of our founder. Let us contend, not for the creed of holiness, but for the holiness principle. Let us not be merely holiness men; let us be holy men. "In the non-essentials let us have liberty; in the essentials let us have unity; but in all things let us have charity." Let us fulfill the expectations, and make real the hopes of the court and public by showing, in the pending election, a Christian spirit of brotherhood towards one who is most worthy.
>
> Standing on these principles, let me say that I have a vision of a time, a blessed time, when men shall beat their swords of slander into plough-shares of gospel truth, and their spears, which they are wont to thrust at the mote in their brother's eye, into pruning-hooks with which to pluck the beam out of their own eye; and men shall learn the war of tongues no more.

J. C. BLACK: ACCUSATIONS OF HORNER

J. C. Black titled his circular "A Review of a Review." Like a tenacious lawyer, he set out to dispute, one by one, statements and allegations made by the Horner camp concerning what had taken place since the opening of the Carleton Place General Conference 1916. Black sought to prove that many of the statements made were "misleading" and deemed it his duty to "present the matter in its true light before our brethren who will, in the near future, be called upon to poll their vote." He questioned the sincerity of Rev. Horner's proposal for submitting to a church Court of Appeal outside the civil courts and abiding by such a decision; he pointed to the so-called special Annual Conference called by Horner at Stittsville, "notwithstanding its protest against the same," as necessary reason to take steps "to protect the interests of the church."

Rev. Black painted an opposing picture to that of Herman James. Rather than pointing to Horner's work as founder and organizer of the HMC, he presented Mr. Horner and company as "totally setting aside, or trampling under foot, and rejecting the authority of last General Conference." Rev. Black concluded his circular by writing, "We trust that each voter will prayerfully and carefully consider the great question at issue previous to casting his vote. If God leads we are, and will be satisfied with the results. We have prayed and still pray that whatever is most for the glory of God, and the best for the future of our church will be done."

END OF CONFLICT

Time ticked as slowly as the falling snow throughout the winter of 1917–1918. Of the one hundred ballots sent, all were duly marked and returned with the exception of two, one of which was sent to R. C. Horner, who did not vote. On the twentieth of March 1918, the Master at Ottawa proceeded to count the votes in the presence of the solicitors for each party. On March 26, the Master published and filed the results: A. T. Warren—58; R. C. Horner—40. Interestingly, Horner received thirty-five of the fifty-eight eligible votes from the Ottawa Conference, only one of eighteen from the Manitoba Conference, four of eight from the Alberta Conference, but zero of sixteen from Egypt.

The conflict was over for Bishop Horner and his men. They had agreed to the ruling by the Supreme Court of Ontario, and lost the vote. Rev. A. T. Warren was declared the properly elected bishop of the HMC, and all the proceedings at the General Conference held at Carleton Place were deemed valid and binding.[32] An injunction restraining the defendants was ordered upon Horner and Monahan from acting as bishop and secretary-treasurer; moreover, they were to account for, transfer, and deliver up to the plaintiffs all property, assets, documents, and money belonging to the Holiness Movement Church.

LIFT UP A STANDARD

The decision to replace Ralph Horner as bishop of the Holiness Movement Church had tremendous ramifications. The HMC in Canada was divided almost equally into two separate camps. Both sides were adamant in their support of either Warren or Horner for bishop. Neither side would budge. The only recourse was to separate into two churches, both holding to the doctrines set forth by the HMC but diverging to accommodate two leaders—two visions of church polity and two views on the inclusiveness of lay representation.[1]

In 1918, a sizeable number of ordained preachers from the HMC set out to organize under the banner of the Standard Church of America. Oral history suggests Rev. Horner was reluctant to form a new denomination, but was strongly encouraged to do so by close advisors desiring to provide a home for those who wished to continue along the old paths and uphold the old ways. Many were also adamant that the bishop had been severely slighted and were unwilling to see him callously cast aside—it was, after all, Ralph Horner who had been the founder and visionary of the HMC. Regardless of the strong nucleus of preachers and people forming the breakaway Standard Church, they acquired no deeded HMC properties and little in the way of finance as ordered by the injunction of the Supreme Court of Ontario.

The division had been difficult and disillusioning for many. Unfortunately, acrimony and animosity developed between various church members and adherents—even some families were divided. There were several disputes about church property. Some members simply walked away and built new churches nearby. Vaida Woodland Armstrong told how the Standard Church in Roblin, Ontario, was built diagonally across the street from the Holiness Movement Church. A humourous story spread that one church would sing, "Will there be any stars in my crown, in my crown?" and the other church would sing in reply, "No not one, no not one!"

On a serious note, there was a certain tragedy in this division as observed some seventy years later by Free Methodist Superintendent Rev. Robert Buchanan: "The Holiness Movement was the first 'break away' from the newly formed Methodist Church of Canada. The 'Holiness Movement' was clearly established to keep alive evangelistic zeal and raise up a 'holy' people in Canada. The division that developed was very sad in that it was a violation of the Biblical and Wesleyan injunction of 'perfecting perfection' of love for God and neighbour."[2]

ORGANIZATION OF THE STANDARD CHURCH OF AMERICA

A special meeting was called by breakaway preachers for July 9, 1918, to be held at Lake Eloida campground. Their goal was to organize the Standard Church of America. They requested Rev. R. C. Horner to attend.

The roll was called and fifty-six preachers and evangelists answered and were organized into the Kingston Annual Conference of the Standard Church of America.[3] The minute book indicates a number of other ministers could not be present but would join at a later time. The number present indicates how strong the support for Bishop Horner had been along the Ottawa Valley and vicinities.

The business of the Conference was fourfold: the passing of ministerial character; the unanimous election and ordination of R. C. Horner as bishop; the establishment of a missionary fund followed by the election of a missionary board; and the appointment of a committee in charge of selecting Sunday school lessons.

The Standard Church began to experience the excitement and exhilaration of beginning anew. There was the anticipation of new potential and a vision for growth and expansion. Unfortunately there is no report from a stationing committee and there are only a few recorded accounts to tell where the fifty-six preachers and evangelists dispersed during the summer of 1918. Did they hold revivals and camp meetings and establish churches? A few scattered records tell us they did. Obviously, there was a flurry of activity to form societies and find places to worship.

Regrettably, a few overzealous individuals set out to establish what they claimed to be "just and fair." As to be expected, such demands only resulted in churches torn apart by divided loyalties. Rev. William Woodland recalled that while Rev. Price was preaching in the Metcalfe Holiness Church, his furniture was removed from the parsonage and he came home to an empty house.[4] When Rev. Monahan arrived at his Holiness Movement Church in Cobden, he found the door bolted and locked, forbidding him to conduct services and continue as pastor.[5] Such foolhardy behaviour was cause for some pastors and members to withdraw from Holiness Movement *and* Standard churches and begin to minister and worship elsewhere.

Although the division was disappointing, it was not the conclusion of ministry for either church. Both churches continued to minister with strength and influence. In fact, it spurred the Standard Church to become aggressive in church planting and opening up new works both at home and in missions. One hundred years later many of these same Holiness Movement and Standard churches have not only survived the ordeal of their division, but have thrived in sharing the gospel in their communities and beyond.

The name Standard Church was based on Isaiah 62:10: "Lift up a standard for the people." Rev. W. J. Watchorn explained the inspiration for the name in the denominational periodical, the *Christian Standard*, which had been published since 1917:

LIFT UP A STANDARD

This command was given to the people of Israel, and handed down to us. There is a great responsibility laid on all God's people, especially on the standard bearers of the Gospel. . . . There are standards in the Bible to be held up as a pattern or model, hence the great responsibility. . . .

Scripture teaches not only regeneration, but also sanctification, called by some the second blessing. . . . There is much modern theorizing on this subject. . . . [I]t requires the present definite experience to lift up the Bible standard on this point. Those who attempt it otherwise make a sad failure . . . How sad to see brilliant minds, useful talents and precious time squandered.

When the standard is low, experience and the work done is low accordingly, and beneath what God requires. . . . Nothing but the best and richest experience is sufficient. . . . God's standard is above all. . . . It makes God's people all one. . . . God wants the standard lifted so high, men will see that the almightiness of Jesus and His blood is alone sufficient. . . . Be not deceived, this is the latter end of the last days and perilous times they are.[6]

SECOND KINGSTON ANNUAL CONFERENCE

The second Kingston Annual Conference convened less than two months later at the Stittsville campground, a few miles west of Ottawa, on August 26, 1918. This Conference would be interesting for three reasons.

1. THE PRESSING NEED FOR A COLLEGE TO TRAIN PASTORS AND LEADERS

A very special part of R. C. Horner's legacy includes his belief in training and educating preachers and workers through the establishment of Bible colleges. Two locations were discussed at length: Belleville and Prescott. The bishop was authorized to inspect both locations and choose according to his judgment the place most suitable. Rev. Horner favored the Bradley House, located in Prescott, Ontario (the building was rented from 1918 to 1920). An educational board was appointed to hire teachers and direct the business of the college.

2. THE REPORT FROM THE COMMITTEE ON UNIFORMS

Standard Church preachers and people would be recognized by their conservative uniforms and dress. The report would be sent as a memorial to the first General Conference.

Item one stated that the uniform would be black. But after lengthy debate and amendments to the original motion, Rev. B. McRoberts moved that the colours would be navy blue, medium grey, dark grey, and black. The item was finally adopted. This, however, was only the beginning of reporting and discussions on dress.

After discussion it was decided that more time was needed and the men's uniform would be detailed more fully in the upcoming General Conference.

The section on women's uniforms (submitted by a committee of women) was the most controversial and extensive: full skirts, blouses without cuffs, black square-crowned sailor's hats, plain shoes, and hair dressed plainly and parted in the centre or combed straight back. These were some of the standards to be upheld for women's dress codes.[7]

What was the motivation and desire for such severity of dress? Four reasons emerged:

1. Some wished to be recognized as distinct, much like the Salvation Army.

2. Others wished to exemplify modesty and simplicity as a means to outwardly express their spirituality. For them dress was an opportunity

to demonstrate complete dedication to God and withdrawal from all that belongs to the world.

3. For some it was a matter of dealing with their flesh and pride of life. They believed the entirely sanctified were "dead to self" and simplicity of dress was a sign of that humility.

4. A small minority wished to prove they were more spiritual than their friends in the HMC.

Unfortunately, the decisions about dress would have ramifications for future growth and beleaguer the Standard Church for the next three generations.

3. THE ELECTION OF DELEGATES TO GENERAL CONFERENCE

Only eight preachers were elected as delegates to General Conference from the fifty-six preachers and evangelists who had assembled at the organizational meeting at Lake Eloida. The Standard Church would remain episcopalian in church government, and ecclesiastical power would rest in the hands of a few ordained clergy.

CONGREGATIONS ESTABLISHED

The fall of 1918 saw the fledgling denomination continue the work of rebuilding churches and congregations. There was almost a race in some places to claim disputed properties and buildings. Churches were planted and established in many different ways using a variety of facilities. Some early examples are recorded below.

BLOOMFIELD

The Holiness Movement Church in Bloomfield, Ontario, did not have possession of a church building. They worshiped in the red schoolhouse at the edge of town on the road to West Lake. In 1916 word of the division within the HMC had reached the small congregation in the red schoolhouse. The people were undecided about what to do. Should they remain Holiness Movement, or should they join with the new Standard Church headed by Rev. R. C. Horner? The congregation put out a fleece. Two ministers—Rev. R. C. Raymond, a follower of Rev. Horner, and Rev. William Grundy of the Holiness Movement— were invited to attend the same service. The people decided that the minister who was inspired to speak first in the service would decide which group the Bloomfield church would follow. Rev. R. C. Raymond arose first and delivered a sermon, so the congregation followed Rev. R. C. Horner and became the Bloomfield Standard Church.[8]

The congregation decided to move location to the living room of Rev. Raymond's rented house. Since pastors were stationed in a church for only two years, a new young couple soon arrived, Rev. and Mrs. George Kelley. Rev. Kelley became a respected and well-loved preacher and evangelist within the Standard Church and holiness circles. Two years later, in 1920, Norman and Minnie Wager were the first appointed pastors of the newly incorporated Standard Church of America.

FORESTERS FALLS—FIRST BUILDING

The first actual Standard Church building was dedicated in Foresters Falls, Ontario, on December 6, 1918, as part of an evangelistic campaign held from December 6–15. This history is of personal interest because on June 28, 1969, your appreciative author married Faye Montgomery, whose home church was the Foresters Falls Standard Church—a connection to the very beginnings of the Standard Church!

The launch of the Foresters Falls Standard Church, however, was rooted in the division that had taken place in the HMC. Rev. G. L. Monahan, pastor of the Cobden Holiness Church, had been a supporter of R. C. Horner. The nucleus for the Foresters Falls Standard Church was mostly supporters of Rev. Monahan, and they helped form the new society within the newly inaugurated Standard Church of America. In 1919, this fledgling society purchased the property of Dr. McKillop at the corner of Queen and Harriet Streets for the sum of four hundred dollars. With only limited professional help and mostly volunteers from the church, the former harness and veterinary shop was remodeled into a humble chapel. The interior was neatly paneled with knotty pine. The old livery stables at the back sheltered the horses of the worshipers. The absence of paint and carpet and the addition of uncomfortable, narrow pews did not in the least dampen the spiritual fervor of "these zealous Standard folk" (as my father-in-law called them), and the church prospered and grew numerically. God blessed the people and pastors, for out of this new congregation two young men were soon called to missionary service: Earl H. Thompson to Egypt and John W. Johnston to China.[9]

In 1920, tent services were held in the neighbouring village of Beachburg. Two women formed an evangelistic team: deaconesses C. Hazzard and L. Richardson conducted the services. A sufficient number of families were touched with the gospel message that a Standard church was also built in Beachburg about six miles down the road from "the Falls." Beachburg church likewise prospered and, because the towns were close in proximity, the two congregations mingled cordially for several decades. Eventually both churches were led by one pastor who alternated between Sunday school and worship services. During the ministry of Rev. Sylvester MacDonald, the two congregations mutually agreed to sell the Beachburg Standard Church; and since several families were also coming from the North Cote area near Renfrew, a building program was initiated in Foresters Falls. In 1970, the congregations joined together in Foresters Falls until 2007, when they moved to a new location and beautiful facilities — Whitewater Wesleyan — near Cobden under the leadership of Rev. Lloyd and Doris Reaney. From humble beginnings in a veterinary-harness shop, this church is a beacon of light to the Ottawa Valley.

Richmond Standard Church

The Richmond Standard Church near Ottawa was also organized in the year 1918 by the Rev. A. A. Smith. A house on McBean Street was purchased to be used as a parsonage. Services were held in the parsonage as well as in the homes of those who lived in the Goodstown area nearby. In 1919, Rev. J. G. Nussey became the pastor. True to Hornerite tradition, the very next summer, in 1920, he helped organize the Richmond Camp Meeting held in a grove of trees owned by Alton Trimble one mile south of the village. This grove was purchased and became the site of an annual camp meeting, which continued until it eventually closed in the 1960s.

A property was also donated by James Trimble on McBean Street, and a church was built under the leadership of Rev. G. W. Oldford. During the next few years, membership increased and two congregations were formed—Richmond and North Gower. Today, many of the descendants of those early church founders have formed a vibrant church, Cornerstone Wesleyan, which is prominently situated in the village of North Gower and ministers to the growing sprawl of Ottawa, Canada's capital.

Revival Services in Kingston

The Kingston Standard Church also dates back to the fall of 1918. Rev. J. G. Nussey, the short, blunt preacher who wasted no time on nonessential chitchat, pitched a tent in what is now known as McBurney Park to hold revival services. Again, the traditional tent services that had served R. C. Horner so well gave birth on October 14, 1918, to the Kingston Standard Church. The newly formed congregation purchased its first property for worship, a house at 66 Main Street, in 1919. The congregation eventually erected a traditional holiness church on Barrie Street in 1926 and held the dedication service on February 13, 1927.

By the late 1960s, the facilities had become outdated: Christian education facilities were cramped and limiting; office space was practically nonexistent; parking space was at a premium. Wisely, the church relocated to the corner of Sydenham and Sunnyside Road. Dedication of the new building occurred on June 22, 1975, under the leadership of Rev. Arnold Rigby. Since opening the new church, the congregation has more than doubled and continued to enlarge the building's facilities. The church is led by Pastor Arnold's son, Rev. Dr. Peter Rigby and his wife, Cindi.

THE CHALLENGE AHEAD

A great challenge lay before the aging bishop and his followers. With the division behind, Bishop Horner and his loyal adherents were embarking on a plan to rebuild and grow a new denomination. Ralph Horner was a man of boundless energy and great organizational ability who stopped at no obstacles. The first General Conference of the Standard Church was called, and the new constitution spelled out the direction of the church for decades to come.

FIRST GENERAL CONFERENCE

The first General Conference was set to be held at the Bradley House in Prescott, Ontario, over Christmas. A ten-day indoor camp meeting, in keeping with the Hornerite tradition of revival services, was also scheduled in the Prescott Town Hall, commencing on December 24 in conjunction with the General Conference.

Minutes from the Journal read: "The first General Conference, having been duly called, met in the Standard Church College in Prescott, Ont. on Dec. 23rd, 1918 at 3:30 P.M. according to announcement." The following members were present: A. A. Smith, R. H. Wiley, Jas. Smith, J. L. Armitage, T. A. Seale, W. J. Watchhorn, Geo. Oldford, R. C. Horner.

Three additional members were present in the second sitting at seven o'clock and added to the roll: G. L. Monahan, J. G. Nussey, and F. J. Mayhew.[10]

Bishop R. C. Horner occupied the chair.

W. J. Watchhorn was appointed secretary.

The following committees were nominated by the chair and accepted by Conference: Uniform and Dress, Missionary, and Book Room.

During the first General Conference, only eleven qualified as eligible ministerial delegates and elders to sit within the Conference bar. There were no lay delegates. Only eleven elders, following the episcopalian polity Bishop Horner favoured, would set the tone and direction for the entire church and its people. As previously noted, there were many more preachers and evangelists who had attended the Annual Conferences, but only a handful of elders were eligible to sit within the bar of that first General Conference. In the 1923 historical photograph, taken only five years later during the Kingston Annual Conference at Lake Eloida campgrounds, sixty-three fully uniformed ministers and evangelists, nineteen of them women, stood proudly to be photographed.

General Conference continued diligently the next morning, Christmas Eve, at eight o'clock until the evening. Three topics were discussed:

1. The Book Room. A great deal of time was spent discussing the stock and maintenance of the book room. Much of the stock consisted of books and pamphlets written by Bishop Horner.

2. Foreign Mission Field. J. G. Nussey submitted the missions report on behalf of the committee. The first item: What field should the church endeavour to enter? G. L. Monahan and F. J. Mayhew proposed that Egypt be considered as the first mission field and that in preparation a man be sent to investigate. Obviously, the knowledge of Egypt from experience with the HMC would make this field particularly appealing; on the other hand, the Egyptian elders had voted unanimously against the leadership of Bishop Horner.

3. Committee on Uniform and Dress. The Kingston Annual Conference had set the tone for dress, sending a memorial to General Conference. G. Oldford was appointed to have the requirements for uniform in dress printed in pamphlet form for easy reference.

There were two sections to consider:

1. Uniform for women: Eleven items specified dress codes for evangelists and preachers' wives. Colours were to be black, grey, and navy blue; laywomen might wear dark brown. Ten more items specified how the uniform would be sewn, the style of hats and shoes worn, and how hair should to be combed and left unadorned.[11]

2. Uniform for men: The list of requirements for male preachers was shorter but still exacting: "Preachers shall wear no colors but dark grey, navy blue or black. No box back coats. No patent leather, tan, narrow-toed, or high heeled shoes. No clarence or double banded high collars, other than clerical. No broad Quaker-rim silk or castor hats."[12] Trousers were to be "not shorter than two inches from the ground, medium width without rolls or strips. No cuffs or cuff links."[13] A small pamphlet later printed in 1926 stated specifically that "shirts shall be dark in color, black, blue or grey. White collars may be worn, but no neckties. Preachers shall wear clerical collars. No gold or gold-plated collar buttons or shirt buttons."[14]

DISCIPLINE AND MANUAL

The Discipline and Manual (Section VIII), adopted by the Conference and printed for public use, stated the rationale for the codes on dress and furniture. It is presented in question-and-answer format:

Question: Should we insist on plain dress?
Answer: Certainly. We should not on any account spend what the Lord has put into our hands, as stewards, to be used for His

glory, in expensive wearing apparel, when thousands are suffering for food and raiment, and millions are perishing for the word of life. Let the dress of every member be plain. Let the strictest economy be used in these respects. We will have a uniform for men and for women. We will have a committee on uniform for men and another for women.

Question: Should our furniture, as well as our dress, be plain?

Answer: By all means. Let the strictest economy be observed in both. Let no expensive furniture or high-priced carriages be used while there is a single individual for whom Christ died, hungry, or naked, or without the word of life. And let the same principle of saving all we can, that we may have to give to those who need, govern us in renting or building houses to live in.[15]

Thus, like many primitive holiness churches emerging in the early twentieth century, the Standard Church became mired on the road of austere legalism. Legalism hindered growth. Moreover, numerous children of members and adherents either turned against their church in rebellion and bitterness, or looked to other less legalistic denominations for spiritual growth and service. Jessie Steenburg, daughter of Rev. George Shadbolt, often reflected that even though her parents had been gracious and accommodating, the church standards and legalism were cause for many childhood frustrations; even as an aged woman, she would shudder about the strict dress standards imposed upon her as a teenage girl attending public school.[16]

There was another underlying but less understood reason contributing to why legalism held grip over holiness churches: many were reacting to modernism (Darwinism, higher criticism, and forsaking the doctrine of biblical inerrancy), which was beginning to infiltrate some of the larger denominations in North America. In 1910, General Superintendent Albert Carman of the Methodist Church of Canada lost a long-standing battle to keep German higher criticism out of Methodist educational institutions such as Victoria University, Horner's alma mater, which had moved from Cobourg to Toronto in 1910. Canada's largest Protestant denomination was lost to evangelicals. Wayne Kleinsteuber explains in his book *Coming of Age: The Making of a Canadian Free Methodist Church* that not only the church, but the age itself seemed to be careening out of orbit:

> After years of peace and prosperity, optimism and stability, the nations lurched into World War 1. The innocent, fresh-faced youngsters sent off to make the world safe for democracy returned from the trenches as battle-hardened, worldly-wise men with shrunken souls harboring secrets known only to them and God. Anguish and confusion held home-folks and war veterans in their grip. There was a deep yearning for old, familiar landmarks.
>
> For the theologically and morally conservative, who found themselves out of tune with theological higher criticism and the post-war "flapper era," the temptation to abandon the world to its own devices, raise the barricades as high as possible, and retreat into their own cozy subculture was almost irresistible.[17]

THE BOOK ROOM

General Conference continued all Christmas Day from eight o'clock in the morning until late evening. The book room occupied most of the discussions. The next day, December 26, two more sessions centered mainly on the status and state of the book room. Finances were a major issue—the new church had few dollars to spare. Nevertheless, Conference moved to reimburse Bishop Horner $2,670.05 for his financing of church literature and supplies: two thousand hymnbooks (Conference also requested an order for five hundred more), hymnbook plates and permissions, and numerous tracts and books. Finances were in short supply (G. Oldford reported, "we have no capital"), but $500 was received serendipitously from the estate of the late Geo. Bird of Stirling, Ontario, and designated by Conference for use by the book room.[18] It was decided that Conference borrow $800 from G. L. Monahan and pay that amount immediately to Bishop Horner; it was decided that $500 more would be paid on or before Jan 15, 1919, with the remaining $870.05 to be paid in installments of $50 with interest at 5 percent. Conference resolved that "all our preachers and workers take a special interest in this branch of our work, and labour to make it self-sustaining by dealing (as much as possible) with . . . books, hats, calendars, stationery, Sunday School supplies, etc."[19] Ralph Horner invested in and believed in the power of books, tracts, and magazines; he was willing to invest his personal time and money to print literature promoting the doctrine and preaching of the holiness message and he expected his preachers to do so as well.

The afternoon session adjourned to meet at the call of the chair. Members of Conference filed forth from the Bradley House with a fresh fire of determination: new church, new hymnbook, new articles of distinction, new mandate.

NEW CHARTER

During the beginning of 1919, Rev. Ralph Horner sought to obtain a charter from the Canadian government for the new church to be called the Standard Church. The federal government, however, rejected the application on the grounds that this was Horner's third attempt to charter a church after his applications to incorporate the Wesleyan Methodist and Holiness Movement churches. Not to be denied, Rev. Horner and his men applied to the United States, where the Standard Church of America was incorporated in the city of Watertown, county of Jefferson, state of New York. It followed that the Canadian government could hardly refuse a charter for a church already chartered in the United States, and on January 5, 1920, the Standard Church of

America was incorporated in the Dominion of Canada and granted a federal charter.

Some years later, about 1940, Rev. W. B. Fleming was appointed to assist Rev. Irwin Brown in obtaining recognition of the Standard Church of America for the New York Conference. After consulting a lawyer, they discovered that all US trustees of the Standard Church of America had died, and new trustees had not been elected. This meant the Standard Church of America had dissolved and the charter could not be renewed with that name. The name the Standard Church was suggested and a new charter was obtained. Oddly enough, the church was called the "Standard Church of America" in Canada, but in America, the name was simply the "Standard Church."[20]

New Beginnings

Bishop Horner was a tireless, boundless worker. His pace was exhausting. At sixty-five years of age he began the determined task of consolidating his preachers and people under the banner of the Standard Church of America. Several five-day holiness conventions were conducted early in 1919: Roblin, Campbellford, Inverary, Seeley's Bay, Madoc—all in eastern Ontario.

The Feast of Pentecost was once again scheduled for May on the historic north shore campgrounds of Lake Eloida, near Athens, Ontario. The camp had not been retained by the HMC; the owner, Andrew Henderson, had only leased the grounds to the Holiness Movement in 1899, but after the division he transferred ownership to the Standard Church.[1] Lake Eloida was brimming with memories of Hornerite services and victories, and retaining the camp provided the rallying place Ralph Horner needed for equipping and indoctrinating ministers and evangelists and, thereafter, sending them forth on fire to new fields of labour.

A special session of the Kingston Annual Conference convened on May 22, 1919, during the Feast of Pentecost. Most of the early sessions dealt with the examination and passing of ministerial character and the recommendation of probationers to the ministry. Sixty-three men and women were accepted to be enlisted on the Conference roll on the condition they pass examinations on doctrine.

THE SEMINARY

A major item dominating the Conference agenda was the seminary.[2] The minutes record an impassioned, but optimistic presentation by Bishop Horner relating to the school year in the Bradley House at Prescott during the past winter. There was, he emphasized, the necessity of a larger school in the very near future. He reported the work was prosperous, but the church was missing a great opportunity by not being prepared for up to one hundred students in the school next winter. He believed a building should be erected immediately to accommodate at least fifty prospective students preparing for ministry. The bishop made an earnest appeal to the Conference for a good donation, for, he predicted, it would depend upon the generosity of Conference as to what churches would contribute. Conference has the opportunity to encourage laypeople to give, he declared. Bishop Horner reported that he himself had given much to the school this past winter, but was certain he would be well rewarded: he believed God for $100,000 in hand before he would commence building—a major sum of money in 1919 on the heels of World War I and the deadly Spanish flu. "Donations are already coming in," the bishop reported, "and I want to know how much this Conference will give before I leave this Feast of Pentecost."[3] Subscriptions and offerings were received, and the next day the Special Committee reported that ministers and workers on the campgrounds had made a commitment of $6,700—an offering of supreme sacrifice from those who had so little!

GENERAL CONFERENCE ENDORSES SEMINARY

A special session of General Conference convened on May 26 following the ten-day Feast of Pentecost and the adjournment of the Kingston Annual Conference. The new seminary again was the priority on the agenda.

Most of the discussion concerning the need for a new college and church headquarters had occurred beforehand in the Kingston

Conference. Bishop Horner and his leaders were well aware that the Standard Church would need a ministry center to train preachers and workers, provide a headquarters for administration, and give the new movement a focal place of identification. The special session of General Conference lasted only for the afternoon of May 26, and little is recorded in the minutes concerning the discussion and launching of the new seminary. But the decision to build was momentous for the new denomination. James Smith and R. H. Wiley moved that Rev. Horner nominate a committee to select a site for a new Standard Church seminary. The committee would consist of W. J. Watchorn, James Smith, and T. A. Seal.

FATIGUE AND HEALTH ISSUES APPEAR

Bishop Horner's furious pace, however, was beginning to affect his general health and level of fatigue. The *Athens Reporter* noted on August 28, 1919, that, "Camp meeting is in full tide this week with a good attendance and will continue over Sunday, 31st. Bishop R. C. Horner, the veteran of many hard fought battles and crowning victories, is in charge at the Camp Ground. Owing to recent illness he is forced to spare himself his usual supreme effort." Later the next week the *Reporter* noted, "The camp meeting closed, Sunday, 31st. The participants claim very satisfactory results. It is estimated that about 1,500 were in attendance Sunday afternoon." The conventions, preaching, crowds of people, emotional services, conferences, and organizational responsibilities were obviously exhausting, and Horner's tired body was beginning to show the wear.

SEMINARY PLANS PROCEED

On November 1, 1919, fourteen beautiful acres of farmland were purchased for $10,000 on Perth Street, known as Schofield Hill, in Brockville, Ontario, for the purpose of erecting a new college and headquarters for the Standard Church of America. Plans for a three-story college building at 243 Perth Street were drawn by architect A. Stuart Allaster. A bold appeal for $100,000 was made throughout the church to finance the new project. This was a big dream in a difficult time. Canada and the United States were struggling economically, attempting to revamp a wartime economy and deal with a world in a shaky peace. The cost of living had spiraled. At one point in 1920, prices had increased 100 percent over the prewar cost of living in 1913. Workers, many of whom earned less than one dollar per hour, were asked, in spite of rising costs, to take pay cuts. Despite the times, Bishop Horner was asking the new church for the astronomical amount of $100,000 to build the new seminary. The wisdom of such a venture was doubted by some. This project would test the faith and mettle of the newly emerging Standard Church.

Rev. G. Oldford, secretary for the seminary fund, later reported he had encountered difficulty raising the money, being "repudiated" by some.[4] The drive for funds caused a great deal of public discussion and deliberation, he said, but added, "We have not undertaken this weighty matter ostentatiously, but with much deep consideration and prayer. We think our brethren and friends throughout Canada and the United States will agree with us that our church would fail her duty not to have a seminary of learning. Such an institution is the want that is felt by every religious community of any extent of intelligence."[5]

SACRIFICES FOR THE SEMINARY

Amazingly, the Standard Church people reached their goal within a year! But it was not without considerable sacrifices. Some, we are told, mortgaged their farms. Rev. Earl Thompson wrote of one boy who asked his mother, "Could we not do without milk and give the money we spend on it to help build the seminary?" Thompson also recalled church members donating one day's salary per month to the fund, and others who sold fowl, calves, sheep and pigs, and turning the money over to the church.[6]

The Standard Church, like the people in Nehemiah's day, "set their hands to do this good work."[7]

Excavation and construction began early in the spring of 1920. That fall the building was well advanced; students moved in and classes commenced in the red-brick seminary even before construction was completed. Rev. James Smith was appointed manager.

Bishop Horner called for a five-day midwinter convention to begin January 1, 1921. He promised a large staff of teachers to preach at the convention "in demonstration of the Spirit and of power." He used the convention as a springboard to dedicate the new college and declared, "The whole building is dedicated to God as a place in which missionaries, preachers, and evangelists are to be trained and baptized with fire to go and rescue the perishing masses."[8]

In a departure from his usual procedure, Bishop Horner asked laymen, rather than clergymen, to be the keynote speaker and chairperson for the dedication service. Mayor David Lewis of Brockville was the guest speaker, and the architect, A. Stuart Allaster, acted as chairman. The dedication service was the only function of the convention held in the new college. All other meetings and sessions were held at Victoria Hall, the home of the town's administration. In a statement issued when the college marked its sixtieth anniversary in 1981, the Standard Church reminisced:

On the fifth night, after the last sermon had been preached and the last 'Amen' uttered, the people returned home to face the challenges of life. The significance, however, of that first service at the mid-winter convention in Brockville remains. Today, the school is still part of the Standard Church. It speaks of a dream and testifies to a people who were willing to sacrifice for a future which they claimed for God.

Final cost of the three-story red brick seminary was $65,000. Amazingly, the entire goal of $100,000 had been raised, so the college had funds left over for future use. Later, in 1924, a high school department was set up at the seminary, and a publishing house was built in 1928 at the foot of Schofield Hill. Between the publishing house and the seminary, the fertile green fields became flourishing gardens to support the work of the college.[9]

REVIVALS CONTINUE

From all appearances, the Standard Church was flourishing at the beginning of the new decade. There was excitement and anticipation because the denomination was new and facing challenges that called for prayer and faith. But local churches were mainly rural and small-town in culture, and the traditional methods of reaching the unconverted continued mainly through evangelistic revivals, conventions, and camp meetings. Preachers were trained and mentored to emphasize evangelistic preaching, exhorting seekers to come forward and kneel at an altar of prayer. Horner had written in 1910, "Every pastor is expected to 'do the work of an Evangelist.' In this way he 'gives full proof of his ministry.' The work of a Christian minister is to commence and to promote Scriptural revival. There is no Christian minister apart from this."[10] Hence, Sunday's preaching was evangelistic in style, with the specific goals of converting sinners, restoring backsliders, and leading members into the experience of entire sanctification. Weekdays were spent making calls on members, visitors, and contacts in the neighbourhood to enquire of their spiritual welfare. Home visits usually concluded by kneeling for a closing pastoral prayer. Pastoral calls were made on those who were sick or in crisis. A midweek prayer meeting gathered the faithful (either in homes or the church) to share testimonies and pray for the concerns of the congregation, loved ones, and the community. To keep revival flames burning among churches, the Discipline stated that after counseling with the presiding elders, the bishop or president must appoint pastors to their fields of labour annually, and not for more than two consecutive years.[11] The Discipline also stated that "wherever possible, the society will hold at least three services a week for the conversion of sinners and the entire sanctification of believers."[12]

The episcopal system of church governance, however, continued to cause anxiety and insecurity among a number of the preachers. Each year pastors wondered where they might be stationed. A list was published at the end of Annual Conference—Rev. Albert Risby of Calgary reminisced that in the early days of the Western Conference, the Stationing Committee would pin a list to a tree, and at the end of Conference preachers gathered about the tree to see where they might be moving. The diary of Bessie Wager Seiter, a pastor's daughter during the 1920s, indicates it was reasonable that some pastors ought to have remained longer in their charges, because for some, work on buildings had not been completed and some churches were having obvious success and growth under the existing pastor. Regardless, after two years the preacher and his family followed the dictates of the Discipline and were assigned to a new circuit even if it meant moving while the school year was already in session. In a special memorial edition of the *Christian Standard*, it was reported that Rev. F. J. Mayhew was stationed in twenty-two circuits during his years of ministry from 1906, when he was ordained deacon by Bishop Horner, until his death on August 20, 1930, while serving in his latest circuit, the Madoc Standard Church.

Eventually, the wisdom of the two-year rule began to be openly questioned. The General Conference minutes, January 1931, record that a memorial from the Kingston Annual Conference requesting permission for the Stationing Committee under certain conditions to extend the length of time a pastor might be stationed in a circuit for up to one year longer than was customary, when "in the judgment of the Stationing Committee, the state of the work demands it."[13] The item was referred to the Committee on Discipline. No recorded recommendation by the Committee on Discipline was found; the practice prevailed for many years, but began to change with the times, for in the 1956 Manual and Discipline, we read that the presiding elders under the chairmanship of the Conference superintendent were the Stationing Committee to appoint ministers to their fields of labour, and no time limit was specified.[14]

The practice of moving preachers every two years also gave rise to another problem—the rise of local leadership that superseded the pastor's authority. The General Rules of the Discipline stated that "in every society there must be at least one service a week where none are permitted to meet but members of the Church in good standing. In each society one person will be appointed leader by a majority vote of the society for a term not exceeding three months, but may be re-elected."[15] This practice was obviously an attempt to duplicate the class meetings, which the Methodist Church under John Wesley organized for accountability and personal spiritual growth. However, the practice often gave rise to the emergence of a lay leader who became the local "strong man." Over time society leaders held considerable power and influence in the local congregation. Such men could and did cause power struggles with the new incoming pastor. Who would lead the church? The pastor or the society leader?

MISSION FIELDS

EGYPT[16]

The first General Conference of the Standard Church in 1918 mandated a new mission field to be established in Egypt. A board of missions was appointed and an annual Missions Sunday designated for November 10 of the same year. But who would go to the mission field?

In 1919, Rev. Risk Bishay, a former Holiness Movement pastor in Egypt, wrote a letter to Bishop Horner requesting a missionary. There was a speedy response: "A missionary called F. R. Webster is appointed to Egypt. I pray he will have success."

Ray Webster was a farm boy and the only child of Russell and Charlotte Webster from a small community called Owls Head, New

York. Ray Webster had been converted under the ministry of a lay preacher, Ma Brownell. He received a dramatic call to the ministry with a vision of a lost world and a deep passion for lost souls. When he told his invalid, widowed mother of his missionary call, she told him to go.

In late autumn of 1919, Rev. F. Ray Webster sailed from New York City, arriving in Alexandria shortly before Christmas. He traveled southward to Nikhela, a village 230 miles south of Cairo. Here Ray Webster began his labours in a small rented house, with services held on the ground floor and a room above for his dwelling. He faced a new culture, a strange and difficult language, a hostile climate, and hordes of flies and mosquitoes. Nevertheless, missionary Webster praised God for the privilege of sharing the gospel message. His first message was "The blessing of the Lord, it maketh rich, and he addeth no sorrow with it" taken from Proverbs 10:22 (KJV).

Ray Webster was a demonstrative preacher and large crowds came to hear and watch him preach. He was both expressive and emotional, punctuating his messages with ringing exclamations: "Hallelujah! Praise the Lord! Glory to God!" (later in Arabic, once he learned words to express the same). What fascinated many was that when he expressed his exuberant shouts of glory, he would also leap high into the air for joy. Rev. Earl Thompson, who succeeded him, reported that many souls were converted through Webster's ministry. Rev. Webster would round up as many listeners as possible and lead them like the Pied Piper from one street to the other singing and clapping their hands into the meeting place where he would conduct a church service and deliver the words of life. Many responded to his messages and were converted.

What was the secret of his success? The Egyptian brethren reported they were told by Rev. Webster, "Do not call me before eight in the morning because I spend two hours in daily fellowship with God." Ray Webster was a man of prayer.

On Sunday, March 8, 2009, Rev. Webster was on our minds as we bounced along a bumpy Egyptian village street in our rented van. Nagy, our trusted driver, skillfully maneuvered through a maze of beeping sedans, clover laden donkey carts, rumbling transports, skittish tuk tuks, and darting pedestrians. Amazing! I was in Egypt on a mission's tour with Rev. Earl Conley and team, enjoying the ministry and fellowship of our Egyptian churches— 25 in all, and I was on my way to preach in Nikhela, the first Standard church in Egypt. If Rev. Webster could see us now! Nikhela was Nagy's hometown where his mother lived, and as we dodged the traffic along the road, he explained to me that this was the village where the first Standard Church had been planted. Nagy also related an interesting story about Rev. Webster that had not been forgotten among the Egyptian brethren. Apparently, one of the brothers from the church had seen a vision: he saw a man clothed in a long white robe, riding on a white horse, leading a congregation clapping their hands for joy, marching around a church. That man, said Nagy, was Rev. Webster.

Today there is an established church in Nikhela, and the work in Egypt has grown much beyond the humble beginnings when Rev. Webster first arrived in 1919. Our Missions Safari was duly impressed with what God was doing. Some of the churches are large (300+) and filled with young people. Many are undertaking steps of faith that are great spiritual challenges, especially in a country where freedom to build churches is curtailed by the government. Rev. Ray Webster would be amazed and fulfilled . . . he might even do one of his leaps for joy![17]

CHINA

The Standard Church continued to support missions in Mainland China under the brave leadership of Tillie Danford and Lydia Connaughty. Both had remained loyal to Bishop Horner and continued their ministry at length in the Standard Church. Miss Connaughty had not been in good health and returned home from China in 1910, spending three years taking care of her mother and brother; she returned to China to assist Miss Danford in 1923. They encountered great difficulties but continued their labours, eventually establishing work in two villages and a mission home in Teng Huang Ting. The work of these two female missionaries was hampered by famine, flood, and poor health, but they were undaunted. More will be told about the China mission in a later chapter.

WORK PROGRESSES

Such were the faith adventures of many in the early days of the Standard Church. They were pioneers and often faced incredible odds and hardships to serve the Lord and the church. Many young women were sent in pairs to hold revival services in out-of-the-way places. They faced dangers, sacrificed, and gave everything they had. They often had very little to survive on but faith.

The story is told of two young women, Miss Mina Eastman and Miss Blanch Caldwell, who founded and established a church at Seeley's Bay, Ontario, in 1919. "The Bishop told us that we would go to Seeley's Bay," they reported. When asked where they would be staying since there was no existing church at Seeley's Bay, Bishop Horner replied that the corner of a crooked rail fence would do. Their motto: "Our extremities are God's opportunities. Do the best with what you have." God did bless their efforts with converts for the kingdom, and a Standard Church was eventually built in Seeley's Bay.[18]

IVANHOE CAMP MEETING

Camp meeting tradition continued to be strong among the Hornerites, but after the division, the Standard Church lost its stronghold of Ivanhoe Camp Meeting. Not to be deprived of their spiritual oasis, the fledgling congregations in Eldorado, Madoc, Belleville, Toronto, Bloomfield, and Ivanhoe came together in 1918 and purchased a new twelve-acre site from farmer Samuel Tanner, set in the mature maple woods north of the village of Ivanhoe, Ontario, about six miles distant from the original HMC camp. Mervin Cooke reported the Standard Church people swarmed Tanner to request the land, and he responded enthusiastically, "Yes, I will sell you a piece of land; swarm me again and I will sell you more!" According to Fred Crawford of Syracuse, New York, whose father was a participating pastor at the early Ivanhoe Camp Meeting, campers lived in large circus-like tents, slept in feather ticks, and cooked in the open on wood-fuelled cook stoves; the setting was described by one as being "as close to heaven as you can get."[19] A large tent was erected in the centre of the clearing where the gospel meetings were conducted. The railway companies added special trains to Ivanhoe Station to handle the numbers wanting to get to the camp. The old railway bed, a short distance from the entrance to the camp tucked off Highway 62, can be seen to this day.

PIONEER SPIRIT CONTINUES

Despite pressure, stress, and declining health, Bishop Horner continued his work of building the seminary in Brockville, sending out missionaries to pioneer works, establishing a mission field, publishing a magazine, and raising funds to maintain the work. By the close of 1920, churches had been established in Quebec, Ontario, Alberta, and British Columbia, and there were also pioneer works in Michigan, Pennsylvania, Vermont, and New York State. The Standard Church was enthusiastically pressing forward, "lifting up a standard for the Lord."

FOUGHT A GOOD FIGHT

Everyone began to notice that the incredible strain and pressure was taking its toll on Bishop Ralph C. Horner. But though in failing health, Bishop Horner continued to be intensely active in the stressful work of building, financing, preaching, and teaching. Rev. Earl Thompson recalled that Bishop Horner preeminently believed in "redeeming the time": at four or five o'clock in the morning he was in his study pursuing Conference work and dispensing with his correspondence. While in Prescott, suffering from weakness and high blood pressure, he was called to the Watertown Conference. His physician told him he should be in the hospital and that it was quite possible he would be found dead in bed any morning. In spite of this he insisted on going. Rev. Thompson was appointed to travel with him. Crossing the border, they learned from the authorities that to proceed further, a vaccination was required. Despite the doctor's advice to the contrary, Bishop Horner, rather than turn back, met the vaccination requirements and pressed on to the Conference.

DEATH OF A BISHOP

As late summer began to set in during September 1921, it was noticeable to all that Bishop Horner had become considerably more feeble and frail. When he arrived at his beloved Ivanhoe campgrounds many of his

Ivanhoe District friends were ready to lavish every kindness and comfort upon him. When walking to and from his tent he was assisted by some of the brethren. On his arrival at the camp, he was asked whether or not he wished to bear the responsibility of taking full charge and appointing the various preachers. He said that he wanted to do his part.

George Oldford recalled that no one was surprised, though people did wonder if he was up to the task. Oldford recorded what took place during the next twenty-four hours:

> The service was opened with the ordinary devotional exercise of singing, prayer and reading of the Scriptures, after which Bishop Horner walked briskly from the front seat and gained the platform without assistance. In his usual manner he gave out his text—Acts 4:20, "For we cannot but speak the things which we have seen and heard." After preaching for about four or five minutes he drew the chair to him and sat down, saying, "I have preached as long as I can standing; I will preach as long as I can sitting." In this posture he finished his last and, what we may call his dying message to about one thousand people. Though very feeble in body, and his voice so weak that not more than half the audience could hear him distinctly, yet his memory was clear and his mind active. In his sermon he clearly distinguished the doctrines of the Baptism of the Holy Ghost, Entire Sanctification, and Conversion, and as his manner has been, called on those who had the experience to stand up. He then invited those who wanted salvation to come to the altar, emphasizing his call by shouting in an unusually strong voice, "Hurry! Hurry! Hurry!" A good season of prayer followed.
>
> While in conversation with him just before he retired, we asked him if he were tired after preaching, and he replied, "You never heard me say I was tired." When he was retiring a brother asked him if he could sing something for him, and he sang the stanza:

Take hold, hold on
Hold fast and never let go,
No matter how the wind in the tempest may blow,
Take hold and never let go.

He went to sleep in ease and as peacefully as usual. At three o'clock he was taken with smothering and a severe pain in his hip. He called, and presently a number were gathered at his bedside. While at prayer, the pain instantly left him. He then expressed a desire to be left alone, thinking that he could go to sleep. All retired except one brother. At six o'clock it was noticed that his strength was failing, but he refused to call the doctor.

Early in the morning, the dying bishop sent for Myrtle Morris. As soon as his eyes fell on her he said, "Myrtle, can you get hold of God for me?" She dropped to her knees and God filled her soul with these beautiful words:

O God, our help in ages past,
Our hope for years to come,
Our shelter from the story blast,
And our eternal home.

Later it became evident that immediate action must be taken and accordingly the doctor was called, but he gave no hopes. At his own request the dying warrior was propped up in bed with pillows, in which position he remained while his breath grew shorter and shorter and his pulse fainter, till without a struggle or sigh his noble spirit took its flight—on the beautiful morning of September 12, 1921, at twenty minutes after 10 o'clock, the death messenger silently visited Ivanhoe Camp Ground and bore softly from our midst the soul of our dearly beloved Bishop. The last battle was fought and the unparalleled career of Bishop R. C. Horner was ended. Many of his friends—preachers and laymen—stood around watching the end, and were so deeply affected that from silent tears they broke into loud weeping. Just as his spirit was passing out the heart-broken gathering sang part of that beautiful hymn, "Say will the angels come?"

Death came so suddenly that it was impossible for his family to reach him before he passed away. We met his bereaved wife in Belleville, and when the sad news was broken to her, she mournfully said, "My darling is gone." After a slight pause she added, "Take me to him." Then standing on the station platform with her heart lifted in solemn resignation to the will of Him that doeth all things well, she quoted:

Servant of God, well done!
Thy glorious warfare's past,
The battle's fought, the race is won,
And thou art crowned at last.
And then she added, "And I know it."[1]

Bishop Ralph Horner had passed on to his eternal reward. His rich, full voice would no longer be heard echoing forth on the revival circuits or in the big gospel tents exhorting sinners to repentance and believers to seek entire sanctification. He would no longer cast a vision for young preachers to reach out to a perishing world with the hope of the gospel through faith in Jesus Christ. He had passed the torch on to his holiness children in the Holiness Movement and Standard churches. They would carry on his legacy.

FUNERAL SERVICE AT IVANHOE

A funeral service was conducted for Bishop Ralph Horner the next day, Tuesday, September 13, 1921, in the large gospel tent on Ivanhoe Campgrounds. The sermon was preached by Rev. James Smith. The preacher expressed his sense of inability to do justice to the occasion, but his discourse to the mourning audience was inspiring and encouraging and a fitting tribute to the life of Bishop Horner. The following is a summary of the sermon preached by Rev. Smith:

HE FOUGHT A GOOD FIGHT

Text: "I have fought a good fight, I have finished my course, I have kept the faith, henceforth there is laid up for me a crown of righteousness, which the Lord, the righteous judge, will give me in that day" (2 Tim. 4:7–8 KJV).

Introduction: Bishop Horner was converted when a young man, and at that time made such a complete surrender to God that he could be trusted with every grace and blessing through life. He was sanctified standing on his feet, and we have heard him tell how God poured out the Holy Ghost upon him while praying under a tree, before he ever heard the doctrine preached. Like Paul, he became a flaming evangelist.

In the Beginning: In the beginning of his labours, it would seem that life was to be a pleasant one. His pathway was strewn with flowers. We well remember his early labours up and down the land, hundreds flocking to hear him, and scores testifying to being saved and sanctified wholly. But he was soon to realize that instead of flowers, thorns would cover his pathway, because the carnal nature is at enmity with the doctrine and experience of real holiness.

He Never Wavered: Through evil report as well as through good he kept pressing on. His saying was, "You never saw me when I was not blest."

His Courage Was Undaunted: There were times when the world might say "He was defeated," but you never can defeat a man when God is at his back. The world might say he was, but this army of preachers and people are here today to testify to the fact that he has not been defeated.

He Finished His Course: It is a great thing to be able to look back over our lives at the last and say, "I have fought a good fight." It is also a great thing to be able to say, "I have finished my course." Our Bishop could say this. His work is accomplished. Only three years ago one of weaker faith and vision could see no future hope before us as a church. We had no churches, no parsonages, no campgrounds, and no institution of learning. But with his anointed vision he could look out into the future and see great possibilities, and not only see them but with his undaunted courage and perseverance he has brought these possibilities to pass. We are once more an army moving on to take the country for God. We are organized; we are incorporated; we are not embarrassed by his death. He has left us in good standing. We are moving along.

The Seminary Was His Last Work: [The Seminary] is the crown of his earthly life. For years he desired a suitable place where young people whom he loved so well might receive a proper education, and thus be fitted for their great calling in life. No one not in close touch with him knew what it has meant to him to prepare such an institution — the exhausting hours, the mental strain and self-denial. But he has realized his desire. He has seen it completed. He has finished his life's work, and now, like a great and brave general, he has gone without leaving a command behind.

His Faith Was Strong: His was not a dead, a formal faith, but a living one that brought to pass. How often we have heard him say he knew nothing about doubt. In the hours of deepest trial his faith never wavered; he was strong in faith, giving glory to God. His was a faith that brought every virtue and grace to his heart and life, and this continued to the last. He could truly say, like Paul, "I have kept the faith."

Our Tears Flow Freely: Our tears are not tears of sorrow. We are not sad. We think of our beloved bishop now not walking with feeble step and weakened body, but already he is treading the golden streets with elastic step and with a glorified body. He will be looking down over the battlements of glory upon us in the conflict here. Let us be faithful to the cause of holiness he so nobly defended, and uphold the doctrines that he preached.[2]

SAD FAREWELL

George Oldford continued his narrative of the sad and tearful farewell as the casket was slowly carried and loaded onto the waiting train at the Ivanhoe station:

After the service, the sorrowing multitude followed the remains to the station where they gathered around the casket and with swelling hearts sang, "Shall we gather at the River," "What a Friend we have in Jesus," "When the Roll is called up Yonder," and "Rock of Ages." While the casket was being placed on the train, the hymn "Meet Me There" was sung. Then came the saddest moment of all, when the train moved slowly away while the gathering again broke out in song, "Parting to meet again at the Judgment."

We returned to the Camp Ground feeling that the same spirit that had animated his Christian life and ministry was possessing our breast and that the God of our Father in the Gospel would be the Captain of our host and lead us on to victory.

One of the many things that shall ever remain in our memory of him is that in his last sermon he quoted the stanza so appropriate to the life-long ambition of his holy soul:

Happy if my latest breath,
I may but grasp His name,
Preach Him to all and cry in death,
Behold, behold the Lamb.[3]

FUNERAL SERVICE AT BISHOP HORNER'S HOME

A second funeral service for family and close friends was held at Bishop Horner's home, 16 Cameron Street, Ottawa, one o'clock, September 15, 1921. Rev. J. G. Nussey led this service and again read from 2 Timothy 4. His message declared that Bishop Horner stood out as one of the great men of the day. Words of tribute were given by Rev. A. A. Smith, Rev. S. S. Lindsay, Rev. R. J. Mayhew, Rev. Wesley McGaw, and Deaconess E. James. After her address, Deaconess James sang "Beyond the Silent River."

Most moving were the words of his sorrowing wife. As she stepped up by the casket and stroked his hand, she said, "Ralph, you have left me alone. Thou holy man of God, dearest of all husbands to me." Stroking his face, she said, "My precious clay, my precious clay. No more advice, no more counsel, no more rebukes, no more letters, my precious husband. Thy God is my God, thy people shall be my people. Farewell till we meet again."[4]

A large procession of sorrowing friends and family followed the casket to the cemetery at Merivale, just outside Ottawa. The remains of Bishop R. C. Horner were tenderly lowered into the grave in a grassy plot beneath two beautiful shade trees, there to await the general resurrection.

MEMORIAL SERVICE AT KINGSTON

A memorial service was held by the Kingston Conference at one thirty, September 28, 1921, at Kingston, Ontario. Rev. G. L. Monahan led the tributes to Bishop Horner by various men and women of the church by saying, "There has been a tremendous gap made in our ranks by his departure, but the Lord who made the gap will fill it, and the work will go on and prosper till the world is girded with salvation."

The tribute by the bishop's younger brother, Rev. George Horner, who had accompanied Ralph on so many campaigns and had been his close companion and guardian, was stirring:

I can go back farther than any of you. I remember way back when my father died. We grew up together on the farm, worked together, and served the enemy of our souls together. But the time came when we heard the noise of the shouting Methodists three miles away. My brother and I made up our minds to go and see them. The first sight which met our eyes as we came to the road was a banner over the gateway, "Clarendon for Jesus," and oh, the thrill that passed through my nature as I passed under it. . . .

The revival went on, and every one of us (Horner family) got saved . . . [and] it was not long after that I found my brother was called to preach. I thought it was all right, but wondered how he could manage, because neither of us could speak plainly, but God helped us through.

My brother's first appointment was his home circuit, where he remained two years. It was a flaming revival all the time. . . . The next meetings I attended . . . he told me to take a meeting, and we have laboured together ever since. . . .

Some think it was an awful calamity when he was put out of the church, but I do not. I have a feeling of gladness that my brother, who has gone to glory, has left a band all united. [Drowned in shouts for two or three minutes.]

Let us stand together by the old landmarks and be true to the doctrines of justification, sanctification and the baptism of the Holy Ghost and fire, and if we do this we shall see flaming revivals in which many souls will be born again.[5]

Letter of Tribute to Mrs. Horner

Dear Mrs. Horner,

Word has reached me of the sudden departure of your dear husband, the Rev. Bishop Horner, B. D. I hasten to extend to you our deepest sympathy in this your day of trouble. We feel that we have lost a great man, the holiness cause has suffered a severe shock, and the kingdom of our risen Lord has had its ranks weakened in losing such leadership. Many will rise up and call him blessed. A giant has fallen in our midst. . . .

Now I commend you to God and the word of His grace. You do not know me, but your dear, revered husband knew me. I pray that a leader will arise to lead the holiness forces to victory, and take up the great work that your husband so nobly commenced and carried through. May God sustain and bless you and your family.

Yours in His love.
Rev. John Stark
Methodist minister, Marbleton, Que.[6]

Press Releases

Newspapers announced Bishop Horner's death and departure with glowing praise for what he accomplished during his lifetime. Many were immediate, some much later. Three have been selected.

Brockville Recorder and Times

The day after Horner's death, the *Brockville Recorder and Times* published an announcement of his death claiming he suffered a paralytic stroke.[7] The newspaper also included a detailed synopsis of R. C. Horner's life: his birth in Clarendon, Quebec, his conversion at a Methodist camp meeting nearby, and his subsequent ministry in the Methodist, Holiness Movement, and Standard churches. There was glowing admiration for his accomplishments in ministry: "The late Rev. Mr. Horner was a man of marked energy and great organizational ability. He was stopped by no obstacles and successfully overcame every one which he encountered."[8]

OTTAWA JOURNAL

Charles Lynch writing in 1960 for the *Ottawa Journal*, summarized Ralph Horner's legacy nearly fifty years after his death:

Ralph Horner was the first of the Pontiac Horners to attain fame. . . . Before his death at 68 years, he had founded two churches and his spiritual influence was felt in Canada, The United States, and far distant countries. . . . This flashback of Bishop Ralph Horner shows him to be a controversial figure. . . . He was a convincing speaker and with his red beard and nearly six-foot frame was an inspiring revivalist.

Towards the end of the 19th century a spiritual revival took place in the Ottawa Valley. An outgrowth of this religious awakening was the Holiness Movement Church in Canada, organized in Ottawa in December 1895. Within five years the young Church, under the dynamic leader of Ralph Horner, had 118 places of worship, 5,643 members and adherents, and 80 ministers and evangelists. . . . [W]ork spread to all provinces of Canada except the Maritimes, as well to New York State, China, Hong Kong, the Sudan and Egypt. In Egypt, missionaries have been especially successful in establishing schools, teaching evangelism and pastoral activities. A flourishing Church in Belfast, Northern Ireland has supplied a record number of young men to the ministry of the Church.

In 1919, the Standard Church of America was formed and incorporated and within a few years congregations were formed in several states. . . . In 1920, the church was incorporated in

Canada and congregations were established in Quebec, Ontario, Saskatchewan, Alberta, and British Columbia. Missionaries were sent to China and Egypt. . . .

A strict but fair man he preached forgiveness and saw to it that his own family attended church four times on a Sunday. . . .

Bishop Horner and his flock did not drink or smoke, did not play cards and the men did not wear ties. No dishes were washed on Sunday and the food for Sunday was always prepared on Saturday. There was no work on Sunday of any kind. There was no travelling on Sunday and Bishop Horner would get off a train rather than travel on the Sabbath.

Bishop Horner died at a meeting at Ivanhoe Camp, Ont., after five strokes in September 1921.[9]

SHAWVILLE EQUITY

The *Shawville Equity* honoured their native son in the 1967 Centennial Edition that celebrated Canada as a nation by publishing a summary of the "illustrious, but controversial conversion and career" of Bishop Ralph Horner. The story concluded with a quote from Ralph Horner's memoirs: "Preachers, who are filled with power by the spirit of the Lord, and judgment, and might, are a terror to formal preachers." The writer ended with this comment: "Bishop Ralph C. Horner must indeed have been a terror to formal preachers and in the book his trials as such make entrancing reading."[10]

LAYPEOPLE MOURNED HIS DEATH

Despite the awareness of his failing health, the death of Bishop Horner sent shockwaves across the Standard Church and beyond. Many extolled the life and legacy of the late R. C. Horner. Jane Conley wrote in her memoirs:

In the fall . . . we were shocked and saddened to hear of the death of our beloved Bishop R. C. Horner. His passing was a great loss to the church. We mourned as for a Christian father, but the Lord, who is too wise to err, and too kind to be unjust, took him from his earthly toil. We believe he will reap a glorious harvest. He passed to his reward from the Ivanhoe camp ground, where he had fought many battles against sin and the Devil, and had won many souls for Jesus. He had said he wanted to die in the harness, in other words, at work for the Lord. He preached the day before his death and we are told he had to set down to finish his sermon. . . . A memorial stone was erected on the spot, and eventually the R. C. Horner Memorial Tabernacle was built.[11]

Family Mourned His Death

Very little has been written about Ralph Horner's family. Left to mourn were his faithful wife and coworker, Annie, and a family of seven: three sons—Ralph Jr., James, and Arnold; and four daughters—Myrtle Hale, Delma (Nettie) Galello, Annie Ray, and Hulda Ellison. The Horner children paid a price to have a famous father. They were called upon to sacrifice their father because of the busy life and demands placed upon him. Jim Wood had opportunity to interview Ralph Junior, the oldest son. Although Ralph Junior had a great deal of respect for his dad, he sadly related how his dad sold Ralph Junior's pony for two dollars to give the money to a needy mission. That was hard for him to accept, he said, and he left home at age fifteen. When asked if the prostrations in the services were real, Ralph replied, "They were real: I watched the people fall." The children often watched the services from outside the tent. None of them joined the church. Three of the daughters moved to California. They watched their dad—who had sacrificed everything—turned out of the church he had helped found, and they had difficulty accepting that treatment as fair and just.[12]

POSTLUDE

Dr. Peter Marshall once said, "The measure of a life is not its duration, but its donation." That worth is usually not assessed until after our death (and then only God is the ultimate appraiser). Who will carry on our memories? How many people have been touched in a positive manner? How many of these went on to touch others because of our actions? This is the measurement of a life—a legacy. The measure of Ralph Horner's life is being assessed to this day. His legacy is being carried on by his spiritual children and their churches: the HMC has since merged with the Free Methodist Church, and the Standard Church has merged with The Wesleyan Church; a small remnant remains as the Independent Holiness; various Pentecostal Assemblies of Canada have Hornerite holiness roots. Horner's legacy today numbers thousands of Christians and scores of churches across Canada, some even in the United States; the ripple effect has been felt in other countries such as Ireland, Egypt, China, Mexico, and Ghana.

Ralph C. Horner at time of ordination, 1887

Coworkers Chas. McInnis, R. C. Horner, J. V. McDowell, and John Waddell

Bishop R. C. Horner, May 1917

Bishop R. C. Horner with wife Annie

Annesley College, Ottawa

Missions HMC Rev. H. E. Randall,
first missionary to Egypt

Missions HMC Rev. A. Van Camp, China

Missions HMC Miss Sarah Longhurst, Egypt

Missions Rev. Earl and Annie Thompson
and family, Egypt

Missions SCA Rev. Ray Webster, Egypt

Missions SCA
Rev. Irwin L. Brown, Egypt

Missions SCA Rev. Martin and Ella Slack, Egypt

Stella Brown, Egypt

Missions SCA Rev. Kingsley and Dorcas Ridgeway and family, Egypt

Missions SCA Miss Irma Ergezinger, Egypt

Missions SCA Rev. Harold and Mary Berry, Egypt

Missions SCA Rev. Earl, Doris, and Henry Conley, Egpyt

Missions SCA Rev. Arnold, Evelyn, Peter, and David Rigby, Egypt

Missions SCA Rev. Eldon, Francis, Sharon,
and Merri-Lyn Craig, Egypt

Missions SCA Lydia Connaughty,
China

Missions SCA Tillie Danford,
China

Missions SCA Rev. William, Glenna,
and Evangelyn Wagner, China

Missions Rev. John Johnston,
China

Missions SCA Josephina, Soccoro, and Elva, Mexico

Missions SCA Rev. Joe, Jermima, Albert, and Diella Ocran, Ghana, West Africa, 1990

Missions SCA Naomi Green, Founder Missionary Society

Excavating and building Brockville Bible College, BBC, 1920

Brockville Bible College students, about 1936

Harold Moyles, resident
gardener and caretaker at BBC

Brockville Bible College and Seminary,
1921–1981

Selling produce to support BBC

Harold Moyles, BBC's corn man!

Reminiscing, Irwin and Jennie Brown
with Uretta

Reminiscing, Western Conference Preachers, 1930

Reminiscing, Kingston Conference, Standard Church, 1923

Reminiscing, Western Conference, 1950s

Reminiscing, Rev. David Parks and James Pring,
Newbrook Camp Meeting

Reminiscing, Rev. Joe Ocran and Jemima,
Ghana

Reminiscing, Rev. and Mrs. G. MacGarvey,
general superintendent

Reminiscing, Rev. Earl and Doris Conley,
Henry, Sandra, and Mary Lou, missionaries
to Egypt, general superintendent

Bishop, Rev. G. L. Monahan

General Superintendent
Rev. J. G. Nussey

General Superintendent
Rev. E. H. Thompson

General Superintendent
Rev. J. B. Pring

General Superintendent
Rev. I. L. Brown

General Superintendent
Rev. E. R. Conley

Reminiscing, R. C. Horner Memorial Tabernacle, Ivanhoe Camp Grounds

Historic, Standard Church General Conference, 2002

General Superintendent
Rev. G. MacGarvey

Historic, superintendents Rev. Don Hodgins
and Rev. George MacGarvey sign merger agreement

New home of District Headquarters for Central Canada District
of The Wesleyan Church, Brockville, Ontario

MOVING FORWARD

Who could fill the shoes of Bishop Horner? It was obvious no one would ever take his place, but the Standard Church was determined to carry on his legacy and work. A special session of General Conference was called at 44 Main Street, Kingston, Ontario, on September 26, 1921, to deal with the leadership void. The Conference opened at seven thirty by singing "A Charge to Keep I Have"—a fitting hymn for those who would carry the banner after the death of the founding bishop. The secretary, W. J. Watchorn, presided as chairman pro tem. Eleven of fourteen eligible elders answered the roll call. The Standard Church would organize according to the episcopal governance model that Bishop Horner adhered to. None of the deacons and deaconesses (sixty plus in the Kingston Conference alone) was present to help set the sail for the future of the church, and, for certain, no lay delegates attended.

The Conference recognized the necessity of electing a president to chair the meetings and lead the church. After a "lengthy and free discussion," there was an impasse. It was decided to adjourn and meet in the morning to reconsider the leadership and direction of the church.

The next day, Tuesday, it was the pleasure of Conference to elect a president by ballot. There were no nominations—each member of General Conference was considered an eligible candidate for election. Conference voted four times, and each time there was no election. Obviously, there was no general agreement among the eleven elders as to whom the leadership mantle should pass. Each time, Rev. G. L. Monahan and Rev. J. Nussey were separated by only one vote, but neither received the necessary 50 percent plus one majority. What should they do? Finally, Rev. G. L. Monahan was elected chairperson pro tem to preside over the Conference. It was not until a later special sitting of General Conference held on October 3—again at 44 Main Street, Kingston—that the unfinished business of choosing a president was addressed. Rev. G. L. Monahan was elected by a margin of 11 to 2 to become president of the Standard Church of America.

A committee was also launched to establish a memorial fund in memory of the late Bishop R. C. Horner. Further to this, a special committee was formed to enquire into any financial settlements necessary between the former Bishop Horner and the Standard Church, and to see that the needs of Mrs. Horner were provided for. The Conference also began to make provision to continue the work and ministry of denominational matters. Committees were formed to deal with the book room, the Standard Church Seminary in Brockville, and missions. Rev. James Smith was appointed by Conference to be editor of the *Christian Standard*, the official publication of the Standard Church, and G. Oldford, editor of the *Young People's Leader*, a weekly Sunday school paper distributed each week in the churches.[1]

THE MONAHAN YEARS

Rev. George L. Monahan proved to be an able administrator and leader. He was impressive, charismatic, and had an air of authority about him that reminded the church of Bishop Horner. He had black wavy hair, grew a moustache (even attempted a beard, which jokingly was referred to as a "matter of prayer"), and he stood on the platform like the old bishop when he preached. His grandson, Rev. Paul Johnston, recalls that Rev. G. L. Monahan was a fiery preacher with a deep resounding voice.[2] In 1925, he was elected bishop, having received almost unanimous approval from members of General Conference, certainly above the 75 percent as set forth in the Discipline of the church.[3] Rev. G. L. Monahan had obviously won the approval and respect of the Conference, for W. J. Watchorn reported in the October 30, 1925, edition of the *Christian Standard* that, "A notable characteristic of this Conference session which we must not fail to report, was the spirit of unity and harmony which prevailed. We believe this will yield a bountiful harvest of victory and success."

The church prospered under Rev. Monahan's able leadership. Bert Montgomery of Foresters Falls recalls Rev. Monahan as very personable, always giving advice, encouraging, solving problems, and walking about between services at camps and conventions with other ministers (especially the younger ones) to counsel and motivate them in their work. He remembers Monahan's favourite saying was, "We expect the tide to rise!"[4] In his tenure as president and bishop between 1921 and 1933, Monahan dedicated nineteen churches. By 1928, the Kingston and New York conferences totaled fifty-three churches with forty other appointments (many pastors had more than one circuit) for a total of ninety-three preaching stations. The tide was indeed rising for the Standard Church!

The 1925 October and November issues of the *Christian Standard* published encouraging reports from thirty-six Kingston Annual Conference churches. Many churches were small in number but were busy conducting revival services and reaching out to nearby communities and towns. Published reports included: Madoc Circuit (Madoc and Eldorado), Belleville, Bloomfield, Stirling, Cambellford, Harlowe, Elm Tree, Peterboro, Havelock, North Marmora, Toronto, Brockville, Athens, Smiths Falls, Bishops Mills, Seeley's Bay, Ottawa, Richmond, Kingston, Inverary, Yarker, Violet, Roblin, Pembroke, Foresters Falls, Beachburg, Renfrew, Chesterville, Morrisburg, Arundel, Montreal, Millfield, Covey Hill, Shawville, and North Clarendon.

The following reports are typical of submissions printed in these special editions of the 1925 *Christian Standard* during the Monahan days:

Bloomfield: We have some good material in the County of Prince Edward. Things are very encouraging. A new appointment has been opened in the prosperous town of Picton. Praise God! Three new members have joined the Bloomfield society. A real good convention was held in February followed by two weeks of revival services which were productive of much good. Some precious souls were born into the kingdom. We are looking forward to a great revival this winter. Pastor: Rev. Bert McRoberts.

Toronto: In the large, wicked city of Toronto we have a band of very faithful people. Despite the fact that the band is small it is large enough to stem the wicked tide of iniquity. Not one man, woman, or child has been turned away from the Standard Church Mission hungry. On very many street corners the gospel story has been preached to hundreds. Toronto is a great missionary field. Many poor souls have wept their way to the altar of prayer. We need your prayers and help in fighting such wickedness and penetrating such darkness. Pastor: E. Adams.

Pulaski Circuit (New York Conference): The work in Pulaski is coming along fairly well. The attendance is very good and the blessing of the Lord is in our midst. . . . The outlook for a revival is good and promising, as the people are willing to obey God.

Altmar: The work at Altmar is getting along better than in the past. The people have greater zeal to see God's work prosper and souls born into the Kingdom of God. Praise His holy name. A tract of ground has been purchased for the creation of a new church. The outside people are very much interested in seeing God's work growing in this place. The people are getting along well spiritually. Pastor: Rev. W. R. Young.

Feast of Pentecost Continues

Standard Church preachers and evangelists continued the tradition of meeting yearly at Lake Eloida during the Feast of Pentecost for renewal and doctrinal teaching on entire sanctification and the baptism of the Holy Ghost. Preachers were exhorted to pray for the experience and seek the infilling. Irwin Brown tells of attending his first Feast of Pentecost in May of 1921:

[The camp] was located on the north shore of Lake Eloida. Being shallow, with a muddy bottom, [the lake] was not conducive to swimming. It simply formed a picturesque background for the cottages on the shore. A large tent served as the place of worship. A liberal supply of straw served as the floor, and planks served as seats. There was a platform composed of two foot by eight foot planks. It had a narrow carpet along the side next to the congregation. A small table and two chairs were all the furniture needed. There was no pulpit. Such a thing as a pulpit was considered worldly. The preacher was expected to read the Bible, announce his text, then lay the Bible on the table and preach his sermon. No article of furniture separated him from his people. He must not have any notes for his sermon. All he had was a text. The altar consisted of a preaching platform. You went forward and knelt in the straw. The praying around the altar was loud; tears flowed; testimonies broke out spontaneously when the worshippers arose to go to their seats. Testimonies consisted of confessions, of stories and victories, of praised to God for His wonderful mercies. Feelings ran high, and testimonies were punctuated by shouts of "Hallelujah," "Glory to God," and "Praise the Lord, brother." Those were truly happy times of close fellowship and mutual concern for "the work" as the running of churches was frequently called.[5]

FOREIGN MISSIONS

Foreign missions have always had a special place in the hearts of Standard Church people. Recall that at the time the church was officially organized in 1918, an annual Missions Sunday was designated for November 10 of the same year and a board of missions was appointed with Rev. James Smith as treasurer. Rev. Earl Conley, long-time missionary to Egypt, diligently recorded the history of Standard Church missionary endeavors and most of the following is gleaned from his careful research.[6]

EGYPT

Rev. Ray Webster had heeded the call to go to Egypt and began to establish the work there.[7] Work was established in Nikhela, and news spread to other villages of the services. Nezlet el Milk and Berba, villages about ten miles from Nikhela, requested and were granted a lay pastor. Long days of toil, extensive travel, especially by donkey, and lack of proper diet resulted in serious deterioration of Rev. Webster's health, and he left for a much needed furlough in the homeland in 1922.

Earl Thompson, a Bible school boy just twenty-one years old, was welcomed to Egypt a short time before Rev. Webster's departure. His first sermon was "The Son of Man Is Come to Seek and to Save That Which Was Lost." Opposition to the gospel was gaining momentum, and his life was in danger at various times. On one occasion, after preaching a message, the brethren, fearing that harm would come to him, formed a protective wall around him and carted him on their shoulders to his room. Tuberculosis threatened to end his missionary career. The American doctor advised him to return to his homeland. However, fellow missionaries and the home church began to pray, and Rev. Thompson was healed and able to return inland and resume his ministry.

These were difficult days in missions! After weeks of seasick travel by freighter, early missionaries boarded dusty, drafty, uncomfortable trains, which moved inland at what seemed like a snail's pace. They were quickly introduced to a hostile climate where mosquitoes and flies never went away and fleas made their unwelcome appearance every winter. Often they lived in homes which we might describe today as humble huts, where they shivered in drafty, unheated rooms in the winter and sweltered in summer heat up to 45° and 50° C. Water was brought to their dwelling in goatskin bags, to be stored in a corner in large earthen vessels (*zeers*). Nights were brightened by light from a small kerosene lamp. Letters, which took weeks to arrive, reminded them of the distance between them and loved ones in the homeland. Loneliness and illness were never far away. The battle to conquer a strange and difficult language at times seemed hopeless. Days of toil and travel were followed by times of frustration, confusion, and stress.

In the fall of 1924, Martin and Ella (Hunt) Slack arrived in Egypt. They proved to be a valuable addition to the missionary staff in every aspect and greatly assisted in the expansion of the work. For a time the three missionaries shared a mud brick house in Nikhela. New villages were opened for the gospel, and day schools were established.

Rev. Thompson began a work in Sahil Tahta, twenty miles to the south. A small school for beginners was started, which broke down a great deal of prejudice. Many of these students became brethren in the church in later years. Several schools were established in other villages until government regulations made it impossible to continue. A lot was purchased in Nikhela for the purpose of building a mission home.

In 1924, there were three national workers in Egypt with three mission stations and four other villages where preaching services were conducted.

In 1925, the Slacks took up residence in Sahil Tahta and many souls were won to the Lord through their labours.

Plans were made for the construction of a chapel and mission home on the lot purchased at Nikhela. A chapel was also built at Nezlet el Milk. The work of Berba was being carried on by nationals.

The people of Egypt were receptive during this period. The government welcomed and even assisted missionaries in opening day schools. A new church was dedicated in the village of Nezlet el Milk in 1926. Revival services were in progress in Nikhela when Deaconess Stella Brown arrived in the fall of the same year. She joined right in and held services for women and children. Her home was always open to the village women and she did a very personal work among them, strengthening the Christians in their faith and encouraging them to mature in the things of God.

Each missionary's life had a great impact upon the Egyptian believers. One pastor tells of a service which Mrs. Slack took, and how she was anointed with the power of the Holy Spirit as she announced her text, "Ye shall receive power."

On January 4, 1927, the first Egyptian Conference was held with four missionaries and eight nationals. A revival at Nikhela was reported, with attendance of 300 to 500 nightly in an open courtyard. There were 125 conversions.

A property was purchased in the village of El Berba for the purpose of building a church. Construction was progressing on a new church in Nikhela and a parsonage at Nezlet el Milk. In 1928, Rev. Earl Thompson left Egypt for a much-needed furlough.

The Slacks spent two years of splendid pioneer work in Sahil Tahta. In December 1929, Mrs. Slack gave birth to her fourth son. Complications arose and she became seriously ill. On December 29, she went to be with the Lord while her husband was holding a convention in a tent in Tahta. She was buried in the cemetery at Drunka, just outside Assiut. Three months later her husband left for home with a broken heart and four motherless boys.[8]

Ten years had passed since the work had begun in Egypt. Congregations had been established in Nikhela, Nezlet el Milk, El Berba, Sahil Tahta, Mallawi, Naga Hamadi, and Zerabi.[9]

CHINA

Pioneer missions work in the name of the Standard Church was begun in mainland China under the dedicated ministry of Tillie Danford and Lydia Connaughty. These brave women felt God calling them to labour in inland Hunan Province, a mountainous area which had been decreed forbidden territory for foreigners and their religion.

In the spring of 1923, Miss Danford was accompanied by a Chinese evangelist who began a search for a house. The mayor had forbidden anyone to rent a building to foreigners. The only building he could secure was a small shack on a street outside the wall. This street formed the residential section for all the carpenters in the city and was often called Carpenter Street. The front room, with its earthen floor, served in the daytime as a shop in which furniture was made. At night the planks were returned to their places and securely fastened so that thieves could not enter. The Chinese evangelist set up housekeeping in the building and turned the shop into a room for him, so that his wife and Miss Danford might share the back room.

Lydia Connaughty, on furlough from China, had been looking after her aged mother. She accepted the challenge and started out to join Miss Danford in August of 1923, reaching the interior in October. After a lengthy trip of almost three hundred miles by riverboat and other means of transportation up the Yangtze River, the last stage of the tedious journey was made by mountain chair carried by coolies. Great difficulties were experienced as they attempted to establish a work in this remote area. The missionaries' first residence was a two-room shack at the river's edge furnished with boxes and borrowed benches. A property was eventually purchased outside the East Gate of Feng Hwang T'ing to be used as a mission home, with enough land to build a future chapel. In addition to local prejudice and suspicion, the ladies endured many other unfavourable circumstances. In spite of all this, they reported a successful year, and a new station opened in January 1924 at Kaotsun. They now had three national workers.

Famine, flood, civil war, and poor health hampered the missionaries during 1925. A larger building was rented for worship inside the city walls to meet the demands of the expanding work. The building, an old dilapidated one, blackened from the smoke of twenty or thirty years, was leased for a term limited to three years. The walls were first whitened with lime, some white paper was put over the old cupboards in the Chinese evangelists' two rooms, and two other rooms were used for inquirers and Sunday school classes. When finished it looked like a new place. The chapel had seating for nearly two hundred. Most of the floor was earth.

Foreigners, and missionaries in particular, were not welcome in China during the late twenties. Anti-foreign sentiment, which had accompanied the Nationalist Movement in China, was growing. Officials were unfriendly, and people on the streets were afraid of them. It was rumoured that the "foreign devils" were involved in the sale of opium and young girls. It was common to be reviled and cursed as they walked the streets. The exchange of currency was almost impossible. The lady missionaries in Feng Hwang T'ing endured all this during their years of labour. In addition there were the hazards of civil war, which at times was almost waged on their doorstep.

At a meeting of the missionary board on December 9, 1925, it was decided to send another missionary to China. Rev. John Johnston joined the team in ministry in the fall of 1926.

The turmoil in China was expanding as the communist forces were attempting to take control. The governor of Hunan Province was engaged in a campaign to drive them out. Many older people died as the famine spread.[10] Conditions in China were deplorable, owing to civil war and famine. Thousands were starving and dying. The sisters who had been faithfully labouring to establish a flourishing mission of the Standard Church in Feng Hwang T'ing, were greatly hindered from pursuing their regular work by the distress. God stood by His servants as they labored faithfully to assist the large numbers who were succumbing to famine and plague. A letter received from the field reported: "A large part of China is in the grip of an intense ant-Christian agitation and has resulted in widespread persecution." Early in 1927, a telegram was received from the British Consul ordering the missionaries to leave Hunan Province for their own safety and advised them to seek a place of safety in the security of Shanghai. More than five thousand missionaries were compelled to evacuate their stations. The board of missions decided that personnel should go home on furlough.

By the fall of 1928, reports indicated it was safe to return. The situation in China was still tense when Danford and Connaughty returned accompanied by two qualified teachers, Rev. William and Glenna Wager and daughter, Evangelyn. Rev. Johnston joined them at Hankow. A day of fasting and prayer was proclaimed by the board on behalf of China which represented one quarter of the world's population at the time.

The Wagers and Rev. Johnston witnessed the siege of Changteh. In May of 1929, they proceeded upriver, arriving after a seventeen-day journey, and joined the pioneer women, Danford and Connaughty, at Feng Hwang T'ing. After their return, the missionaries reported a sweeping revival.

With the outbreak of a new war, the mission board again made the sad decision to withdraw missionary personnel and close the work in China. In spite of wars, persecutions, and difficult circumstances, the work of the Lord in China goes on.[11]

CHINA EPILOGUE

The question might be asked whether the missionary endeavor by the Standard Church in China was worth it. Was the money sent from North America as well as the effort and sacrifice by faithful missionaries worth the cost? There are two answers to the question.

First, one must understand the passion and urgency of the missionaries' call. Lydia Connaughty wrote the following in her book that she coauthored with Tillie Danford to heighten the awareness of the need in China:

The so-called dark China has a dim light of our Lord Jesus shining upon her now. Do you want to help these people for Jesus' sake? . . . The city of Feng Hwang T'ing and the surrounding country are in dense heathen darkness. Women and girls are sold as you would sell cattle. Baby girls are often smothered or drowned at birth, as you would do away with kittens. A constant slave trade is being kept up, taking the girls to fill the houses of ill-fame, just for the lustful and evil passions of men. . . . What if it were your wife, or that sweet little innocent girl of yours? . . . Men, women, boys, and girls are taught that idols made of wood, brass, and earth can save them from their sins and give their souls rest and happiness. Yet they are miserable. Little Book, we send you forth with prayers and tears to do work for the Master in arousing concern for His lost ones.[12]

Second, one must see the work in China from a God-view. Time provides perspective not usually seen in the immediate present. The *Ottawa Citizen* carried an interesting report on China, May 14, 1994:

The meeting takes place in an unofficial house church outside the authority of the government recognized "patriotic" church movement. It is illegal, after China passed a law in February on religious activities. On the house porch you might find a foreign missionary denouncing idolatry and leading in prayers. His presence is also illegal.

Official statistics concede there are well over 1 million converts in Hunan province—which has a total population of 51 million, mostly poor peasants. There are mass meetings at night on hilltops, with tears and prostrations. Mass baptisms take place, again by night, in cold mountain waters. Hands are laid on the sick and crippled: miracles are attested. . . .

A couple of decades ago, says Balcombe, "missionaries spent a lifetime winning a few converts. Today the churches in every country grow by tens of thousands yearly."

Dr. Alton Gould, former Holiness Movement and Free Methodist missionary to Egypt, informed Rev. Earl Conley in about 1995 that the work started by the Standard Church in the early twenties in Ansiang (pronounced Anchung) was really expanding. He said they had out-grown their original meeting place so they purchased an old factory that became jam-packed. St. Paul understood the growth principle many years ago, writing to the Corinthians, when he noted, "I have planted, Apollos watered; but God gave the increase" (1 Cor. 3:6 KJV). The Standard Church mission planted in China, many watered, but God has given the increase which has multiplied many times over into a mighty church for God's kingdom.

THE WEST JOINS IN

As previously noted, the HMC had made considerable headway in western Canada—largely a reflection of westward migration from the Ontario heartland between 1896 and 1905, when the railway opened land for settlement. Pioneers moved to homesteads and took with them their holiness faith and practices and established about twenty-five churches—mostly in rural Saskatchewan. Many were located at either a rural crossroads or in a small hamlet; but eventually, children of homesteading pioneers moved to get jobs and employment in the cities, where they established churches from Winnipeg to Vancouver.

When the division took place in 1918, most western Holiness Move-ment churches remained with the mother denomination. Thus, if the Standard Church was to have a presence in the West, the new church was forced to establish mission works in new locations. This was good, for there was not the same sense of rivalry and competition between the two denominations in the West, but rather a greater sense of cama-raderie and fellowship. New fields of opportunity were opened to the Standard Church to share its message, and new areas were reached that otherwise might have been left untouched. Evangelists A. B. Carson,

David Parks, and W. J. Jackson conducted revivals in Alberta and began new churches in the communities of Newbrook, Vegreville, Athabasca, Mosside, and Amber Valley; works were also established in the cities of Calgary and Edmonton. The revivals were carried eastward to Carievale, Saskatchewan.

GOOD HOPE

The Good Hope Church and Campground, a 1.75-acre corner of land purchased from William Burnett a few miles east of Fort Saskatchewan, near Bruderheim, Alberta, belonged to the Holiness Movement Church. However, after the division in 1918, the congregation wished to join with the newly organized Standard Church. Obviously this was controversial and, as Ruby Steiert recalled, there was squabbling over this desire. But in the end, the Holiness Movement agreed to sell the church and campgrounds to the Standard Church. The local people said squabbling would never happen again, so they burned the deed—literally! Good Hope was the first Standard Church in Alberta and was an important centre because it had a campground where pastors and workers could congregate for spiritual invigoration and vision casting. It was an equipping and sending center for young men and women to enter the new fields of evangelism opening up to the western church.

Ruby (Cripps) Steiert, whose family farm was one-half mile north of the church, recalled that her father was very much put out that the Standard Church people were required to purchase their own church. However, the church continued as usual, and Ruby related that each Sunday services were judged "by the number of people who fell prostrate on the floor under the blessing of God." [13]

CALGARY

The next Standard Church established in Alberta of which we have record did not begin officially until seven years later. In the May 8, 1925, edition of the *Christian Standard*, an unnamed writer gave praise to God for the arrival of a pastor (unnamed) in Calgary during the extreme cold on December 20, 1924. The new pastor found a small flock of believers who were sheep without a shepherd. The writer continued by saying there had been no place in which to worship except homes since they had been without a pastor for some time. "On the first of January, God opened up a small hall . . . with nice living rooms for the pastor and his family. Meetings were started in earnest and the gospel was preached with no uncertain sound. . . . Since that time the congregation has been slowly increasing." Three other cottage prayer meetings were held "which had a stimulating effect" on the main services each Sunday.

SEVEN YEARS OF PROGRESS

By 1925, Rev. G. L. Monahan was enthusiastic in his report of the progress that had taken place within the Standard Church:

The Standard Church was organized seven years ago. It is indeed marvellous in our eyes what God has done for us since that time. Many prophesied that it could not even be incorporated, and even if it did, that it could not exist. . . . The Church is now incorporated in the Dominion of Canada, and in the United States of America. The ministerial ranks have almost doubled in numbers since it was organized. A beautiful property in Brockville, consisting of fourteen acres of land and a large brick house, was purchased for the Seminary, and a large three-story fire-proof building has been erected on it, valued at over fifty thousand dollars. . . . Nearly all the old appointments are now furnished with either newly built churches or churches bought from other denominations. . . .

Some camp grounds have been bought and paid for. Others have been leased for a long period of time. Besides these there will be a number of tent meetings conducted, opening new work in new places. . . .

It can be safely said that every branch of the work is progressing. Three churches have been dedicated during the past winter. One more is about ready. Others are under construction.

It is inspiring to the work to have so many young workers entering the ministry.

The revival spirit is greatly increasing throughout the whole connection. The end is not yet, praise the Lord forever! "Onward Still, is Jehovah's Will." If God be for us who can be against us? All things are possible to those who are apostolic in faith and power.[14]

THE PUBLISHING HOUSE

From the beginning, the printing press had been an important arm of Bishop Horner's ministry. He was a prolific author of church literature and doctrinal books; year after year, hundreds of softcover booklets containing his "Feast of Pentecost" sermons were distributed.[15] In the early years he had been the editor of the *Era*, which was published weekly—a mammoth undertaking! Even before the Standard Church had officially formed, Horner had begun publishing the *Christian Standard* on February 10, 1917, contracting the work out to the Jackson Press of Kingston, Ontario. In 1921, the young denomination purchased a small hand press and began operations in the new Standard Publishing House, which consisted of one room set up in the girls' dormitory at the college in Brockville. Type was set by hand for the four-page *Christian*

Standard, and the letter press was powered by the foot-pumping of several boys from the seminary. Mrs. Monahan became responsible for printing the paper. As the circulation of the *Christian Standard* increased and the popular Sunday school paper the *Young People's Leader* began to be distributed weekly, an electric motor was installed to run the press. Later the press was moved to the basement of the new Brockville Standard Church at 100 Perth Street. A linotype was purchased, and contract printing in the community became necessary to cover the cost of the church publications.

In 1928, a building was erected for the publishing house at 195 Perth Street, and the machinery was moved to that location. A horizontal press was purchased; soon a new linotype was installed; next a high-speed, automatic letter press; and later an automatic horizontal press. The Standard Church was continuing Bishop Horner's tradition of printing and distributing Christian literature to the churches and members.

LOOKING BACK

During the 1920s, the Standard Church ministered to many of the rural people in the Ottawa Valley and eastern Ontario. Progress was made in similar areas of the West, especially northern Alberta. Foreign missions continued to be strongly supported in Egypt and China. They were good years for the Standard Church. Years later, in the 1990s, Bessie Wager Seiter, a now-retired school teacher, reflected on those years of beginnings she experienced with her parents, Rev. and Mrs. Norman and Minnie Wager, in early Standard Church pastorates and wrote:

As I sit at my desk, I hear the drone of an airplane passing overhead. I am reminded of the different life we live in the nineties compared to life in the twenties. Then we had just begun to hear of airplanes and radios, and electricity was a luxury enjoyed by those living in town. We knew nothing of television, air conditioning, and computers, and travel was a slow process. We couldn't fly halfway around the world in a few hours. But we were content. . . . [We] were content because we didn't know about these modern conveniences. One thing we did know was about God. He was the same then as He is today. The Bible tells us that Jesus Christ is the same forever. If we commit our way to Him, He will be with us regardless of our circumstances.[16]

Called to Preach
(the 1920s)

A call to preach in the Standard Church was not for the faint of heart. Many young preachers and their families were deeply dedicated and committed and gave their lives sacrificially to preach the gospel. This chapter is about two of those preachers. Events and details are based on personal diaries in an attempt to help the reader enter into the life of a Standard Church preacher during the 1920s.

Norman Wager—Church Builder[1]

Norman and Minnie Wager lived in Rosebush, Michigan, and attended church with their family. Norman was Sunday school superintendent and very active in music. The Wagers had been content with their life until two female evangelists—Miss Christie and Miss Watchorn—were invited to Rosebush to hold revival services. The Wagers attended the services and soon found they desired something they did not have—a personal experience with Jesus Christ as Lord. Conviction pricked Norman's heart, and one day while alone in the horse stable he gave his heart to Christ. Minnie resisted, but eventually she too yielded and accepted Christ as Lord of her life.

A short time later, in the summer of 1920, the Wagers sensed an unrelenting call to full-time Christian ministry and volunteered to serve in the Standard Church. They were promptly stationed without mentoring or Bible college training at Bloomfield, Ontario. Norman and Minnie rented out their farm, sold some of their household goods, and began to pack their Model-T Ford. The car was loaded to capacity: suitcases tied to the outside of the vehicle, Minnie's copper boiler strapped on one side of the car, and bedding piled so high on the backseat there was scarcely room for the three Wager girls to find room to sit.

Five hundred bumpy miles and three long days later, the Wagers finally arrived at their first destination: Ivanhoe Camp Meeting. They were cordially greeted by several families from Bloomfield. Beds were made, and the Wagers were informed they were to have their meals with Mrs. Edward Cannon in a large tent set up for cooking.

After the evening meal, everyone knelt on the ground around the table, and another gentleman, also a guest, led in prayer. The Wager girls were fascinated because he prayed so loudly—he could be heard to the distant recesses of the camp. Moreover, he rocked back and forth vigorously on his knees as he prayed. This was the Wagers' introduction to the first Standard Church missionary, Rev. F. R. Webster.

BLOOMFIELD

On the Monday following Ivanhoe Camp, the Wagers stuffed themselves back into their heavily laden Model-T and chugged off for Bloomfield, only to learn their goods from Michigan were not yet there. Again, accepting the hospitality of the Cannon family, the Wagers were lodged until their luggage finally arrived.

The parsonage in Bloomfield was rented and consisted of three medium-sized rooms downstairs and three upstairs. Since there was no church building, the small parlor in the pastor's house served as the meeting room for the growing congregation. Sunday school not only took up the parlor but the dining room and kitchen as well. It was not long until Norman Wager persuaded the congregation to rent a hall downtown until such time as a church could be built.

Soon the Wagers moved across the street into a more comfortable house as well. They did not have running water, but they did have the luxury of electricity. The electricity was not metered, so the electrical company would send a man once a month to count the light bulbs, and charge the household a minimal fee per bulb.

Bloomfield, Ontario, is a rural community located on an island in Lake Ontario, a few miles from Belleville and surrounded by the natural beauty of orchards and vineyards. The Wagers picked strawberries and cherries in season and worked occasionally in the canning factories. Wages were used to supplement the Wager income since Standard Church ministers did not receive a salary but were dependent upon the Sunday offerings for their living. Their daughter Bessie recalled that much of what her father earned, however, was deposited into the building fund for the badly needed new church.

Soon a small building lot by the creek owned by the Mabel Thompson family was purchased. More sacrificial donations began to arrive. Mrs. Wilmot (Eulah) Steenburgh purchased a cottage on Beaver Lake for one hundred dollars from her meager savings. The owners sold the cottage to Mrs. Steenburgh, knowing any profit was to be used for a church. The property was resold for five hundred dollars and the entire amount donated to the new church fund.

Mr. James Molyneaux donated trees on his farm for lumber. His son, Ralph, Rev. Wager, and other volunteers from the community cut trees and hauled them to Cooper's Mill in Bloomfield to be sawed into lumber.

Building began as early as possible in the spring of 1921. The lot was cleared and cleaned, and Rev. Wager, Ralph, and men of the church began the work of putting up the walls. The first gravel was drawn, one yard at a time, by Edwin Steenburgh, a teenager, with his pair of ponies. Cement was mixed by hand. Edwin also drew the cement and finishing lumber for the church from the Dayton Lumber Company in Picton.

By fall the church was completed and ready for the dedication service. A district convention was held in the new church. Host churches usually provided food and lodging for the guests who attended three services each day during these five-day events. Most churches had a kitchen in the basement where the meals were prepared, but the Bloomfield church was not yet completed, so people were fed in various homes.

The dedication service was set for Sunday afternoon. The president of the Standard Church, Rev. G. L. Monahan, was in charge. The church was packed to capacity and the children were seated around the altar at the front. It was an occasion to be celebrated and remembered by the congregation who had worked so diligently for this moment.

But alas! Pastors were stationed for no more than two years on a circuit. In her diary, Bessie said, "Only a miracle could extend that stay to three years." Two years passed very quickly, and it was with anxiety and anticipation that Norman Wager attended Conference in September just after school had started. Suspense reigned as pastors did not know where they might be sent. Saturday afternoon, the closing day of Conference, finally arrived, and Norman heard his next appointment read: Norman Wager, Belleville. His family waited with anticipation at home for the news.

BELLEVILLE

Belleville was only about twenty miles away, but to the three Wager girls it was the other side of the world. The Wagers' new home was one side of a duplex in the north end of Belleville on Grier Street. The owner lived in the other half. The house was small—three rooms downstairs and two small bedrooms upstairs. There was no electricity, running water, or indoor plumbing. A small barn outside was available, and since the Model-T had seen better days, Norman sold the car and bought a horse and buggy.

Church was held in a downtown hall on Bridge Street. A Chinese restaurant was on the first floor and the owner of the restaurant lived on the third floor. The Standard Church was sandwiched in between. There was a front stairway from the street that was used by most attendees who came to the church. The Wagers, however, usually entered through a back entrance because there were places in the alley to hitch horses and buggies. They climbed an outside stairway to a flat roof and entered through a window, which was easily opened. Conditions for the church were far from ideal, but Norman Wager continued his work of preaching and calling along with his usual burden of prayer.

Two miracles took place in Belleville that made an indelible impression on the Wager family. Norman's suit was wearing out, especially at the knees. Minnie was an experienced seamstress—she had been a dressmaker—but mending the suit had nearly come to an end. All the same, the Wagers did not have the extra money to buy a new suit. Yet, neither Norman nor Minnie told anyone, except God in prayer, about this pressing need. One Sunday morning after church, one of the women from the congregation stepped up to the preacher and said, "Brother Wager, the Lord tells me I should buy you a new suit. Go to the tailor shop, have one made, and send me the bill." Now a tailor-made suit was a luxury the Wagers could not afford. To the family, it proved that God gives abundantly above and beyond all we could ever ask for.

There was also a miracle of healing. Rev. Wager suddenly became ill one Sunday night after church. He was in such pain that a doctor was summoned. After examining him, the doctor diagnosed a severe case of kidney stones. The pain continued for three days and the doctor finally said, "Tomorrow we'll have to take you to the hospital and I'll operate." In the 1920s, any surgery was serious. Besides, how would the Wagers pay for the surgery? There was no health insurance and money was scarce. Norman Wager prayed, "Lord, why can't You heal me now?" Suddenly, Rev. Wager heard the Holy Spirit say, "Get up and dress; go out to the kitchen and tell your wife you aren't going to have another attack." Norman obeyed and never had another kidney stone attack as long as he lived!

Minnie Wager did not usually volunteer for jobs at the church. Her ministry gift was hospitality. She enjoyed entertaining company at home. Nevertheless, one warm summer morning Minnie called her daughters into the kitchen and announced that they were to take care of the house that day. With tears coursing down her cheeks, she removed her apron, faced her girls, and declared, "I am going out to raise money to build the new church." She took a small pad and pencil and started down the street. Minnie Wager tramped over the city with the message, "God has sent me to raise money to build the new church." Needless to say, later that evening, she returned home with enough pledges and cash to start building a new church.

One day, Rev. Wager heard about a family living on a farm near Cannifton, who had once been in the ministry and following the Lord. Minnie and Norman called on this family and, after prayer and persistent love, the W. H. Shadbolt family returned to the church. Mr. Shadbolt tore down a barn that had some fine timbers and donated them to the new church building. Since Rev. Wager was a gifted carpenter and the people knew how successful he had been at Bloomfield, the pastor was chosen to lead the building committee. Again, Rev. Wager and many dedicated people spent countless hours with hammers and saws working on the new building. But finances were tight, so Rev. Wager made a quick trip to Michigan, mortgaged his farm, and used the money to continue building the new Belleville church.

The building was almost completed when the two-year rule came into effect. When the stationing list was read at Conference, Rev. Wager was appointed to the Ivanhoe Circuit and he was unable to finish the interior of the Belleville church. Many regretted that Rev. Wager was not permitted to remain for the dedication service, but such was the discipline and custom of the Standard Church.

IVANHOE

The Ivanhoe Church was situated near the Ivanhoe campgrounds, but the parsonage was in the tiny village of Crookston. The house consisted of three rooms downstairs and two upstairs. There was no indoor plumbing, water, or electricity. A long woodshed and little barn, where Molly the horse lived alongside the buggy and cutter, was fastened onto the kitchen. The kitchen was a wing on the back of the house built on posts with no foundation under it. Needless to say, it was unbearably cold in the winter. On warm winter days, Minnie would cook batches of homemade beef stew and vegetable soup to put aside for the cold snaps when the kitchen would be closed off. On cold winter evenings, the prepared food was reheated on the woodstove used for warming the house.

When the Christmas season arrived, one of the parishioners gave the Wagers three frozen, dressed geese to enjoy. But a few days later, Norman decided to visit a family who was attending the Ivanhoe church; he packed a box with vegetables, fruit, nuts, and one of the frozen geese. He invited his daughter Bessie to go along with him to deliver the Christmas gift. Bessie had never in her entire life seen a home like the one at which they arrived. It consisted of one room with a cook stove, an old cupboard, a table with broken chairs, and some homemade bunkbeds in two corners. Bessie would never forget the children's faces as they saw the Christmas treats. "It made me feel very rich indeed," recalled Bessie.

Bessie loved Ivanhoe and wanted to stay there forever! She attended a good school, had good friends, and attended a church she enjoyed very much. She often stayed after school to clean blackboards for Miss Blue, her teacher; the two would then enjoy the walk home together along the country road. But again, Conference decided her father's skills were needed to build another church, so after only nine months at Ivanhoe, immediately after Pentecost, the Wagers moved to Madoc. Norman decided to sell Molly, the horse, to buy another Model-T, and Bessie said good bye to her friends, her school, her teacher, and her pet horse, and moved with her family to the Madoc Circuit.

MADOC CIRCUIT

Madoc consisted of three appointments: Madoc, Eldorado, and Plane Settlement. Plane Settlement met in the country schoolhouse; Madoc held services in the Orange Lodge Hall; Eldorado owned a small church at the north end of the village and represented the largest attendance of the circuit.

Rev. Wager's schedule on the Madoc Circuit was rigid. Each Sunday morning there was a Sunday school and preaching service at Eldorado (Minnie stayed in Madoc to help in the Sunday school). Mr. and Mrs. Allie Fox provided Sunday dinner for the minister so he need not return home. After a quick meal, Norman would hurry off for the afternoon Sunday school and church service at Plane Settlement. Later, tired and fatigued, he would return home with just enough time to relax a short while before the evening service in Madoc. People from the three appointments gathered in Madoc for an old-fashioned Sunday evening revival meeting of singing, preaching, praying, and testimonies. Sunday was exhausting, but Monday morning Norman would continue his pastoral calling and preparation for three prayer meetings to be held during the week!

Madoc was a large farming area. Church members brought in crocks of homemade butter, cans of maple syrup, pork hams, and various in-season produce from their gardens. The Devolin family at Plane Settlement donated one gallon of milk each prayer meeting night; this was fine in cool weather and the milk would stay sweet for some time, but in warm weather, Minnie would boil the milk and keep it in sealers to be stored in the cellar.

At other times, parishioners would donate a half beef. This would create quite a process as the meat was always canned—a major task of cutting the meat and stuffing it into sealers. Norman would bring out the old copper boiler Minnie had brought from Michigan and place the sealers in the boiler filled with water. While the meat was boiling on the kitchen stove, the suet was cut into small pieces, placed in pans to "fry out" in the oven, and later set aside to be mixed with Gillette's lye in an iron kettle to make white bars of soap used for washing clothes. Canning meat was a lot of work, but when Minnie served canned beef with gravy and mashed potatoes, nothing surpassed it for flavor.

Norman Wager had been sent to Madoc to help build another church. A sizable lot beside the parsonage had been designated for the new building. A large load of used lumber had been donated and placed in the backyard of the parsonage. The three Wager girls, along with their mother and a neighbour, Mrs. McDonald, busily hammered out the old nails so the lumber could be reused in the new church. The people of the church were very generous in helping as much as they could, but the responsibility of the project was on Norman Wager. He spent long hours working on the building as well as preparing for three services each Sunday. Many days when he retired, he was so weary he could barely function, only to follow the same schedule the next day. Often he would say to Minnie, "It's very hard to build a church and be a pastor, too." Moreover, there were always the persistent parishioners who did not realize the heavy load he carried and would expect frequent pastoral visits as well.

The Madoc church was completed in 1926. A convention had been scheduled as a lead up to the Sunday dedication service. Sunday morning was the climax, and sitting on the platform were all the people who had come to help dedicate the church Norman and the congregation had built.

The dedication service was inspiring, but the tantalizing odor of food cooking in the basement wafted throughout the congregation and promised more good things to come. Downstairs, Mrs. R. J. Druce, assisted by her minister husband, was busily preparing dinner. The Druces were a delightful couple known for friendly conversations, jokes, and a wonderfully winning way with children and youth. When the service was finally over, which lasted longer than usual because of the dedication, dinner was served. And what a meal: roast beef, mashed potatoes and gravy, vegetables, and all topped off with homemade pies! This was Standard Church heaven!

The Wagers drove their Model-T as long as possible that fall. But when snow began to fall and temperatures began to drop, a change of transportation was needed because there were no snowplows to keep the drifted roads open. Norman drained the Ford's radiator and placed the wheels on blocks for the winter. A kind gentleman who operated a tailor shop downtown owned a horse. He asked the Wagers if they would like to drive the horse in return for giving the horse care through the winter. The Wagers had a horse to drive for two winters. On cold Sunday mornings, Bessie, laden with such heavy clothes she was scarcely able to move, climbed into the cutter beside her dad. Minnie added a flat iron to keep feet warm, and off trotted father and daughter over the winter roads to conduct the Sunday services in the little churches that belonged to Norman's circuit. Bessie said, "I really enjoyed these cold winter Sunday mornings with my dad."

The Wagers were just becoming well acquainted with the people of their circuit, when in the spring of 1927, the stationing committee of Annual Conference announced Norman Wager would be appointed to Arden. Arden had experienced a revival during the winter of 1925–1926 under the ministry of Rev. Frank C. Harris. Another church needed to be built.

ARDEN

Arden was a wilderness paradise: a beautiful land of lakes, rivers, forests, hills, and colourful rock formations a few miles off highway 7 between Kaladar and Sharbot Lake. The Arden congregation had rented a house on the main street of town across from the mill pond. But the mosquitoes and black flies were horrendous. Early in the spring, Minnie purchased several yards of woven cloth, the consistency of window screening. With her hammer and box of tacks, she tacked the netting in each window until all of the windows were screened and ready for the onslaught of vicious insects.

Wild blueberries grew in abundance on the rocky hillsides, and raspberry canes grew in many of the brush piles along the edges of properties. Many quarts of fruit and preserves were placed on the shelves; more berries were spread on clean sheets to dry and later became ingredients for delicious cobblers and pies.

The work in Arden had only begun in 1926. Rev. Frank Harris had conducted revival services in Elm Tree during the winter of 1925–1926 and the revival spread to Arden. Revival services were held in the Arden town hall.

A camp meeting, part of Hornerite culture, was planned for that summer. When Rev. Wager arrived late in the spring of 1927, he was appointed to be in charge. That summer, the big gospel tent was pitched not in the woods, but in an open field adjacent to the town. During the heat of the day, the tents on the grounds became so hot they were almost unbearable. The Wagers were fortunate—the camp was located near their home and they enjoyed the luxury of sleeping in their own comfortable beds each night. The camp was well attended, although not nearly the size of Ivanhoe.

Work on the new church began, and Norman Wager led in the construction of the building. John Hayes, better known as Jack Hayes, donated the property. He was not a regular attendee of the church, but his wife was a devout Christian and a faithful member of the Arden church. Mr. Hayes also loaned money to purchase the necessary materials to begin construction, and the foundation was dug and cement poured. Logs were donated, lumber sawed, and gradually the Arden Standard Church began to be erected.

Many local people were generous in doing all they could to assist. Mr. and Mrs. Charlie Snyder were special friends and worked hand in hand with Norman. Sometimes Rev. Wager became concerned that Charlie was working too hard, so together they would take a few hours and go fishing in the abundant lakes nearby.

A number of volunteers from other districts came to help. One such visitor was Rev. H. S. Hornby from the new Brockville Seminary. He stayed about three weeks. The Wager girls enjoyed his visit because he was a great conversationalist and they enjoyed his intellectual discussions. During his stay, he would rise early each morning before anyone else was awake and go for a swim in the mill pond across the street. He said it invigorated him for the day.

Minnie faithfully cooked for those who were helping to build the church. It did not matter how many were working on a particular day, Minnie would prepare dinner for all: a full noon table was the norm and God blessed her with a marvelous ability to take little and make a delicious meal. Some would stay overnight, and Minnie with her gift of hospitality always found rooms and made them feel at home.

Norman also kept up his busy schedule of preaching at three different charges: Sunday morning he helped in the Sunday school and preached at Elm Tree; Sunday afternoon he preached at Dead Creek (Borden-wood); Sunday evening service was held at Arden in the old town hall, and everyone from the district was encouraged to attend. Many came. However, the town hall was not a pleasant place to hold church services since a dance was usually held on the premises Saturday night and the hall was in dire need of cleaning before the service could begin. Norman also conducted three prayer meetings each week and summer found him fulfilling his responsibilities for the camp meeting. There is little wonder that many nights Norman and Minnie would retire exhausted.

The church went up in record time and was almost completed when Norman and Minnie suddenly were required to return to Michigan to put their farm and finances in order after so many years of renting and neglect.

ROSEBUSH, MICHIGAN

Upon returning to Michigan, the Wagers became pastors of the Rosebush Standard Church. Soon, a new family began attending. Their son was converted, and a few years later he married Bessie, the Wagers' daughter. They became high school teachers and spent many summers as children's workers and singers at summer camp meetings. Bessie stated in her memoirs: "If my parents had not served the Lord with all their hearts, I would not be a Christian today." What better legacy could Norman and Minnie Wager leave behind!

IRWIN BROWN—MAKING OF A LEADER[2]

Irwin L. Brown became one of the most prolific writers in the Standard Church. His writings not only describe the church culture and methodology, but also recall the hardships faced by many of the young men and women who pioneered churches.

Irwin Brown was born on June 25, 1904. His mother, Martha (nee Jackson), died when he was two years old and he was left with no memory of her whatsoever. His six-month-old sister, Verna, was adopted by Martha's older sister, Catherine Post. The three other children, Orville, nine; Mable, seven; and Irwin were left at home in the care of their father. Irwin's father did not remarry—he worked every day to support his family, leaving early in the morning and not returning until about six thirty each evening. Irwin recalled that Orville and Mable managed the house and got the meals. The three children saw little of their father except in the evenings and on weekends. "How we children survived is a mystery to me!" Rev. Brown wrote in his memoirs.

When Irwin was sixteen, he went to work with his brother Orville on a highway project in Michigan during the summer of 1920. One day he received a letter from his sister Verna, who was living with his aunt Catherine near Belleville. She told Irwin in her letter how the Lord had saved her. This was foreign to anything in Irwin's thinking, and he did not understand what she was telling him. Upon returning home to Belleville in December, Verna called and invited him to go to church with her. The church was a large room on the third floor of a building on Bridge Street. Irwin said he started going to church with his sister and liked to walk home with her to Cannifton.

The services in the Standard Church were different from anything Irwin had ever experienced. The congregation prayed simultaneously out loud, sang enthusiastically, and repeatedly responded with hearty amens to show approval to the preaching. The minister's name was Tom Seal, and Irwin described him as a big, good-natured Irishman. It took him five minutes or so to get preaching, but once he got into his sermon, his thoughts flowed smoothly. His voice was pleasant and he was always smiling as he preached. "I liked him," remembered Irwin. "When he shook your hand he pumped your whole arm as if it were a pump handle."

Whenever he went to church, recalled Irwin, the people were always kind and friendly. "They talked to me about getting saved, but I did not have the remotest idea what they meant."

Winter came, and Naomi Brown and her sister Bessie invited Irwin to attend a convention on January 12, 1921, held in the village of Eldorado. People were attending from Belleville, and Irwin sat with his friends at the back of the primitive church filled to capacity with those who had come to hear Rev. G. L. Monahan preach. Monahan was a gifted preacher and orator, mentored by Bishop Horner to be a revival evangelist. Irwin later recalled his conversion experience:

I do not remember what he preached about, but my heart was strangely moved. At the end of his sermon he gave an altar call. Hardly realizing what I was doing, when the people started singing, I started for the altar. The Spirit was moving on my heart, I know that now. . . . People gathered around me to pray for me and with me. I did not how to pray, but in my heart I was saying, "Lord, save me." . . . After an hour or two of praying, I decided to really believe that Jesus did forgive me. I straightened up, closed my eyes and said to Jesus, "I do believe You save me now." It was like leaping off a cliff and falling upon jagged rocks; but, just as I neared the rocks, I felt warm arms beneath me. They were the arms of Jesus. I had cast myself upon Him.

Later on, all who had prayed at the altar were asked to give their testimonies. I had never done anything like that in my life.

I stood up and said, "Jesus takes all the starch out of me!" A strange testimony you may say, but it worked for me. My soul rejoiced, even if I had no words to express it.[3]

CALL TO MINISTRY

Irwin Brown faced a conflict two months after his conversion. The people in the Belleville church began to pray that God would call him to preach. It was true, Irwin confessed, he did feel an inward impulse that said in his heart, "God has called me to preach." One day, the pastor, Rev. Seal, said to him, "I have to be away this Sunday, and I want you to take the morning service for me." Irwin was stunned, but he consented to do so. He would always remember that service. He preached a half hour and surprised himself. Truly the Lord helped him. This service confirmed his conviction that God had called him to preach or at least be involved in some kind of ministry. In response to that call, Irwin Brown gave his life, not only to preaching and evangelism, but for many years teaching in colleges and training hundreds of young men and women for the Christian ministry.

Irwin made known his call to preach and attended the Feast of Pentecost that spring at Lake Eloida. He was assigned a partner, William Snow, and the two teenagers were appointed to preach for the summer in Malone, a country village about six miles west of Eldorado, where there was no church—only a general store, a railroad station, and couple of outbuildings. The boys made contact with Mr. and Mrs. Fox and stayed with them for a short time. They went visiting around the countryside and preached in farmhouses where friendly people offered hospitality.

Eventually, the two young preachers acquired a tent about fourteen by fourteen feet in size. They pitched the tent in the commons, a large area owned by the government. Farmers used the commons for pasturing calves and cows. Unknowingly, the boys had pitched their tent across a cow path. One night, while the boys were sleeping, something startled the cows and they came stampeding along the path on which the tent was pitched. The boys were rudely awakened by the stamping of hooves, and the snorting and bellowing of frightened cows as they trampled over the tent, knocking it to the ground. Fortunately, Irwin and William were not injured. The boys lit their lanterns and surveyed the damage. Miraculously, the tent was not torn nor the center pole broken, and soon they had repitched the tent—this time, just a little off the cow path! The next day, the young preachers dug postholes, cut small trees for posts, and erected a strong fence as a fortress around their tent.

Services were moved to a drive shed—a place where buggies and wagons were stored out of the rain, sun, and snow. It was a fairly large shed and accommodated about thirty people. The young preachers made plank seats, placed a preaching table at one side of the shed, and decorated it with cedar boughs for fragrance. Irwin reported that many people were invited to the old drive shed and were converted to follow the Lord.

BACK TO SCHOOL

Rev. G. L. Monahan informed Irwin and William that they were to attend the seminary in Brockville that fall. Irwin was dumbfounded. He had no idea how he could buy the necessary books for his studies. He was in his eighteenth year and had never finished public school. Undaunted, he trusted God to make up for lost time and finish high school. During the year, his clothes became so patched and his shoes so badly worn that someone gathered an offering of twenty dollars and gave it to him so he could purchase shirts, socks, shoes, and other needed clothing. Irwin's clothes had become so ragged that all he had to wear for his preaching was a sleeve and preacher's collar to which he attached a dickie (preacher's front) to hide his bare chest. New clothes meant no more need for the dickie—God had provided and he was now well dressed!

SUMMER REVIVALS

When the school year ended in 1922, Irwin Brown was once again appointed for service by Rev. G. L. Monahan: he would aid Rev. J. B. Pring in revival services at Beachburg, Ontario. A tent was pitched in a sheltered grove on a lot at a crossroads location. Meetings were held every evening except Saturdays, and twice on Sundays. A surprising number of people attended these services and Irwin was called upon to preach many times. They were joined by Rev. Martin Slack who knew the area and owned a lively horse and a buggy; he took Irwin to visit the people around the countryside. They called on people, prayed with them, and invited them to the services. Many claimed to be converted during those meetings.

After the summer, school again commenced and Irwin was back at the seminary to begin his grade nine. To earn some cash, he was put in charge of the two furnaces at both buildings. He studied hard and passed the government examinations. He was now nineteen years old and ready for more summer evangelism.

MORIN FLATS AND ARUNDEL

When classes were finished that spring, Rev. Monahan said to Irwin, "I want you to go to a place in Quebec called Morin Flats [later renamed Morin Heights].[4] There is a church building which is now empty, but a few people living in Morin Flats used to come to the church. I want you to open up that church and start a work there."

Irwin was dumbfounded. He had no money, and his shoes had again become worn and tattered. How could he possibly go to Morin Flats? When he told Rev. Monahan of his plight, he was given money to buy a pair of shoes and a rail ticket to Montreal. In Montreal, Irwin made his way to the Standard Church Mission, where Rev. Rosco Hawley was pastor. He stayed over Sunday and preached in the mission. Rev. Hawley gave the young preacher enough money to buy his ticket to Morin Flats, and Irwin left Monday for his new circuit.

Morin Flats was an adventure. There were no contacts and no one to meet Irwin at the station. Stopping at a small, white cottage, Irwin asked to come in to read the Bible and pray. The elderly couple, relatives of the Watchorn family, invited him to join them for the evening meal and offered him a bed that night until he could rent a room the next day. The rundown church needed extensive dusting and cleaning to be ready for services. Irwin went to every home in town announcing the opening of the church on Sunday evening. Sunday came and the door was open. But not one person came. Irwin was totally disappointed.

Discouraged, Irwin determined to go to the town of Arundel, about twenty miles north of Morin Flats, where another Standard church was located in full operation. He took his trunk and met the pastor, Rev. Rolland Crozier. He warmly welcomed Irwin and invited him to take his services for two weeks while he went on a vacation. Within two weeks, Irwin received a letter from Rev. Crozier saying his children had measles and it would be a month or two until he returned. Irwin Brown had the church all to himself for the rest of the summer. He received some good offerings and had a congregation to preach to and people to visit. He stayed until it was time to return to Brockville to attend another year at the seminary.

Studies Continue

When Irwin Brown graduated from grade eleven, he was considered to be educated. "Too much education was considered to be harmful to spiritual life."[5] Consequently, at a meeting of the elders of the Kingston Conference, the decision was made to station him at a church. Rev. J. B. Pring, a very close friend and spiritual father who was a member of the stationing committee, informed Irwin of the plan. Irwin objected, insisting that he graduate from high school first. Rev. Pring reported this to the committee, and they agreed to allow Irwin to return to the seminary. It was a difficult year, however: smallpox invaded the seminary and many became ill. The school was fumigated and two or three were sent to an isolation hospital. However, Irwin finished his grade twelve studies that year and continued the next year, graduating from grade thirteen. With this level of education, he was assigned to teach at the seminary under the leadership of the new principal, Miss Elizabeth Convey.[6]

MISSIONARY PASTOR

In May of 1927, Irwin Brown was appointed to his first full-time pastorate in Moira, Ontario, a few miles from Ivanhoe campground. It was a small village consisting of a general store, two or three houses, a blacksmith shop, and a Standard Church. Since he had no car or horse, Irwin made pastoral visits on his bicycle. His congregation numbered about twenty, and consisted of farmers from the country and a few families from the village. One family in particular had a daughter, C. Hazzard, who became an evangelist in the Standard Church. Her companion was Miss Richardson. Both women were excellent speakers.

Irwin Brown stayed in Moira until the fall of 1928, when he was called back to Brockville to teach grades nine and ten geography and history in the seminary. Later that fall, he was appointed by the missionary board to go to Egypt. Irwin recalled, "I was not too anxious to go, but consoled myself by thinking I could be both a missionary and a student and learn a new language, Arabic, and get acquainted with a famous country of Bible times."

MARRIED

In 1933, Irwin Brown returned home to Canada. To his surprise, provisions had not been made for his living accommodations—Bishop Monahan had just resigned—so Irwin had no place of residence except his sister's home in Belleville. Fortunately, Rev. Nussey, the new general superintendent, took pity and invited the young Rev. Brown to stay with the Nussey family in Napanee. That summer Irwin became Rev.

Nussey's chauffeur, driving the superintendent to the various summer camp meetings and assisting in the special meetings.

It was at Ivanhoe Camp that Irwin met Jennie Jackson. She was pretty, a talented singer, and played the piano and Spanish guitar. Rev. Brown recalled that during camp, he asked Jennie to marry him and she consented. Irwin and Jennie were married on December 27, 1933, at Watertown, New York, by Rev. R. J. Druce. Irwin took his new bride to the parsonage in the mountains of Arundel, Quebec, north of Montreal. The winter was cold and the parsonage was not easily heated. On one particular night, Rev. Brown recalled, it was so cold that even with a roaring fire in the large box stove, everyone was shivering; the postmistress informed him the next morning it was sixty degrees below zero. Thus began married life for the newlywed Pastor and Mrs. Brown.

In 1942, the Browns moved to Malone, New York with their two daughters, Uretta and Martha. In 1943, Lavada was born. Jennie was healthy both physically and mentally and able to take care of the children while Irwin travelled and held special services in various churches. During the summer, Irwin attended Winona Lake School of Theology. Upon his return, however, he noticed Jennie's mental health beginning to deteriorate, gradually becoming worse and worse. Sadly, in 1944, it was necessary to admit Jennie to the state hospital. In 1945, she was transferred to Canada and admitted to the psychiatric hospital in Brockville—she was never released. Now, along with church responsibilities, Irwin Brown was sole caregiver for three young girls.

A MANY-FACETED MINISTRY

Despite his personal hardships, the ministry and influence of Irwin L. Brown continued to grow: pastor, teacher, author, missionary, principal. Ultimately, in 1954, Irwin Brown was elected general superintendent of the Standard Church of America. We will read more of him in subsequent chapters.

REFLECTIONS

Norman Wager and Irwin Brown represent many of the young people who sacrificially stepped out in faith during the 1920s to pioneer, conduct revivals, and pastor primitive churches. They are only two examples of what many others did. Their diaries and memoirs give us a glimpse into what it was like to enter the ministry of the Standard Church. The work did not promise ease, nor were the rewards measured by fame and fortune. The ministry was often challenging and living conditions substandard. On the other hand, there was the joy of leading others to sanctification; there were the rewards of ministering to the sick and providing for the needy. Moreover, there was a faith community who joyously gathered at various revivals, conventions, and camp meetings to enthusiastically worship, pray, and share testimonies of victory and triumph.

Revisiting the lives of these saints inspires faith and challenges us to follow in the service of our Lord Jesus Christ. They are part of that great cloud of witnesses cheering us onward to throw off everything that entangles or hinders us and persevere in the race marked out for us.[7]

16

THE GREAT DEPRESSION

The Great Depression hit Canadians and Americans with an unexpected jolt on Black Tuesday, October 29, 1929, when stock markets plummeted dramatically. Also referred to as the "hungry thirties," the 1930s became a decade of desperation for many caught in the grip of a downward economic spiral. Demand for Canadian exports such as wheat, wood, paper, fish, minerals, coal, and base metals fell off sharply; a bushel of no. 1 northern Canadian wheat fell from $1.03 in 1928 to 27 cents in 1932. The prairie wheat farmer was not only caught in a severe economic downturn, but a devastating drought struck the plains of southern Alberta and Saskatchewan, reducing the land to "dust bowl" conditions.[1]

Times were tough and unemployment rampant, but the Depression offered unique opportunities for churches to minister. Despite the hardships, the hungry thirties became a decade of growth for a number of evangelical denominations:

- The Christian and Missionary Alliance in Canada reported church growth during the 1930s "in direct contrast to the depression experienced by the entire country."[2]
- The Salvation Army reported city corps such as the Oshawa Salvation Army, where many people were without work, continued to grow.[3]

• The Pentecostal Assemblies of Canada (PAOC) experienced healthy growth. In 1920 the PAOC listed a total of twenty-seven churches; by May 1, 1939, when the Depression was nearly over, the *Pentecostal Testimony* was able to report over three hundred affiliated assemblies.[4]

OLD-TIME RELIGION

The Standard Church was also poised for growth and expansion at the beginning of the decade. Even the secular press was impressed with the potential. Perhaps the most famous newspaper coverage of the Standard Church was printed in 1930 when *Toronto Star Weekly* reporter A. D. Kean visited Ivanhoe Camp Meeting and wrote a two-page spread, complete with photographs, entitled "Old Time Religion." He reported that on Saturday evening there were no fewer than one thousand campers. But on Sunday the crowd was so large the tabernacle overflowed and people were congregated everywhere on the grounds. Kean's observations and impressions speak of a church on the verge of a favourable future:

"Victory! Victory, at last!"

A peal of triumph came in deep contralto tones from a comely young woman with shining face, who stepped joyously down a straw-littered aisle of the Ivanhoe Tabernacle. "I'm saved!" The vibrant cry of exaltation continued, "Praise be to God. I'm saved!" And the youthful figure swayed and tottered, weaving forward or sideways and round and round towards an area that was spread knee-deep with loosely scattered new-mown hay, before a carpeted platform upon which a minister of the Standard Church of America was speaking.

"Amen, brothers and sisters," the preacher called. "Praise the Lord for the fruits of victory that are so manifest among us."

Then he added in persuasive tones, "Are there any more among you who feel the call of the Spirit? Come on—come on—don't be afraid—let your sins be forgiven, that you may walk forever in the path of righteousness and peace."

A score or more—boys and girls in their teens, grown-ups and aged ones—rose up and went forward.

A high-pitched tenor voice broke into song, which was quickly joined in by the throng, "Stand up, stand up for Jesus, ye soldiers of the Cross," they sang while the penitents pressed closer and closer, up to the preacher and the long platform. "From victory to victory, / His army shall He lead; / Till every foe is vanquished / And Christ is Lord indeed."

The mighty chorus, swelled by now to a thunderous pitch, echoed down from the high-arched rafters of the building, and stretched out across the fields and farmsteads of the hilly countryside.

The singing went on without abatement—those old-time revival tunes, "Bringing in the Sheaves," "Is My Name Written There?" "Work for the Night is Coming," and "Throw out the Lifeline."

By this time there were twenty-three repentant sinners kneeling at the front of the Tabernacle. They were surrounded by at least one hundred of the evangelists and their prayer helpers, who all joined in a ringing chorus of supplication.

A. D. Kean's observation at Ivanhoe portrays the intensity and power of services in Standard Church conventions and camp meetings:

Let me here make an observation. At no other religious gathering, either while attending open-air revivals in south Texas, where 500 baptisms during a single Sunday were not unusual, or amid the "Great Spirit" ceremonies of the sun dance festivals held by the Blackfoot Indians in western Canada; or again, as a participant in the early-day evangelistic meetings of Moody and Sankey on the western coast, has the impression been more forcefully made of a faith more patiently sincere than that portrayed by all who went through the manifestations of the Spirit at the 1930 camp meeting held upon those "Blessed Grounds" under the auspices of the Standard Church of Canada among the maple-clad hills north of Belleville, Ontario on Sunday, September 15.[5]

REVIVALS IN WESTERN CANADA

The Standard Church was expanding westward as well. The church and campgrounds at Good Hope in Alberta, forty miles north of Edmonton, became a hub to send out evangelists, and the work spread to other northern communities. The 1932 State of the Work Report, prepared by D. A. Mow for the Western Conference, was held in the parsonage at Good Hope and effused with enthusiasm: "We are pleased to report advancement in all branches of the evangelistic fields. New fields are opening and a call for workers is coming from the different places. The ministers in charge of the various fields of labour have given favourable reports."[6] A brief review of each circuit was included: Amber Valley, Mosside, Carievale, Vegreville, Good Hope, Calgary, Moose Jaw, Newbrook. The report ended with an enthusiastic exhortation to look toward the future: "Previous years have given great encouragement and inspiration to go forward in this great work, but we are looking forward to the future to give us greater cause for doubling our labours and pressing forward at our King's command. Brethren, pray for the advancement of God's cause in this part of his moral vineyard."[7]

NEWBROOK

In the fall of 1928, William (Bill) Burger Sr., a Christian who farmed near Good Hope, purchased land in Newbrook, seventy-five miles north of Edmonton. The district was largely homestead country and the area was populated with pioneers. There was a spiritual vacuum in this new community and the people were hungry for God. Bill Burger presented the need to Rev. Wilber J. Jackson, an evangelist mentored by Bishop Horner, who was stationed at the Good Hope Standard Church. After prayer and planning, Mr. Burger brought Rev. Jackson in the spring of 1929 to the log schoolhouse at Balsam Grove, about five miles east of the small Newbrook hamlet, and across from the homestead where my dad, Leonard Croswell, was brushing and breaking the land. The revival that began in those meetings would not be forgotten for many years by local residents. My dad often recalled Rev. Jackson's first words in the little schoolhouse: "I may be a stranger to you, but I am not a stranger to God." A religious revival commenced that touched the entire community.

Ruby Mow, years later, wrote for the *Christian Standard* that it was common to see children having prayer meetings at recess and noon hour in the corner of the schoolyard, praying with their friends. Ruby related how her dad was converted: "A six year old girl approached Bro. Jackson and said, 'I feel I should pray in school.' He told her, 'If that is what the Lord is asking you to do, do it.' Upon seeing the girl on her knees, conviction seized Mr. D. Mow, a Roman Catholic teacher, and he prayed through to victory, and later felt his call to Brockville Bible College and ministry. Approximately seventy people were saved in the revival."[8]

In the summer of 1930, the first camp meeting was held on the township line, three miles east of Newbrook, with about two hundred in attendance—a large number for a pioneer community. The campers slept on straw ticks in tents. The preaching tent was filled nightly. Bishop Monahan and Rev. and Mrs. Carson of Saskatchewan assisted Rev. Jackson.

Church services, which had begun in the schoolhouse, were moved a mile down the road to the home of Mr. and Mrs. Bill Croswell. In 1931, George and Elizabeth (Aunt Jenny) Croswell donated five acres of land across the road on the corner of their farm to build a parsonage and church and provide space to conduct the summer camp meeting.

Most of the materials for the church and the parsonage were donated. Ernie Croswell hauled logs for sawing. Construction was a community project and was completed in 1932. Pastor Lawrence Yadlowski, local son and long-time pastor of the Newbrook Standard Church, remembers his dad, John Yadlowski (one of the original Ukrainian settlers in the district), recollecting that so many neighbours volunteered to assist in building that some were told they were not needed and should return home. The congregation formed a strong rural circuit. Rev. and Mrs. Carson were stationed at the new church, and the work continued to be a strong witness under their leadership.

CAMPSIE

One of the highlights of Newbrook Camp Meeting was the arrival of campers and visitors from the various African-American communities west and north of the grounds. Campsie, a community of approximately fifty about ten miles west of Barrhead, was home to the first African-American settlement touched by the Standard Church. About 1930, Rev. David Parks hitched his team of horses to a "Bennett buggy" and conducted services in the area. A revival ensued, making a significant impact on the community. In time, several Campsie converts became preachers for the Standard Church: Andrew Risby, Albert Risby, Napoleon Sneed, and Lena (Sneed) Johnson.

AMBER VALLEY

Amber Valley, about twenty miles east of Athabasca, was home to a much larger settlement of African-American pioneers. Willis Bowen recalls that his father, Bodie Bowen, was one of the original settlers who drove a team of horses to this "land of milk and honey"—a tedious journey along primitive dirt roads from Edmonton to Athabasca Landing and from there along the treacherous trail through muskeg and dense bush that led to Donatville (Pine Creek) and later renamed

Amber Valley for the colour of the trees in the fall. It was an isolated community, "but the settlers in Amber Valley were as tough as their surroundings."[9] Over three quarters of them remained on the land long enough to receive patents for their homesteads, reports the Alberta Heritage Foundation.

It was to Amber Valley, shortly after the revival in Campsie, that David Parks and Wilber Jackson came to hold tent meetings in the clearing of a field belonging to Tim Toles about a half mile down the road from the famous Amber Valley Ball Field and a quarter mile from the Toles Schoolhouse. Evangelist Jackson was the fiery, prophetic preacher and filled the altar with those seeking to escape the "wrath to come." David Parks wooed them with his infectious wit and humour— one moment the audience was weeping, the next moment roaring with laughter. With his guitar slung over his shoulder, his energetic and robust singing, and his unique gift for storytelling, he was an immediate attraction and became revered among the African-American community as "Dad Parks."

Hence, the Amber Valley Revival began to take place among the settlers. In the July 1932 Western Annual Conference minutes, the secretary reported Amber Valley as a new field: "Attendance is good, souls are being saved, and believers sanctified." Indeed, it was from this revival that the famous evangelist, Dorothy Sneed, was saved. Services were later held in the nearby Toles School until about 1950, when a Standard Church was built on the farm of Obadiah Bowen.

The western superintendent at this time was Rev. John Carson. He stationed Albert Risby and Nap Sneed as pastors in Amber Valley the first year after they were saved. Willis Bowen recalls that his uncle, Obadiah Bowen, and Albert Risby became an evangelistic team known as Peter and Paul—Albert preached and Obadiah prayed. There also formed what became known as the "Amber Valley Quartet" composed of Albert Risby with his guitar, Andrew, Dorothy, and Lena; sometimes "Aunt Pearl," Dorothy's mother, joined the singers as well. Aunt Pearl, however, did not sing much past the first verse before she would "get blest"; while the others continued she would dance and wave her hanky, all the while laughing and praising God until she fell prostrate on the tent straw or church floor—much to the humour of the congregation.

BARRHEAD AND DISTRICT

David Parks was used by God to conduct revivals in northern Alberta communities around Barrhead. One young man saved in his meetings was Norman Wiggins; he later became a pastor and superintendent in the Standard Church. "Brother Wiggins," as he was called, remembers those revival services. He said one could feel the difference before opening the door to the schoolhouse.

David Parks was known for his tireless energy, infectious wit, and sense of humour. His Sunday began with a morning meeting at Campsie; he would leave the people praying at the altar and head for Rosalie some seven miles away for an afternoon service; again, after leaving the people praying at the altar, he travelled to Stewartfield for another service, where Norman Wiggins and family lived. That evening a tired Rev. Parks would head back to his little log home by Richmond Lake, where he had the vision to begin the Mosside Camp Meeting.

Revival fires broke out at Mosside Camp. An interesting story is told of Mr. George, who had not been to church for some time, though his wife had been very faithful in attending the meetings. Rev. Parks went to visit Mr. George and said, "You haven't been in church for a while." But Mr. George was quick to tell him why: "I can hear you from where I am!"

VEGREVILLE

In 1932, the Conference minutes reported the work at Vegreville, east of Edmonton, was a promising field. By 1935, work had been established at Vegreville and Rev. Carson had been stationed there. He reported the church was gaining ground with new members joining and a youth service each Friday evening. This field is of particular interest because a local farmer, believing in the message of the church, included in his will to the Standard Church the "mineral rights" to his farm. Years later interest was indicated by a prospective drilling company to search for natural gas; payments to explore were paid that met an emergency of the Western District at a precise time of need. The future potential of the oil rights is unknown.

MOMENTUM SLOWS

The Standard Church rode a wave of momentum leading up to the 1930s. Leadership exuded vision. Doors opened in the east and the west. Young men and women were called to the ministry. Churches were planted. A fine training center in Brockville, Ontario, was in place to equip enthusiastic recruits. Would this new generation of Hornerites continue the momentum of the 1920s, rise to the challenge of the Great Depression, and grasp the unique opportunities set before them? Moreover, would the Standard Church transition to begin reaching an increasingly urban, industrial, mechanized, and secular society?

Unfortunately, growth and momentum began to stall, and it began first of all in the eastern conferences. Pastors and leaders were aware something was amiss as early as 1931: the General Conference Committee on Evangelism submitted a lengthy report consisting of seven items lamenting the decline of evangelistic zeal and suggesting various reasons for the decline. The report began by stating the purpose for the formation of the Standard Church: "Our church was born of revivals. It was organized to promote revivals. Our discipline states, 'Our purpose in banding together is to spread scriptural holiness and save the communities in which we live.'" The report contended the church's mandate was not being fulfilled: "We find that we need to be more aggressive. . . . We see grave cause for dissatisfaction with results of our present labours. Our membership is not increasing, our societies are not reviving, and few sinners are being reached. While searching into the causes of these conditions, we observe that we are not venturing out in soul saving campaigns as boldly, frequently and persistently as we once did."[10]

Recommendations to regain evangelistic fervor included more and prolonged revival campaigns, cooperation with neighboring pastors, taking advantage of appropriate seasons for revival meetings, greater use of women evangelists not simply as special singers but as evangelists, and prevailing in prayer.

Why was the Standard Church not experiencing the growth and vibrancy that other denominations were during the Depression? It was not because of lack of prayer or devotion. These people were sincere and fervent. It had more to do with a culture, traditions, and practices deeply ingrained and assimilated in members and ministers over time. They were difficult to recognize and correct, for human nature is averse to change.

RURAL MINDSET

The suggestions made by Conference to reinvigorate evangelism had merit—for a rural mindset. What it failed to recognize was the changing face and culture of North America: large populations from rural communities migrating to the cities; two million men unemployed in Canada and one quarter of the population in the US; relief camps for the destitute and long soup lines for the hungry. The Kingston Conference of 1936 was still praising conventions and camp meetings as encouraging and fruitful and expressing approval for those members who loved the old fashioned way. But how were they reaching the lost and needy crowding into the cities? As late as 1939, the Kingston Conference was extolling the value of tent evangelism: "In the past gospel tent services have been frequently useful in revival work. We strongly recommend that more tent meetings be held and that each district have a medium sized tent to be used over the district in pioneer evangelism through the summer. This would open doors for young workers and students whom God has called."[11] Even though the 1931 General Conference admitted to waning success, little changed, and by 1939 Conference still remained fixated on tents to reach primarily rural communities.

GOVERNANCE

Creative entrepreneurs and trailblazers were not encouraged and unleashed. Preachers were boxed in by the stationing committee. Sadly, the two-year ruling for pastoral appointments was still in effect. The constant moving, at the discretion of the committee, often disrupted projects and interrupted ministries. Moreover, pastors were not able to set long-term goals. Subsequently, pastors were not motivated to solve problems and lead a church to a higher level of growth and service—they simply looked forward to moving on to the next circuit. The ruling also caused hardships for pastoral families, especially during the severe economic times of the Depression. The ruling obviously was an issue discussed among pastors, since Bishop Monahan's opening address to the 1931 General Conference was "a defense of our form of Church Government." His remarks probably were in anticipation of a memorial being sent up from the Kingston Conference that read, "Whereas there is occasional need for a pastor remaining on a circuit for more than two years, and whereas our present ruling gives the Stationing Committee no power to extend this term, we do hereby memorialize the General Conference to make a ruling authorizing the Stationing Committee to leave a preacher on a circuit six months or one year longer when in their judgment the state of the work demands it."[12] The memorial was referred to the Discipline Committee and tabled for further discussion: there was resistance by the leadership to make the adjustments, and the ruling was left intact.

LEGALISM

Evangelism and growth continued to be encumbered by legalism and dress standards. In the 1931 session of General Conference, a prolonged and close discussion took place in which all Conference members were urged "to a closer observance and stricter enforcement of the dress regulations."[13] Seven years later, in 1938, a memorial was sent to General Conference regarding a uniform for seminary students, stating all persons will dress in the Standard Church uniform.[14] Unfortunately, the clothesline had become a measure of spirituality that set unrealistic parameters for many youth desiring to enter the ministry of the church. The dress code was not compatible with a society becoming more and more urban, educated, and industrialized.

PLANS FOR PROGRESS

Despite concerns about the growth plateau, other reports in the 1931 General Conference were encouraging. A new publishing house had been built on the southern end of the college property at an approximate cost of $13,122, accommodating the book room, the printing plant, a bishop's apartment, room for press workers, and a future classroom for use by the seminary. A committee was appointed to continue working on a new Standard Church hymnal. Rev. E. H. Thompson was designated missionary to Egypt, and a committee formed to investigate purchasing a car. A year later, in a special session called on May 17, 1932, a request was considered regarding the formation of a new annual Conference in Michigan—the committee recommended that a Conference be organized when a sufficient number of preachers were eligible for membership. The Standard Church had some obvious concerns, but there was still much to anticipate and be thankful for.

Would the church adjust and regain its fire and entrepreneurial zeal? It might have, but unfortunately, two events took place that dampened enthusiasm and throttled growth.

Bishop Resigns

The first setback was the unexpected resignation of Rev. G. L. Monahan as bishop.[15] It was a grave loss and a serious blow to the morale of the church, for Monahan was a gifted and energetic leader. A special session of General Conference was called on May 24, 1933, at Athens, Ontario, to deal with his letter of withdrawal. Rev. J. W. Nussey was chosen by the Special Conference to be the chairman of General Conference until a regular session of Conference could be called; Rev. Nussey was subsequently elected president on September 18, 1933. Although Rev. Monahan was later reinstated into the Kingston Conference in 1936, he never again filled an influential role in the leadership of the Standard Church; moreover, he was the last bishop ordained to lead the Standard Church.

Stock Market Scandal

A second blow to morale came in the years 1936 and 1937. Unbelievably, it was a stock market scandal! Times had become difficult for many Standard churches during the financial meltdown of the Depression years. Preachers, evangelists, and laypeople were caught in the desperation of the times and faced hardship and extreme poverty. Destitute men rode the rails from place to place looking for work and better economic conditions. Many Sunday offerings for the country preacher consisted of farm products — eggs, milk, preserves, and garden produce. The Depression gave rise to desperate survival measures, but what took place still remains a mystery difficult to comprehend. Two of Bishop Horner's most trusted men, G. L. Monahan and W. J. Watchorn, both known for their financial acumen and leadership, discovered the name of a stock in western Ontario by the name of Paragon Hitchcock Mines Ltd. (Mud Lake Mines) with promising potential for growth and profits.[16] The two men travelled throughout the church presenting the prospectus to interested investors. Rumor claimed Standard Church money was invested (but there is no evidence of this); however, numerous pastors and people purchased shares. Gordon Hammond remembered some of the stocks were even sold to Holiness Movement pastors and people, including some in his family. That selling the shares was not immediately squelched is truly incredible, since the Standard Church Discipline expressly forbade even the buying of life insurance: "It savours covetousness; the desire for filthy lucre should be repressed, and not permitted to bud, blossom and bear fruit. It is the merchant, the farmer, the teacher, the preacher reaching beyond, and securing more than it has pleased God to give them in their callings."[17] The moment of truth arrived when it was discovered the mine did not even exist. Rev. Earl Conley, subsequent superintendent, looking back, believes it was one of the most damaging things that happened to the church. Every investor lost all he or she invested. The fiasco caused a great deal of harm to the mood within the church: some claim it killed the work in Michigan and it definitely caused disillusionment and hard feelings among many across the conferences. At the 1937 Kingston Annual Conference, Monahan submitted his resignation, and in the 1938 Conference roll, Watchorn's name was listed as withdrawn.

A memorial was sent to General Conference by the 1938 Kingston Conference that read, "Whereas certain members of this Conference have become involved in the mining business and more especially in selling gold mining stock and whereas the general feeling of this Conference is that our ministers should not be engaging in such business . . . we hereby do memorialize the General Conference to take up this matter for consideration."[18] In the subsequent General Conference, the memorial was read, discussed, and tabled.[19] No more is heard of the stock scandal, for everyone had learned a hard lesson, and any stock salesmen roaming throughout the conferences would be ostracized.

MISSIONS CONTINUE UNABATED

Standard Church missions had prospered in the previous decade. During the Great Depression missions were presented with challenges and financial restraints. China missions succumbed to disease and national upheaval, but Egypt overcame challenges and made progress despite the hard times.

CHINA

Conditions in China had become extremely unsettled politically. Moreover, the mission faced a serious outbreak of cholera. After investigation and earnest discussion the 1931 General Conference was doubtful as to whether the China mission should continue or discontinue and decided to leave the decision with the missionary board. Three years later, the Missionary Committee met on October 2, 1934, and reported that, regrettably, the mission closed. Although the mission was closed, the faith of the Chinese believers persisted and bore bountiful fruit in later days (see chapter 14).

EGYPT

Egyptian missions began the 1930s with promise. In January 1930, the *Missionary Ambassador*, a monthly magazine devoted entirely to missions, was launched. Rev. Earl Thompson began a tour of churches in North America for the purpose of fund raising and generating interest in the Egyptian mission field. Rev. I. L. Brown also arrived in Egypt; despite economic hardships, his first text at Nikhela was "I am come that ye might have life." The Egyptian Conference reported seven pastors and a new work begun in El Gharazat.

The next year, July 1931, Rev. Thompson and his wife, Annie (Hill), sailed for Egypt with their son, Glen, bringing along a Chevrolet car and a printing press. There was great rejoicing on their arrival. Rev.

Thompson, a veteran missionary, had almost become a legend, with tales of bravery and hardship endured during his first term. The work in Egypt now consisted of eight stations and a membership of 175. A mission home was completed over the church at El Nikhela: Rev. Thompson had used his influence with the governing body of the village to get permission to build and secure materials.

Stella Brown returned home in 1932 after having spent much time in villages with ministry among women.

Irwin Brown resided in the town of Mallawi. He was noted for his writings and visitation of the villages; he also was a good student of Arabic. After three years, he went on furlough in 1933. The Thompsons were left in Egypt to carry on work alone.

The year 1934 brought activity and challenge. The missionaries were told of seething unrest, deteriorating security, threats, and violence. Four young men were fired upon after leaving the church at Tahta; three were wounded, two seriously. Rev. Thompson reported that the men were recovering, but the shooting had a negative impact on their work. People were afraid to attend services. Nevertheless, progress continued with properties purchased at Naga Hamadi and Shil Tahta. An Arabic magazine was launched. A day school was operated in Nikhela. The Conference now consisted of ten appointments and national workers.

The challenge was finances. The sponsoring church at home was experiencing the bite of the Depression. Rev. Earl and Annie Thompson's extensive report to the missions board was encouraging, telling of how they sensed the prayer by the church at home pulling them through, but they were experiencing progressive cutbacks in their budgetary operating funds from $3,233.39 in 1932, to $1,680 in 1934. In three years, missionary giving had been cut nearly in half. The Thompsons reported that should the deficit of funds continue, various mission stations would be forced to close and preachers would be dismissed. Rev. Thompson reminded the home church of China's closure and warned that unless every preacher took the matter to heart and stirred himself and his people, they feared that Egypt would meet with the same fate.

The Missionary Committee realized emergency measures were necessary to save the Egyptian work. Regardless of a serious deficit of money on the home front, the committee set a generous faith budget of $2,300 for the following year. They set financial goals for each local church. The committee called for additional publicity in the *Christian Standard*. Praise was offered to God for supplying the need during those difficult times, for in 1936, Rev. Thompson reported "a banner year" in the building program! Some of the debts were liquidated, several church and parsonage projects were completed, land was donated by the brethren at Bahaleel, and fifty thousand bricks were prepared for construction of a church there.

A new treaty between Britain and Egypt created changing and uncertain conditions. Rev. Thompson wrote that he was concerned about the protection of minorities and the future of missions in particular. In the past, the British had kept a firm hand on the situation. Now that Egypt had been granted nominal independence, political disturbances, mob violence, and anti-missionary rhetoric increased.

Nevertheless, a new work was commenced in Gena in 1937. Conference statistics showed that the previous six years had been a time of expansion and consolidation. There were now twelve appointments and eleven pastors. A day school had been started at Sahil Tahta. The Thompson family left for Canada on furlough.

In the fall, Kingsley Ridgway and his family arrived in Egypt as interim missionaries with the understanding that they would continue their ministry in Australia. They were greeted warmly by dozens of Nikhela brethren at the railway station. Ridgway and his wife became loved by the people as they were always ready to serve. Mrs. Ridgway, however, was ill much of the time they were in Egypt, and because of her condition they resided in Cairo for a time.

In 1938, work began in Abadda, Sheikh Masaad, and Dishna. Services were also being held in homes in El Wagada. In eighteen years, nine churches had been built with three rented buildings and ten Conference members. Church membership was 416 and there were five day schools.

As war clouds gathered in 1939, Rev. Harold Berry's application for service on the mission field was approved. His travel was delayed until January 1940, because of the outbreak of World War II. Rev. Berry arrived in Egypt after a long, dangerous ocean voyage. The war situation was worsening and spreading to the Middle East, so it was decided that the Ridgways would leave for Australia with their four children.[20]

Despite the war, Rev. Berry remained in Egypt. He was remembered for his strong voice and forceful evangelistic preaching, as well as his laugh. Correspondence from Rev. Berry indicated support funds from home were reaching him with great difficulty because of wartime conditions. Employment was secured with the YMCA in the Royal Air Force, which gave him a regular source of income and provided a supplement for the national pastors. In spite of dire wartime conditions, the work in Egypt not only was maintained but some churches were also built.[21]

HOLINESS MOVEMENT CHURCH EXTENDS HAND OF RECONCILIATION

Back at the home base in North America, Standard Church people were continuing to experience the ravages of a devastating Depression. Inevitably, conversations and discussions returned to reuniting forces with their former brethren, the Holiness Movement Church, to combine resources and personnel. The HMC took the initiative, and a letter of invitation to discuss uniting was sent to the Standard Church in 1938.[22] A committee from the Standard Church was formed to negotiate reuniting. On September 28, 1939, a special session of General Conference was called by newly elected president, Rev. E. H. Thompson, at Lake Eloida. After preliminaries, discussion took place regarding the proposed union. There was a great deal of debate and after referral back to the committee, a letter was formulated and sent to the superintendent of the HMC:

> We feel with you that the preservation of the spiritual unity which exists among all God's people is a matter of highest importance and that loyalty to our Lord Jesus Christ obliges us and each of His followers to support such measures as are calculated to sustain that oneness of heart and mind. We believe, moreover, that organic unity where possible, contributes to that great end.
>
> We are glad to know that as a church you continue to uphold the clear, strong doctrine of Full Salvation and the Baptism of the Holy Ghost, in which we also firmly believe. But in our view of the principles which should govern Christian living, it is evident we have diverged widely and we fear that the spirit of oneness which is shared by individuals and small groups is far from being felt in general by the two churches. These things compel us regrettably to conclude that the proposal for organic union is premature. . . .
>
> The above thoughts express not only the opinion of the undersigned, we find they are shared by our ministers in general, and we trust you will receive them, as they are presented, in the fear and the love of God.
>
> Yours in Christ,
> E. H. Thompson, J. B. Pring, H. S. Hornby

The letter was not a closed door to negotiations but certainly put the lid on immediate union. Many were disappointed. This, however, would not be the last time the Standard Church would talk of union with HMC. In the meantime, they would still interact at camp meetings and conventions often cooperating and sharing resources and personnel.

WAR YEARS

When World War II began in 1939, Rev. Thompson resigned his office of general superintendent to become a chaplain in the Canadian Armed Forces. Rev. Thompson stressed his need for the full support and prayers of the Conference. Looking into the future, he pointed out that "we will at the close of the war be facing a changed world, and will have to adjust ourselves and our methods of approach. . . . Unique opportunities will be before our church, and we should be ready to extend our frontiers."[23]

How correct he was! The church would emerge from the war in 1945 facing a new and vibrant country. Canada became confident of her place and power in the world. Both the US and Canada enjoyed an economic boom with record prosperity. Social values changed as society became more flexible and open. Would the Standard Church have the courage to take advantage of these unique opportunities?

Winds of Change

Having survived the Great Depression and World War II, North Americans began to embrace the good life of the post war years. This new era of optimism and prosperity would influence holiness churches and specifically the Standard Church. Change was inevitable.

After his stint as wartime chaplain in the Canadian Armed Forces, Rev. Earl Thompson was reelected general superintendent at General Conference on Athens campground, May 15, 1945. Upon reassuming the chair, he addressed the Conference and stated that "while we are in a changing world, we need the Spirit of God to lead, guide and bless." Rev. Thompson paid tribute to Rev. James Pring, general superintendent in his absence, who had led on through many difficulties. He assured Conference that while he was away, his interests had been with the church, and though members had decreased, "we can rise by the help of God and come back to God in a greater spirit of cooperation."[1] Rev. Thompson recognized that adjustments were necessary before the church could prosper in the booming postwar age. Some of the issues had been with the church since the beginnings of the Holiness Movement but had run into rigid opposition. In the optimistic winds of the postwar they were again being voiced, but this time recognized as valid.

LAY DELEGATES

The matter of lay representation in conferences returned to the forefront. Evidently there had been plenty of discussion behind the scenes, for a memorial to General Conference from the more conservative Western Conference was read opposing lay representation; the Kingston Conference, however, had become convinced of the necessity of lay leadership and counteracted the Western motion with a memorial of their own. Changes were taking place: General Conference voted to allow one elected lay delegate per church with voice and vote in the annual conferences.[2] It was a window opening for laypeople to begin working with their preachers and pastors in leading and building the church. Only nine years later, in 1954, a memorial was again received from the Kingston Annual Conference requesting the status of lay delegates to General Conference be reconsidered and that lay delegates not only be allowed to vote in General Conference but also be considered eligible for membership on any committee. This time the memorial passed with only one dissenting vote.[3] The narrow confines of leadership imposed by the rigid episcopalian governance that Bishop Horner and his men so tenaciously adhered to were slowly being relaxed and shed, and the vitality of lay leadership was being allowed to blossom.

CHURCH UNIFORM

For years dress and, in particular, the church uniform had been a contentious issue. By 1945, the styles and standards of uniforms for preachers and evangelists were relaxing. The Western Conference, however, noted this relaxation and went on record to request the retention of the uniform. As expected, there was opposition to the stringent dress codes from other conferences: the Kingston Annual Conference sent a counter memorial to General Conference to drop the present uniform;

the memorial requested the issue be referred to the Committee on Uniform to recommend appropriate alterations in the Discipline. To avoid contention and controversy, few specifics were suggested on the Conference floor. Nevertheless, a committee was nominated by the chair to draw up rules for dress and attire.[4] Interestingly, by the time the 1950 General Conference rolled around, the uniform for men and women had become much less an issue. That is not to say standards regarding modest dress, gaudy colours, and showy styles were discarded—they were still upheld. It did mean, however, that many members were recognizing the folly of judging spirituality by the colours and styles of dress that a person wore. The uniform was becoming an artifact of the past.

MUSICAL INSTRUMENTS

Singing had always been a major part of revival services in Holiness Movement and Standard churches. In fact, numerous hymnbooks had been published containing hymns and gospel songs appropriate for revivals and Sunday worship; Bishop Horner, himself, had composed his famous gospel song "We Are Happy Today," used extensively throughout holiness churches.[5] But singing had always been a cappella, and the person with the loudest voice and best pitch would begin the first note of each hymn and the congregation would join in. In large congregations, this singing could be exceedingly moving. But times were changing, and instruments such as guitars and accordions were becoming popular to lead congregational singing and accompany specials during the services. Rev. David Parks especially was known among the rural communities of Alberta for his energetic singing accompanied by his guitar on such popular numbers as "Every Day I'm Camping!" and "Victory in Jesus." The 1945 General Conference, not wishing to cause division or offend any particular group, left the issue of musical instruments open ended, simply stating, "Musical instruments shall not be used in our regular public services without the consent of the congregation, the pastor, and the Presiding Elder."[6] The door had been opened. Musical instruments became more and more common, and many congregations began to use instruments of their choice.

CHURCH UNION

There was another wind blowing. Many members and adherents of the Standard and Holiness Movement churches felt it was time to put the past behind them: the breach must be healed before either could move on. To be sure, some from older generations still nursed perceived injustice and were uncertain as to whether they could trust the other; but a new generation was arising and the division mattered less to them. The two churches began to realize they had much in common doctrinally, ritually, and historically. Indeed they shared personnel and resources at camp meetings and revivals, renewing hopes of reconciling and unifying Bishop Horner's fractured family. A logical first attempt was to cooperate through their schools—Annesley College and Brockville Bible College.

In 1945, with Armistice Day near at hand, Brockville Seminary became known as Brockville Bible College and added a complete high school curriculum leading up to senior matriculation. Rev. I. L. Brown was appointed principal. A major boost to the college occurred when the Canadian government decided to assist young veterans from the war to obtain more education. An inspector came and examined the school's facilities, courses, and teacher qualifications; he recommended Brockville Bible College as suitable for training war veterans who had not obtained a high school education and also as a fitting place for veterans who wanted to enter the Christian ministry. About eighteen veterans came to BBC. The influx of students made necessary the purchase of a large old mansion on Perth Street almost directly across from the college. The government paid almost double the tuition fees for these veterans compared to regular students in the school, and this influx of funds allowed for extensive repairs that otherwise would not have been possible.

COLLEGES AFFILIATE

Rev. Brown worked diligently to reach out to the HMC. As principal of BBC, Rev. Brown invited the students and faculty of Annesley College to visit for a full day. It was an olive branch. Annesley College accepted the invitation, chartered a bus, and came to Brockville Bible College. They attended classes in the high school and theology department. They were pleased with what they saw and heard. Subsequently, during the summer of 1948, the board of directors and trustee board of Annesley College met with the board of directors of Brockville Bible College: it was unanimously decided to affiliate the two Bible schools, use the BBC facilities, and raise the educational standards with a view to eventually conferring theological degrees. It was reported that the first year of affiliation proved very successful. Harold Pointen predicted, "If the affiliation continues to work harmoniously, then sometime within the next four years there will be an amalgamation, which no doubt will eventually lead to a union of the Holiness Movement Church and the Standard Church of America."[7] A number of students who attended BBC during this era of cooperation went on to become successful pastors and leaders in their churches and the evangelical church at large: Dugal Sharpe, Jim Pointer, Roy Kenny, Ross Brown, Harry Hobbs, and Gordon Hammond to name a few. Homer James became a successful gospel singer; David Mainse attended a year of high school while his father served on the Egyptian mission field and later went on to become the highly successful religious TV host of *100 Huntley Street*.[8] Rev. I. L. Brown's editorial in the school's yearbook, the *Lighthouse 1951–1952*, was optimistic and hopeful of future cooperation: "One of the reasons we have as a church, whether Movement or Standard, for operating a training school is to supply our respective mission fields with missionaries who are prepared mentally as well as spiritually for their great work. Through the years that have gone, this school and our affiliate, Annesley College, have been the training ground for many of our missionaries. These men and women have gone chiefly to China and Egypt, where they have laboured with considerable success."

UPGRADE CREDENTIALS

Rev. Irwin Brown sensed his personal educational qualifications were inadequate to meet the standards necessary for administrating and teaching at a higher level college. "Here I was the principal of a college with a staff of teachers all having degrees!" To upgrade his credentials, Rev. Brown began to attend Winona Lake School of Theology during the summers. In the meantime, Miss Ethel Clark, teacher at BBC, had gone to Marion College, Indiana, and had obtained a B.A. degree. Rev. Brown recalled that "it took much effort and sacrifice on the part of my dear children when I went each summer to Winona Lake School of Theology, . . . but I finally finished with a Bachelor of Religion degree in June, 1949!" Rev. Brown continued to take summer school courses at Winona Lake until he finally graduated with an MA in religion. During those years, Ross Brown, Roy Kenny, and Gordon Hammond also received BA degrees from Winona Lake and went on to be successful in the ministry.[9]

MOVES TOWARD MERGER

The joint board of directors for BBC provided the first overtures to further discussion on church union between the Standard and Holiness Movement churches on November 26, 1952. They proposed sharing the BBC property with the HMC for the purpose of promoting a "school of high scholastic standards, both in theology and high school courses . . . [and] provide Bachelor degrees in theology of such quality that our ministerial candidates need not go elsewhere to gain these educational advantages."[10] It was bold thinking on the part of the committee and Rev. Brown: they proposed provisions for cost sharing as well as compensation to the Standard Church for property transferred to the joint college. Surprisingly, Rev. W. J. Stonehouse, general superintendent of the HMC, not only agreed but took the proposal a step further. In his return letter, he replied:

> What would you think of entering into some sort of deliberations regarding church union? There seems to be a growing feeling among our people and preachers that we would be better to get together. There are so many aspects of the wider field of administration that is difficult simply because of our limited reservoir of resources. . . . Two of our preachers said there was talk among the Standard people on their district in favour of church union. I would be so very glad to meet with you and talk the matter over. I am all for church union, not only between the Standard and the Movement but a wider union than that with the Holiness churches.

Both SCA and HMC Conferences and people were abuzz with the exciting possibility of reuniting and joining forces.

New General Superintendent

Rev. I. L. Brown was recognized for his leadership abilities and was elected general superintendent of the SCA in the 1954 General Conference. He had now become an articulate communicator and astute administrator and had become a father figure among many Standard Church people. His leadership would influence the dynamics of talks and negotiations between the SCA and HMC.

Tragic Interlude

Single parent. Principal and teacher. Church leader. Negotiator with the HMC. Could anyone wear as many hats as Rev. Irwin Brown and ask for more stress and pressure? Yet, what was about to take place would break his heart and bring him to his knees in agonizing tears. Lavada Brown, Irwin's youngest daughter brought great joy to him after his long days of teaching and pressures in the ministry. When Lavada was still quite young, Irwin bought her a pair of ice skates and she learned to skate on a pond near the college. She had a natural talent for skating, and within a year Lavada's schoolteacher was surprised at how she had learned to skate so quickly and with such obvious skill—far beyond other children in her class. The Kiwanis Club was informed of her talent and agreed to pay for figure skating lessons. She advanced so rapidly that her skating teacher began to give her personal instruction; on the days of her classes, the manager of the rink roped off half the ice surface so Lavada could practice one half hour entirely by herself without interruption from other skaters. The climax to her lessons occurred when the Ottawa Figure Skating Club came to Brockville for their exhibition and Lavada was asked to give a solo performance. She performed beautifully, and when the audience enthusiastically applauded, several from the Kiwanis Club shouted, "That's Lavada! She's from Brockville! That's our girl!" Rev. Brown was exceptionally proud of his young daughter.

But a horrendous tragedy struck on June 3, 1955. Rev. Brown was preparing to leave that Friday afternoon for the New York annual Conference. He had a strong feeling that he should not depart until Lavada came home from school, shortly after four o'clock. After going outside into the garden for a moment to talk with Mr. Harold Moyles, he went back inside the college to finish some writing and heard a piercing scream. Rev. Brown recounts the horrific details:

I instinctively knew something had happened to Lavada. I dashed out the door and ran toward the place where the scream had come from. Two or three children were standing on the side of the street (behind a large gravel truck) next to our residences. Then I saw Lavada lying motionless on the pavement. I cannot remember any details. I knelt beside her, but there my memory fails. It may be the providence of God that I cannot recollect what I saw. Someone had called the ambulance. I remember it arriving. I know they put Lavada into it and I climbed in and sat beside her until we reached the hospital. Again the details are blurred. I do recall sitting in an office or small room. I vomited. Then a nurse came and told me that Lavada was dead. I seemed to be in a trance. Someone took me home. . . .

Arrangements were made for the funeral. . . . Rev. Rupert Walsh, pastor of the Standard Church preached Lavada's funeral sermon and presided at the grave. When we came out of the church, the hearse was surrounded by the entire Brockville Police Force. They wore white gloves and white caps. They formed two columns and marched ahead of the hearse, slowly. When the procession reached King Street, the police again formed two lines far enough apart for the hearse to pass between them. As it did, they saluted.

But, life had to continue. Miss Olive Pearson of Kingston, Ontario, a member of the Standard Church in that city, loaned us her cottage for a week. Uretta, Martha and I had a chance to be together. We deeply appreciated our stay at the cottage. Olive had also filled the refrigerator and cupboards with food.[11]

LIFE CARRIES ON

After Rev. Brown's tragic loss, his life would return to the church issues at hand. Merger talks between the denominations proceeded and a proposal for union began to be drawn together. Rev. Brown consulted Corbett and Mosclow, Barristers and Solicitors, instructing them to

draw up a statement of opinion. A special session of the SCA Conference met in Brockville on Tuesday, October 16, 1956, to discuss, not
only the printing and publication of a new church Manual and Discipline with changes to governance more acceptable to the union, but
also detailed discussion on how the proposed union might take place.

Three names were proposed by each denomination.[12]

The Holiness Movement Church suggested the following:

1. The Holiness Movement Church
2. The Canadian Holiness Church
3. The United Evangelical Church

The Standard Church put forth the following:

1. The Standard Church of America
2. The Standard Church of the Messiah
3. The Christian Holiness Church

The HMC responded in turn and a special meeting was called with
the SCA on February 23, 1956, to consider the proposals presented by
Rev. Brown. Six proposals were agreed upon. Proposal one was the
most important: that the Holiness Movement Church and the Standard
Church unite under one constitution. Proposal two stated that the name
of the new church shall be acceptable to the general public as well the
people it represents. Another proposal made provision for a generous
time allotment allowing each annual Conference to transition and operate
under the Manual of their respective denominations for up to eight years.
Other proposals dealt with the union and operation of local churches,
camp meetings, schools, periodicals, and missions. Deliberations were
proceeding with a green light.

REASONS FOR MERGER

On April 12, 1957, a paper was presented to the East and West conferences of the HMC to lay the foundation for "Why the Merger of the Two Churches?" The discourse began by paying tribute to the storied history of the Holiness Movement. Interestingly, no mention was suggested that union might heal the old breach that had occurred in 1918. It was as if the new generation wished to erase the embarrassing occurrence from memory. Rather, the paper emphasized that times were changing, and union was deemed a necessity:

> Church Union is now a live issue among our people, and as such it must receive our most careful and prayerful consideration. But, first of all, in paying tribute to our beloved church, let it be said that her history for the past 60 years has been illuminated by many bright trophies, "brands plucked from the burning." She had her origin in Revival fire. Amongst her earliest members were found the very cream of the holiness people in Canada. The revivals which swept over the Country under her banner were unusual and outstanding. A host of mighty preachers was raised up; heroic missionaries crossed the seas to blaze the gospel-trail in heathen lands.
>
> The laity were men and women of deep piety and self-sacrifice. Churches were built in rapid succession, and the denominational polity and government were developed. The Holiness Movement has endeavoured through the years to maintain a glorious doctrinal heritage, and to set a high standard of ethics and morals. Under the direction of the Holy Spirit she has enjoyed much of the signal blessing of God at home and abroad.
>
> However, certain situations developed—to impede the healthy progress of our church and hamper its operations. Because of this we have faced for many years the depletion of our ranks in both pastors and people, consequent murmurings of discontent, and

the disappointing results to our efforts. Yet in spite of these retarding influences much has been accomplished, and for this we humbly thank God.[13]

Despite enthusiasm for union, differences of opinion began to surface and sour the good will developing between the HMC and the SCA. First of all, there still was an underlying lack of trust by older preachers with long memories: Rev. George Armstrong, a young Standard Church pastor at the time, recalled hearing a proposal to construct a second building of equal value to BBC so that if the merger didn't work, each denomination would still have their own property. The Standard Church lost everything in the first division, and it did not want to lose everything again. As well, many on both sides misunderstood the issues: Frances Craig recalled her aunt (Annie Crozier Woodland) remarking, "Well, the Standard Church left, let them come back!" Neither side could understand what the other side was trying to say.

The most troublesome issue, however, that ultimately killed the union arose from a statement in the HMC paper: "[I]n consideration of the momentous issues confronting us it is our considered opinion that these issues can be settled best by effecting a merger with a larger holiness body." It was rumoured that Rev. W. J. Stonehouse, superintendent of the Holiness Movement, concurred with this view. Rev. Stonehouse was a visionary—he believed that to truly heal the breach, the two churches would need to focus on bigger things, in other words a second merger; he naively voiced his speculation that the merger of the Holiness Movement and Standard churches would only be the first step to ultimate union with an even larger denomination, perhaps the Free Methodist Church. There had been distrust already, but to think that Rev. Stonehouse would even suggest such a thing as another union caused many in the Standard Church to be exasperated.[14] To bolster the suspicions, a letter was received by Rev. Irwin Brown, dated April 13, 1957, from R. Boston, secretary for the HMC Union Committee, stating: "[I]t was decided to send a communication to The Standard Church Union

Committee assuring them of our intention to bring the matter of church union with The Standard Church before our Annual Conference when it convenes. However, due to other developments in discussions held at yesterday's union meeting, we are morally bound to inform the Conference of the greater advantages obtainable by uniting with a larger Body." The letter went on to state: "[W]e as a Conference place ourselves on record as favoring a union of Holiness Churches and that we would not wish to participate in any union that would limit such negotiations." The Standard Church committee took Mr. Boston's letter to mean that the HMC was no longer in favour of a simple union with the SCA, but was instead recommending union as a preliminary step to joining with a larger church body. Union talks between the HMC and SCA died on the vine! A return letter was sent by G. W. Armstrong on behalf of the Executive Committee of the SCA to the HMC stating that "since they [the HMC] were no longer interested in negotiating with the Standard Church on the question of union . . . we wish you every success on your future plans, and God's blessing on the same."

Many were disappointed that union did not take place between the SCA and the HMC. Deaconess Lola Willows in particular took it upon herself to help correct what she thought were misunderstandings. In her letter of June 20, 1957, she stated that the Western Conference voted to amalgamate with the Standard Church and not for union with a larger denomination; she said men like Brother Flesher of Edmonton, and Rev. Southcomb spoke strongly in favour of union with the Standard Church. But it was too late. Leaders of both denominations had made up their minds that union between Bishop Horner's two estranged children would not take place.

HOLINESS MOVEMENT JOINS FREE METHODIST

The refusal by the Standard Church did not dampen the aspirations of the HMC leadership for something larger: on October 7 and 8, 1958, a meeting in Kingston of the leaders of the HMC and the Free Methodist Church took place to work out details for a merger of the two denominations in Canada. At a December meeting in Ottawa, a final agreement was made, approved, and signed. The union gave the merged churches greater national coverage, for Free Methodists gained strong churches in the larger cities of Winnipeg and Ottawa as well as areas previously vacant in western Canada. The Egyptian Conference of the HMC, which numbered five thousand members and about nine or ten thousand adherents, voted unanimously to become Free Methodist as well. Ralph Horner's first child, the Holiness Movement Church, had become welcome reinforcements within a larger world-wide Holiness Movement.[15]

POSTWAR MISSIONS

Union talks did not stall growth of Standard Church missions. Foreign missions continued unabated. Remember that one of the committees formed at the first General Conference in 1918 was the Committee on Missions, and the field chosen was Egypt. The mission emphasis gained strength as the years progressed. It was unfortunate the work in China was forced to retreat and close, but the work in Egypt continued to make significant progress. As war approached, there were greater challenges and new hurdles to overcome, but the work in Egypt prospered.[16]

HAROLD AND MARY BERRY

After the war, Rev. Berry returned from Egypt and, while on furlough, married Mary Naismith. The couple returned to Egypt in January 1946. They lived in the mission home above the Nikhela church for two years. Soon a baby girl, Dorothy, arrived; and with the responsibility of a small child, the Berrys decided it would be better to take up residence in Assiut near the American mission hospital. In Assiut they would also have access to a good supply of fresh, clean milk from the American mission farm. To her credit, Mary Berry's active ministry among the women in Assiut was a factor in opening up work in that city. Unfortunately, Rev. Berry's health would not permit him to continue his work in Egypt, and the Berrys travelled back to Canada in 1950.

FOREIGN MISSIONARY SOCIETY

In 1945, Mrs. Naomi Green of Belleville, Ontario, had a vision for supporting the work of Standard Church missions. She organized what became known as the Foreign Missionary Society in her home church. Soon there was a call to organize missionary societies in several other churches, and Naomi Green began to travel extensively in Canada and the US, assisting with the organization of societies that would keep missions in the forefront of local churches. Each society set about to inform congregations of ongoing work in the mission field, as well as raise support for various missionary projects. In the years that followed, the FMS played a vital role in the promotion and support of Standard Church missions.

CONLEYS AND ERGEZINGER

By the fall of 1950, the SCA missionary board had formulated plans to send a new couple to the Egyptian mission field: Earl and Doris Conley. The church planned to have them sail in 1951, but concern was raised when several anti-British riots occurred across Egypt and were accompanied by violence, bloodshed, and the burning of several large buildings. Travel was postponed until 1952, when conditions were more settled. In the meantime, the Egyptian monarchy was overthrown in a bloodless coup and the corrupt King Farouk was sent into exile. The Conleys, with their two-and-a-half-year-old son, Henry, were set to sail for Egypt in the summer, but upon arrival in New York

City found their departure had been delayed for two weeks until August 10. The delay allowed Irma Ergezinger to join them, and they sailed together on August 14, on the freighter *Steel Worker*. They arrived at Port Said, Egypt, August 28.

The missionaries arrived in Egypt the month following the Egyptian Revolution. It was the beginning of an era of change: the new government was less hostile to Christianity and missions, and there were promises of reform and freedom of expression. These opportunities were eagerly grasped by the church, and during the next ten years workers entered several new villages and cities to establish works. New places of worship were erected. Twelve young men entered the ministry.

Rev. Conley said that they were busy days for the missionaries. They conducted village evangelism, women's meetings, children's meetings, and a weekly English service, all the while continuing their intense studies of the Arabic language. Irma Ergezinger and Doris Conley took their full share of ministry with the young people and children. Doris bravely drove along narrow back-country roads and lanes to minister in remote villages. She was welcomed to conduct regular public services in churches, as well as speak at various women's meetings. In addition to all of these activities, the missionaries conducted training classes for student ministers. The Egyptian mission gratefully took advantage of this brief interlude of opportunity for rapid growth and expansion. Gradually, however, restrictions were tightened and life became more difficult with the return of heavy surveillance and censorship.

Of great importance to Earl Conley's future ministry in Egypt was his enrollment in the American University in Cairo; after completing several courses, he was granted a BA in 1956 with a major in Arabic literature. Rev. Conley's mastery of the Arabic language greatly assisted his acceptance and respect among the Egyptian brethren and gave him a decided edge in the future leadership of the Egyptian Conference.

Rev. George Oldford, missions board treasurer, visited Egypt during January and February 1954 and held services in the village churches. When he returned home, he collected money for the purchase of a property in Assiut. A lovely church was built on the location. Sandra May Conley was born while Rev. Oldford was there.

New missionaries arrived in Egypt in the fall of 1954: Rev. and Mrs. Arnold and Evelyn Rigby, with sons Peter and David. They took up residence in Assiut in an apartment adjacent to the Conleys and commenced their study of Arabic. The Rigbys also participated in village visitation, evangelism, and in the pastoral training classes. Timothy Rigby was born in Assiut. Rev. Arnold Rigby enjoyed village evangelism—except for the fleas, which gave him an exceptionally hard time. Evelyn enjoyed working with the women and young people.

During the summer of 1955, while the Rigbys and Conleys were on summer holidays in Alexandria and Cyprus, serious troubles erupted. A Greek terrorist group attacked Turkish residents and British soldiers. Newspapers warned of possible massacres. Prayer was requested by the church in North America, and hostilities eased, allowing the missionaries to return to their base in Assiut. However, storm clouds continued to gather, and on July 26, 1956, Egypt nationalized the Suez Canal. This led to a series of critical events. Britain and France assembled troops along with warships and aircraft carriers in preparation to defend their rights. Nasser said Egyptians would fight until the last drop of blood. Israel attacked Egypt on October 29 and advanced to within ten miles of the Suez Canal. Britain and France attacked with air raids. Three Arab nations ordered the mobilization of their forces.

Things were tense in Egypt and the mission work was brought to a standstill. Hostility toward foreigners was inflamed by the media. The Canadian embassy ordered their nationals to leave. Rev. Conley took the Rigby family to Cairo to meet a convoy of persons to be evacuated from the country. Rev. Conley had driven only two hours on his journey back to Assiut when air raids on Cairo began. What should the missionaries do? The few remaining missionaries decided they should remain in Egypt. Meanwhile in the homeland, friends and loved ones searched the newspapers and listened for news on the radio. Hearing of homes being looted and persons being beaten and robbed, they were very anxious. Thankfully, all the missionaries were kept safe. Gradually the situation returned to near normal and visitation of the churches resumed.

In 1957, Irma Ergezinger returned home on furlough, but the Conleys' term was extended at their request by another year. A third Conley child, Mary Lou, was born in 1958 at the American hospital in Cairo. Later that year, the Conley family returned home on furlough. During their stay in Egypt, they had witnessed and experienced not only the upheaval of the political and social scene, but they had participated in valuable ministry and church growth.[17]

PICKING UP THE PIECES

The eleventh regular session of the SCA General Conference was convened on October 1, 1958, in the Belleville Standard Church. The exhausting union debates and negotiations, as stated in the minutes, "were now closed . . . a thing of the past"—for the time being!

The work of the church continued onward. Three items of interest were given approval:

1. A new *Church Manual and Discipline* was printed and ready for sale and distribution. Special thanks and appreciation were extended to Rev. I. L. Brown and the Committee on Discipline for their labours in this endeavour. This concise manual was widely distributed and became the ruling guide for governance and ritual in the Standard Church for the next forty years.

2. A remarkable new hymnal—*Christian Praise*—edited chiefly by Eva James and Earl H. Thompson, was given approval. It was a monumental task for a small church, but a great success, and many denominations began to use the hymnal. When the music edition sold out, prohibitive printing costs spawned the initiative for printing the words-only edition, which is still used in some camp meetings and small churches.

3. Plans were made to develop the ten-plus-acre property surrounding Brockville Bible College. The field had been used for market gardening by Harold Moyles and helped support the college, but there was growing community and civic pressure to expand the usage. Concrete plans were adopted for the development of a housing project on the property. Included in the proposed plan was the building of an apartment building. Rental proceeds would be dispensed as follows:

- BBC would receive income to replace lost revenue from college gardens.
- A pension fund for ministers of the Standard Church would be established and maintained.

A beautiful twelve-unit apartment building was constructed on Schofield Avenue. For many years, the apartments continued to support the Brockville Bible College, but the pension fund never materialized. The apartments have been upgraded through the years and are still used to support denominational ministries.

DEATH OF REV. H. S. HORNBY

Shortly after the Suez crisis and the return of the Conleys to Egypt, the Standard Publishing House mourned the unexpected loss of Rev. Harold S. Hornby, a staunch and steady supporter of the Standard Church and its ministries. For years, the name Hornby had been synonymous with the Standard Publishing House; one might say Rev. Hornby grew up with the Standard Church publishing house. The original purpose of the publishing house was the production of Christian literature and church publications. However, Rev. Hornby's skill as a printer was the chief reason for the large constituency of acquired customers, and he took special delight in turning out high quality printing for the many clergymen patrons of every church in Brockville and vicinity. *Christian Praise*, the highly popular hymnal of the Standard Church will stand as a lasting monument to the genius of this man who could "coax so much out of so little."[18]

Along with the printing department, there was a steady growth over the years of the Christian Book Store and Supply Centre. A considerable volume of local churches were supplied, along with a large volume of mail order business.

Rev. Hornby was the last person to take credit himself for all the growth that had taken place. He had many helpers he taught throughout the years. All of these people had given their time and labour at sacrificial wages. Many of them were trained by Rev. Hornby. They loved him as a devoted Christian and skillful printer.

During 1959, several thousand dollars were spent in renovating and modernizing the press room. Rev. Hornby had supported the vision to modernize the establishment and looked forward to seeing the publishing house expand and continue its ministry of supplying materials to Sunday school, providing religious books for local church libraries as well as carrying a stock of Christian books for students and readers. He represented the winds of change taking place within the Standard Church to become a part of the larger Christian community.

Tragically, on October 28, 1959, Rev. Harold Hornby's printing ministry came to an unexpected halt: he was received into God's presence as the result of a collision with a truck while riding his motorcycle on Perth Street. He was seventy-one years of age.

Rev. I. L. Brown, in his tribute, wrote, "We will miss his cheerful face, his radiant personality, his hearty 'Amens' and his liberal contributions. We miss him at the table here in the College where he has been boarding since 1922.

"He lived the way he preached. His wages were shamefully low, but he would not accept a raise in pay. We often urged him to give up his motorcycle but he would just smile upon us as we talked. I like to think that God sent a chariot from heaven and picked him off his beloved 'bike' and took him soaring to worlds beyond where he met his Saviour face to face."[19]

THE WORK CONTINUES

The death of Mr. Hornby was a loss, but the work of the denomination would carry on: the publishing house would continue printing sacred literature; missions would continue to grow; local churches would continue to conduct services; and new men and women would rise to the challenge of entering the ministry.

In November of 1959, the Conleys returned to Egypt. New churches commenced in Tima, Weilly, and Tanta. Translator courses were conducted in Assiut to prepare young men as future translators for guest preachers and visitors. Rev. I. L. Brown, general superintendent, visited the field in late 1960 and spent Christmas with the missionaries. The pastors and brethren welcomed him back to Egypt after an absence of almost thirty years. Before Rev. Brown left Egypt, Lola Willows arrived, eager for visitation and preaching in village services.[20]

All seemed quiet and peaceful on the home front, but it was only a temporary calm. That was soon to change. The union issue had not died and would emerge for a final showdown.

No Deal, New Day

Despite the failed merger with the Holiness Movement Church, union talk had not abated. The downside of belonging to a small denomination was an issue still alive with many Standard Church preachers. Many still favoured union with another denomination. This time the Committee on Union recommended considering two denominations: the Pilgrim Holiness Church and the Wesleyan Methodist Church. Two files were kept, one for each denomination. The Standard Church simultaneously conducted union talks with both denominations:

- The executive board of the Wesleyan Methodist Church of America resolved on November 4, 1959, after talks and negotiations with Reverends Brown and Slater of the Standard Church that they express themselves as "wholly in favor of such a union if it seemed to our brethren of the SCA that the Lord would be pleased in consummating it."[1]

- Similarly, two-and-a-half months later, on January 18, 1960, an agreement regarding union between the Pilgrim Holiness Church and the Standard Church was drawn up listing seventeen terms of agreement, which included becoming part of the Pilgrim Pension Plan and obtaining comparable ministerial standing in the PHC. This document was signed by the general superintendents of the PHC (Melvin H. Snyder, with whom most of the correspondence and negotiations had taken place, along with William H. Neff, and P. G. Fleron) and the SCA Committee on Church Union (Rev. Irwin Brown, General Superintendent, Arthur Slater, and Ross Brown).

After study and discussion, it was decided that union with the Pilgrim Holiness Church was most suitable for the Standard Church; hence, a special session of the General Conference was announced to be held in the Brockville Standard Church on June 6, 1960, to consider the union with the Pilgrim Holiness Church.

Although Rev. Brown's sentiments appear to have favoured the Wesleyan Methodists, the PHC had a similar dynamic in preaching style that SCA preachers and people identified with. But caution lights were flashing that would need to be addressed.

THE CALL SYSTEM

Standard Church preachers had a measure of security in that they could rely on the Stationing Committee to appoint them somewhere to a church or circuit. There was fear in joining a call system. What if churches did not choose Standard Church preachers to be pastors? Would they be left without places to minister?

THE BUDGET SYSTEM

We know this today as Church Assessment or United Stewardship Fund, which is used to support the ministries of various districts and General Conference. The SCA had not instituted such a plan; hence, the general superintendent had no means of support and was either stationed in a church or appointed elsewhere; Rev. I. L. Brown was supported by his position in the Bible college. The general board of the PHC made concessions that there would be no general budget required for the Standard Church for the first year, and after that it would be instigated at a rate of one-fourth, one-half, and full for each succeeding year. To prepare Standard churches for assessments, a memorial was sent up to the special 1960 General Conference by the Kingston Conference to put in place the budget system whereby SCA churches and camps would contribute to a General Conference fund.

Merger Negotiations

The Pilgrim Holiness and the Wesleyan Methodist churches were also in negotiations to merge. This fact was noted with caution by the Standard Church because it was the very reason they had turned down merger with the Holiness Movement. A memorial was sent to the 1960 special General Conference from the Kingston Conference that the SCA "remain as we are until such time as the Pilgrim Holiness and the Wesleyan Methodist Churches unite."[2]

Leadership

The district superintendent of the Ontario District of the Pilgrim Holiness Church was Rev. John Keith. If the SCA merged with PHC, what would happen to Rev. I. L. Brown? After all, he had sacrificed and invested his life for forty years in the Standard Church, was an exceptionally gifted teacher and preacher, and had quarterbacked the union talks with the PHC. The Ontario District of the PHC consisted of only nine churches, while there were twenty-three Standard churches in the Kingston Conference, eight in the Western Conference, and five in the New York Conference; moreover, the Egyptian Conference consisted of about twenty stations and churches. Regardless, it appeared Rev. John Keith, the district superintendent and pastor of the Toronto PHC, would become the new DS of the proposed union. The financial arrangements appeared ostentatious to Standard Church pastors living on meagre offerings and unaccustomed to supporting a full-time superintendent. Rev. Snyder had communicated that the DS should receive a weekly salary of between eighty and ninety dollars, and also wondered if Rev. Keith might have possession of the Brockville church parsonage rather than one of the units in the new apartment building; Rev. Keith also requested the room above the publishing house, formerly occupied by the late Rev. Hornby, as an office for himself. The requests for supporting a district superintendent of thirty churches were not unreasonable, but the demands still rankled the leadership and pastors in the Standard Church because their leaders had sacrificed for many years on shoestring budgets.

FREE METHODIST OVERTURE

Consequently, it was not entirely surprising that the Executive Committee meeting in the spring came to the following conclusion regarding union with the PHC: "the financial obligations were burdensome," and "the Canadian Standard Church will profit but little from the proposed union." However, it was their subsequent announcement that took many by surprise: "whereas we have received tentative proposals from the Free Methodist Church on uniting with them . . . [we recommend that] findings relative to union with the Free Methodist Church be prepared for presentation at the Annual Conferences."[3] Here was a new wrinkle: overtures by the Free Methodist Church—the very denomination rejected by the Standard Church in their quest to merge with the Holiness Movement Church—were being considered in the midst of talks with PHC! Interestingly, a letter had been received by Rev. Brown, dated February 23, 1960, from Rev. W. R. Schamehorn, Shawville, Quebec, secretary of the Wesleyan Methodist Church, reporting that "Victor Findlay came . . . and told me that Bro. Pring was using all his influence to swing this circuit Free Methodist." Influential men in the SCA were favouring union with the Free Methodist Church.

On April 30, Rev. Brown wrote to inform Rev. Snyder of the executive's decision: that the Standard Church was unable to meet the financial responsibilities involved in the support of the district superintendent. He also informed him that a subcommittee had been appointed to explore the advisability of union with the Free Methodist Church. Rev. Brown concluded, "We realize this will, no doubt, be a surprise to you, but I saw it coming."

Upon receiving the letter, Rev. Snyder grasped what had taken place: he took the matter in hand and telephoned Rev. Brown on May 19 and confirmed the same by letter the same day. He asked Rev. Brown if he would consider accepting the superintendence of the merged conferences in Canada. Rev. Keith, he said, had expressed his desire to continue work on his doctorate at the University of Michigan. Referring to the matter of district finance, Rev. Snyder expressed his sorrow that the discussion of district finance caused such unfavorable reaction on the part of the committee: "It was my understanding that the whole matter was in an exploratory stage." Rev. Brown again replied by letter (May 20, 1960) that, yes, he would accept the appointment as superintendent in the event of a union with the PHC, but "the vote at a recent meeting of our Ministers and delegates was to postpone union until the Wesleyan Church and Pilgrims unite in 1963." He did also report that the move toward the Free Methodists was defeated 39 to 17. "Nevertheless," he said, "17 is a considerable number and we now face a split which did not exist before. It is a great pity that after the smooth way we were moving toward union that it should have met with this obstacle. We are all very disappointed."

SPECIAL GENERAL CONFERENCE OF 1960

The special General Conference called on June 6, 1960, met as announced to consider the matter of union with the Pilgrim Holiness Church. As the special Conference began, Rev. I. L. Brown as chairperson expressed his desire to have "each one speak out of his heart on the present issue and ever keep in view the interests of our Church on the highest level."[4] He further cautioned the Conference to be "careful not to further frustrate our people," and advised a "period of quiet" to "allow our people to gain their self-confidence and lessen any further possibility of disunity." He suggested the Executive Committee would work out ways and means of strengthening its position regarding church union, and advised the adoption of a budget system throughout the whole church.

A proposed draft of union was heard by the Conference and it was adopted. This was a momentous decision on the part of the Conference. The Executive Committee was given direction to consider ways and methods of promoting and giving direction in the union. Furthermore, a motion was passed to establish a budget system for the general church that was based on adult membership and administered by the Executive Committee.[5]

UNION WITH THE PILGRIM HOLINESS CHURCH FAILS

What took place in the next year was pieced together by letters, minutes, and oral tradition. Union talks with the Pilgrim Holiness Church had gone off the rails. The General Executive met immediately after the special General Conference, and a letter was written on June 7, 1960, by Rev. Brown to Rev. Melvin Snyder, general superintendent, expressing the will of the SCA: "In view of the fact that we entered a period of confusion as a result of certain financial demands that were made upon us and which we felt we were unable to meet, it is deemed necessary to postpone the time of union and give the church an opportunity to reconsider the matter. We assume some of the blame in this delay due to the fact that our method of financing created a serious problem. We therefore recommend that we adopt a budget system for the support of the general program of the church."

Rev. Brown's letter goes on to say that he was "satisfied that we returned to our original position as to what body we should join. There is no antipathy toward the Pilgrims in any way, and we did not associate the time of our union with that of the Wesleyan Methodists. Furthermore, our Executive Committee was authorized to promote a greater degree of fellowship with the Pilgrim Church and the Wesleyans."

Rev. Snyder replied on June 14, 1960, to express his disappointment but to assure that "we will be most happy to cooperate with the Standard Church in every way possible." He expressed regret that a PHC leader had not been present to "explain our organizational set-up and answer the questions which they may desire to ask."

The General Executive met on June 6, 1960, to prepare a budget system to be instigated throughout the whole denomination: each church would be assessed twenty-eight dollars per member; a salary and travel allowance was set for the general superintendent. It was in essence preparation for eventual merger talks with a prospective denomination. Churches would understand assessment requirements.

Union Talk Persists

When the General Conference Executive met on February 17, 1961, it was reported that only three students were attending Brockville Bible College—a major decline in attendance since the heyday of the 1950s. The Executive discussed closing the school and moving the publishing house to the BBC premises. A letter of invitation was read from Lorne Park College, the Free Methodist training center located northwest of Port Credit (in what is now Mississauga, Ontario), inviting Brockville Bible College to amalgamate with them. Rev. Irwin Brown was offered a position by Lorne Park College. This, of course, instigated a lively discussion on the state of the church, which ultimately "led to discussion on the question of union as a whole." Again the pros and cons of union with another holiness church were debated and discussed. A letter was read from Bishop L. Marston of the Free Methodist Church regarding union of the two churches, with an invitation to meet the FMC bishops at Winona Lake, Indiana, April 17–20, 1961. The Executive decided to accept the invitation. Moreover, a committee was established to begin preliminary negotiations for the amalgamation of Lorne Park College and Brockville Bible College.

That spring, the SCA delegation—consisting of Reverends I. L. Brown, A. J. Slater, R. P. Voteary, J. R. Walsh, G. W. Armstrong, and Mr. Clem Hobin—began the long motor trip to Winona Lake. A preliminary meeting took place on the way in the Diamond Horseshoe Motel in London, Ontario, to discuss what the agenda for negotiating should include: the Annual Missionary and Sunday School Conventions; provisions for churches not wishing to join the union; and the educational and missionary fund. Upon the delegation's arrival, three meetings were conducted at Winona Lake.

The two denominational committees met on April 18 and the Free Methodist bishops—Marston, Fairburn, Kendall, and Taylor—presented eleven proposals.[6] The Executive minutes record that the SCA committee favoured the proposals and accepted them as a possible basis for merger. The next day, the SCA Executive Committee convened in the Bishop's Room at Winona Lake and recommended that the General Conference of the SCA unite with the FM church according to the terms agreed upon. They also called for a special session of General Conference on Monday, June 5, 1961, at the Brockville Standard Church.

SPECIAL CONFERENCE, JUNE 5, 1961

Events were heating up. There was much discussion again concerning union. Now it was with the Free Methodist Church. But something was happening among the laity of the church: union talk fatigue.

When the Special Conference convened, an unexpected member appeared. The Egyptian Conference had heard of the merger talks with the Free Methodist Church; they were unhappy about any move in that direction. Hence, the Egyptian Conference voted to send Rev. Conley to represent their concerns. Rev. Conley flew home—his first airplane flight across the ocean—and arrived at the Conference to the surprise of everyone attending.

Rev. I. L. Brown opened the special session of General Conference by exhorting the Conference on the need to weigh the forthcoming matters very carefully and make decisions that would benefit the entire church rather than just a local situation. The matter of merger between the FMC and the SCA was placed before the Conference.

The assets of General Conference were listed as follows:

1. Brockville Bible College $125,000
2. Standard Publishing House $75,000
3. The apartment building $120,000
4. Girls' dormitory $20,000

A paper prepared by the Executive Committee listed the benefits of union:

1. Assistance for Brockville Bible College, the publishing house, and foreign missions presently experiencing difficulty and an accumulated debt of $2,000;

2. Increased pool of preachers to help fill needy circuits;

3. Benefit to camp meetings;

4. Assistance for printing establishment of the Standard Church publishing house.[7]

Rev. Casement was in attendance and presented an explanation of the financial obligations and management of the Free Methodist Church. Appreciation for his explanation was expressed by the Conference.

Momentum for the union was gaining, but a note of caution was sounded: Rev. Conley read a report from the Egyptian Conference expressing their opposition to joining the Free Methodist Church. A close fraternal relationship between the Egyptian Free Methodist

Church (all of which were former Holiness Movement churches) and Egyptian Standard churches had not developed in Egypt as had occurred in Canada: there had been a lack of cooperation between missionaries and churches.[8]

It was now time to bring the matter to a conclusion. Papers were distributed reviewing the pros and cons of union. Superintendent Brown summarized what he felt were the issues. A motion was placed before the Conference to join the FMC: it was carried by a vote of thirteen in favour, nine opposed, and one abstention.[9] But the decision to join was not yet final. Conference also decided that a membership vote would be taken by each congregation and a 60 percent positive vote for union with the FMC would be necessary for the union to be consummated. All votes were to be mailed to the General Conference secretary by July 17, 1961.

It was also the pleasure of Conference to discuss the amalgamation of the Brockville Bible College with Lorne Park College. No final decision was made, but Conference agreed to lend BBC's books and furniture to LPC for use with their students—it seemed that BBC was destined for closure and the death Bishop Horner's vision. Miss Ethel Clark, long-time teacher at BBC, was also recognized for her years of sacrificial service and was given a gift of $1,400 in appreciation.

For the last five years, the Standard Church had been consumed by union talk with the Holiness Movement, the Wesleyan Methodists, the Pilgrim Holiness, and now the Free Methodists. Many laity began to wonder if their leadership did anything other than negotiate merger proposals. Some pastors resisted what they felt was being forced upon them by the leadership without their input and consensus.

When the vote was counted, the "no" vote outnumbered the "yes" vote by 333 to 131.[10] Union talk would be dead for a generation.

NEW DAY

During the time the Standard Church was conducting the vote as to whether they would join with the Free Methodists—a union Rev. I. L. Brown strongly favoured—Rev. Brown received a personal letter from the board of directors of Lorne Park College. In it was an invitation to become the director of college affairs at the college. Rev. Brown recalled, "My soul was filled with joy." Immediately, Rev. Brown called the Executive Committee of the General Conference and read the letter of invitation to them. The Executive agreed they would release him to make whatever choice he felt led to make. Rev. Brown told them his choice was to accept the invitation to join the staff at Lorne Park College. Subsequently, Rev. Brown submitted his resignation as general superintendent of the Standard Church, and immediately wrote Lorne Park College informing them of his decision. The college sent a truck to move Rev. Brown and his belongings to Lorne Park, where an apartment awaited him for occupancy. This was June 1961; it was only a few weeks later, on July 17, that the vote to join the Free Methodist Church was tabulated and rejected.

WHERE FROM HERE?

Another special session of General Conference was subsequently held that fall on Sept 5, 1961, at the Standard church on 100 Perth Street in Brockville to deal with the leadership vacuum caused by Rev. Brown's resignation and the rejection by the membership to joining the Free Methodist Church. Rev. A. J. Slater occupied the chair and spoke to the Conference from Hebrews 4 saying, "Let us fear of a promise being left to us of entering His rest."

The first items of discussion were devoted to Brockville Bible College. What should be done with the building and contents? There were no teachers available at present: Miss Ethel Clark had also accepted a position with Lorne Park College. Word was received that

LPC had rejected receiving the books and furniture on loan from BBC. Conference decided to leave BBC's books and furniture intact for the time being. It would prove to be a good decision.

The general tone of the Conference was dispiriting: the resignation of Rev. I. L. Brown, the death of BBC, a dearth of available preachers for assignment to circuits; the lack of a pension plan for retiring preachers; churches in need of reviving; an empty home missions fund; the search for an editor for the *Christian Standard*. So acute was the need for ministers on the home front that Conference requested the missionary board to release Rev. Earl Conley from Egypt to help fill pulpits in the church at home. Rev. Conley indicated that the Egyptian Conference was indeed moving toward self-government and was able to continue for a time without a missionary on the field; but he did not advise leaving the field permanently without a missionary.

The church struggled on for a year until the next General Conference, which was held in the Brockville Standard Church on September 11, 1962. The roll was called and fifteen elders and eight lay delegates answered to their names. The first item of business was the election of a new general superintendent. Rev. Earl R. Conley, only thirty-four years of age, was declared elected receiving nineteen of the twenty-three votes cast. Assistant superintendents were also elected: Rev. Arnold Rigby would serve the Kingston Conference, Rev. B. W. Fleming the New York Conference, and Rev. J. B. Pring the Western Conference. The annual Conferences reported eight Circuits in the Western Conference, four in the New York Conference, and eighteen in the Kingston Conference for a total of thirty churches and preaching points. It was the beginning of a new era in the Standard Church that lasted for nearly forty years.

During the Conference sessions Rev. I. L. Brown returned to report concerning Lorne Park College. He was cordially received and reported that three Standard Church students were in attendance at LPC: Clark Caldwell, Gary Walsh,[11] and Reta Holmes.

New Approaches

The Home Missions and Church Extension Committee of the SCA endeavored to inject optimism into the 1962 General Conference. The committee made an attempt to pinpoint reasons for and then rectify the seemingly forlorn state of the church: "We feel the condition of our Church today is to a great extent due to our lack of an aggressive Home Missions and Church Extension program. We, therefore, feel it is an imperative that a Church extension program be instituted and put into operation immediately."[12] A fundraising plan was suggested whereby each church would contribute three to four dollars per week and receive pledges to launch new churches.

Personal evangelism in homes began to receive attention as a method of bringing converts to a saving faith in Christ. The Napanee Standard Church hosted a seminar and invited Nate Krupp to teach his course on how to lead a person to Christ. During the Friday evening session, as part of the practicum, he took one of the pastoral students, Robert Gamble, to visit the George MacGarvey family. The evangelists were just about to ask the MacGarveys to receive Christ when the doorbell rang and visitors arrived, calling the session to a halt. But the converts were not lost. Pastor Nelson Peters stopped by the next day and made an appointment to visit that evening. He and his wife, Nellie, led the conversation, while their daughter, Linda, took care of the MacGarvey children. Nelson and Nellie led George and Shirley through the steps of repentance and acceptance to a saving faith in Jesus Christ. George MacGarvey later became a pastor in the Standard Church and ultimately was elected to the office of general superintendent in 1986.

Sharing one's faith through personal evangelism offered an alternate approach to the traditional Standard Church methodology of saving sinners, responding to the altar call of a revival service. The success of the Napanee seminar encouraged the 1963 Kingston annual Conference to recommend that pastors and delegates read Nate Krupp's book, *You Can*

Be a Soul Winner: Here's How, as well as other supplemental books on the "how to" of personal evangelism.

There were, however, some discouraging turns of events that might easily have cast a blanket of gloom over the 1963 Annual Conference: letters of resignation from Rev. I. L. Brown, Rev. J. R. Walsh, and Rev. A. J. Slater. All three resignations were accepted with regret and each man was requested to reconsider his decision and maintain his affiliation with the church. But all was not dispiriting. The disheartening letters of resignation were offset by the encouraging requests of four enthusiastic young men desiring entrance into the ministry: William Milligan, Barney Wood, Wilbert Bertrim, and George MacGarvey.

The Standard Church would continue. Rev. Earl Conley, as the new general superintendent, was a young man with a big challenge ahead of him. But he was determined and resolute to carry on. The church needed a new vision along with new recruits to fill pastoral vacancies and he believed with God it was possible.

EARL AND DORIS CONLEY

Earl Conley was the youngest son of George and Sarah Jane Conley. He was born on August 31, 1928, in Montreal, Quebec. His family had lived on a farm near Morin Heights, but when the mill closed in 1921, his father moved the young family to Montreal where he had been hired by local contractors. Earl's mother was deeply religious, a dedicated follower of Jesus Christ; she also had been an unabashed supporter of Bishop Horner from his early days in the Holiness Movement Church until his death in 1921 at Ivanhoe. She was unquestionably the spiritual leader in her home and Earl from his boyhood was especially attached to her. Earl was raised in the early Standard Church practice of attending camp meetings and conventions from his childhood until his teens. At a young age he became an earnest Christian and at age eight in a service conducted by Rev. W. J. Watchorn, in the Standard Church Mission at

1475 Mountain Street, Montreal, he felt the call of God upon his life for missionary work.[13] In 1945, he shared with his mother that he thought he should attend Brockville Bible College. Earl had obtained a good job in the office of the Canadian National Railroad; his mother was supportive of Earl's desire to attend Bible College but suggested, "Perhaps you should stay awhile and save some money." Earl replied, "The cattle on a thousand hills are the Lord's." His mother recalled, "I was glad he was obeying the Lord but it hurt to see the last of my children leaving home. I had such a lonesome feeling, but I kept praying and when tears would flow unbidden, I would say, 'Lord, Thy will be done. He is Thine. Take him and use him if it kills me.'"[14]

That fall, in September of 1945, Earl registered at Brockville Bible College. The teaching staff included Rev. I. L. Brown, Miss Clark, and Miss Convay. He also became acquainted with Harold Moyles, a "fascinating character," who served as gardener, caretaker, and handyman around the college.[15] Rev. Conley recalled, "The student body consisted of a fine group of young people."

In May of 1947, the young and promising minister Earl Conley joined the Conference of the Standard Church, which was convened at Lake Eloida. In early July, he was assigned to a summer pastorate at Roblin, Ontario, where he recalled riding on his bike over gravel roads to make pastoral calls. In September of that same year, he was assigned to Belleville to assist Rev. J. G. Nussey, who was in his fiftieth and last year of ministry. "I learned a lot from his ministry," reported Rev. Conley. Rev. Nussey wasted no time in small talk—when he felt a home visit was complete, he would abruptly call for prayer, kneel, and after prayer be on his way.

On November 20, 1948, Earl Conley married Doris Brownell in the North Gower Standard Church with Rev. R. Hawley and Rev. J. G. Nussey officiating. Doris had indicated she had received a call to missionary work. That, of course, was important to Earl but along with that, she was a gifted piano player, singer, and speaker; moreover, she had roots in the Holiness Movement and Standard churches from her grandmother, Ma Brownell. They made the perfect team. Over fifty years later, Rev. Conley, looking back over the years of his marriage, made this tribute to his wife and wrote, "From that day Doris has become not only a companion and friend; she has been my partner in every aspect of my ministry. We have rightly been called 'The Conley Team.' I could not have carried on through the years without her help and patience. Thank God for the gift of a wonderful wife!"[16]

Despite his youth, Rev. Conley's experience and education had made him a worthy candidate for the position of superintendent. He was mature, articulate, and well acquainted with Standard Church history and culture. Moreover, he had proven himself a man of action and vision in the church, both at home and Egypt.

THE CONLEY ERA

Rev. Conley knew that members and adherents of the Standard Church needed to be revived with positive news. Much of that would come through providing new personnel to fill the pulpits of churches. But here was the dilemma: how would young men and women respond to the call of God into ministry and where would they be trained?

In late spring of 1963, Rev. Conley, with the approval of his executive committee and other like-minded pastors, determined to revive the traditional "Feast of Pentecost" and conduct a four-day pastors' retreat on the old historic grounds of Lake Eloida camp. It was an opportunity for new recruits to respond to the call of God and also to revive and renew the fundamental teachings of the church on entire sanctification and the baptism of the Holy Spirit. It was also a venue for instilling new vision and hope for the future. It began small: doomsayers had forecast it would be a funeral. But after a small group of about six met for prayer on Thursday morning, the services gained momentum and by the end of the weekend a large number of laypeople also joined in the services. The services on Sunday were well attended; the old tabernacle rang with praises to God. Rev. James Smith looked about at the crowd of people and remarked, "We were told it would be a funeral, but this doesn't look like a funeral to me!"

BROCKVILLE BIBLE COLLEGE

Another indication a new wind blowing was the reopening of Brockville Bible College in 1963. Rev. Conley and his executive committee recognized that if the church was to have new men and women trained for ministry, they would need a training centre to be taught, mentored, and endowed with a positive attitude for the Standard Church and her work. The 1966 General Conference minutes recapped what took place:

> In 1963, it was concluded that in spite of numerous difficulties the College must be re-opened. As plans were finalized for the re-opening, a bequest was received which was taken as a confirmation of the course upon which we had decided and for which we had been praying.
>
> During the first year that the College was re-opened there were six students. During the second year there were eight students. During the third year the number increased to ten students.
>
> The teachers during the past three years have been Rev. Elgan Armstrong, Rev. E. Conley, Mrs. E. Conley, Rev. A. Rigby and Rev. J. B. Pring. Most of these teachers have had to commute from circuits.[17]

NEW COLLEGE PRESIDENT

The enthusiasm of BBC was indicative of a renewed enthusiasm within the Standard Church during the 1960s. Rev. Elgan Armstrong was appointed dean of the college in 1966 and two years later, in 1968, Elgan was asked to relocate from his pastorate at Watertown, New York, and become full-time resident dean on the BBC campus. Rev. Armstrong immediately began a construction project of a three-story addition to the existing girls' dorm to serve as residence for the dean, new dormitory facilities for the girls, and a small gymnasium in the basement for recreational activities and student assemblies. Elgan was extremely gifted and versatile: "As a professor, he is ably qualified in the fields of Greek and Bible literature. As a job superintendent, the entire building project has been under his supervision."[18] He also began an aggressive deputation schedule and travelled with students to represent the college in churches and conventions. The college was blessed with a new influx of young students fresh out of high school who were talented and gifted at music. The BBC quartet—consisting of Faye Montgomery (pianist), Elsie Barnard, Margo Crozier, Marvin Croswell, and Ross Hobin—was extremely talented, and Elgan saw to it they were provided with appropriate sound equipment to enhance their presentations. Elgan's wife, Verda, served not only as mother to her daughters Donna Rae and Joanne, but became dorm mother to the young students fresh out of high school; she also served as college administrator and secretary. More students were drawn to the college, many from the western provinces. A 6,700-mile tour of churches in western Canada took seven students travelling for fourteen days in ten services with stops in Saskatchewan, Alberta, and British Columbia. As the 1968 *Key Yearbook* reported, "The trip was a complete success as the East and West were drawn much closer together. The crowds were excellent and the team received a spiritual uplift. The College is looking forward to a bigger and better trip next year with a larger bus to accommodate more students. Come to BBC and travel with us." New gifted students were attracted forming new trios and quartets. Records were recorded and yearbooks were distributed. BBC had become a unifying element across the church at large, and a generator of positive feelings about the denomination.

New Churches

Following Rev. Conley's election as general superintendent, the Standard Church began to build, buy, and renovate churches, tabernacles, and parsonages; it was a period of peace and renewed enthusiasm. Pembroke had already led the way in 1958 by selling the old mission church and building the new Broadview Chapel under the leadership of Rev. J. R. Walsh. Rev. Conley encouraged building and progress: Shawville purchased new land and in 1965 a new church was constructed. In the meantime, Rev. Conley proposed relocating the North Gower church: in 1966 the North Gower Standard Church dedicated a beautiful new sanctuary and educational facility on a strategic location at the edge of the village along Highway 16 leading into Ottawa. Waterbury Centre in Stowe also relocated and built a new church in the picturesque mountains of Vermont. Three new churches were a boost to Standard Church morale. The Conley years were times of building and growth.

New Church Dedications

- Shawville (1965); Rev. E. S. Craig, pastor
- North Gower (1966); Rev. E. R. Conley, pastor
- Stowe/Waterbury Centre (1966); Rev. Fred Clow, pastor
- Kingston (1975); Rev. A. A. Rigby, pastor
- Brockville (1980); Rev. L. W. Croswell, pastor
- Belleville (1981); Rev. L. B. Moore, pastor

Church Extensions

- Stockdale (1971); Rev. N. Peters, pastor
- Pembroke (1974); Rev. G. H. MacGarvey, pastor
- Wilton (1976); Rev. P. A. Rigby, pastor
- Foresters Falls (1977); Rev. V. S. Scott, pastor

- Bloomfield (1979); Rev. L. W. Hart, pastor
- Napanee (1979), Rev. J. W. Bertrim, pastor
- Harlow (1980); Rev. R. S. Martin, pastor
- Bloomfield (1981); Rev. L. W. Hart, pastor
- Slave Lake (1983); Rev. M. Crouse, pastor

BUILDINGS PURCHASED FOR RELOCATION

- Calgary (1964); Rev. A. G. Risby, pastor
- Toronto (1964); Rev. G. H. MacGarvery, pastor
- Ivanhoe (1967); Rev. N. Peters, pastor
- Thompson (1971); Rev. R. T. Clark, pastor
- Vancouver (1972); Rev. Lena Johnston, pastor
- Pickering (1984); Rev. J. W. Bertrim, pastor

ADDITIONS TO EXISTING CHURCHES

- Stockdale (1971); Rev. N. Peters, pastor
- Wilton (1976); Rev. P. A. Rigby, pastor
- Foresters Falls (1977); Rev. V. S. Scott, pastor
- Napanee (1979); Rev. G. H. MacGarvery, pastor

NEW PARSONAGES BUILT OR PURCHASED

- House purchased in Brockville (83 Stewart Blvd.) for general superintendent (1970)
- Watertown parsonage purchased (1972); Rev. J. W. Bertrim, pastor
- Kingston (1973); Rev. P. A. Rigby, pastor
- Brockville (1976); Rev. L. W. Croswell, pastor
- North Gower, acreage purchased for parsonage (1977); Rev. E. Craig, pastor
- Foresters Falls extension (1983); Rev. J. J. Plaizier, pastor
- Pickering (1984); Rev. J. W. Bertrim, pastor

- Harlow (1985); Rev. J. J. Plaizier, pastor
- Malone (1981); Rev. Howard Ross, pastor
- Shawville (1986); Rev. B. J. Wood, pastor

New Camp Meeting Tabernacles

The new Horner Memorial Tabernacle had been erected on the Ivanhoe, Ontario, campgrounds just prior to Rev. Conley's election. It was designed by Clem T. Hobin and constructed under the supervision of Rev. R. P. Voteary (1961).

Carson Memorial Tabernacle was built on the Newbrook, Alberta campgrounds (1964).

Years later, in 2011, upon reviewing the number of buildings constructed, renovated, or purchased during his tenure as general superintendent, Rev. Conley was amazed. He gave glory to God and shared the words of Jesus: "One sows and another reaps" (John 4:37–38).

Publishing Responsibilities Shift

As already noted, the death of Rev. Hornby suddenly and unexpectedly shifted the heavy responsibilities of printing to other shoulders. The board of directors found an able and consecrated young woman in the person of Miss Ruby Jamieson. Ruby had served the church for many years as the manager of the Standard Church Book Store. While serving there, she also learned the operation of the printing plant, as well as the comprehensive knowledge of the business associated with it. She was handed a heavy load but, as Rev. Brown reported, she did it "cheerfully and vigorously." Assisting her were Arnold Kelly, who became Ruby's right hand printer and machinery operator, and Myrna MacDonald (Arnold and Myrna were later married) who looked after the book store. Ruby Jamieson's 1962 General Conference report for the publishing house read: "Our duties as manager have been heavy, the hours long, and often the physical taxed to its capacity; but the results have been rewarding."

Printing Tradition Continues

When Rev. Conley assumed the role of general superintendent in 1962, he continued to encourage the publishing ministry. He became an avid writer and editor of the *Christian Standard*, as well as publishing several historical booklets such as *Anniversary Reflections, 1917–1987*, *70 Years of Missions 1919–1989*, *Missions in Review*, and *Glimpses*. He also published numerous historical articles, photos, and memorabilia from past issues of the *Christian Standard* and Horner publications. Indeed, without his diligent recording of various events and historical documentations, much of the Standard Church history would have been lost and forgotten. He also supervised reprints of the word edition of *Christian Praise* for camp meetings and paperback editions of *Ralph C. Horner, Evangelist*.

Superintendent's Home in Brockville

As the church progressed, Rev. Conley was moved to full-time status as superintendent in 1970, and a two-story duplex was purchased at 83 Stewart Boulevard in Brockville for the general superintendent's residence. The Conleys, now living near the church headquarters at the college on Perth Street, were free to take a full load of teaching at BBC (Doris and Earl Conley taught courses ranging from theology and Bible courses to Sunday school methods and pastoral counseling). Rev. Conley was also freed to visit churches, travel to the Egyptian mission field, edit the *Christian Standard*, and attend camps throughout the summer (usually as the morning Bible teacher). Also, beginning in 1971, he organized home missionary endeavors into northern Manitoba (Pioneer Summer Evangelism), which led to purchasing a house with room to begin a pioneer work at Thompson under the leadership of Western superintendent Rev. Russell T. Clark. Rev. and Mrs. Walter and Margo Perry were assigned to Thompson in 1972.

The Future Ahead

Rev. Conley had earned the respect of the denomination and had the leadership of the church firmly in hand. But where would the church go from here? Rev. Conley had become general superintendent in a period of despondency and self-doubt. His goal was to consolidate, console, and rebuild. Under his leadership the church was gaining confidence. A new generation of pastors was maturing to think and consider new perspectives on how the ministry should take place. In 1978, the sixtieth anniversary of the Standard Church was celebrated in the modern, newly built sanctuary of the Kingston Standard Church and hosted by Rev. Arnold Rigby.

Something new again was in the wind that would catch the excitement of the church and stretch her vision. But the dream would also lead to a reality check. The denomination faced limited resources, too few sponsoring churches, the failure of the denomination to plant churches, the inability of many to switch ministry paradigms, and limited career opportunities in the ministry for a generation of young people with an expanding worldview.

19

Clash of Old and New

New winds were again blowing through many Standard churches, bringing in fresh life but also stirring up controversy. There were those nurtured on the old revivalist diet of camp meetings and conventions who were entrenched in their thinking of how the church should be conducted. They were unable (or unwilling) to switch ministry paradigm to the new church growth movement taking place in the 1960s. The facilitator for change was Brockville Bible College and the new president, Elgan Armstrong. Armstrong had graduated with a BA from Marion College and had experienced a campus revival of confession and prayer among students and staff. He, in turn, exposed the BBC students to large interdenominational events such as the international Sunday school conventions in Detroit and Toronto, and the Institute for Basic Youth Conflicts in Cleveland, Ohio. Students from BBC learned about churches like First Baptist Church of Hammond, Indiana, led by well-known pastor and innovator Rev. Jack Hyles, whose bus ministry brought thousands each week from the surrounding towns to his Sunday school and church. Most in the Standard Church had been converted (saved) in camp meetings or revival services, but BBC students were learning that many in the large churches featured at conventions were converted in Sunday school or brought to faith through personal visitation in their homes, as taught by James Kennedy in his Evangelism Explosion course from Corral Ridge Presbyterian

Church in Fort Lauderdale, Florida. As BBC prospered, a new generation of graduating pastors began to look beyond their traditional past and challenge the revivalist methods taught by their forefathers.

Hence, the "New Complex" was born in 1978—a bold plan to consolidate Brockville Bible College, the church headquarters, and the local Brockville Standard Church on a forty-two-acre bush lot on Centennial Road just outside the Brockville city limits. The 1979 Kingston annual Conference minutes reported: "God has done wonderful and marvelous things for the Brockville Bible College during 1978. There has been a spirit of enthusiasm, optimism, and loyalty among students and staff. The future is looked forward to with great anticipation as we all work together under God's direction." During graduating exercises held in the Brockville Standard Church on March 17, 1978, twenty-three graduates received awards from the college. The Educational Committee enthusiastically reported the purchase of the Centennial Road property and the potential of the New Complex proposal. The New Complex served as an arch joining the old and new with their different approaches and philosophies: old Standard Church loyalists loved to build (Horner was a builder); the younger aggressive element became enthused because it represented a break from the past into something new with the dream of ultimately providing accreditation for BBC courses.

Unfortunately, in the end, the two could not reconcile. Where would the generation of new pastors minister? Ultimately, many looked beyond the Standard Church and joined other denominations; those remaining began to urge merger with a larger denomination with wider horizons. The flow of students began to diminish. To understand how this took place, allow me to take you on my personal journey, for I was part of the new generation who became involved in the merger process. I had been inculcated by my friendship with Rev. Ken Bombay and his students at North West Bible College in Edmonton, and the booming growth and expansion years of the Pentecostal Assemblies of Canada during the 1950s and 1960s.

PERSONAL JOURNEY: LAURENCE CROSWELL

Many will remember 1967 as one of the most notable years in Canada because it was Canada's centenary and celebrations were held throughout the nation. There was a sense of optimism and pride throughout the country. It was also the year in which I (Laurence) sensed God's call on my life to leave my teaching position at Hazeldean School in Edmonton, a job which I loved, and follow God's strong direction to enter the ministry of the Standard Church. That fall my younger brother, Marvin, and I pointed my '54 Ford Customline eastward on the Trans-Canada Highway and began the long, arduous drive to Bible college in Brockville. We looked forward to a year of excitement and challenge with new horizons before us. We arrived in time to sing and lead the music at the historic Ivanhoe Camp Meeting; Rev. Eldon Craig, a young, budding Standard Church preacher, was the evangelist. I had been appointed as weekend pastor for the 1967–1968 church year to Wilton and Violet, near Odessa, Ontario, a small country circuit of two churches. The members were especially kind to us and adopted Marvin and me as their western sons, serving us many after-church dinners and lunches. Carmel and Lyle Lasher lived near the Violet parsonage, and on many occasions we stopped by and heard how Carmel's father, Rev. George Kelly, had ministered as pastor and evangelist in the early days of the Standard Church. I well remember listening to one of his sermons recorded on a reel-to-reel tape entitled "The Potter's Wheel" and the effect his message and preaching had on me as a twenty-three-year-old preacher. Gracious hosts such as Pauline and Allan Dafoe served many Sunday roast beef dinners, and we listened to Pauline's stories of her dad, Rev. Nelson Peters, a converted farmer and icon in Standard Church circles during the 1950s and 1960s. Though he was not Bible college educated, he could recount a repertoire of convicting stories that would fill his altars full of seekers. He was much in demand for special services and camp meetings. Others, too numerous to mention, provided hospitality and love, but I cannot not fail to mention Mrs. Chile's apple pies: they were never-to-be-forgotten fabulous and famous, and she took us into her home like a mother hen gathers her chicks.

But deep in my heart I knew this wonderful country pastorate was not my life calling. I had a deep conviction that God wanted me in Brockville with the college church—I was a teacher and educator. I determined to wait on God's timing, but the opportunity came soon. The present college church pastor, Rev. Eldon Craig, his wife, Frances, and their two girls, Sharon and Merri-Lynn, had been temporarily stationed at the Brockville church in 1967 while waiting to move to Egypt as the first on-field missionaries since the Conleys had returned in 1961. The Craigs left for Egypt in November of 1968, and I was appointed interim pastor.

The Brockville Standard Church was a challenge; the attendance was small but it was home church for the college student body. The church had begun as a direct outgrowth of the Standard Church Seminary. The students of the seminary first met in 1921 for regular worship services and prayer meetings in the house at 245 Perth Street and later in the dining hall of the seminary. When a few people from the community began to join for worship, the necessity for a separate building became apparent. It was decided in 1923 to purchase a property at 100 Perth Street across the tracks from the college property. It was a postage-sized lot with on-site parking in the narrow driveway and rear for perhaps five cars if they squeezed in tightly; a hydro pole had been placed about one-third of the way across the driveway to complicate driving in or backing out onto Perth Street. The only reason expressed to me for not building on the large Bible college acreage a short distance north on the Perth Street Hill was that the south side of the railroad tracks represented being in the city of Brockville.

I was full of enthusiasm but extremely naïve. The small wage offered was no hindrance to me. I had a definite "call," so I simply found a half-time job at the local Prince of Wales Public School teaching the boys' physical education program from grades four to eight (in retrospect one of the best things I could have done to help our ministry). Overseeing the entire boys' physical education program was a challenge my training in educational gymnastics had not prepared me for, but my principal, Mr. David Cotie, was patient in supporting me, and I had three good years in that position (concluded by "my boys" winning the Leeds Grenville County Junior Track Meet). The next year I was placed in a grade three class (the only year I taught full time at POW) to qualify for my permanent Ontario teaching certificate. I am thankful for the twenty-four years at Prince of Wales. God was good: thirteen teachers from POW at one time or another attended our church during the following years, including my principal, David Cotie, and his wife, Bea, who later became members of our church and personal friends. Moreover, my part-time teaching job helped support our family during the building years at the church, allowing us to remain long term in Brockville to lead and guide the church through various stages of growth and development without personal financial stress. Suffice it to say, I am a strong advocate of "tent-making ministries" for young pastors seeking to plant new works or grow small churches.

When Annual Conference was held in 1969, the stationing committee appointed me to continue as pastor of the Brockville Standard Church. I was engaged to Faye Montgomery, a talented young woman from Foresters Falls, Ontario, who had graduated from BBC, was enrolled in Ottawa Teacher's College, and would definitely be an asset to the church and college ministries. We married on June 28, 1969, on a hot, humid day in the Foresters Falls United Church. The Kingston Conference superintendent, Rev. Arnold Rigby, believed in us and did his utmost to encourage us in every way possible. Our gratitude to him will not be forgotten.

The Brockville church was a challenge. Rev. George Armstrong had been pastor of the church from 1962–1966. He had been a tireless Sunday school worker and used his car to bring children to the church from the city and countryside. Sunday school attendance rose to more than sixty and new people began to attend. When Rev. Armstrong was stationed in

Napanee, Rev. J. Pring temporarily filled in until the Craigs came to Brockville in 1967. Eldon and Frances Craig began to emphasize a family approach to the ministry, and a number of young couples began to take leadership and serve in the church. The Armstrongs and Craigs were responsible for beginning the transition of the Brockville Standard Church from serving primarily BBC staff and students into a church reaching into the broader community and countryside.

When I began my ministry in Brockville, I was busy to say the least. I was teaching part time at the POW school, finishing my Bible college courses for ordination (I already had my BEd from the University of Alberta); getting the parsonage ready for a new bride; teaching an English course at the college as well as leading a small college choir; and I began to emphasize the Sunday school as a means for expanding our ministry into the small city of Brockville and neighbouring hinterland. The emphasis in the 1960s was highly influenced by Jack Hyles. I had read his books and travelled with BBC to Detroit: "bus ministry" was promoted as an effective means for church growth. Believing we could do it too, I purchased an old Pontiac station wagon and filled it with children. We soon had a used school bus painted green and were bringing over thirty children and youth to the church on Perth Street. That, however, upset the status quo of the church and surprised many of the congregation that on rally Sundays we could have 100 (on one Sunday, 150) in attendance, many of them wiggling, unchurched children and youth with little experience in church protocol. I continued to be involved helping in the college ministry with Rev. Elgan and Verda Armstrong, the principal and administrators of BBC. The college was flourishing (in 1969–1970 attendance reached a peak of thirty[1]), the church was growing, and there was a positive sense across the denomination. The Armstrongs recognized the need for a strong local church to attract students and in turn were extremely helpful in the Brockville church: Verda played the new Hammond organ, giving the church services a completely different atmosphere; Elgan applied his building expertise and headed up the major renovations and modernization of the church sanctuary. (In fact, we were finishing the carpeting and installation of new seats literally an hour before the funeral service of former general superintendent and church icon Rev. J. B. Pring in March 1971.[2]) Soon new young families were attracted to attend the little church on Perth Street.

We realized, however, that in order for the church to experience continued growth and expansion, we would eventually have to move. In 1975, the church purchased a three-and-a-half-acre lot from Mr. Bill Van Dusen just outside the city limits on County Road 27, the extension of Centennial Road, on the way to Lyn. We were planning to build a church that would seat approximately two hundred people—but with adequate off-street parking that did not involve a hydro pole blocking the entrance.

THE NEW COMPLEX

As the local church partnered with BBC, a larger vision began to emerge: Why not combine the assets of Brockville Bible College and the church headquarters together with the local church and cooperatively build a facility that would be larger than anything we had attempted before? Everyone would benefit. We had a dream and a vision and soon we were negotiating with Bill Van Dusen for a forty-two-acre strip of land beside and behind the new church lot on Centennial Road. He offered it to us for $71,000, a great deal of money for the denomination in 1977. Elgan Armstrong engaged an artist to draw a visionary conception of an ultramodern building complex that would house the denominational headquarters, the Bible college, and the local church. Rev. Conley passionately shared the vision at the annual Feast of Pentecost, and gifts and pledges were received. Applications and minor variances to accommodate a church and college were made to the Elizabethtown Township, and on August 11, 1978, the deal was signed and the Standard Church became owner of a large parcel of land on Centennial Road with a dream to become a teaching-administrative centre that would also become home to a vibrant local church reaching out to the greater St. Lawrence Valley. The vision became known as the "New Complex."

But enthusiasm for the New Complex began to sputter soon after the land was purchased. Prospective students to BBC began to look beyond the limited possibilities of opportunity at BBC and ministry in the Standard Church. Larger colleges such as Bethany Bible College (Sussex, New Brunswick), Emmanuel Bible College (Kitchener, Ontario), and Ontario Bible College (Toronto) were enrolling Standard Church students. Many of these students at one time might have attended Brockville Bible College. Where would the graduating students find places to minister? Where would they find churches that would accommodate and understand their philosophy of ministry? Some who applied for ministry in the Standard Church stayed for a short period of time but later went elsewhere.

This is not to say that activity and enthusiasm in the Standard Church had ceased. On the contrary, churches and parsonages were still being built and renovated during the 1980s (see chapter 18). Moreover, the Sunday school as a means for church growth began to take on new excitement and importance, especially in the eastern Canadian churches. Wilton, Kingston, and Brockville were sending out Sunday school buses to gather students. Laypeople were travelling with BBC to attend the international Sunday school conventions. Every year a Sunday school convention was held at a local church and the climax was the annual presentation of the Sunday School Cup and Shield which was won for increases in attendance, number of memory verses learned, and hours spent in teacher training. Kingston was the most aggressive church and won the cup three years in succession.

However, by the mid-1980s, a desire to move beyond the status quo began to permeate a number of churches and pastors that would eventually lead again to talks of merger.

In 1983, BBC president Elgan Armstrong resigned and a driving force for the completion of the New Complex dream was removed.

Attendance at BBC began to dwindle. Rev. Wayne Briggs, who had been pastor of the Brockville Wesleyan Church, was appointed Bible college dean and took over leadership of the struggling student body that was left in 1984. Rev. Briggs became a healing balm to many in the denomination and travelled to churches and camp meetings applying his ministry of counseling to pastors and laypeople alike. Despite the fact that college enrollment had declined to a small number, the College board decided to proceed with relocating BBC to the new campus on Centennial Road. The relocated Brockville Standard Church was doing well, topping attendances of 250, and was able to provide classroom and library facilities. In 1985, the dean's residence was sold and a new president's home was built for Rev. Briggs on the New Complex property. The remaining Brockville Bible College buildings, consisting of the girls' dorm and the seventy-five-year-old administrative building at 243 Perth Street were sold in 1986 to facilitate the transfer to Centennial Road. A house dorm was constructed, and the college had a new campus and a fresh look. Hopefully, new facilities coupled with the enthusiasm of Rev. Briggs would be a draw to prospective students.

In 1986, the new Standard church on Centennial Road began to make plans for another cooperative effort with the denomination to build phase two of the New Complex: the General Conference would loan funds at a low rate and also provide funds to build a balcony which would include a library and denominational archives to store records and display Standard Church history. The new addition was actually a future, full-sized gymnasium and balcony. However, an interior designer was hired to suggest possibilities for the interior décor that would be pleasing in arrangement, style, and colours: creatively patterned carpet was installed providing for individual seating arranged in a semicircle around a large corner stage fashioned with creative lighting and rich, hanging drapery; the ceiling was lowered and the drab grey gym was transformed into a magnificent sanctuary, equipped with a professional sound system that created an ambiance for worship and praise. Few could recognize the new sanctuary as the ultimate gymnasium it would later become in 2005.

NEW SUPERINTENDENT, NEW FOCUS

A new era in the Standard Church of America was again being ushered in. A number of Standard churches adjusted their style and presentation of ministry and found their congregations could grow without any compromise to doctrine or beliefs. Change was evident in 1986 when the Quadrennial General Conference convened on May 19 in the Centennial Road Standard Church at the conclusion of the last Feast of Pentecost held on the historic Lake Eloida campgrounds. Rev. Earl Conley declined serving a seventh term as general superintendent. Rev. George MacGarvey, formerly the general secretary and pastor of the Pembroke church, was elected to the office; he was seen as a bridge between the traditional and those desiring change. Rev. Conley was elected missions director, a newly created position that would have positive effects on the growth of foreign missions. Major changes were taking place in the direction and organization of the Standard Church.

Foreign missions had always been close to Rev. Conley's heart and after his election as missions director, he began working to expand projects he had already begun.

MEXICO

In June of 1985, Elmer Brown of Ottawa and Rev. William Davis introduced Rev. Conley to two sisters from Mexico: Josefina Dominguez and Socorro Tapia. They desired to help establish mission work in the area of Tijuana, Mexico. In December of the same year, a week-long gospel crusade was conducted by Rev. Conley and Bill and Dorothy Davis in a small hilltop chapel at Sierra Colorado (Tijuana) that had been arranged by the Mexican sisters. Subsequently, after

General Conference in Brockville, Rev. Conley organized the first "Mexico Missions Safari" with twelve participants. Mr. and Mrs. Jim Atchison of San Diego were instrumental in helping those who visited Tijuana in 1986 and two more safaris in 1987 and 1988. They provided generous hospitality and wonderful Christian fellowship.

In 1989, a weekly outdoor ministry for women and children was launched by the Mexican sisters in Mariano Matamoros (Tijuana) with distribution of food, clothing, literature, and medicine, along with hygiene instruction. This was a working-class community, originally known as Buenes Aires. There were no evangelical churches in the area. A daily vacation Bible school was held with an enrollment of forty. As the ministry continued, there were faith commitments and requests for baptisms.

In 1992, the land was purchased at the corner where services had been held. A building was designed to be used for a chapel and multi-purpose ministry. The plans were drawn by David Lopez, a fine Christian architect. He designed the building to withstand earthquake shocks that might occur in the area. Construction was delayed because of a heavy rainfall that lasted for almost two weeks, causing the city reservoir to overflow. Roads were washed away, bridges destroyed, residences damaged, and hydroelectric and telephone systems were interrupted for days. Several buildings slid down steeply terraced hillsides. Some thirty lives were lost.

When work finally resumed, construction began on the cement block chapel. By September of 1994, the first floor was 60 percent complete. By request of the missions director, a Spanish sign was placed on the property that, translated, read "Church of the Open Door."

On June 25, 1995, the Mariano Matamoros chapel was dedicated with the building filled to capacity and a group from the Kingston Standard Church in attendance. The Kingston group sang several songs they had learned in Spanish and English and shared their testimonies. The Kingston mission team also conducted a three-day vacation Bible school along with services for adults in the new church with approximately eighty in attendance. The group also had an opportunity to minister at an anniversary service in a downtown church and an orphanage for boys. In 1996, a parsonage and several Sunday school rooms were built above the church.

By 1999, the Mariano Matamoros congregation celebrated official registration with the Mexican government with a congregation of sixty families assuming full pastoral support. They continued their outreach into other nearby communities through Bible clubs, and in 2000 a daughter congregation was established at Ejido Altiplano.[3]

GHANA

Joe and Jemima Ocran immigrated to Canada from Ghana and had spent several years in Calgary before committing their lives to Christ in the Calgary Standard Church. Soon after, they sensed a call to return to their homeland as missionaries. In 1986, they moved to Brockville, settled in the new college dorm on Centennial Road, and began attending classes at BBC. It was a one-year stay but in that time they endeared themselves to the Brockville congregation who adopted them as its own. In the years following, the Brockville church would become one of the major supporters of the Ghana mission. The following year, Joe Ocran, accompanied by Rev. E. Conley, visited Ghana to investigate the possibilities for beginning a new mission. During their travels, they were privileged to speak in a number of Methodist churches, and for the first time Joe had an opportunity to share his testimony with relatives and friends.

The next year, Joe Ocran enrolled in Ontario Bible College, Toronto, and he and Rev. Conley continued planning for a ministry in Ghana. They visited Ghana again in 1989 and made several important contacts, gathering valuable information that would assist in laying the groundwork for the proposed launching of a Ghanaian mission work in 1990. They received an enthusiastic welcome from church leaders and were given opportunity to preach in some of the largest churches in the country.

Joe Ocran returned to Ghana in February of 1990 with the purpose of finding a home that would also serve as headquarters when his family took up residence. A place was secured in Tema, fifteen miles from Accra (the capital of Ghana). Tema is a busy, industrial community with an ocean port and a population of 100,000. On August 28, 1990, the Ocrans with their two children, Albert and Diella, left Toronto to commence pioneering the Ghanaian mission.

It was a readjustment for the Ocrans to return to Ghana after living in Canada for so many years. In a letter to the church back home, Joe wrote:

Albert and Diella are both in school finally. I certainly understand the culture shock that the children might encounter. Albert especially had problems getting used to the school life and even the people here. By God's grace, he is adjusting steadily. Both Albert and Diella are speaking the local language now (not fluently, mind you). We are holding Sunday morning services in our home. We have had to restrict the number of people since we are in a residential area and such activities are not allowed and could mean trouble for us if reported to the authorities.

Tema became the hub of the Ocrans' activities. The first official services were held in the Redemption Valley School, commencing in January 1991. Large signs advertising services had been placed in three areas of the community. In addition to the Sunday morning service, there was a midweek gathering. Monday was designated as a day for door-to-door visitation. A very effective outdoor campaign was held. Attendance slowly increased. A tremendous opportunity opened when they were invited to provide religious instruction for six hundred elementary students and one hundred fifty high school students at two separate schools. On April 26–29, another successful outdoor crusade was held with large crowds and one hundred commitments. The Sunday morning attendance had greatly increased and Sunday school commenced with forty children. Construction on a new chapel began in 1991, and the first service was held in the new building on January 19, 1992, with a Sunday morning worship attendance of ninety.

But Joe Ocran was not content to simply build one local church. He had a vision that included all of Ghana. Soon the Ocrans were planning a special outdoor Easter crusade in Ashale Botwe (a village where Jemima's brother, Seth, who had recently come to faith, lived). Joe reported good prospects for commencing a church in this new community. To their encouragement, the chief of the village designated land upon which a temporary building might be constructed for worship.

Before departing for Ghana, Pastor Joe had hurriedly put together a draft organizational plan for the development of a holistic ministry to the impoverished people of Ghana—a *must*, he said, for the mission to be accepted and registered in the country. The organization sputtered until Carole Tanney, an experienced and qualified nurse from Brockville, Ontario, took over leadership. She organized a board and incorporated Project Reach Out as a nonprofit organization. She exuded boundless energy, organizing fundraising projects (garage sales, spaghetti dinners, silent auctions, bake sales); moreover, she organized field trips to Ghana for practical assistance in clinics, services, and building projects. Participants came back to Canada enthused and determined to contribute in some way to the budding mission. A major boost to the mission occurred when Sheldon Gilmer, former missionary to Congo, joined the PRO board in an advisory role. As a member of Help for the Aged, he helped formulate applications to the Canadian International Development Agency (CIDA). Funds were matched by CIDA which provided opportunities to purchase a medical van, construct a clinic, develop a vocational school, and purchase land for growing seedling fruit trees. Programs were launched into new communities which resulted in the expansion of churches. Volunteers from Canada participated in the expansion of the work: preaching and field seminars by pastors, and practical projects by nurses, dentists, and builders. Brian and Sherrie Davis also provided valuable motivation with their enthusiastic support, field visits, and generous hospitality to Rev. Ocran on his yearly return visits to Canada, providing a home base for him in Brockville to launch his deputation travels to churches, camps, and conventions.

Forward twenty years to Easter 2011. The mission in Ghana celebrated its twentieth anniversary in Sakumono: from its humble beginnings of one church, the Ghanaian mission totaled over forty-five churches (including six developing churches) and stretched from Ghana's southern to northern regions. Many of these churches got their start under a mango tree.

As a tribute to what God had done, Rev. Conley wrote, "The Missionary Societies of the Standard Church have borne a large share of the responsibility for launching and maintaining the work in Ghana. Their efforts have been supplemented by many individuals and congregations across the denomination. It has been a combined effort under the dedicated labours and leadership of our missionaries—Joe and Jemima Ocran—with the faithful labours of the national pastors."[4]

EGYPT

The oldest mission field of the Standard Church was not neglected during these years. Rev. Conley had already begun to organize his annual Egyptian safaris. During February of 1986, his last year as general superintendent, he sent an evangelistic team of four pastors—Walter Hegadorn, Alvin Lasher, Vernon Scott, and Larry Hart—to conduct seventy-one services in twenty churches to conclude with a final rally in the Shoubra, Cairo church on February 26. They would meet up with Rev. Conley's safari group (the author was a member) to arrive on February 25. The rally did not materialize because of rioting during the night of February 25 around the Pyramids Holiday Inn where the safari group was lodged. The riot was crushed by the Egyptian army after paramilitary internal security troops stormed out of their barracks near the Great Pyramids in protest, setting fire to dozens of markets and shops, destroying cars and trucks, and shattering the dining room floor of the Holiday Inn. Guests fled to their rooms before being escorted at about nine thirty to the roof for safety, where they remained for the duration of the night. The Egyptian staff calmly kept the almost three hundred guests from panic despite the sporadic rattle of gunfire, beeping smoke alarms, and raging fire in the dining room. Later that morning, they were able to lead all guests to the courtyard garden below, where they were met by a bus and taken to another hotel.

The incident did not dampen enthusiasm for Rev. Conley's Egyptian safaris and visitors were not subjected to an ordeal of this kind again. In fact, in 1988, another team from Canada visited several of the Egyptian churches and this time Rev. Conley, as the new missions director and his wife, Doris, stayed behind for almost two months to give leadership, teaching, and encouragement to the churches.

A rally was held in 1989 at the Nikhela church to celebrate the seventieth anniversary of the launching of the Standard Church mission by founding missionary Rev. F. R. Webster. Representatives from almost every Egyptian congregation attended in addition to a safari group of ten from Canada.

Perhaps one of the greatest losses to the Egyptian churches took place in 1995. Rev. Awad, the popular and charismatic Egyptian superintendent, was experiencing serious health problems. Doctors in Egypt and Canada prescribed their best medicines to help him. By August of that year, he appeared to have improved dramatically and determined to return to his work in the Tima church. He and his wife arrived in Tima Thursday morning, September 7. Later that afternoon in his home, he suffered a fatal heart attack and went to be with the Lord.

Rev. Ibraheem Hanna Soltman became superintendent of the Egyptian Conference. He was born in Mallawi, Upper Egypt, and began his training for ministry in 1960, enrolling in the Wesley Theological College, Assiut. The work in Egypt made remarkable progress under the leadership of Rev. Ibraheem. He was eager to see the work of God advance and had a vision for the future. A pioneer ministry was launched in Alexandria with a parsonage built above the church and another floor for Sunday school and future hostel for university girls. Several young men enrolled as candidates for the ministry. A new work in Cairo was also opened in a new community called Sixth of October City.

Ninety percent of Egypt's population is Islamic, but the Christian church continues to make steady progress, sometimes under difficult circumstances. At the time of publication, there are twenty-four Standard (Wesleyan) churches. Many of them have exciting ministries led by young men and their families who have directed aggressive outreach ministries, new building additions, and dynamic worship services.

SIGNS OF COMING CHANGE

A sense of discontentment began to permeate the Standard Church during the mid-1990s. Local churches in North America began to feel isolated from one another without a passionate vision for the denomination as a whole. On one hand, those who reflected the traditional ways theologically and evangelistically were slowly diminishing in influence, while churches that were thriving began moving out of the traditional Standard Church ethos. Some suggested the denomination was one generation from becoming a decentralized conglomeration of churches joined together only by their properties held in trust for the Standard Church of America.

The Pembroke Standard Church reignited the merger flame. They sold their existing church and purchased the former Pentecostal Assemblies Church on Renfrew Street, a large spacious building in downtown Pembroke with plenty of room for Sunday school and fellowship facilities. The dedication service was held on May 24, 1987, with Rev. E. S. Craig, the pastor, in charge. It was a giant step of faith for the Pembroke congregation because it involved a major commitment and monetary investment for the people of the church. Moreover, it moved them out of their small church mentality and broadened their potential for ministry. But it also raised concerns: What was the direction and future of the Standard Church to which they belonged? Who would provide leadership? Where would their youth find appropriate Bible college training and opportunity for service? Furthermore, how would the Standard Church provide future pastoral candidates for their church? Hence, the Pembroke Standard Church wrote a letter to the General Executive requesting their property deed with the ultimate desire to transfer them to a larger denomination. It was a repeat of the early 1960s, except this time it began on an individual church basis—no other church had ever requested their deed. The difficulty with their request, however, was this: according to the episcopal mode of ownership in the Standard Church, the granting of property by the General Executive to an individual congregation was not possible. According to the Manual and Discipline of the church, "All properties, real and personal of the Corporation, shall rest in the General Conference."[5] Only an amendment to the constitution would allow such a transaction.

SPECIAL GENERAL CONFERENCE 1987

In light of Pembroke's letter, the Executive Committee requested verification that the motion, vote count, and date of the society's resolution be sent to the committee for further consideration. Upon receipt of the motion's proceedings, it was decided that a special session of General Conference be called May 16, 1987, to deal with the request of the Pembroke society. Upon convening, the Executive presented General Conference with three possible options for consideration as to the future of the Standard Church:

1. That we investigate the elements necessary for the strengthening and advancement of our denomination as an instrument of God;

2. That we associate/affiliate with another denomination /organization in terms of specific ministries (i.e., college, missions, publications) while maintaining our own identity and government;

3. That we consider amalgamation with another denomination. During the sessions, it was proposed that an investigation by the Executive along with a representative body of seven laypersons be elected as a Special Committee to bring a report to the next General Conference. However, a motion to delete the last item, "that we consider amalgamation with another denomination," was carried by a close vote of 20 to 17. Merger was temporarily rejected.

The motion, however, did not solve the Pembroke dilemma. Moreover, the North Gower church also indicated they had the same concerns. Conference commissioned the General Executive and seven laypeople to study the first two proposals, as well as resolve the difficulties arising between the denomination and the Pembroke and North Gower societies. The investigation would not include outright amalgamation with another denomination but did include the process of exploring affiliation.

Pembroke did not gain possession of its deed, but it had reopened the discussion of merging with a larger denomination. Pembroke knew it had strong support.

20

MERGER

The 1987 special General Conference set in motion a process that eventually produced amazing results. The process was often ponderous and tedious, but slow and patient progress produced mutual benefit for both conservatives and progressives. Both were loyal to the Standard Church and desired to preserve the work, history, and traditions of the church—and, yes, the vision, sacrifice, and accomplishments of Ralph Horner and his band of pioneering Hornerites.

After the special session of Conference, the Special Committee was authorized to investigate two possible resolutions to stave off what was perceived as a potential division within the church precipitated by Pembroke's request for its deed.

COMMITTEE MEETING ONE

Superintendent MacGarvey wasted no time in calling the Special Committee together. The first meeting was held on October 3, 1987, to set the parameters of the study. The committee agreed to study the past and present with a view to make corrections to fulfill the purpose of the church in the future.

COMMITTEE MEETING TWO

The following meeting was scheduled for January 9, 1988. The committee was presented with a statistical overview of the Standard Church. The committee learned, for instance, that in 1928, the Kingston Conference (which at that time included the US churches) was composed of fifty-three circuits (churches) and forty other appointments for a total of ninety-three preaching points (excluding western Canada). However, in the 1929 Kingston Conference minutes, the Committee on Evangelism and Church Extension had already recognized a disturbing observation of church closures and declines in attendance; they "strongly recommended that where churches are closed and the work is dying out, very special efforts be made to revive them." The committee applauded churches for "an increase in revival efforts through the past year. There have been more than one hundred weeks of special meetings. . . ." But statistics reveal that revival meetings were not producing growth, for there was an alarming decline in attendance and membership during the next forty-five-year period: by 1975 there were only twenty-eight churches in the three North American conferences.

That was not to say, however, that recent trends of the 1980s had not indicated a turnaround in many areas. There was much positive news to report: attendance increased significantly in a number of churches; budget goals for missions, camps, and churches were met; and churches, parsonages, and camp buildings were renovated. There had also been efforts to begin new works in Gananoque, Pickering, and Slave Lake. And the mission work in Egypt was doing well, reporting new churches and revival. One member of the committee pointed out:

> Yes, we may from time to time have a problem but churches outside our denomination have their problems as well. They too have country churches as we do, and they have churches that show no growth. As a matter of fact, they are decreasing in number because the area or town they are located in is also decreasing

because people are moving to larger cities. . . . Yes, others do have problems. We have problems and needs, and, of course, some changes should be made. We are small but let's continue to build.[1]

For the next meeting, each member was requested to present a paper with observations and insights on the state of the church, and offer advice for solving the issue at hand.

COMMITTEE MEETING THREE

The Special Committee assembled for the third time on April 23, 1988, at the Brockville Standard Church to present thoughts and observations. Superintendent MacGarvey opened with an exhortation to "accept one another as we are even if we do not meet one another's standards or preconceptions. . . . [W]e are one in the body of Christ. . . . [Let us] honestly talk about our feelings, ideas, hopes and doubts."

The meeting was then opened to hear reports. Various members spoke to issues ranging from losing Standard Church heritage to reevaluating the purpose and vision of the denomination. Rev. Vernon Scott spoke candidly of coming to grips with the issue. John Hewitt of Pembroke was frank but prophetic: "Is there a glimmer of possibility that we have sparked a little spark that if fanned could be the beginning of a new and exciting day for us all?" Others spoke of the potential of the Standard Church and exhorted the committee to "Rise up and build. . . . The God of Heaven will prosper us."

Perhaps the most insightful report was that of Rev. Peter Rigby. He began by tracing the roots of the Standard Church from the very beginnings of the Horner movement. "The new denomination (the Holiness Movement) which began with a flurry of activity and success soon found itself divided over the leadership of Horner. Another denomination (the Standard Church) resulted in 1918." Rev. Rigby tactfully pointed out three historical realities:

1. The division that resulted in the Standard Church was not a special move of God, but was a conflict among brothers over the issue of leadership. The truths of Christianity were not at risk.

2. Horner as a leader was innovative, pragmatic, and charismatic. . . . He was not restricted to outworn methods but responded to needs. As a leader who made things happen he attracted people who also wanted to see things happen. This resulted in church growth. But not all the leadership who followed Horner had the same dynamic zeal to see the lost won for Christ. As a result the Standard Church failed to be an innovative organization (as Horner was) able to reach out past its own boundaries.

3. Horner applied his theology pragmatically. What convinced people was not so much his logic but the power of God in Horner's life and Horner's ability to apply his theology so that practical results were seen. This aspect of his theology has not been followed.

Rev. Rigby concluded by outlining the task at hand to be considered: "We need a new consensus. It must be a consensus which is able to build on the past without idolizing it. . . . The new consensus must be made with the realization that the denomination is in transition theologically and culturally. Yet, in the midst of this diversity the common elements must be discovered and brought together. . . . If the problems and the struggles we have encountered will help us better do the task to which God has called us, we can give praise to the One who has assured us that 'all things work together for good.' God is sovereign. Let us be willing to trust Him wherever He leads."

MORE COMMITTEE MEETINGS

The Special Committee realized that time was of the essence and set the date for the next meeting for September 17, 1988. Subcommittees met in the interim to prepare further reports on five areas of concern: involvement of laypeople, outreach, education, healing of differences, and statement of purpose. The reports and suggestions were a time of soul searching and honest evaluation of practical areas such as the inclusion of laypeople in planning and decision making, and how Conference should be conducted. It also recognized that if the church was to experience wholeness, there must be respect for distinctions that exist that we must be bound together by the lordship of Christ, as well as remember that we are called to operate within the Wesleyan perspective, which is a call to holiness of life and power for service.

One more committee meeting was held a year later on September 30, 1989, to discuss the possibilities of affiliation with other educational institutions. It was generally agreed upon that Brockville Bible College was not able to provide for the church's educational needs in its present status.

There was little that could be acted upon until the General Conference in 1990. Reports were prepared for General Conference.[2]

GROWTH AND PROGRESS

One of the interesting observations during the meetings of the Special Committee was that growth in a number of churches, as well as growth of foreign missions, was not hindered by talks of merger or affiliation as they had been in the 1960s. Reports were shared and discussions held but they did not consume the participants and deter their focus from ministry. In fact, there was a growing sense of brotherhood. Perhaps because local churches and foreign missions realized they must continue the work of ministry regardless of what eventually would take place within the bureaucracy of the Standard Church of America, congregations and pastors recommitted to reaching their communities; and communities and missions under Rev. Conley's leadership expanded to include Ghana and Mexico. As a result, local churches that began to adjust worship styles and community focus began to reach new attendance highs. Foreign missions became fresh and exciting: missions in Egypt continued to flourish (Rev. Conley conducted his annual mission safaris), and the budding works in Ghana and Mexico provided new interest and focus.

GENERAL CONFERENCE 1990

The 1990 General Conference was convened on June 18 in the Brockville church. Rev. Awad, superintendent of the Egyptian Conference, was in attendance. All participants anticipated the importance of the Conference.

- The Special Committee presented recommendations that would give special recognition to lay members. Conference approved the recommendations in a major shift from Bishop Horner's long-preferred episcopal mode of governance: the Executive Committee would be made up of at least one-third but not more than one-half lay members; the board of missions and college board of directors would include an equal number of lay members and elders.
- Church planting received special recognition: Conference recommended that the mission board and missionary societies study the possibility of designating a specific percentage of mission offerings for planting new churches. Ten thousand dollars had been received from the estate of Sidney Crawford and designated for church planting in the Western Conference to purchase a property or to establish a revolving fund for the same.
- Conference recognized that Brockville Bible College was in transition. In 1988, Rev. Wayne Briggs resigned as dean. Rev. Laurence Croswell became interim dean. The BBC board established a new mandate for the college: A two-year program was developed offering short one- or two-week-long courses; students were also given opportunity to take inter-session courses at other Bible colleges.

Conference ended on a positive note. Changes were made to the governance and methods of conducting business, and lay delegates were made to feel part of the workings in the denomination. But there was no mention of any plans for merger or affiliation with another denomination, though the issue was not dead. The process would continue another eight years until 1998.

In the meantime, however, the Standard Church of America continued to make progress. North Gower overcame adversity: a fire badly damaged the church on March 20, 1992, but the congregation rose up in faith, renovated the burned-out ruins, and added a new sanctuary and foyer which were dedicated on October 3, 1993. Five new Ghanaian churches were visited by Rev. E. Conley and Willis Bowen in 1993, and land was purchased for a headquarters at Sakumono (Tema). By 1997, the work in Ghana reported eleven congregations. The seventy-fifth anniversary of the Standard Church of America was celebrated August 27, 1993, in a joyous afternoon service at the Ivanhoe campgrounds. Seeley's Bay Standard Church celebrated the dedication of a fine new church building on September 15, 1996, with Rev. Walter Hegadorn as pastor. The Brockville Standard Church was reaching attendance highs of six hundred. The Standard Church was actually showing healthy growth for the first time since the 1930s.

This growth, however, did not deter those who believed a merger must eventually take place. They were of the opinion that continued health, growth, and ministry in the future could only be maintained by an eventual merger with a larger organization with greater educational and human resources. But this time they believed the Standard Church could negotiate union from the standpoint of strength rather than weakness. Merger would be sought to continue the momentum in the Standard Church and add to the strength of a sister denomination.

WATERSHED—1998 GENERAL CONFERENCE

The 1998 General Conference became the watershed Conference that heralded momentous changes. Rev. Conley requested to be relieved of his duties as editor of the *Christian Standard*. A denominational newsletter would take its place. There was a detailed strategy for church planting presented with plans for financing and training. The three annual conferences of North American Standard Churches would merge and function as one Conference under the name General Conference and convene every two years. But the most monumental and far-reaching decisions arose from two recommendations posed by the General Executive.

Recommendation One

Congregations who choose, after a 51 percent majority membership vote, may be allowed to affiliate with the Free Methodist Church, The Wesleyan Church, or the Brethren in Christ Church. The Standard Church would retain deeds.

After a two-year affiliation, church deeds may be transferred upon request after a two-thirds percent majority vote by the membership. The vote would be conducted by the superintendent. The deed would be transferred at the congregation's expense, providing no monies were owed to the denomination.

Recommendation Two

That a yes/no vote be taken concerning merger with another denomination. In the event of a yes vote, a second vote would follow asking which denomination—namely, the Free Methodist Church in Canada or The Wesleyan Church—the Conference would prefer to negotiate with.

This vote signified momentous change. There was much discussion and the motion was amended to read "Are you in favour of affiliation/ merger?"

Both motions carried as a whole: thirty-eight approved; twenty opposed.

After the resolution of these two issues, recommendation regarding preference for denominations came to the floor. Results of the Conference vote were Wesleyan, 24; Free Methodist, 15; other, 17; spoiled, 1. From this juncture on, the Standard Church would continue cooperation and negotiations with only one denomination, the Central Canada District of The Wesleyan Church.

Merger was not decided upon immediately—only a *preference* for affiliation/merger—but the wheels were in motion. Recommendation one became of utmost importance in the appropriate procedure and protocol local churches must follow should they wish to take ownership of their deeds before and after merger was decided upon with The Wesleyan Church in 2003. In fact, not following the protocol as outlined at General Conference would nullify any other procedure that churches might attempt. It would eventually save two churches and a campground from being lost to the merger.

New Millennium—New Affiliation

The year 2000 not only marked the celebration of a new millennium, but it marked the beginning of a new relationship for the Standard Church with The Wesleyan Church. When General Conference 2000 convened, the General Executive presented an Affiliation and Missions Agreement with The Wesleyan Church for the approval by the membership. The Executive had received input from pastors and worked with the superintendent of The Wesleyan Church, Rev. Hodgins, to incorporate suggested changes and were now ready to hear the voice of Conference. After lunch break, Conference resumed with prayer by Ellard Perry, and the recommendation was adopted by a "yes" vote of 45, and "no," 6. It was an overwhelming vote to proceed with a closer union of the two churches.

Other interesting business transpired. The two remaining American churches, Waterbury Center and Watertown congregations, advised Conference of motions by their respective congregations to affiliate with The Wesleyan Church, and the superintendent advised them of the proper procedure. Two other churches presented plans for major building campaigns: Foresters Falls was taking the visionary step of purchasing a prime property near Cobden to relocate, and Brockville presented plans for a two-million-dollar expansion. Both churches were given permission to pursue their deeds for financing purposes. But again Conference clarified the process necessary for requesting deeds for the purpose of affiliation. Foresters Falls purchased their new property under the ownership of their local trustees; Brockville continued with their present status of ownership under the trusteeship of the Standard Church. No congregational vote was taken, but the church began to pursue what affiliation with The Wesleyan Church might look like.

Pastors and lay delegates went back to their churches. A new day was dawning for the Standard Church of America.

General Conference 2002

Members of the Standard Church waited with anticipation and expectation for the next General Conference to convene at the Centennial Road Standard Church on Friday, May 24, 2002. A number of significant events had taken place in the two-year interim of Conference:[3]

1. The Belleville Standard Church on Cloverleaf Drive (New Hope Fellowship) was sold to the Brethren in Christ Church for $150,000. The parsonage was also placed on the market.

2. The Bloomfield church was placed on home mission status and an arrangement worked out with The Wesleyan Church to reestablish the ministry.

3. The Brockville church began the third phase of its new addition to include a new sanctuary, a foyer/boulevard, and office and boardroom space. The church received a $100,000 loan from Conference, which became available from the sale of the Belleville church. In lieu of interest, the Brockville church would commit 7 percent of the initial loan

amount to Ghana missions in addition to regularly budgeted mission's allotments.

4. The Standard Church at Malone, New York, was authorized to proceed with the sale of the church and parsonage.

5. In February of 2001, the Pembroke Standard Church (Wesley Community Church) voted to merge with The Wesleyan Church. This was ratified in June 2001 and was conducted according to procedure by Superintendent MacGarvey.

6. Burke Camp, New York, drafted its own constitution and was seeking to establish its own board and membership in an effort to facilitate an ongoing ministry.

7. The Kingston Standard Church received approval to renovate and extend the entrance to include a lift and spacious office facilities.

8. Two other churches requested their deeds: the Standard church at Seeley's Bay, Ontario, and the Standard church at Newbrook, Alberta, which also included the Newbrook Camp facility. Both churches would be required to follow the procedures as outlined in the General Conference of 1998, which would require a two-thirds majority vote by members before deeds might be returned.

MERGER NOT AFFILIATION

It was part two of the Executive Report that was the most surprising. The Executive recommended that the Standard Church "continue with the affiliation agreement with The Wesleyan Church for another two years, building on the co-operation already begun." However, a member of Conference moved in amendment that Conference not only continue with the affiliation agreement, but also empower the Executive to work with The Wesleyan Church to draft a merger agreement within the next year. To the surprise of everyone, the amendment carried! Straightaway, another motion directed General Conference to convene in the next year, 2003. In preparation for this Conference, a copy of the merger draft would be sent to all pastors and local churches at least one month prior to Conference. The road to merger with The Wesleyan Church was set.

Time was of the essence and much work needed to be completed before the coming Conference. A joint meeting of the Wesleyan District Board of Administration (DBA) and the Subcommittee of the Standard Church met on December 10, 2002. Important resolutions were ironed out:

1. It was recommended that the Standard Church as a denomination merge into The Wesleyan Church, but each congregation be given opportunity to pursue one of three options:

- Merge.
- Affiliate with The Wesleyan Church on the basis of established Wesleyan policies for affiliate churches.
- Pursue an independent course.

2. No church would be forced into a relationship it did not wish to pursue.

3. A tool kit would be supplied to each church with regard to change of denominational identification and legal particulars, (i.e., transfer of deeds; Revenue Canada Registration; bank accounts). Each congregation merging would be valued as an equal member and would receive voice and vote on the direction and administration of the Central Canada District (CCD).

4. Credentials of all Standard Church pastors would be transferred to The Wesleyan Church.

5. There would be a transition district board of administration composed of leaders from the incoming Standard Church and the welcoming Wesleyan district.

6. Standard Church missions would retain their Canadian Charter from the perspective that support for the works in Ghana and Egypt were currently supported by donations from Canada. Since The Wesleyan Church had already established work in Mexico, the single Standard

Church mission church would be better served through Wesleyan World Missions oversight.

7. United Stewardship Fund (USF) payments would begin at 5 percent and increase by at least one percentage point annually up to the established USF annual rate, with a goal to be paying at the annual rate within five years.

MERGER AGREEMENT COMPLETED

The special session of General Conference of the Standard Church of America was announced and convened at the Centennial Road Standard Church in Brockville, which was now in the midst of a multimillion-dollar building project, on May 24, 2003. When the roll was called, forty-one members were present consisting of elders, executive lay members, lay delegates, and Conference organizational representatives.

The Conference began with a time of silence in memoriam of Standard Church members of Conference who had recently passed away. Rev. Conley led in a prayer of thanksgiving for their lives and work. Two were ministers who had been icons in the early work of the Standard Church: Rev. Andrew Risby, pastor of the Calgary Standard Church for fifty-six years; and Rev. Robert Gamble, pastor, evangelist, and church builder in the Kingston Conference for many years as well. Two others had been pioneer pastors' wives: Nellie Peters and Phoebe McDonald.

PANEL DISCUSSION

The business of Conference began with a panel discussion to address questions concerning merger with The Wesleyan Church. The panel was composed of Rev. Dr. Holdren, general superintendent of The Wesleyan Church; Rev. Donald Hodgins, superintendent, Central Canada District,

The Wesleyan Church; Rev. George MacGarvey, general superintendent, the Standard Church; and two members of the Standard Church Executive, Kelly Wieler and Rev. Peter Rigby.

Questions ranged from the deadline for local churches to pursue independence (September 15, 2003), to the role of Standard Church missionary societies (they would continue) to a variance in teaching the doctrines of entire sanctification and the baptism of the Holy Spirit.[4]

FINAL THINGS

Everyone waited with anticipation for what they knew would be the final item of business on the agenda: the vote to merge with The Wesleyan Church. But first, two historical items were brought to the attention of Conference:

1. August 26, 2003, would mark the eighty-fifth anniversary of the organization of the Standard Church of America, and each church was encouraged to set aside a day of celebration to commemorate that date.

2. Hillside Chapel at Morin Heights, Quebec, was designated as a Heritage Building and as such to be maintained and continued to be used in the ministry of the Word. The Morin Heights Chapel had been built in 1895 by followers of Rev. R. C. Horner and was the oldest remaining structure within the Standard Church currently being used for services of worship.

THE VOTE

Dr. David Holdren then addressed the Conference with some final remarks acknowledging the momentous significance of this Resolution for the denomination. He stated, "This is an opportunity to offer thanksgiving to the Lord for our denomination's story and journey to date.

The Standard Church brings to The Wesleyan Church a passion for God's Kingdom. We all gain by this merger."

The Executive recommended that General Conference adopt the following resolution: "Be it resolved that the Standard Church of America merge with the Central Canada District of The Wesleyan Church, and that the Standard Church Executive be instructed and authorized by this General Conference to implement the wishes of Conference in this regard."

The final vote on the motion was counted: 49 Yes; 6 No.

The motion carried.

The merger would occur officially on January 1, 2004. Each local church was given opportunity to choose immediate merger, affiliation, or independence according to Conference protocol. Many of the local churches had already voted. Others had not but would be required to do so. That is another story for the next and last chapter.

Epilogue of Final Things

After the merger of the Standard Church of America with the Central Canada District of The Wesleyan Church, January 1, 2004, there was still work to bring the union to completion. The charter for the Standard Church was not annulled and was still registered by the federal government of Canada—likewise, the charitable status of Standard Church Missions and Brockville Bible College. Most churches conducted congregational votes to join the merger before the January deadline. Two churches voted to pursue independence: Vancouver and Seeley's Bay followed the protocol as set out by the 1998 General Conference and received possession of their deeds. But there remained the issue of properties owned by General Conference, namely the apartment buildings and General Conference houses in Brockville, and other remote properties and abandoned churches scattered across Canada.

The West Joins In

The death of Rev. Andrew Risby in 2002 was a leadership loss to the western churches—he had ministered in Alberta for sixty-six years, fifty-six of which were spent in Calgary.[1] But the vacuum was capably filled by Rev. Lawrence Yadlowski, who moved to Calgary on September 6, 2002, after retiring from teaching. Rev. Yadlowski, a native Albertan, had been born and educated at Newbrook, Alberta. He had been converted in the little Standard church near his home under the discipleship of Rev. Myles Goudy. After attending the University of Alberta, Rev. Yadlowski had become bivocational and taught in the Newbrook Public School while pastoring the Newbrook Standard Church and Campground for thirty-three years. He had a wide and extensive ministry in the district. Pastor Yadlowski was also appointed Western Canada leader for the Standard Church. He carried a great deal of influence and his leadership would be needed.

When General Conference voted to merge with The Wesleyan Church, the task of bringing in the West was placed upon the shoulders of Rev. Yadlowski. The Calgary church discussed its options and voiced concern over the young people and what there would be to offer them should the church not become part of the merger. The membership vote for merger surprisingly was almost unanimous: 29 Yes; 4 No; 8 adherents voted to remain independent. Calgary was in.

Slave Lake, under the leadership of Pastor Gilbert Conners, voted favourably to join the merger. Slave Lake, Alberta, had been pioneered by northern missionary, Miss Irene Ingram.[2]

But it was Edmonton and Newbrook that provided interesting drama. Both had become small churches with few members. Emotions were divided concerning merger with The Wesleyan Church. When Rev. Yadlowksi conducted the vote, both churches registered tied votes—equal support for merger versus independence. Rev. Yadlowski was decisive, however, immediately informing the societies that merger would take place since the negative vote was not equal to the two-thirds majority required by the General Conference of 1998.

The West owes much to the leadership and vision of Rev. Lawrence Yadlowski, his wife, Glenys, and their family. They have been tireless workers, first as members of the Standard Church, and then as supporters of the union with The Wesleyan Church. They were honoured at the Homecoming Celebration of Newbrook Camp in 2010 for their forty years of service to the church and camp meeting.

The Vancouver Standard Church was in transition at the time of the merger. Long-time pastor, Lena Hutchings, like her brother, Rev. Andrew Risby, had been pastor of the church for many years. For health reasons, "Sister Lena," as she was known, moved to Seattle to live with her niece. Rev. Hutchings had not favoured merger, and the church voted to follow her lead and remain independent. However, the Vancouver congregation did not cut itself off from fellowship with its former sister churches in the West. It continued to attend the Newbrook Camp and Calgary Easter Convention. There are many ties between the Vancouver society and its former Alberta church family.

BRINGING IN THE HOMESTEAD[3]

Centennial Road Standard Church (Brockville) was in a unique position during the merger talks. The assets of the local church were linked to the assets of Brockville Bible College and the denominational headquarters in Brockville—the New Complex. The Standard Church had been generous in lending monies, donating property, and making concessions to CRSC to make possible a beautiful campus for the local church and housing the denomination's headquarters. The facilities were testimony not only to the generous giving of the local congregation but also to the Standard Church of America. In reality, the New Complex was an extension of the vision and sacrifice of Bishop Horner and those who laboured with him to purchase land in Brockville and provide a school and headquarters in 1919. The New Complex was in a sense an extension of Horner's homestead.

During merger negotiations, CRSC was in the midst of a multimillion-dollar addition (the final cost was near three million dollars) and there was the stress not only of construction, but also providing finances to complete the project. Barry Hobin, a former student of Brockville Bible College and award-winning architect in Ottawa, had drawn up plans for the final phase of the administrative building and church that tied together phases one and two into an architecturally and artistically pleasing structure. Opinions about merger among the local congregation and leadership were divided, and further discussions at this juncture had potential to divide the church and thwart the momentum of fundraising and construction.

To add to the controversy, a philanthropist offered to build a million-dollar prayer garden on the one-acre site in front of the church (over the tile bed, no less!) to provide a refuge of healing for hurting people, and a place to meditate for the spiritually thirsty. Initially, few members were enthusiastic about the project, thinking it too ostentatious for the church. However, having led through many controversial projects, I believed the garden to be a once-in-a-lifetime opportunity that would eventually become a blessing for the church and communities beyond. I pressed ahead to see the project become a reality. Scott D. Windham of Florida, drew up plans for what eventually became the Garden of Hope and Faith Walk. Beautiful bronze sculptures of various Bible themes were designed to be set in place by renowned artist Beverley Paddleford and husband, Monte of Lander, Wyoming. Another project had been added to my responsibilities.[4]

As pastor, I believed it best to keep merger talk low key until a more appropriate time after construction was completed and finances stabilized. Some issues, specifically membership, needed to be resolved with The Wesleyan Church before we proceeded. I announced to our congregation the decision of our denomination to merge with The Wesleyan Church. CRSC agreed to pursue affiliation, and a letter dated September 11, 2003, informed the Wesleyan District of our intention. According to The Wesleyan Discipline this would allow us a five-year window before a vote was necessary to decide upon full merger.[5] A constitution was drawn up stating our affiliate status with The Wesleyan Church and a vote was conducted with the congregation on Sunday, December 21. It was accepted unanimously. However, in our haste to get on with buildings, gardens, and ministry we had neglected to follow the appropriate protocol. Rev. G. MacGarvey pointed out to

CRSC in his letter of November 2, 2006, that we had proceeded to vote without his participation as superintendent and chairman of the meeting. Our proceedings had not been conducted according to procedures as set forth by the General Conference of 1998, and thus were null and void. No consenting signatures had been attached to transfer property deeds and, as our lawyer Mr. Neville Johnston explained, all property was still legally held in trust for the Standard Church of America.

Something else began to take place in the fall of 2004 as we neared the end of construction. I began to experience overwhelming fatigue. Was it burnout or something more serious? I had always been full of energy and vigour. Shortly after Christmas, I began to experience a low-grade fever that persisted for several weeks, and despite an examination by my doctor in early January, I could not shake the nightly chills and sweats. We dedicated the new addition with Rev. MacGarvey and Barry Hobin as honorary guests on January 30, 2005, but I was lethargic, feverish, and losing weight. It was not until mid-February that I was diagnosed with bacterial endocarditis, a bacterial growth on the mitral valve of my heart, which if left untreated would have been fatal within a year. Thus, I was removed from active ministry for much of the next year. I was immediately hospitalized for a week, administered heavy doses of antibiotics intravenously for the next three months, and scheduled for open heart surgery in the fall of 2005 to correct the defective valve.

When I came back in the winter of 2006, new leadership was in place. They had different goals and different denominational aspirations. I began to realize affiliation meant little to anyone who wished to remove CRSC from our Standard Church tradition and Wesleyan family. It would only take a two-thirds vote by the membership of the congregation. I came to the realization that it would be morally wrong, but I was still weak from treatments and surgery. Nevertheless, I made a commitment that with God's help I would finish the task, follow our sister Standard churches, and lead CRSC into full membership with The Wesleyan Church. It was not an easy undertaking: physically, I battled lingering fatigue; and emotionally, our church suffered the loss of some leaders and members. But on September 16, 2007, CRSC, under the supervision of District Superintendent Rev. Don Hodgins, voted almost unanimously (this time following proper procedure) to join the merger. Final vote: 178, Yes; 12, No. Bishop Horner's heritage homestead for which he laboured so diligently and sacrificially would remain in the church family and his vision for Brockville would continue.

In our 2008 District Conference at Silver Lake, it was my joy to present the campus and facilities of CRSC to the Central Canada District of The Wesleyan Church to be used by God for His glory. I stated that I believed we would be an asset to one another and that God had a wonderful future for us as we shared together in the exciting work of furthering the kingdom of our Lord and Saviour Jesus Christ in Canada—and yes, into the uttermost parts of the world.

NEW CHURCH

Rev. Don Hodgins summarized the merger this way: "On January 1, 2004, the Central Canada District of The Wesleyan Church and the Standard Church of America became a new church to the glory of God!" Central Canada District had been a small district with limited capacity and resources for expansion and growth much like the Standard Church. But with the merger, the newly enlarged district enjoyed a critical mass (about forty-five churches) that enhanced ministry potential. Not only did the two churches espouse the same mission to embrace the work of Jesus Christ and expand God's kingdom, but by sharing resources (human, financial, and material), they increased their potential beyond what either church had ever dreamed. The addition of the Brockville campus renewed dreams of the former Brockville Bible College to serve as a teaching centre for church-planting seminars, leadership training, ongoing adult education, and the very first opportunity in Canada to receive seminary courses for accreditation in The Wesleyan Church (FLAME).[6] Moreover, the BBC scholarship fund was united with the

Spearman scholarship fund to help students who qualified for ministry and was extended to include the training and equipping of pastors on former Standard Church mission fields.[7]

DISTRICT OFFICE

Another exciting decision of the newly merged district was the relocating of the district office to the Brockville campus on Centennial Road. It had been the dream of the Standard Church New Complex to combine the facilities of the local church with the Bible college and headquarters into one functioning campus that would make a statement of progress and vision. It is interesting, in fact, to realize that, long before the merger, the first office of the Central Canada District of The Wesleyan Church was in Brockville before later moving to Belleville. The central office of the combined district was relocated in the fall of 2010 to the new, modern office space on the campus in Brockville; it was a statement of the District's desire to forge ahead with aggressive growth and church planting. It was in keeping with the dream and vision of Bishop Horner and his followers that the property so many had sacrificed for would be used to train and reach a new generation for Jesus Christ.

EMERGING REGIONS

In 2009, a bold new strategy was placed before Central Canada District to reach Canada for Christ. The plan was to divide the existing district into three zones: Central Canada, Lake Region, and Western Canada. Zone leaders would be placed in charge of sharing the vision, creating infrastructure, and laying the groundwork to facilitate future church plants. During the 2010 District Conference, the plan was adopted and Rev. Mark Parker was appointed zone leader of the Lake Region and Rev. Laurence Croswell, Western Canada. Both leaders set about to cultivate relationships with existing pastors in their regions, develop a working knowledge of communities, and identify potential church-planting locations. There was a desire to see Wesleyan churches planted from sea to sea in significant locations across Canada. The future alone will reveal the success of this faith venture as God's people volunteer for this visionary, pioneering thrust to spread the gospel.

LEGACY OF BISHOP RALPH C. HORNER

One is tempted to ask what we can learn from our past—especially when former methods and values are openly questioned and in some cases ruthlessly discarded. To answer this question, it is important to understand that the past is only relevant if it tells us something useful about the future. Two denominations sprang from the revival ministry of Ralph Horner: the Holiness Movement Church and the Standard Church of America. But without Horner at the helm, both movements eventually faltered. Whatever the reasons—lack of vision, loss of zeal, bondage of legalism, or the restrictions of confining governance—neither could sustain momentum and passion. Both denominations eventually realized they would need to merge into the infrastructures of larger, more established denominations to retain their identities, continue to grow, and even survive. The Free Methodist and The Wesleyan churches provided the necessary denominational frameworks. But lest one think the mergers were simply sinking ships reaching out for lifelines to be saved from drowning, such was not the case. Both welcoming denominations gained strength from the Hornerite recruitments, and some of their largest churches trace their roots to Bishop Horner and his adherents.

What can we learn from Ralph Horner's life and ministry? Like his preaching, the lessons are simple. They might be summarized by four statements:

1. Followers of Christ, who are entirely sanctified and baptized by the Holy Spirit, possess dynamic power to build God's kingdom.

In his memoirs, Horner recalled his personal experience. One Saturday night, about eleven o'clock, he was "looking for victory for the Sabbath" when Micah 3:8 "was conveyed by the Spirit" to his mind: "But truly I am full of power by the Spirit of the Lord." With the verse Horner described what took place: "The power of God fell on me and I could not stand, sit or walk. The tent seemed too small for me. . . . When I was able, I went to the house where I slept; but every step of the way, my whole nature cried out, 'Truly I am full of power.' The first time I preached, I had to cry out, 'Truly I am full of power. . . . The congregation was obliged to believe it. Some who had opposed me from the time that I went there, rushed to the penitent form after listening to the sermon. . . . The power and fire fell on the people, and they were melted at the feet of Jesus."[8] Horner had a dynamism that expressed itself in powerful preaching and tireless work for God's kingdom.

2. Spirit-filled men and women overcome difficulties, discouragement, and opposition.

Horner never questioned his calling and vision. He knew in his heart that God had called him to preach in evangelism and nothing—not accusations, hecklers, or impossibilities—could cause him to waver from that calling or succumb to obstacles thrown across his path. He knew where God had called him to go and he trusted God to provide His power to get there.

3. God is faithful in keeping His promises.

Bishop Horner's dream and legacy is still alive over a century later among third and fourth generation offspring who trace their spiritual roots back to the early Hornerites and their work of evangelism and preaching the doctrine of holy living. When God establishes a covenant with His people and confirms it, with "signs and miracles,"[9] there is nothing that can destroy it—the vision will come to pass!

4. God provides the appropriate time for changing leadership without human intervention.

The division of the HMC in 1916 centred upon Horner's leadership, his declining health, and a new generation of holiness preachers. Critics and detractors, unwilling to wait for God's timing, were determined to dethrone him. Rev. Horner was offered the role of honorary bishop, which seemingly would have conferred upon him influence in the church while freeing him to do what he did best: preach and write. For reasons we can only speculate, the bishop was unable to accept that role and relinquish leadership. His life was testimony that he was God's anointed and deserved respect. The bishop died five years after the first murmur of division and two years after the incorporation of the Standard Church in Watertown, New York. The impatient needed only wait five years. A division might have been avoided.

Methods come and go. What was once new eventually becomes old. Gradually everyone and everything must be cleared away to make room for new leaders and new ways of doing things in a new generation—it is the ebb and flow of life and death. But one thing never changes: the motivation that drives the church to preach the gospel to the far ends of the earth is constant. Few in this age would pitch a tent at the edge of town and expect throngs to come and be converted. Nevertheless, Ralph Horner's vision during his great tent revivals along the Ottawa Valley remains intact: to see men and women come to faith, experience the cleansing of sanctification from sin, and welcome the dynamism of the Holy Spirit's infilling to send them into the world to share the good news of Jesus Christ. This desire lives on in the hearts of hundreds of men and women who trace their spiritual roots to the Hornerite movement that first ignited during the latter half of the nineteenth century in Clarendon, Quebec. Revival fires caught in towns and villages along the valley, spread throughout rural Canada and the northern US, jumped across denominational lines, and ultimately were carried across two oceans into remote villages of China and Egypt.

HORNERITE ROOTS

Many who trace their spiritual roots to Bishop Ralph Horner and his movement have made significant contributions to their church, community, country, or mission. They may have ministered in Holiness Movement or Standard churches, or moved on to other denominations and ministries, but they have remained sympathetic to their holiness Hornerite roots. More importantly, they were loyal to the church of Jesus Christ and the building of His kingdom whether they were publically acclaimed or laboured faithfully in some unheralded corner of the harvest field. Regardless, their roots need to be remembered and honoured and their stories expanded. Only a select few were brought to our attention. Certainly, many have been overlooked or forgotten. Some will not be honoured until they stand before the great white throne on that day when Jesus returns. They are listed in no particular order of influence or importance.

MISS SARAH LONGHURST

In 1907, Miss Sarah Longhurst, at age forty-six, while living at home in Canada, volunteered for missionary service in the Egyptian Conference of the HMC and was unexpectedly accepted. That fall she and Miss Clara McLean arrived in Alexandria, Egypt, and began serving in 1908 at the Girls' School in Assiout, which had recently opened for boarding pupils (having been a day school until then). Although Miss Longhurst also served in the villages, her work was mostly in schools. In 1920, she was sent to Port Said to take charge of the Peniel School for Moslem Girls, which was financed by a group of concerned and caring supporters in California. Miss Longhurst remained there until her death in 1940 at the age of eighty—after thirty-three years of continuous service! During her later years, Miss Longhurst spent much time publishing and distributing Christian literature in the Arabic language. In 1945, a memorial to her long and faithful service was set up by Mrs. J. C. Black, to print Gospels in two new African dialects for distribution.

MISS ELLA BIRDSELL

Miss Ella Birdsell became one of Rev. Horner's first influential female evangelists who had a great deal of success on the eastern Ontario revival circuit (often teamed with Ida Mason). She testified to being converted in the fall of 1880 at the Methodist Episcopal Church in Athens, Ontario, in a revival conducted by Rev. W. Service, the minister in charge at the time. However, she struggled with her conversion because she found, to her sorrow, that her heart had become very hard for one her age. She claimed not to have assurance of salvation until she received counsel from Rev. D. Winter—Horner's fellow Conference evangelist (see chapter 2)—at a subsequent revival service. After much prayer and help she claimed, "light came to my soul," and she was able to sing, "My God is reconciled." Subsequently, after "a severe struggle with the man of sin, as he did not want to die," she testified that "God wholly sanctified my soul. . . . And God has not only asked me to be true to my testimony, but to walk in all the light I could get in matters of dress, eating, drinking, conversation, and every doubtful thing." Ella Birdsell started to work in the church in 1881. She received the baptism of the Holy Spirit "on receiving light from Rev. Bro. Horner," before testifying that she was "on the road for greater things."[1] She became a member of Conference along with Ida Mason, Frank Coleman, and Robert Stacy on December 31, 1916, in a special session of the Holiness Movement Church held in the Mission Hall on Concession Street, Ottawa.

REV. R. MALLETT

Rev. R. Mallett was an ardent supporter of R. C. Horner's early ministry. He testified that as a little boy his mother had led him to pray that he might be converted and become a preacher. "I was, thank God, powerfully converted when I was about fifteen years old. I soon found that I had doubts and fears; that anger, envy, pride, love of praise, selfishness, and other works of the flesh gave me a great deal of trouble. I felt sure there was something better for me than so much sinning and repenting, but knew not how to get it." While teaching school in 1865, Mallett attended a revival meeting and felt the call to preach. He entered this work in June 1872. On his journey to entire sanctification, Rev. Mallett was privileged to hear Rev. S. P. Jones in Toronto preach from 1 John 3:9, which helped him much. He also got "a mighty lift toward entire sanctification by hearing General Booth speak; I saw it was my privilege to live 'holy,' to do those things that are pleasing in His sight." In June 1891, Rev. Mallett attended tent meetings in Wilton, Ontario, held by Rev. R. C. Horner and was led "to see that the old man must be crucified, that I must present my 'body a living sacrifice, holy and acceptable unto God,' and that I must do my best to purify myself 'even as He is pure.'" Mallett's testimony to holiness is quite profound: "How blessed the freedom—how sweet the rest—how abounding the love—how safe to let God keep me, fill me, lead me, and use me as He wills. What a blessed exhilaration to preach pardon, purity and power as the privilege of all through the Lord Jesus Christ, and see hundreds converted, scores sanctified and baptized with the power the first year of my establishment in this unspeakable experience of perfect love!"[2]

REV. ALBERT T. WARREN

Depending on perspective, Rev. Albert T. Warren (April 15, 1865 – June 6, 1925) might either be vilified or venerated. But for those who knew him, he was a godly man caught between a rock and a hard place during the division that took place within the HMC between 1916 and 1918. He was loved and respected with true affection by members of both the Holiness Movement and Standard churches. Rev. G. L. Monahan shared affectionately at Bishop Warren's funeral service and related how "Brother Warren had spoken to him about his calling to preach and asked him if God was not showing him white harvest fields somewhere." During the time of the division, Rev. Warren was a conciliator; his desire was to keep the church from dividing. He was also pastor to many of the ministers going through a difficult time of disillusionment. Rev. Peter Wiseman, in his funeral address on June 9, 1925, at Fifth Avenue Holiness Movement Church, spoke of Rev. Warren as someone you could approach: "He was always ready to talk things over." It seems evident Rev. Warren accepted the position of bishop reluctantly: "[H]e never wanted prominence. [H]e loved the church . . . he loved his men and loved the people of God." Rev. Wiseman recalled in his remarks that Rev. Warren "made a great sacrifice for the cause of Christ. He entered the ministry in a time when circumstances were not so inviting as today; a time when men had to make their own circuits. . . . No person was more ready to take a hard place, a hard battle, a hard problem, a hard circumstance, than was Brother Warren. . . . He succeeded as leader by the noble qualities of a humble obedient servant."[3]

MR. HAROLD MOYLES

No one attending Brockville Bible College after 1931 forgot Harold Moyles. His life was one of dedication to the work and ministry of the college. He became an icon in the Standard Church to which BBC and the Brockville Standard Church (now Centennial Road Standard Church) owe a great deal of respect and gratitude.

Harold Heson Moyles was born on Queen Victoria's birthday— May 24, 1907—to a young barmaid named Annie Moyles in the District of Nottingham, England. The poor, single mother had little to offer her infant son, so in 1910, three-year-old Harold was taken to a Roman Catholic orphanage. The nuns were good to him. They helped him cultivate an appreciation for God and good music and helped Harold develop his singing voice. At the age of sixteen, Harold was placed on a French ship—the *Montcalm*—with three other orphan boys and sent to the unknown land of Canada. The teenagers were part of an immigration policy to relocate more than seven thousand children to Canada, where they were employed as labourers and domestics and often stigmatized, becoming known as "home children." Many were sent initially to holding houses at Belleville and Brockville before being dispersed to often arduous lives on farms and homesteads where they were contracted for up to two years and used as farmhands. Harold lived with the John Condron family for three years before heading out to find work on his own in the bustling town of Peterborough. Harold worked on farms until 1929, when he went to work for General Motors in Oshawa. He earned enough money polishing cars to purchase his first brand-new motorbike. He made friends with the Robinson family and for the first time in many years had a real home.

In 1931, Harold was again working in Peterborough, where he attended some evangelistic services conducted by Deaconess Eva Alexander, a Standard Church evangelist. One night in April 1931, Harold made his way to the altar and committed his life to Jesus Christ as Lord and Saviour. He never regretted that evening, and he returned home full of joy and peace—an experience he never forgot. On September 17, 1931, Harold entered the Brockville Seminary as a student in the high school. His farming experience gradually took on more and more significance as the school depended upon that income for its survival during the Depression years. Harold never left Brockville Bible College and made the college dorm his home. He was remembered by students for his hard work in the gardens and his boisterous laughter ringing throughout the college. Harold had a great sense of humour. Sometimes his laughter was ill-directed, and ill-timed, but it carried him through many difficulties and hardships. Students in the 1970s also remember Harold for his evening ritual of relaxation in a comfortable lawn chair in the Armstrongs' German shepherd dog kennel, reading the *Recorder and Times* or sharing his Thanksgiving or Christmas turkey with the dogs.

Harold was also known as the "con man" on the streets of Brockville where he could be seen selling his famous corn to the residents of the city. His tractor and cart were well-known icons of the city.

Sunday mornings would find Harold in the Brockville Standard Church, his hearty voice singing the hymns of faith he enjoyed so greatly. Throughout the week, Harold was the handyman and janitor around the college, cleaning and sweeping and doing odd repairs. During the spring and summer he was in his gardens planting and harvesting corn and strawberries to support the work of BBC. Harold's labours contributed thousands of dollars to the work of the college. He did not receive a wage for himself, but after a day of sales he would bring the entire proceeds to the college treasurer so a bank deposit might be made. The college often survived financial hardships because of Harold's garden proceeds. When Harold Moyles died in the St. Lawrence Lodge on March 6, 1997, he had few personal possessions. His bank account of $3,236.71 (saved from his pension cheque allowance) was released to the Brockville Bible College Scholarship Fund. He had little to his name in earthly possessions, but great spiritual rewards in heaven. His funeral service was attended by former teachers and students of BBC and conducted by his pastor, Rev. Laurence Croswell. Rev. Mrs. Doris Conley gave his tribute: "Harold, do not think that your labours have been in vain. . . . You have touched and blessed many lives of those who are now all over the world serving as missionaries, pastors, architects, construction engineers. Harold, as a former student / faculty member and present BBC Board Member, I want to thank you for being there all these years. We love you and we are your family."[4]

REV. ANDREW RISBY

Rev. Andrew Risby, known for his powerful preaching, was one of Calgary's longest serving ministers. His roots were in Alberta's early black communities. He not only ministered to his own congregation, but also to the entire black community throughout western Canada.

Rev. Risby was born August 11, 1917, at Campsie, one of the northern Alberta communities near Athabasca and settled by black immigrants from the United States in the early twentieth century. He was called to the ministry when he was nineteen and devoted the rest of his life to service in the church.

After pastoring at Amber Valley and Edmonton, he came to Calgary for a special meeting and stayed in the city from that time on. He married Edith Smith who had moved from Regina. They were married fifty-five years. Although the Calgary Standard Church served many members of Calgary's black community, Rev. Risby sought to build a multiracial, multicultural congregation. "When the Black Achievement Award Society wished to honour him, he was puzzled; he didn't do what he did for publicity."[5]

Pastor Risby served the Standard Church as pastor, evangelist, district superintendent, and chairman of Newbrook Camp Meeting.

Rev. Gary Walsh

On August 30, 2008, Gary Walsh delivered the keynote address at the ninetieth anniversary celebration of Ivanhoe Camp Meeting. He spoke eloquently and gratefully of his years as a young person growing up in the culture of the Standard Church, and of course, attending Ivanhoe Camp. Gary was a pastor's son who demonstrated great leadership abilities. His father, Rev. J. R. Walsh, had been the pastor of the Pembroke Standard Church during the late 1950s and early 1960s. As a young man, Gary demonstrated scholastic and leadership gifts and sensed a call to enter full-time Christian ministry. When he was ready to enter Bible College in 1961, the college had closed, and Gary enrolled in the Free Methodist College at Lorne Park. After graduating, he furthered his studies at Asbury Theological Seminary in Wilmore, Kentucky, eventually completing his doctorate of ministry. Gary did not return to the Standard Church. He became a successful minister with the Free Methodist Church and served congregations in Ontario, Kentucky, and New York. Later he became denominational superintendent in western Ontario and missionary-teacher in Hong Kong. In 1993 he was elected bishop of the Free Methodist churches in Canada. After serving four years as bishop, Rev. Walsh was named president of the Evangelical Fellowship of Canada in 1997. On becoming EFC's new president, Gary Walsh had expanded his vision for Canada from his small-tent Hornerite roots to a larger vision of encouraging and empowering local communities, promoting leadership development (especially among newer Christians) and providing a "big arch under which evangelicals can share basic beliefs, cherish their diversity and work together to impact Canadian society."[6]

Rev. David Mainse

Sitting down with David Mainse on Sunday afternoon, November 28, 2010, to chat about his holiness roots was a particular opportunity that doesn't come along every day. I had listened to him preach during the Sunday morning service at the local Highway Pentecostal Church, noting his unmistakable holiness references to sanctification and death of the old man of sin. That afternoon after a traditional Sunday roast beef dinner at Pastor Rick and Joyce Lott's home, David sat on the couch with me and related how his dad, Rev. Roy Lake Mainse, was sent to Egypt in 1938 by the Holiness Movement Church to support the pastors who were being persecuted for their Christian faith. Rev. Mainse planned to locate a suitable place for him and his family to live and send for them to join him in Egypt. Unfortunately World War II broke out and it became too dangerous to travel in the Middle East. Thus the Mainse family was left in Canada without a father. It was not until December 1944, near the end of the war, that Rev. Mainse returned unexpectedly and was welcomed home by his family. Little David was eight years old at the time, and after more than six years of being separated from his father, they were complete strangers. David recalled hiding in some bushes nearby and being dragged out by his sisters to meet his father. There were hugs and kisses all around for mother and daughters, but in true Victorian tradition, David got a handshake (men did not show any physical affection to their sons).

That evening as the family gathered around the table, Rev. Mainse conducted his first devotional with the family since departing for Egypt. He opened his Bible and read, "And every one that hath forsaken houses, or brethren, or sisters, or father, or mother, or wife, or children, or lands, for my name's sake, shall receive an hundredfold, and shall inherit everlasting life" (Matt. 19:29 KJV). Rev. Mainse then pulled out a worn black book, faded by the scorching Egyptian sun. "God promised a hundredfold increase," he said as he began to weep, showing his family well over twelve hundred Egyptian names he had written in the little black book.

Little did David's father realize that this promise of God would continue to be fulfilled through the international ministry of his small, frightened son who barely knew his father. David's childhood was filled with emotional trauma: His father had been absent from home

many years in Egypt, his mother died when he was twelve, and his
father later remarried and returned to Egypt two weeks after the wedding, leaving fifteen-year-old David to the care of Rev. I. L. Brown
and the staff at Brockville Bible College during the period when the
Holiness Movement and Standard churches were considering union.

David was resentful and bitter at the loss of his mother and being
left alone at boarding school. One day he motorcycled to Montreal to
get a job aboard a ship that would take him to Egypt so he could visit
his father, and say, "Here I am, Dad! I'm your son you left in Canada."
But the employment agency was not fooled into believing David was
eighteen, and he made his way back to BBC and the continuing chagrin
of Rev. I. L. Brown at David's ongoing shenanigans.

David returned to Pembroke the next year a discouraged, defeated
teen who needed God. It was the witness of three Christian boys at his
high school, and Sid Healey, who tricked him into attending a Youth
for Christ rally in Ottawa, that turned David's life around. When the
invitation was given, his old school chum from Brockville Bible College, Homer James, met him and said, "David, doesn't it make sense
to give your heart to Jesus?" Homer placed his arm around David's
shoulders and walked him down the aisle. "It finally made sense to
me," recalled David as we sat comfortably on the chesterfield. "It was
more than an emotional response—it was a rational response that what
Jesus said was true." David's life was never the same thereafter.

David attended Peterborough Bible College and became the Pentecostal pastor in Deep River. He began a fifteen-minute TV program
following the late night news in Pembroke, Ontario, that later became
Crossroads, an international ministry reaching into many countries
around the world. His son-in-law, Nizar Shaheen, became founder and
president of Light For All Nations Ministries, which produces Arabic
language television programming seen worldwide via satellite and the
Internet. The legacy of holiness missionary Rev. R. L. Mainse, who
simply claimed the promises of God, is still being fulfilled and carried
on to the third and fourth generations.

"I am very thankful for my holiness roots," David assured me, his eyes moistening. "People like the two sisters, Holiness Movement evangelists Miss James and Mrs. Willows, had a phenomenal impact on my life."[7]

REV. JAMES B. PRING

Rev. J. B. Pring was born in Haliburton, Ontario, December 22, 1883. The family moved west and homesteaded in Saskatchewan. As a young man he was converted and entered into the ministry of the Holiness Movement and Standard churches. He pastored churches in Quebec, Ontario, Saskatchewan, Michigan, and New York. He was elected general superintendent of the SCA (1940–1945; 1950–1954), became editor and writer for the *Christian Standard*, served as dean of Brockville Bible College, was a Western Conference superintendent, and a church evangelist. He was known for his godly life, his model preaching, and his friendly demeanour. He was quick to encourage and slow to criticize. When visiting Egypt, he so impressed the brethren they referred to him as the apostle John.

DEACONESS ELNORA BURNS

Elnora Pearl Burns was saved at Lake Eloida camp in 1913 and vividly recalled leadings to preach at age twelve. She attended the first Standard Church Bible School in Prescott in 1918 when there were fifty-two students. She recalled a revival started in the school during that first year. Miss Burns ministered to the needs of a number of circuits in Ontario and knew many of the very primitive hardships endured by the early female Hornerite preachers. She later nursed both at nursing homes and private homes, and cooked at the Fulford Home and Psychiatric Hospital in Brockville while she cared for her aging parents. Bishop Horner often visited the Burns's home for rest and respite from his busy schedule. Through many years of strenuous labour and sacrifice, Miss Burns became crippled with severe arthritis and was confined to her home on Broadway Avenue in Brockville. She ministered to numerous people, including this young pastor, who would stop at her home for prayer and spiritual help.[8]

DEACONESS IRENE INGRAM

Miss Irene Ingram began her first Sunday school in Slave Lake in 1952. There was no parsonage and no support. She was offered a small, one-room skid shack about ten feet by sixteen feet that had no insulation and no skirting around the bottom to keep out the cold. It had a cook stove but no heater. Miss Ingram would dig firewood out from under a pile of snow, saw it into blocks by hand, and split it for the heater. Despite her hardships she testified to wonderful manifestations of the glory and power of God. She made arrangements to move a little building from Athabasca to use for a church in Slave Lake, about a block away from her shack. Years later she remininced, "I had many wonderful experiences here in Slave Lake, praying with drunkards, visiting the sick and shut-ins and parents of the children who attended my Sunday school." Although she took a temporary position as cook at Brockville Bible College, then moved back to minister at Two Hills and Hairy Hill, Alberta, her heart was in Slave Lake, where she returned to conduct Sunday school. Sometimes as many as forty-three children gathered in her second eleven-by-fourteen shack. It was not until Rev. Larry Spinner, pastor of the Edmonton Standard Church, took it upon himself to lead in the construction of a new chapel in 1983 that the Slave Lake Mission was able to expand to the ministry it now enjoys.

DEACONESS LOLA JAMES WILLOWS

"Sister Willows," as she was known, became a holiness icon at Holiness Movement, Free Methodist, and Standard Church camp meetings and conventions.

Lola Willows' parents had settled in northern Ontario where the village of Stittsville now stands. They were staunch members of the Methodist Church. But as time passed, they came to believe the church had become cold and formal. Lola was born in 1890, and while she was still a young girl, Rev. R. C. Horner came to hold meetings in the area. Lola recalled, "Holy Ghost conviction settled on the people so much that some were prostrated by the power of God. Both father and mother were gloriously converted. My mother would get so happy she would dance, and father would run around the church." In a camp meeting nearby at Munster, Ontario, Lola, at the age of eleven years, "prayed through." She said joy filled her soul.

Family altar was conducted three times a day and ministers of the gospel were frequent visitors. On Sunday morning twenty cows had to be milked before members of the James family were in their places by 9:30 at the little white church four miles away. Her father was the Sunday School Superintendent and his rule was never to be late.

A meeting was held every month in the James's home and on that day, usually Thursday, Lola's father, John, would prepare the large dining room with chairs and planks, and his wife would set the table for all who came from a distance. Lola remembered that the yard was filled with horses and buggies and the house was often so full that many had to stand outside. Lola wrote, "Many sinners were saved in those meetings and they will rejoice all through eternity. The country was stirred for miles around. Our home was always open to receive the 'prophets of the Lord.' And many times, I think, we 'entertained angels unawares.'"

Despite such a home, Lola recalled becoming cold and indifferent. She attended the Conservatory of Music in Ottawa for four years and became a music teacher. At age nineteen, she married Lloyd Willows.

They were invited to an old-time revival and felt the Spirit's dealings. He said to Lola, "You lead the way and I'll not be long after you." But she failed to yield.

Lola and Lloyd moved to the newly opened homestead territory of southern Saskatchewan, where two boys, Gerald and Ross, were born to them. From the homestead, the Willowses moved to Calgary and then on to Vancouver.

Lloyd Willows developed pneumonia, and at six o'clock one morning the doctor was called. Friends said they never expected him to walk out of the house alive. But Lola remembered her mother's parting words: "If you ever get in trouble, pray." Lola came to terms with God and promised God that if Lloyd got well, she would seek salvation and bring her family up right. Lloyd recovered, but still Lola lingered in her step of faith, "afraid to leave and start for Heaven alone." But when another move was made to Moose Jaw, Saskatchewan, Lola came to a decision that she would start for heaven and attend the little Free Methodist church even if she had to go alone. One morning she testified, "the Light of Heaven broke through, and the witness came that my sins were washed away. My mouth was filled with the praises of God. Joy unspeakable filled my soul." Lola established a family altar and began to call in the neighbors' homes to pray with them.

Eventually, Lloyd's business moved the family to Battleford, Saskatchewan. As Lola became better acquainted with the people, they would ask where she attended church. The burden was laid upon her to open a mission. A building was secured that had been used as a dance hall and relief center. Seats were installed, a piano brought in, and services announced. Lola and son Ross learned to preach in that mission.

Some years later Lloyd developed cancer and died. Lola's older sister was in evangelism, and the two sisters decided to form a team and travel full time. They sang together and took turns preaching. Eva played the guitar and accordion. Some summers they attended as many as seven camp meetings. Their evangelistic work took them to Ireland, Egypt, and the United States, as well as all across Canada.

Over a period of more than fifty years, Lola Willows became a familiar figure at holiness camp meetings and conventions. Because she testified of "anointing for service" she was sometimes called the "third blessing woman." She carried a burden for family, friends, and neighbors, people in every field where she preached. She was known as a "giant in intercessory prayer." Joy was her trademark, and while on her deathbed in 1988, too weak to speak, she wrote in quavering letters on a notepad brought to her bedside, "I'm still praise God."

Lola Willows is best remembered for her songs and exhortations. She continually testified what the Lord had done for her. Songs for which she is best remembered are "You Had Better Dig Deeper," "My, Didn't It Rain," and "My Ship Came In."

Her last trip was to an Easter convention at Calgary Standard Church in 1988. Though ninety-eight years old and weakened by a viral infection, she stood on the convention floor and exhorted the gathering, not only to "be true to the ancient landmarks," but also to "keep the vision and go forward. There are great things ahead."[9]

ELIGIBLE VOTERS IN GENERAL CONFERENCE (1916)

Ruling of the Supreme Court of Ontario: *Holiness Movement versus R. C. Horner*. Ordained ministers of the Holiness Movement Church eligible to vote for bishop:

OTTAWA ANNUAL CONFERENCE

1. J. L. Armitage
2. F. G. Armitage
3. C. M. Arksey
4. E. J. Bishop
5. W. H. Bradley
6. C. F. Bowen
7. J. C. Black
8. J. Brownrigg
9. S. S. Buell
10. P. Bennett
11. J. W. Campbell
12. R. Collins
13. E. H. Claxton
14. S. G. Caswell
15. G. A. Christie
16. Geo. Chambers
17. F. W. Crawford
18. R. J. Druce
19. F. Dalin
20. R. E. Featherstone
21. Wm. Grundy
22. S. A. Graham
23. R. C. Horner
24. R. M. Hammond
25. John Hunter
26. E. R. Holley
27. H. R. James
28. John Jarvis
29. Henry Jarvis
30. S. H. Jeffrey
31. W. Jackson
32. S. S. Lindsay

33. Ed. Lindsay
34. G. L. Monahan
35. F. J. Mayhew
36. W. J. Major
37. B. McRoberts
38. H. R. McMillan
39. W. A. McCracken
40. A. Moors
41. J. G. Nussey
42. G. Oldford
43. J. Price
44. M. C. Pritchard

45. J. B. Pring
46. R. C. Raymond
47. R. Radford
48. T. O. Roe
49. I. E. Smith
50. Jas. Smith
51. A. A. Smith
52. T. A. Seale
53. A. A. Wells
54. W. J. Watchorn
55. R. Webster

MANITOBA ANNUAL CONFERENCE

1. A. T. Warren
2. S. J. Shields
3. G. R. Horner
4. B. E. Cowan
5. J. Cooke
6. S. G. Caswell
7. D. Caswell
8. J. Mott
9. David Gebbes

10. David R. Gebb
11. Russell Warren
12. S. A. York
13. E. F. Smith
14. B. Van Camp
15. Wm. Clark
16. E. R. Quick
17. D. C. Reed
18. H. H. Childrerhose

ALBERTA ANNUAL CONFERENCE

1. W. J. Dey
2. R. J. Dey
3. W. J. Tompkins
4. W. F. Leedy

5. A. B. Carson
6. J. A. Stark
7. I. B. Johnson
8. H. S. Hornby

Egyptian Annual Conference

1. C. W. Trotter	9. Ashan Khaleel
2. A. Moore	10. Shenshoon Fanuse
3. A. A. Caswell	11. Ghaly And-is-Saved
4. F. Kendell	12. Hanna Ghobriel
5. C. Van Camp	13. Shaker Yusif
6. C. Reynolds	14. Abd-el-Messiah Feltus
7. Habeeb Bushara	15. Saverus Seedhorn
8. Tofik Girgis	16. Azeez Rapahael

Members Added by Hon. Justice Clute

1. W. J. Ketcheson	3. G. L. Ralph
2. W. G. Burns	

Totals from Each Conference

Ottawa Annual Conference	55
Manitoba Annual Conference	18
Alberta Annual Conference	8
Egyptian Annual Conference	16
Added by Justice Clute	3
Total members	100

PUBLICATIONS BY R. C. HORNER
(listed chronologically by year of publication)

1. *Voice Production*, introduction by N. Burwash (Toronto: William Briggs), National Archives of Canada, 1888.

2. *Gospel Tent Hymns*, compiled by R. C. Horner and J. V. MacDowell (Toronto: W. Briggs), National Archives of Canada, 1889.

3. *Entire Consecration*, introduction by A. Carman (Toronto: W. Briggs), National Archives of Canada, 1890.

4. *Pentecost*, introduction by Hugh Johnston (Toronto: W. Briggs; Montreal: C. W. Coates; Halifax: S. F. Huestis), National Archives of Canada, 1891.

5. *To, Before, and On the Altar*, introduction by A. M. Phillips (Toronto: W. Briggs), National Archives of Canada, 1891.

6. *From the Altar to the Upper Room* (Toronto and Montreal: W. Briggs; Halifax: S. G. Huestis), National Archives of Canada, 1891.

7. *Notes on Boland*, introduction by J. V. McDowell (Boston and Chicago: McDonald & Gill; Toronto: W. Briggs), National Archives of Canada, 1893.

8. *Original and Inbred Sin* (Ottawa: Rolla L. Grain), National Archives of Canada, 1896.

9. *Fragments from the Feast, 18 Sermons* (Belleville: The "Cruse of Oil" Tract Repository), National Archives of Canada, 1902.

10. *Saved to the Uttermost* (Ottawa: Holiness Movement Publishing House), National Archives of Canada, 1903.

11. *The Children of the Bible* (Ottawa), National Archives of Canada, 1903.

12. *The Feast: 14 Sermons, Exhortations and Experiences*; Fourth Annual Feast of Pentecost of the Holiness Movement Church (Ottawa: Holiness Movement Publishing House), National Archives of Canada, 1903.

13. *The Root* (Ottawa: Holiness Movement Publishing House), National Archives of Canada, 1904.

14. *Seventeen Sermons and Addresses* (Ottawa: Holiness Movement Publishing House), 1905.

15. *Bible Doctrines No's 1 and 2* (Ottawa: Holiness Movement Publishing House), 1908.

16. *The Sunday Scholars' Guide*, rewritten and reprinted, 1908.

17. *The Second Commandment*, seven sermons preached at the June camp meeting, Chesterville, Ontario (Ottawa: Holiness Movement Publishing House), National Archives of Canada, 1909.

18. *Revival Sermons: Feast of Pentecost*, 6 volumes, 1910 and various dates.

19. *Ralph C. Horner, Evangelist: Reminiscences from His Own Pen, Also Five Typical Sermons* (published by Mrs. A. E. Horner, Standard Church Book Room), posthumous publication circa 1922.

"WE ARE HAPPY TODAY"

APPENDIX 5

MISSIONARIES

A. HOLINESS MOVEMENT MISSIONARIES WHO SERVED UNDER R. C. HORNER'S LEADERSHIP (1897–1918)

EGYPT

1. Rev. Herbert E. Randall: 1899–1906
2. Miss Edith A. Burke: 1899–1907; China: 1909–1920; Sudan: 1931–1949
3. Miss Cora Van Camp: 1899–1905; 1912–1919; 1930–1931
4. Miss Carrie Reynolds: 1899–1910
5. Miss Elma Cannon: 1901–1910 (became Mrs. Trotter in 1904); 1913–1916
6. Rev. W. C. Trotter: 1901–1911; 1913–1916
7. Miss Lydia Bradley: 1904–1911; 1912–1914 (became Mrs. Caswell in 1912)
8. Miss Emma Barkley: 1906–1912 (became Mrs. P. C. Bennett)
9. Miss Ethel Clark: 1906–1913 (became Mrs. A. Joyce)
10. Miss Sarah Longhurst: 1907–1940 (thirty-seven years without furlough)
11. Miss Clara McLean: 1907–1919 (became Mrs. Kendall in 1910)
12. Rev. A. Moore: 1909–1913; 1914–1922
13. Mrs. A. Moore: 1909–1913; 1914–1922

14. Miss Jennie Sinclair (not sent by board): 1910–1921
15. Rev. A. A. Caswell: 1911–1914
16. Miss Jennie Werry: 1912–1923

CHINA

1. Rev. Asa Van Camp: 1904
2. Miss Edith Burke: 1909–1920
3. Miss T. Danford: 1910–1921
4. Rev. S. G. Caswell: 1910–1920
5. Rev. S. G. Graham: 1910–1918
6. Miss M. Irwin: 1913–1922
7. Mrs. S. G. Caswell: 1913–1920
8. Mrs. S. A. Graham: 1913–1918

B. STANDARD CHURCH MISSIONARIES

EGYPT

1. Rev. Ray Webster: 1919–1922
2. Rev. Earl Thompson: 1922–1928
3. Rev. Earl and Annie Thompson: 1931–1937
4. Rev. Martin and Ella Slack: 1924–1930
5. Rev. Irwin Brown: 1926–1932
6. Miss Stella Brown: 1930–1933
7. Rev. Kingsely and Dorcas Ridgway: 1937–1940
8. Rev. Harold Berry: 1940–1944
9. Rev. Harold and Mary Berry: 1946–1950
10. Miss Irma Ergezinger: 1952–1957
11. Rev. Earl and Doris Conley: 1952–1958; 1959–1962
12. Rev. Arnold and Evelyn Rigby: 1954–1956
13. Rev. Eldon and Frances Craig: 1968–1970

China

1. Miss Lydia Connaughty: 1923–1927; 1928–1934
2. Miss Tillie Danford: 1923–1927; 1928–1934
3. Rev. John Johnston: 1926–1930
4. Rev. William and Glenna Wager: 1928–1934

Ghana

1. Rev. Joe and Jemima Ocran: 1990–

Mexico

1. Socorro Tapia: 1989
2. Miss Josefina Dominguez: 1989–

APPENDIX 6

HISTORIC PHOTOGRAPHS

A. KINGSTON STANDARD CHURCH CONFERENCE 1923

Names supplied by Mrs. Mina (Eastman) Armstrong (left to right):

1ST ROW

R. Horner, J. Johnston, W. Wagar, H. Leedy, B. Ross, S. Cooper,
R. Hawley, J. Gibbs, R. Wagar, G. Rhodes, T. Connell, I. L. Brown
Children: Clifton Watchorn, Herman Arksey

2ND ROW—WOMEN

E. Convay, M. Eastman, C. Hazzard, L. Richardson, M. McCutcheon,
M. Kennedy, E. James, D. Potter, Miss Kussie, J. Young, B. Brown,
E. Alexander, E. Dack, M. Holbrook, I. Giffin, B. Wagar, A. Argue,
B. O'Hara, D. Haggerty

3RD ROW

E. Adams, F. Armitage, L. Tomlinson, G. Crawford, F. N. Crawford,
G. Horner, F. Mayhew, J. Carson, R. Raymond, G. Monahan, J. Nussey,
T. Seale, R. Druce, W. Watchorn, G. Oldford, R. Featherstone

4TH ROW

R. Crozier, R. Schamehorn, H. Winters. W. McQuaig, D. Parks, C. Arksey, B. McRoberts, J. Pring, S. Lindsay, H. Hornby, R. Webster, N. Wagar, J. Hunt, E. Burtch, E. R. Holley, G. Veal

B. WESTERN CONFERENCE MID 1930S

Men: J. Holst, W. Jackson, A. Risby, D. Parks, A. M. Goudy
Women: First two unknown, "Sister" J. Carson far right

C. WESTERN CONFERENCE 1949

1ST ROW

A. Carson, E. Brown, D. Sneed, M. Spies, M. Shouldice, P. Jackson

2ND ROW

L. Johnson (sitting), D. Parks, A. M. Goudy

3RD ROW

A. S. Risby, A. Bortnick, J. Carson, A. G. Risby, W. N. Wiggins, Joan Risby, Laura Wiggins, S. Steiert

D. GENERAL CONFERENCE 2002

1ST ROW

S. Cuddy, W. Martin, J. Horner, J. Ocran, J. Plaizier, H. Ibrahim, G. MacGarvey, D. Hodgins, E. Conley, D. Conley, M. Traviss, M. Bertrim

2ND ROW

R. Hopkins, R. Kingston, W. Barnes, R. Gamble, C. Lapointe, A. Pybus, C. Burtch, B. Moore, F. Craig, D. Plaizier, S. Lovelock, F. Druce, L. Croswell, D. Greer

3RD ROW

A. Woodworth, R. MacGarvey, D. Moffat, E. Mallory, P. Armstrong, A. Lasher, D. Vine, J. Zilkie, E. Craig, B. Bertrim, L. Yadlowski, M. Rice, P. Rigby, R. Martin, E. Perry, B. Moffat, D. MacPherson, L. Reaney

TOP ROW

J. McElhinney, A. Buckingham, C. Peters, L. Sneed, W. Bertim, W. Hegadorn, K. Tapper

STANDARD CHURCH CAMP MEETINGS

Standard Church Camp Meetings at time of merger with The Wesleyan Church, 2004:

1. Zion Hill Camp Meeting, Foresters Falls, Ontario
2. Bethel Camp Meeting, Odessa, Ontario
3. Ivanhoe Holiness Camp Meeting, Ivanhoe, Ontario
4. Burke Camp Meeting, Burke, New York
5. Newbrook Camp Meeting, Newbrook, Alberta

NOTES

PREFACE

1. C. Roy Fortune, "Ralph Cecil Horner: Product of the Ottawa Valley" (master's thesis, Carleton University, 1999).

CHAPTER 1

1. C. Roy Fortune, "Ralph Cecil Horner," 3. Records in the Clarendon Circuit of the Wesleyan Methodist Church confirm the first son of James Horner and Ellen Richardson died September 20, 1851, at the age of eighteen months.

2. Ibid., 25. The Shawville United Church parish registers 1851–1904, M. G. 8, G 53; National Archives of Canada. Ralph Horner's wife, Annie, recorded his date of birth as December 22, 1854 (Ralph C. Horner and Annie Horner, *Ralph C. Horner, Evangelist: Reminiscences from His Own Pen* [Brockville, Ontario: Standard Church Book Room, date of publication probably in the 1920s], xii), but the earlier date is more in keeping with events recorded in his memoirs: Horner reported that he was twenty-five when he returned to school after his conversion and call to preach.

3. Ibid.

4. Ibid., notes from chapter 2, "Ralph Horner's Ottawa Valley."

5. Ibid., 17.

6. Horner and Horner, *Ralph C. Horner, Evangelist*, 5.

7. Ibid.

8. Ibid., xii.

9. Charles Lynch, *Ottawa Journal*, May 14, 1960.

10. Horner and Horner, *Ralph C. Horner, Evangelist*, 17.

11. Fortune, "Ralph Cecil Horner," 36.

12. Hugh Horner, interview with Mark Croswell, 2008.

13. Keith Dagg, *Those Hornerite Preachers* (self-published); Keith Dagg, great-grandson of George Horner, interview by Mark Croswell, 2008.

14. *Ottawa Journal*, May 31, 1894.

15. Hugh Horner, Mervin Cooke (heard his dad tell the story many times), and Keith Dagg (retold from the version written by a great-granddaughter of George Horner), interview with Mark Croswell.

16. Chad Gaffield, *History of the Outaouais* (Quebec: Les-Presses de l'Universite Laval, 1997), 208, cited in Fortune, "Ralph Cecil Horner," 53.

17. Fortune, "Ralph Cecil Horner," 39.

18. Goldwin French, *The People Called Methodists in Canada* (Toronto: Ryerson Press, 1963), 73, cited in John Dunlop Craig, "Out and Out for the Lord" (master's thesis, Toronto School of Theology, 1969), 62.

19. John Micklethwait and Adrian Wooldridge, *God Is Back* (New York: Penguin, 2009), 21.

20. George A. Rawlyk, ed., *Canadian Protestant Experience, 1760–1990*, census (Kingston: McGill-Queens University Press, 1993), 102–104.

21. Micklethwait and Wooldridge, *God Is Back*.

22. Ibid., 128–129.

23. Ibid., 132.

24. Fortune, "Ralph Cecil Horner," 39–40.

25. Horner and Horner, *Ralph C. Horner, Evangelist*, xi, 3–4.

26. Annie Horner reported that Ralph Horner was converted in July, 1872, which would make him eighteen years old (Horner and Horner, *Ralph C. Horner, Evangelist*, xii). However, *Dictionary of Canadian Biography Online* reports the date as July, 1876, which would make Ralph twenty-two years old at conversion. The later date seems more in keeping with events, for after receiving his call to preach, Ralph reported that he reenrolled in public school at age twenty-five (Horner and Horner, *Ralph C. Horner, Evangelist*, 25).

27. Horner and Horner, *Ralph C. Horner, Evangelist*, 5.

28. Ibid., 5–8.

29. Ibid., 8.

30. Ibid., 9.

31. Ibid., 10–11.

32. Ibid., 13.

33. Ibid., 22.

34. Ibid., 15–19.

35. Ibid., 23–42.

36. William F. McDowell, interview by Mark Croswell, Clarendon, Quebec, 2008.

37. Ralph said his parents had taken him to a surgeon, but the problem persisted. It took tree operations by a skilled surgeon to correct the problem, and years to overcome the force of habit. Ralph was also helped after attending one year at the National School of Oratory and Elocution at Philadelphia, graduating in 1886.

38. Horner and Horner, *Ralph C. Horner, Evangelist*, 23–24.

39. R. C. Horner, *Conference and Evangelistic Relations* (Ottawa, Ontario: Holiness Movement Publishing House, 1903), 3.

40. Ibid., 41.

41. Ibid., 50.

42. William F. McDowell, interview by Mark Croswell.

CHAPTER 2

1. S. D. Clark, *Church and Sect in Canada* (Toronto: University of Toronto Press, 1948), 368.

2. Ibid., quote from John Webster Grant.

3. Micklethwait and Wooldridge, *God Is Back*, 67.

4. Albert Carmen, "Holiness Our Hope," *Methodist Quarterly Review* 21, July, 1884, 572.

5. Marguerite Van Die, "The Double Vision: Evangelical Piety as Derivative and Indigenous in Victorian Canada," cited by Mark A. Noll, David W. Bebbington, and

George A. Rawlyk, eds., *Evangelicalism: Comparative Studies in Popular Protestantism in North America, the British Isles and Beyond, 1700–1900* (New York: Oxford University Press, 1994), 254.

6. Semple, "Decline," *Lord's Dominion*, 217.

7. Ibid., 10–12.

8. Horner and Horner, *Ralph C. Horner, Evangelist*, 138.

9. Lola J. Willows, *The Two Sisters* (Brockville, Ontario: Standard Publishing House, 1957), 19.

10. Rev. S. A. York, in a letter to Rev. H. W. Pointen, December 10, 1949.

11. Melvin E. Dieter, "Wesleyan-Holiness Aspects of Pentecostal Origins: As Mediated through the Nineteenth-Century Holiness Revival," *Aspects of Pentecostal-Charismatic Origins* (Plainfield, N.J.: Logos International, 1975).

12. Horner, *Conference and Evangelistic Relations*, 3.

13. Horner and Horner, *Ralph C. Horner, Evangelist*, 66.

14. Ibid., 4.

15. Ibid.

16. "Journal of Montreal Conference 1887," 199, cited in Harold William Pointen, "The Holiness Movement Church in Canada, bachelor's thesis, Victoria University, 1950, 25.

17. Ibid.

18. Ibid.

19. Horner, *Conference and Evangelistic Relations*, 4.

20. Horner and Horner, *Ralph C. Horner, Evangelist*, 76.

21. Horner, *Conference and Evangelistic Relations*, 6.

22. Horner and Horner, *Ralph C. Horner, Evangelist*, 77.

23. Semple, *Lord's Dominion*.

24. "Minutes of the Montreal Conference" 1888, 57, cited in Pointen, "Holiness Movement Church in Canada," 29.

25. Horner and Horner, *Ralph C. Horner, Evangelist*, 81–82.

26. Micklethwait and Wooldridge, *God Is Back*, 66.

27. Horner and Horner, *Ralph C. Horner, Evangelist*.

28. R. C. Horner, *Bible Doctrines* (Ottawa, Ontario: Holiness Movement Publishing House, 1908), 170.

29. Ibid., 174.

30. Ibid., 14.

31. Ibid., 39.

32. Kevin Bradley Kee, *Revivalists: Marketing the Gospel in English Canada, 1884–1957* (Montreal and Kingston: McGill-Queen's University Press, 2006).

33. Clark, *Church and Sect in Canada*, 372.

34. *Ottawa Journal*, Friday, September 14, 1888, 34. Quotes from the story were later reprinted in the *Pembroke Observer and Advertiser*, December 13, 1889.

35. Glen Lockwood, "The Rear of Leeds and Lansdowne," *Athens Reporter*, January 28, 1890.

36. Reprinted in the *Christian Standard*, November, 1981 (supplied by Mrs. Luella Hartley).

37. *Ottawa Journal* (summary), Friday, September 14, 1888, 34, cited in the *Pembroke Observer and Advertiser*, December 13, 1889.

38. Horner and Horner, *Ralph C. Horner, Evangelist*, 120.

39. Ibid., 77–78.

40. "Singular Religious Movement," *Pembroke Observer and Advertiser*, September 14, 1888.

41. Horner and Horner, *Ralph C. Horner, Evangelist*, 83–84.

42. Clark, *Church and Sect in Canada*, 370.

43. Ibid., 373.

Chapter 3

1. See appendix 1 for a biography of Ella Birdsell.

2. Horner and Horner, *Ralph C. Horner, Evangelist*, 110–111.

3. Brian Ross, "Ralph Cecil Horner, A Methodist Sectarian Deposed 1887–1895," *Journal of the Canadian Church Historical Society*, vol. xix no. 2, 98.

4. George W. Brown, David M. Hayne, and Frances G. Halfpenny, *Dictionary of Canadian Biography* (Toronto: University of Toronto Press, 1976).

5. Semple, *Lord's Dominion*, 391.

6. Rev. William McDowell, United Church minister, Shawville, Quebec, interview by Mark Croswell. Rev. McDowell reported that the Portage-du-Fort circuit was a strong church because of river traffic; people from Shawville and Starks Corners travelled there for supplies. William's father, Dr. McDowell, worked with R. C. Horner in Shawville and was a sympathetic Methodist.

7. Ross, *Journal of the Canadian Church Historical Society*, 98.

8. Horner and Horner, *Ralph C. Horner, Evangelist*, 115.

9. Ibid., 124–125.

10. Ibid., 126.

11. Ibid., 132.

12. Ibid., 133.

13. Ibid., 135.

14. Brown, Hayne, and Halfpenny, *Dictionary of Canadian Biography*.

15. Marilyn Fardig Whiteley, *Christian Guardian*, September 30, 1891, cited in Charles Edwin Jones, "Cyclones of Power/Noisy Display: The Holiness Conflict in the Methodist Church," in *A Guide to the Study of the Holiness Movement* (Metuchen, N.J.: Scarecrow Press, 1974), 12–13; also see "Papers of the Canadian Methodist History Society," June 1997.

16. Ibid.

17. Ibid.

18. "The Reporter," *Athens Record*, September 27, 1892.

19. Pointen, "Holiness Movement Church in Canada," 72–75.

20. *Christian Guardian*, February 7, 1894, 84.

21. "Report of Evangelistic Committee, Minutes of Montreal Conference of the Methodist Church," 1892.

22. See appendix 1 for a biography of Rev. R. Mallett.

23. A. Blackburn, B. Sandford, and A. Moorcroft, *Pilgrimage of Faith* (Madoc, Ontario: Madoc Review Ltd.), 226.

24. Rev. R. Mallett, "Report from Eldorado Circuit," *Canadian Methodist and Holiness Era*, vol. II, Toronto, Wednesday, March 15, 1893, no. 6, 46.

25. Blackburn, Sandford, and Moorcroft, *Pilgrimage of Faith*, 226–227.

26. "Cyclones of Power," *Christian Guardian*, 14.

27. Ibid., 15.

28. "Minutes of Proceedings of Montreal Conference of Methodist Church" 1893, 73, 46; cited in Pointen, "Holiness Movement Church in Canada."

29. Ibid.

30. "Cyclones of Power," *Christian Guardian*.

31. R. C. Horner, *Notes on Boland*, entered according to Act of Congress in the year 1893, in the office of the Librarian of Congress, at Washington, 1893; entered according to the Act of the Parliament of Canada in the year 1893, in the Office of the Minister of Agriculture, at Ottawa.

32. Semple, *Lord's Dominion*.

33. Horner, *Conference and Evangelistic Relations*, 2, 5.

34. Ibid., 9–10.

CHAPTER 4

1. "Cyclones of Power," *Christian Guardian*, 15.

2. Ibid.

3. *Ottawa Evening Journal*, May 31, 1894.

4. "Montreal Conference of the Methodist Church 1894 Minutes," 89–90.

5. Ibid.

6. Ibid.

7. "Cease as a Minister: Rev. R. C. Horner Asked to Return His Parchment," *Daily British Whig*, Kingston, Ontario, Saturday, June 2, 1894.

8. Notes of Conference session are based on a report from the *Toronto Globe*, June 4, 1894.

9. Horner, *Conference and Evangelistic Relations No. 2* (Ottawa, Ontario: Holiness Movement Publishing House, 1906), 2–3.

10. *Toronto Globe*, June 4, 1894.

11. Ibid.

12. *Daily British Whig*, June 2, 1894.

13. R. C. Horner had reason to be concerned about doctrinal drift. During Conference, Rev. A. M. Phillips lectured on "Christ the Model Man." His thesis was that the church had not comprehended the Christianity of Christ. The early church so emphasized the divinity of Christ that it eclipsed His place as an example. Neither the Reformation nor the Methodist revival restored Christ to His true position. The impression many have regarding the salvation of the cross is that of an escape from righteousness rather than from sin. The preachers of Christianity should realize that their mission is to make heaven on earth, not to populate some vague hereafter. The lecture was followed with great interest and was greeted with loud applause.

14. Horner, *Conference and Evangelistic Relations No. 2*.

15. "Bishop Horner Is Suddenly Called Home at Camp Meeting," *Recorder and Times*, Tuesday, September 13, 1921.

16. "Proceedings of the Montreal Conference of the Methodist Church" 1895, 66; cited in Pointen, "Holiness Movement Church in Canada."

17. "Bishop Horner Is Suddenly Called Home," *Recorder and Times*.

18. Horner, *Conference and Evangelistic Relations*, 14–15.

19. "Bishop Horner Is Suddenly Called Home," *Recorder and Times*.

20. Rev. Nelson Burns was born March 22, 1834, in Niagara, Ontario. At about fourteen years of age, he read Phoebe Palmer and experienced the "blessing of holiness." As a young preacher, he became known as a "circuit smasher" because of the disruption provoked by his emphasis on holiness. Burns and others formed an association on December 30, 1879, and affirmed the Methodist commitment of John Wesley "to spread Scriptural holiness over the earth."

21. Pointen, "Holiness Movement Church in Canada."

22. *Christian Guardian*, June 6, 1894, 78.

CHAPTER 5

1. Pointen, "Holiness Movement Church in Canada," 82.

2. "Report on Methodist Conference," *The Toronto Globe*, June 4, 1894.

3. Pointen, "Holiness Movement Church in Canada," 83.

4. Blackburn, Sandford, and Moorcroft, *Pilgrimage of Faith*, 74. No date of dedication or purchase is available, but the first group called themselves "Wesleyan Methodists" and the church was owned by the Holiness Movement Church for many years after.

5. Ibid., 77.

6. Ibid., 296.

7. Fortune, "Ralph Cecil Horner," 116.

8. See statistics later in chapter 5 submitted for incorporation.

9. James R. Kennedy, *South Elmsley in the Making 1783–1983* (Corporation of the Township of South Elmsley, 1984), 294. (Book supplied by Ray MacFadden, former Brockville police chief.)

10. *Recorder and Times*, September 13, 1921.

11. Blackburn, Sandford, and Moorcroft, *Pilgrimage of Faith*, 74.

12. S. A. York in a letter to Harold W. Pointen for work on his thesis, December 10, 1949.

13. Ibid.

14. Pointen, "Holiness Movement Church in Canada," 98–99.

15. John Eades (grandson of G. A. Christie), "George Alexander Christie—Early and Public Life" (unpublished paper).

16. The fraternal name "Brother" was used to refer to any who were not fully ordained.

17. Carman papers 1852–1917, box 14, file 96, United Church Archives, Victoria University, cited in Fortune, "Ralph Cecil Horner," 119–120.

18. Ibid., see notes 118–120; "Debates of the Senate of the Dominion of Canada 1896" (Ottawa: S. E. Dawson, 1896).

19. See chapter 1. Methodists remained the largest Protestant group in Canada from 1871 until 1911, when they were marginally surpassed by the Presbyterians. At the time of Church Union in 1925, there were 418,352 official members as well as many adherents, an impressive gain in little over a century from the 2,550 Methodists in Ontario in 1812.

20. *Athens Reporter*, June 10, 1896.

21. Pointen, "Holiness Movement Church in Canada," 89.

22. *Holiness Era*, March 24, 1897; cited in Louise A. Mussio, "The Origins and Nature of the Holiness Movement Church: A Study in Religious Populism," *Journal of the Canadian Historical Association 1996*, New Series Vol. 7.

23. Fortune, "Ralph Cecil Horner," 119–120.

24. Ibid.

25. Ibid., 120.

26. Ibid.

27. Ibid.

28. Earl R. Conley, "Glimpses," citation: "The Holiness Movement Church in Canada."

29. Pointen, "Holiness Movement Church in Canada," 111.

30. Ibid., 110.

31. "Special Conference of the HMC in Canada Minutes," Ottawa, December 29, 1896.

32. "Horner Suspended," *Athens Reporter*, March 31, 1897.

33. "A Defense of Mr. Horner," *Athens Reporter*, June 2, 1897.

34. "Holiness Movement Conference Special Committee Minutes," April 5, 1897.

35. "Third Annual Holiness Movement Minutes," March 18, 1897.

36. "Holiness Movement Conference Special Committee Minutes," April 5, 1897.

37. "Holiness Movement Conference Special Committee Minutes," May 27, 1897.

38. "Conference of Special Committee Minutes" (Ottawa, Ontario: Holiness Institute, March 2, 1899), 118.

39. Blackburn, Sandford, and Moorcroft, *Pilgrimage of Faith*, 80.

40. *Evening Star*, Toronto, December 4, 1897.

41. "Minutes of the Fifth Annual Conference of the Holiness Movement Church," Mission Hall, Ottawa, December 3, 1998, 107–108.

42. Collection of Dr. Carman Letters (archives, dept. of Victoria University); cited in Pointen, "Holiness Movement Church in Canada," 113.

43. Doug Warren, "The Closing of a Church, Fifth Avenue Free Methodist Church, Ottawa, Ontario" (unpublished research paper, March 10, 2003).

44. Pointen, "Holiness Movement Church in Canada," 113–114.

CHAPTER 6

1. Ma Brownell was a grandmother of Doris Conley, wife of Rev. Earl Conley, general superintendent of the Standard Church.

2. *Experiences and Writings of Ma Brownell* (Brockville, Ontario: Christian Standard Publishing House, 1932).

3. Fortune, "Ralph Cecil Horner," 63.

4. Fortune, "Ralph Cecil Horner," 108–110.

5. *Holiness Era*, December 29, 1897.

6. John Wilkins Sigsworth, *The Battle was the Lord's: A History of the Free Methodist Church in Canada* (Oshawa, Ontario: Sage Publishers, 1960), 45.

7. R. Wayne Kleinsteuber, *Coming of Age: The Making of a Canadian Free Methodist Church* (Canada: Light and Life Press, 1980), 34.

8. Fortune, "Ralph Cecil Horner," 130.

9. Jim Wood, interview by Mark Croswell, 2008.

10. *Discipline: Holiness Movement Church*, Section XV, July 28, 1897, 34–35.

11. Horner and Horner, *Ralph C. Horner, Evangelist*, 122.

12. Ibid., 127.

13. Ibid., 129.

14. Ibid.

15. "Victim of Senseless Fashion," *Holiness Era*, October 6, 1897, 158.

16. *Discipline: Holiness Movement Church*, Section XVI, 83.

17. Michael Tapper, "Assessing Social Sin: A Critical Task in Contemporary Methodism," Second Annual Wesleyan Studies Symposium, March 15, 2011, Tyndale University, cited from The *Works of John Wesley*, "A Farther Appeal to Men of Reason and Religion (Clarendon Press, 1975).

18. S. Jane Conley, *My Walk with God* (Brockville, Ontario: Henderson Printing).

19. Keith Dagg, interview by Mark Croswell.

20. Blackburn, Sandford, and Moorcroft, *Pilgrimage of Faith*, 74–75.

21. Kennedy, *South Elmsley*, 294.

22. Ibid., 296.

23. Ibid.

24. R. C. Horner, *Entire Consecration* (Toronto: W. Briggs, National Archives of Canada, 1890), 26.

25. Willows, *Two Sisters*, 19–20, 22–23.

26. Rev. S. A. York in a letter to Harold W. Pointen, December 10, 1949.

27. Grandparents of Laurence Croswell.

28. Rev. J. H. Southcombe (1914–2008), *Life and Times of the Holiness Church* (self-published, 1980).

29. See appendix 4 for a copy of "We Are Happy Today," popularly known as "It Is Good to Be Here."

30. Notes from "The History of Lake Eloida," *Athens Reporter*, August, September, October, 1961.

31. *Athens Reporter*, August 1902.

32. Margery Callen, "Letters Back Home to Caintown," citation: by Harold (surname unknown).

CHAPTER 7

1. Nettie M. Hill and Norma A. Eves (compilers), "A Brief History of Holiness Movement Missions 1899–1959," Young People's Missionary Society, prepared by Hill and Eves on motion of the Annual Missionary Convention, Athens, Ontario, 1948.

2. Ibid., 4–5.

3. Ibid., 6.

4. Ibid., 8.

5. Ibid., notes on "Egyptian Missions." Miss Sarah Longhurst was sent to Port Said to take charge of the Peniel School for Moslem Girls, which was financed by a group of interested and concerned people from California, USA. She remained at the school until her death in 1940 at the age of eighty after thirty-three years of continuous service. She also spent much of her time publishing and distributing Christian literature in the Arabic language. In 1945, a memorial to her long and faithful service was established to raise funds to print and distribute Gospels for two new African dialects.

6. Hill and Eves, "Brief History," notes on "Egyptian Missions," 10.

7. Ibid.

8. Ibid., 21.

9. Rev. Asa B. Van Camp, *Diary* (Ottawa, Ontario: Holiness Movement Publishing House, 1905).

10. Hills and Eves, "Brief History," 21.

11. Rev. Asa B. Van Camp, *Gems of Thought* (Ottawa, Ontario: Holiness Movement Publishing House, 1906).

12. T. Danford and L. E. Connaughty, *Introducing Christianity into Feng Huang T'ing, Hunan, China* (Brockville, Ontario: Standard Church Book Room, 1928).

13. Hill and Eves, "Brief History," 28.

14. Ibid.

15. Ibid., 25.

16. Ibid., 26–27.

17. Ibid., 16.

CHAPTER 8

1. "General Conference Minutes," February 1, 1905.

2. "General Conference Minutes," Stittsville, Ontario, May 14, 1907, 102.

3. Ibid., 102.

4. Horner had indicated to the committee that he felt the need for an absolute rest physically. He also felt he needed their hearty cooperation relative to the work in general. The bishop indicated he would not take responsibility for appointing the president.

5. "Special Committee Minutes," October 30–November 2, 1907.

6. "General Conference Minutes," 1907, 104.

7. Statistics from Conference Minutes, 1896–1909.

8. Thomas William Miller, *Canadian Pentecostals: A History of the Pentecostal Assemblies of Canada* (Mississauga, Ontario: Full Gospel Publishing House, 1994), 25.

9. Rob Clements, "Remembering the Holiness Movement," *Free Methodist Herald*, July–August, 1998, 8; cited in Warren, "Closing of a Church."

10. Gordon Francis Atter, *The Third Force* (Peterborough, Ontario: College Press, 1962), 19.

11. Ibid.

12. John McAlister, "Report from Western Canada," *Pentecostal Testimony*, no. 1, December 1920.

13. James Craig, "The Father of Canadian Pentecostalism, Robert McAlister, 1880–1953," *Canada Portraits of Faith* (Mississauga, Ontario: PAOC Archives).

14. Fortune, "Ralph Cecil Horner," 203. The 1901 census lists Robert McAlister's oldest brother, James of Cobden, and his family as "Hornerites."

15. Atter, *Third Force*, 35.

16. Eades, "George Alexander Christie," 12.

17. Fortune, "Ralph Cecil Horner," 203.

18. Roy C. Fortune in a letter to Gordon Atter, July 15, 1996.

19. Rev. Ken Bombay, interview by Laurence Croswell, November 25, 2009.

20. Eades, "George Alexander Christie," 36.

21. Atter, *Third Force*, 36.

22. *Pembroke Advance*, December 13, 1889.

23. Glenn J. Lockwood, *The Rear of Leeds & Lansdowne: The Making of Community on the Gananoque River Frontier* (Lyndhurst, Ontario: Corporation of Rear and Lansdowne, 1996), appendix 13, 596.

24. Ibid., 474.

25. Claire Fuller, *The Effect of the Pentecostal Movement on Canadian Methodist and Holiness Churches, 1906–1930*; cited in Eades, "George Alexander Christie," 12.

26. Miller, *Canadian Pentecostals*, 66, 126.

27. "Light on Troubles Existing in the Holiness Movement Church," adopted at the Laymen's Camp Meeting, Ottawa, September 14, 1915.

28. Atter, *Third Force*, 37.

29. Ibid., 205.

30. Clare Fuller, "Holiness People in Early Canadian Pentecostalism, 1906–1919" (unpublished essay, 1988).

31. Douglas Rudd, *When the Spirit Came upon Them* (Mississauga, Ontario: Pentecostal Assemblies of Canada, 2002), 125–126.

32. Miller, *Canadian Pentecostals*, 63.

33. Horner, *Bible Doctrines*, 134.

34. Donald W. Dayton, *Theological Roots of Pentecostals* (Metuchen, N.J.: Scarecrow Press, 1987), 98–100; cited in Eades, "George Alexander Christie."

35. "General Conference Minutes," May 10, 1910, 12.

36. Ibid., 124.

37. James E. Wilson in a letter to the Board of Directors Committee, February 28, 1914.

38. "The Holiness Movement Church Discipline," 1907, 83.

39. Ibid., 60.

40. W. T. Purkiser, *Called unto Holiness*, vol. 2 (Kansas City, Mo.: Beacon Hill, 1983), 269.

41. S. Lewis Johnson Jr., "The Paralysis of Legalism," *Bibliotheca Sacra*, April–June 1963, 109.

42. "General Conference Minutes," 1903, 87.

43. "Fifth General Conference," Ottawa, Ontario, 1910.

44. "Special Committee Minutes," HMC, January 24, 1911.

45. Herman R. James, "Circular Letter to the Ordained Ministry of the Holiness Movement," 1917.

46. "General Conference Minutes," Kingston, Ontario, 1913.

47. James, "Circular Letter."

48. Eades, "George Alexander Christie."

CHAPTER 9

1. Pierre Berton, *The Promised Land: Settling the West, 1896–1914* (Toronto: McClelland and Stewart, 1984), 440; quotes from Albert Hubbard.

2. Wilson, February 28, 1914.

3. "Special Committee Minutes" (General Conference), Stittsville, Ontario, May 18, 1914.

4. Committee members present: E. H. Claxton, D. Anderson, W. J. Watchorne, M. C. Pritchard, W. A. McCracken, Johnston Price, G. A. Christie, and P. Wiseman.

5. "Special Committee Minutes," May 19, 1914.

6. Ibid.

7. "Light on Troubles," 13.

8. "Special Committee Minutes," May 22, 1914.

9. Ibid.

10. Ibid.

11. Fortune, "Ralph Cecil Horner," 186, interview July 5, 1996, with Rev. William McDowell, retired United Church minister, Shawville, Quebec. Rev. McDowell, whose parents and grandparents were close friends of Horner, believes Rev. Horner was a fine, honest man but speculates he may have suffered from presenile dementia.

12. "Light on Troubles," 15.

13. "Minutes" 1914, Ottawa Annual Conference, 120, 125.

14. Ibid., 125.

15. "Light on Troubles," 17.

16. Membership in 1914 Ottawa Annual Conference reported in Conference minutes— full: 1164; members on probation: 110; adherents: 1309; average attendance: 3721.

17. "Light on Troubles."

18. Ibid., 7–8.

19. Ibid.

20. Ibid.

21. Ibid., 12.

22. Ibid.

23. Ibid.

24. Eades, "George Alexander Christie."

25. Ibid.

26. "Ottawa Annual Conference Minutes HMC," October 24, 1916, 158–159.

27. "Cross-Examination of Mr. G. A. Christie on His Affidavit," Supreme Court of Ontario, July 17, 1917, 17.

28. "General Conference Minutes," 1916, 12.

29. "Examination of R. C. Horner by Mr. McCormick," Supreme Court of Ontario, September 19, 1917.

30. "Affidavit of G. L. Monahan," Supreme Court of Ontario, July 19, 1917.
31. "General Conference Minutes," 1916, 12.
32. Eades, "George Alexander Christie."
33. Ibid.
34. "General Conference Minutes," 1916, 16.
35. Ibid., 17.
36. Ibid., 27.

CHAPTER 10
1. *Experiences and Writings of Ma Brownell*, 83–85.
2. A letter was sent to Rev. R. C. Horner, April 13, 1917 (Metcalfe, Ontario).
3. The issue of publishing the *Christian Standard* is interesting because J. C. Black claimed that G. A. Christie had refused to publish articles in the *Holiness Era* on either side of the controversy, and had received significant criticism from both sides of the dispute for his decision.
4. "Special Committee Minutes," May 9, 1917.
5. Ibid.
6. The minutes of this Special Conference are important because they contain the charges and proceedings concerning the removal of R. C. Horner from the bishopric and Bishop Horner's repudiation of the proceedings and charges.
7. "Special Session of the Ottawa Annual Conference Minutes," May 15, 1917, 185.
8. "Ottawa Conference of Holiness Movement Church 1917 Minutes" (Horner Conference), 183.
9. Some of these persons later became icons in the Standard Church and made significant contributions: Eva Alexander, David Parks, W. Jackson, and John Carson.
10. "Ottawa Conference of Holiness Movement Church 1917 Minutes," 188.
11. In the August 15, 1917, edition of the *Athens Reporter*, a letter to the editor informed readers that a camp meeting announced for Lake Eloida, August 12–19, Bishop Horner in charge, was "entirely misleading." The meeting was not authorized by the Committee. The regular and authorized Annual Camp Meeting of the District was to be held from August 26 to September 2, Rev. J. C. Black, assistant to Bishop Warren, in charge.
12. Supreme Court of Ontario (Oral) Judgment, J. Sutherland.
13. Supreme Court of Ontario findings.
14. Conley, *My Walk*, 46.
15. Paul Johnston, interview by Mark Croswell.
16. Conley, *My Walk*, 47.
17. Summary from the Supreme Court of Ontario.
18. Ibid.
19. "Affidavit of G. L. Monahan," Supreme Court of Ontario, filed July 19, 1917.
20. Affidavit, June 20, 1917, Kemptville, Ontario, filed July 9, 1917.
21. "General Conference Minutes," 1916, 12.
22. Eades, "George Alexander Christie."
23. "Affidavit of George A. Christie," Supreme Court of Ontario, filed July 9, 1917.
24. Ibid., 16.
25. Ibid., 10.
26. Ibid., 13.
27. "Examination of Defendant, R. C. Horner," Supreme Court of Ontario, filed September 28, 1917, 30.
28. "The Holiness Movement Church in Canada; A. T. Warren and S. A. York, Plaintiffs; R. C. Horner and G. L. Monahan, Defendants," Supreme Court of Ontario, October 3, 1917.

29. Ibid.

30. For a list of voters, see appendix 2.

31. James, "Circular Letter."

32. See appendix 1 for a biography of Bishop Albert T. Warren.

CHAPTER 11

1. The Holiness Movement officially voted to replace the office of bishop with that of general superintendent in 1926. At that time lay representation was adopted, and presiding elders were elected by ballot instead of appointed by the bishop. The Standard Church continued with the traditional conservative episcopalian model of governance.

2. Robert J. Buchanan, Free Methodist Church Superintendent, "Memorandum," commenting on proceedings of the HMC of Canada General Conference, Carleton Place, Ontario, December 15–22, 1916.

3. "Minute Book, Organization of the Standard Church of America, Kingston Annual Conference Journal," 1918–1927.

4. Fortune, "Ralph Cecil Horner," 196; interview with Rev. William Woodland, Kingston, Ontario, February 16, 1998.

5. Rev. Paul Johnston, grandson of Rev. G. L. Monahan, interview by Laurence Croswell, January 2009.

6. E. R. Conley, ed., *1917–1987 Anniversary Reflections*, a booklet of remembrance prepared to celebrate the seventieth year of publication of the *Christian Standard*.

7. "Second Annual Conference Minute Book," Stittsville, Ontario, August 29, 1918.

8. Bessie Wager Seiter, *Just Remembering: My Life in the Twenties as a Preacher's Kid in the Standard Church in Ontario* (self-published).

9. Bert Montgomery and Mac Coughlin, "History of Foresters Falls Standard Church, Eightieth Anniversary."

10. "General Conference Journal," 1918–1950.

11. Ibid.

12. Ibid.

13. Ibid.

14. "Uniforms for the Ministry and the Laity," approved by the 1926 General Conference, the Standard Church of America.

15. "Dress and Furniture," *Doctrine and Discipline of the Standard Church of America*, Section VIII (Kingston, Ontario: Jackson Press, 1918), 29.

16. Pastoral visits, Laurence Croswell.

17. Kleinsteuber, *Coming of Age*, 34–35.

18. "General Conference Journal," December 26, 1918.

19. Ibid.

20. Irwin L. Brown, *The Story of My Life* (self-published), 48.

CHAPTER 12

1. "Leeds County: Village," *Recorder and Times*, November 1, 1938 (Athens, Ontario).

2. "Kingston Annual Conference Journal," 1918–1927, 7–9.

3. Ibid., 8.

4. G. Oldford, *Christian Standard*, February 6, 1920.

5. Ibid.

6. Harry Painting, "Bible College: Reunion of Old Time Students, Staff, Held," *Focus on the District—Brockville Recorder TV-Travel Times*, May 22, 1987, 8.

7. Nehemiah 2:18.

8. Painting, "Bible College."

9. Ibid.

10. R. C. Horner, *Pastoral Evangelism, the Magazine of the Holiness Movement Church*, Ottawa, Ontario, May 1, 1910, 31.

11. *Doctrine and Discipline of the Standard Church of America* (Kingston, Ontario: Jackson Press, 1918), question 3, answer 3 (1), 86.

12. Ibid., number 5.

13. "General Conference Minutes," January 31, 1931, "Memorials from Annual Conferences," item 1.

14. *The Manual and Discipline of the Standard Church of America*, authorized and published by the General Conference, 1956, "Election and Duties of Presiding Elders," 84.

15. "General Conference Minutes," January 31, 1931, "Memorials from Annual Conferences," items 4 and 5.

16. Rev. E. R. Conley, compiler, *Missions in Review*, Standard Church of America (2000), notes and quotes.

17. Laurence Croswell, missions safari in Egypt, 2009, led by Rev. E. R. Conley.

18. *Christian Standard*, July/August, 1979.

19. "Interview of 87-year-old Fred Crawford," *Community Press* (Easter Edition, September 11, 1990), 10.

CHAPTER 13

1. George Oldford, *Christian Standard*, Friday, October 7, 1921, vol. V., no. 35.

2. Ibid. We have taken liberty to organize the message by Rev. James Smith into sermon format for ease of reading. Capitalizations are mine. Some material was omitted, but the main body has been recorded for the reader's challenge and inspiration.

3. Oldford, *Christian Standard*, vol. V., no. 35.

4. Ibid.

5. Ibid.

6. John Stark, *Christian Standard*, October 7, 1921.

7. "Bishop Horner Is Suddenly Called Home," *Recorder and Times*.

8. Ibid.

9. Charles Lynch, "Controversial Figure Founded Two Churches," *Ottawa Journal*, May 14, 1960.

10. "Mighty Outpourings," *Shawville Equity*, October 12, 1967.

11. Conley, *My Walk*, 61.

12. Jim Wood, interview by Mark Croswell.

CHAPTER 14

1. "General Conference Minutes," September 26, October 3, 1921.

2. Rev. Paul Johnston, interview by Mark Croswell, 2008; and by Laurence Croswell, 2009.

3. "General Conference Journal," 1918–1950, 44.

4. Bert Montgomery, interview by Laurence Croswell, Foresters Falls, Ontario, 2010.

5. Brown, *Story of My Life*.

6. Conley, *Missions in Review*, compilations and gleanings from issues of the *Christian Standard* and *Missionary Ambassador*; also from notes by Rev. Fadil Ibraheem and Rev. Earl Thompson, the Standard Church of America, 2001; June Hegadorn, Doris Conley, and Janet Hegadorn assisted in preparation.

7. "Two Bishops," chapter 10.

8. Ella Slack was the sister of Sadie Montgomery, Faye Croswell's grandmother. The four Slack boys were met along the railroad by "Aunt Sadie" near Cobden and stayed in her home until Martin Slack remarried.

9. Conley, *Missions in Review* (minor adjustments for ease of reading).

10. *Christian Standard*, January 7, 1926.

11. Conley, *Missions in Review* (minor adjustments for ease of reading).

12. Danford and Connaughty, *Introducing Christianity*.

13. Ruby (Cripps) Steiert, telephone interview by Laurence Croswell, 2009. David Wieler pastored the Good Hope Church, 1962–1967. Ruby Steiert and her husband, Simon Steiert, were Standard Church pastors until he entered the Armed Forces during World War II and served overseas for three and a half years as a stretcher bearer. The ravages and memories of the war were difficult for him to overcome, and when he returned in 1946 he did not reenter the pastoral ministry.

14. "Reflections," *Christian Standard, Anniversary Edition*, 4.

15. See appendix 3 for list of writings by R. C. Horner.

16. Seiter, *Just Remembering*.

CHAPTER 15

1. Based on Seiter, *Just Remembering*.

2. Brown, *Story of My Life*.

3. Ibid.

4. The property for the Morin Flats church was donated by Abraham Watchorn, father of Rev. W. J. Watchorn in 1885, and the church was built in the fall of that year. The Watchorn family held the deed until Mrs. Watchorn ultimately signed the deed over to the Standard Church. In 1958–1959, Rev. E. R. Conley and brother-in-law Clem Hobin renovated the church and began holding summer Sunday evening services. Mrs. Jane Conley supervised the schedule until the fall of 1969; she died in 1970. Summer services were not continued until 1987, when Rev. E. R. Conley resumed scheduling. The Morin Heights church is the oldest standing Standard church.

5. Brown, *Story of My Life*.

6. Convey Crescent in Brockville is named after Elizabeth Convey.

7. See Hebrews 12:1.

CHAPTER 16

1. P. W. Bennett et al., *Canada: A North American Nation* (Columbus, Ohio: McGraw-Hill, 1989).

2. *Christian and Missionary Alliance in Canada*, "History, 1930s," http://cmalliance.ca/historyc1420.php.

3. *History: The Salvation Army Oshawa*, "April 2010 Marked 125 Years of Ministry in Oshawa," http://www.google.ca/oshawa+history.

4. *Pentecostal Testimony*, December 1920; May 1939.

5. *Toronto Star Weekly*, September 27, 1930.

6. "Western Conference Minutes," July 21, 1932, chairman: Bishop Monahan, 25.

7. Ibid., 27.

8. "Newbrook Standard Church," *Christian Standard*, April, 1972.

9. Mikell Montague, "Fixing Obadiah Place," *Alberta's Cultural Heritage Magazine* — Summer 2000; Willis Bowen, interview by Laurence Croswell.

10. "General Conference Minutes," January 6, 1931, Kingston, Ontario, 90–91.

11. "Kingston Conference Minutes," 1939, 184.

12. "General Conference Minutes," 1931, 69.

13. Ibid., 76.

14. "General Conference Minutes," 1938, 168–169.

15. Brown, *Story of My Life*, 41.

16. Laurence Croswell: during pastoral visits Miss Eleanor Burns (retired deaconess, Brockville) shared stories about early days in the Standard Church. She said news of Bishop Monahan's resignation cast a discouraging pall throughout the church.

17. Paragon Hitchcock Mines Ltd. sold by R. F. Walker and Co., Suite 503—211 Kings St. W. Toronto, Ontario. Rev. Bob Buchanan, Rev. Eldon Craig, and Rev. Gordon Hammond; interviews by Mark Croswell.

18. "Discipline of Kingston Annual Conference Minutes," 1938, item 7, 152.

19. "General Conference Minutes," 1938, item 6, 172.

20. Conley, *Missions in Review*.

21. Ibid.

22. "General Conference Minutes," 1938, 179.

23. "Special Session General Conference," Minute Book, 1940, 199.

CHAPTER 17

1. "General Conference Minutes," May 15, 1945, 224.

2. Ibid., 231.

3. "General Conference Minutes," 1954, 20, 24.

4. "General Conference Minutes," 1945, 226–232.

5. See appendix 4 for a copy of "We Are Happy Today."

6. "General Conference Minutes," 1945, 232.

7. Pointen, "Holiness Movement Church in Canada," 143.

8. See appendix 1 for the story of David Mainse, his conversion, and ministry.

9. Brown, *Story of My Life*.

10. Minutes, Joint Board of Directors, November 26, 1952.

11. Brown, *Story of My Life* (slight modifications made for ease of reading).

12. Special General Conference, October 16, 1956, Conference Minutes, 65.

13. R. Boston and W. A McMillan, paper on "Church Union" presented to joint meeting of Church Union Committees, East and West Conferences, April 12, 1957.

14. Rev. E. Craig, interview by Laurence Croswell. Rev. Craig recalls that while he was a student at BBC, he had conversations with Rev. I. L. Brown and Rev. G. Armstrong regarding early Standard Church memories.

15. A small number of HMC churches in Saskatchewan and Ontario did not merge with the Free Methodist Church and formed the Independent Holiness Church under the leadership of Rev. John Woodland.

16. Conley, *Missions in Review*.

17. History of Egyptian missions based on notes and quotes from Conley, *Missions in Review*.

18. Rev. I. L. Brown, "Special Memorial Edition," *Christian Standard*, February 1, 1960.

19. Ibid.

20. Conley, *Missions in Review*.

CHAPTER 18

1. Executive Board, the Wesleyan Methodist Church of America; signed: Rev. B. H. Phaup, Chairman; Rev. Kenneth Dunn, Secretary, November 4, 1959.

2. It is of interest to note that on June 26, 1968, the Pilgrim Holiness and the Wesleyan Methodist churches did unite to become The Wesleyan Church. Amazingly, it took another thirty-six years for the Standard Church to join this union (2004).

3. "General Conference Executive Minutes," April 30, 1960, 120.

4. Special General Conference Minute Book, June 6, 1960, 109.

5. Ibid., 111.

6. "General Conference Executive Minutes," 1947–1962, 144–145.

7. "Special General Conference Minutes," 118.

8. Ibid., 119.

9. Ibid., 128.

10. Recording Notebook, General Conference Vote, re: Merger.

11. See appendix 1 for biography of Gary Walsh.

12. "General Conference Minutes," 1962, 165.

13. Earl Conley, *Memoirs* (self-published).

14. Conley, *My Walk*, 97.

15. See appendix 1 for biography of Harold Moyles.

16. Conley, *Memoirs*.

17. "General Conference Minutes," 1966, 30–31.

18. *Key Yearbook*, 1968, Brockville Bible College.

CHAPTER 19

1. "General Conference Minutes," 1971, 275.

2. See appendix 1 for biography.

3. Conley, *Missions in Review*.

4. Ibid.

5. *Manual and Discipline*, The Standard Church, 90–91.

CHAPTER 20

1. Special Committee of the Standard Church, January 9, 1988.

2. Special Committee of the Standard Church, September 17, 1988.

3. "General Conference Minutes," May 24, 2002.

4. Appendix A was attached to the merger agreement, which read: "Although the understanding of the process between the two denominations tends to be different, the desired results harmonize. Both denominations teach Entire Sanctification and empowerment for ministry is what God desires for believers. Both teach that what God desires He makes possible through His grace and the power of the Holy Spirit. The Wesleyan Church . . . recognizes that the Standard Church doctrine does not identify the baptism of the Holy Spirit with Entire Sanctification and that her people may maintain the distinction in their understanding and preaching between Entire Sanctification and the Baptism of the Holy Spirit for empowerment."

CHAPTER 21

1. See appendix 1 for the biography of Rev. Andrew Risby.

2. See appendix 1 for the biography of Irene Ingram.

3. Autobiography: Laurence Croswell.

4. The prayer garden was officially dedicated by Rev. Laurence Croswell, assisted by Rev. Earl Conley, and the congregation of Centennial Road Standard Church on October 26, 2008.

5. *The Discipline of The Wesleyan Church 2000*, Appendix II, Article IV, 474.

6. FLAME: Fellowship of Leaders Acquiring Education. FLAME is an intensive weeklong conference of classes for those students twenty-eight years of age and older (special approval may be admitted with DBMO approval) working toward ordination,

transfer of ordination, lay ministry commissioned ministry, or special worker. A typical week is divided into two sections so that a student can complete two courses in one week. Well-qualified professors in their field of study are brought in and class time is combined with worship, fellowship, and fun.

7. The Six Pack: Program developed to teach pastors in Ghana the basics of theology, ministry, and church governance and bring them to a basic level worthy of ordination. Six pastors from the CCD of The Wesleyan Church were supported and sent by their congregations to conduct two-week classes at various times during the year to specific locations across Ghana. Ghanaian pastors are assisted by the college scholarships.

8. Horner and Horner, *Ralph C. Horner, Evangelist*, 98–99.

9. Ibid., 11.

APPENDIX 1

1. *Canadian Methodist and Holiness Era*, October 11, 1893, 198.

2. *Canadian Methodist and Holiness Era*, May 24, 1893, vol. II, no. 11, 86.

3. *Canadian Methodist and Holiness Era*, 1925.

4. Doris Conley, "Tribute to Harold Moyles," *Christian Standard*, September 1991.

5. David Bly, "Passing of Rev. Andrew Risby Leaves 'A Big Hole in Our City'" (interview with Cheryl Foggo), *Calgary Herald*, June 28, 2002.

6. News release, "The Evangelical Fellowship of Canada Names New President," *EFC*, 1997.

7. Dr. Roy Lake Mainse, *A Happy Heart . . . One Man's Inspiring Story of God's Fulfillment in His Life* (Toronto, Ontario: Crossroads Christian Communications Inc., 1988).

8. Notes from Robert Tanney, *Acts of Modern Apostles* (self-published).

9. Willows, *Two Sisters*; Anita Brechbill, "20th Century Spiritual Giants," *The Satisfying Portion* (Mahefey); *Christian Standard*, July/August 1988.

BIBLIOGRAPHY

Anniversary Reflections, Christian Standard, 1917–1918. Brockville, Ontario: Standard Church Publishing House.

Atter, Gordon Francis. *The Third Force*. Peterborough, Ontario: The College Press, 1962.

Blackburn, Alma, Blanche Sandford, and Alma Moorcroft. *Pilgrimage of Faith: 150 Years of History of the Churches in Madoc Township and Village 1824–1974*. Madoc, Ontario: Madoc Review Ltd.

Brown, Irwin L. *The Story of My Life*. Self-published.

Christian Standard. Brockville, Ontario: Standard Church Publishing House, various issues.

Conference Minutes: Minutes of the Proceedings of the Wesleyan Connection Canada; Minutes of the Proceedings of the Holiness Movement Church; Minutes of the Proceedings of the Standard Church of America.

Conley, Earl. *Glimpses*. Brockville, Ontario: Henderson Printing, 1998.

———. *Missions in Review, the Standard Church of America*. Brockville, Ontario: Standard Publishing House.

Conley, S. Jane. *My Walk with God*. Brockville, Ontario: Henderson Printing.

Craig, James D. "Out and Out for the Lord." Master's thesis. Wycliffe College and Toronto School of Theology, Toronto, 1995.

Danford, T., and L. E. Connaughty. *Introducing Christianity into Feng Huang T'ing Hunan, China*. Standard Church Book Room, 1928.

Eades, Tom and Grace Eades. "George Alexander Christie—Early and Public Life." Unpublished paper.

Fortune, C. Roy. "Ralph Cecil Horner: Product of the Ottawa Valley." Master's thesis. Carleton University, 1999.

Hill, Nettie M., and Norma A. Eves. "A Brief History of Holiness Movement Missions, 1899–1959." Papers prepared and given at regular meetings of the Ottawa Young People's Missionary Society.

Holiness Era. Ottawa, Ontario: Holiness Book and Publishing House, various issues.

Horner, Ralph C., and Mrs. A. E. Horner. *Ralph C. Horner, Reminiscences from His Own Pen*. Brockville, Ontario: Standard Church Book Room.

Kennedy, James R. *South Elmsley in the Making 1788–1983*. Corporation of the Township of South Elmsley, 1984. Supplied by Ray McFadden.

Kleinsteuber, R. Wayne. *Coming of Age: The Making of a Canadian Free Methodist Church*. Light and Life Press Canada, 1980.

Newspapers: *Shawville Equity*; *Ottawa Journal*; *Athens Reporter*; *Pembroke Observer*; *Toronto Star*; *Kingston Whig Standard*; *Toronto Globe*; *Brockville Recorder and Times*; *Kinston Daily British Whig*; *Tweed News*.

Pointen, Harold William. "The Holiness Movement Church in Canada." Bachelor's thesis. Emmanuel College of Victoria University, 1950.

Seiter, Bessie Wager. *Just Remembering: My Life in the Twenties as a Preacher's Kid in the Standard Church in Ontario*. Self-published.

Sigsworth, John Wilkins. *The Battle Was the Lord's*. Oshawa, Ontario: Sage Publishers, 1960.

Van Camp, Asa B. *Diary*. Ottawa, Canada: Holiness Movement Publishing House, 1905.

Willows, Lola J. *The Two Sisters*. Brockville, Ontario: Standard Publishing House, 1957.

INDEX